Paths Not Taken

Political Pluralism in Post-War Singapore

edited by

Michael D. Barr and Carl A. Trocki

NUS PRESS
SINGAPORE

© 2008 NUS Press
National University of Singapore
AS3-01-02, 3 Arts Link
Singapore 117569

Fax: (65) 6774-0652
E-mail: nusbooks@nus.edu.sg
Website: http://www.nus.edu.sg/npu

ISBN 978-9971-69-378-7 (Paper)

National Library Board Singapore Cataloguing in Publication Data

Paths not taken : political pluralism in post-war Singapore / edited by
 Michael D. Barr and Carl A. Trocki. – Singapore : NUS Press, c2008.
 p. cm.
 "Most of the papers in this book were first presented in 2005
 at an international symposium hosted in Singapore by the
 National University of Singapore's Asia Research Institute (ARI)
 ..."--P. 2.
 Includes bibliographical references and index.
 ISBN-13 : 978-9971-69-378-7 (pbk.)

 1. Singapore – Politics and government – 20th century –
 Congresses. 2. Cultural pluralism – Singapore – History –
 Congresses. 3. Social movements – Singapore – History –
 Congresses. I. Barr, Michael D. II. Trocki, Carl A.

 DS610.6
 959.5705 -- dc22   OCN154714418

The cover photograph is from the Tan Kok Kheng Collection, courtesy of National Archives of Singapore

Typeset by : SC (Sang Choy) International Pte Ltd
Printed by : Print Dynamics (S) Pte Ltd

*This book is dedicated to
the memory of Oliver W. Wolters,
a great historian and teacher
whose suggestion inspired this book.*

Contents

Abbreviations

ABL	Anti-British League
Angkatan 45	Generation of 45
API	Angkatan Pemuda Insaf or Generation of Aware Youth
ASAS 50	Angkatan Sasterawan Lima Pulahan or Generation of the Writers of the 1950s
AWARE	Association of Women for Action and Research
bang	Chinese dialect group
BS	Barisan Sosialis or Socialist Front
CC	Community Centre
CCC	Citizens' Consultative Committee
CCP	Chinese Communist Party
CO	Colonial Office or Community Organisation in Chapter 12
CORD	Coalition of Organisations for Religious Development
CSS	Catholic Students' Society
CUF	Communist United Front
CWS	Catholic Welfare Services
DBP	Dewan Bahasa dan Pustaka
DP	Democratic Party
EACC	East Asia Christian Conference
FMS	Federated Malay States
FO	Foreign Office
FUEMSSO	Federation of the United Kingdom and Ireland, Malaysia and Singapore Student Organisation
GCC	Geylang Catholic Centre
GLU	General Labour Union
GMD	Guomindang
HDB	Housing and Development Board

huiguan	Chinese clan group
ISA	Internal Security Act
ISC	Internal Security Council
ISD	Internal Security Department
JIM	Jurong Industrial Mission
JPC	Justice and Peace Commission
KMM	Kesatuan Melayu Muda
KMS	Kesatuan Melayu Singapura
LBM	Lembaga Bahasa Melayu
LEKRA	Institute of People's Culture
LF	Labour Front
MCA	Malayan Chinese Association
MCP	Malayan Communist Party
MCS	Malayan Civil Service
MDU	Malayan Democratic Union
MEC	Malay Education Council or Majlis Pelajaran Melayu
MEWC	Malay Education Working Committee
MNP	Malay Nationalist Party
MP	Member of Parliament
MPABA	Malayan People's Anti-British Army
MPAJA	Malayan People's Anti-Japanese Army
MSC	Malaysia Solidarity Convention
MUIS	Majlis Ugama Islam Singapura or Islamic Religious Council of Singapore
NBLU	Naval Base Labour Union
NCCS	National Council of Churches of Singapore
NGLU	Nanyang General Labour Union
NGO	Non-government organisation
NPPA	Newspaper and Printing Presses Act
NTI	Nanyang Technological Institute
NTU	Nanyang Technological University
NTUC	National Trades Union Congress
Nusantara	Malay World
NUS	National University of Singapore
NUSS	National University of Singapore Society
NUSSU	National University of Singapore Students' Union
PAP	People's Action Party
PERSAMA	Persatuan Artis Malaya or Malayan Artists Union

PKMM	Partai Kebangsaan Melayu Malaya
PMCJA-PUTERA	Pan-Malayan Council of Joint Action or Pusat Tenaga Ra'ayat Alliance
PMFTU	Pan-Malayan Federation of Trade Unions
PMU	Peninsula Malay Union
PP	Progressive Party
PPSO	Preservation of Public Security Ordinance
PRS	Partai Raayat Singapura or Partai Rakyat Singapore
PWD	Public Works Department
SAR	Singapore Annual Report
SATU	Singapore Association of Trade Unions
SBHEU	Singapore Business Houses Employees' Union
SBWU	Singapore Bus Workers' Union
SCBA	Straits Chinese British Association
SCCC	Singapore Chinese Chamber of Commerce
SCHFEU	Singapore Commercial House and Factory Employees Union
SCM	Student Christian Movement of Singapore
SCMSSU	Singapore Chinese Middle School Students' Union
SCW	Singapore Council of Women
SCWO	Singapore Council of Women's Organisations
SFSWU	Singapore Factory and Shop Workers' Union
SFTU	Singapore Federation of Trade Unions
SGEU	Singapore General Employees' Union
SHB	Singapore Harbour Board
SHBSA	Singapore Harbour Board Staff Association
SHBWU	Singapore Harbour Board Workers' Union
SITC	Sultan Idris Training College
SLAD	Singapore Legislative Assembly Debates
SMNO	Singapore Malay National Organisation
SMTU	Singapore Malay Teachers' Union
SOCANSA	Singapore Overseas Chinese Anti-Japanese National Salvation Association
SPH	Singapore Press Holdings
SSCS	Straits Settlements Civil Service
SSLC	Straits Settlements Legislative Council
SS(S)A	Straits Settlements (Singapore) Association
STC	Singapore Traction Company
STUC	Singapore Trade Union Congress

TNA, PRO	The National Archives of the United Kingdom, Public Record Office
UIM	Urban and Industrial Missions
UMNO	United Malays National Organisation
UN	United Nations papers, Cambridge University Library
USSU	University of Singapore Student Union
WP	Workers' Party
YCW	Young Christian Workers Movement

Contributors

SUNIL AMRITH is a Lecturer in History at Birbeck College, University of London. He completed his Ph.D. in History at the University of Cambridge, and was subsequently a postdoctoral research fellow at Trinity College, Cambridge. He is the author of *Decolonizing International Health: India and Southeast Asia, 1930–65* (Palgrave, 2006). His current research is on the history of Tamil migrant communities in Southeast Asia. s.amrith@history.bbk.ac.uk

TIMOTHY P. BARNARD is an Associate Professor in the Department of History at the National University of Singapore. His research focuses around Malay cultural and social history, and he is currently working on a history of Malay film from 1945 to 1965. His publications include *Multiple Centres of Authority: Society and Environment in Siak and Eastern Sumatra, 1674–1827* (KITLV, 2003), and the edited book *Contesting Malayness: Malay Identity across Boundaries* (Singapore University Press, 2004). histpb@nus.edu.sg

MICHAEL D. BARR is a Lecturer in International Relations at Flinders University. He was formerly an Australian Research Council Postdoctoral Research Fellow and Lecturer at The University of Queensland (2002–2006), and a Queensland University of Technology Postdoctoral Research Fellow (1999–2002). He is the author of *Lee Kuan Yew: The Beliefs Behind the Man* (Routledge, 2000), *Cultural Politics and Asian Values: The Tepid War* (Routledge, 2002, 2004), and co-author with Zlatko Skrbiš of *Constructing Singapore: Elitism, Ethnicity and the Nation-Building Project* (Nordic Institute of Asian Studies Press, 2008). His articles were published in *The Pacific Review, Asian Studies Review, Asian Ethnicity, Journal of Contemporary Asia* and *Journal of Health Politics, Policy and Law*. michael.barr@flinders.edu.au

C. C. CHIN alias Chen Jian was born in 1940 in Singapore. A graduate of Nanyang University (1965–66), he is an independent researcher and was a visiting scholar with the Centre for the Study of the Chinese Southern Diaspora, Australian National University and a Research Fellow of the Institute of South East Asian Studies, Jinan University, in Guangzhou, China. His research interests are on the history of the Chinese in Southeast Asia, and on the Hakka dialect group. He was a council member of the National Archives of Singapore (1990–2000), Adviser to the Society of Asian Studies, and a Council member of the South Seas Society, as well as Chief Editor of the *Journal of the South Seas Society*. He has written articles and book chapters in both English and Chinese on the history of the Japanese Occupation and the Malayan Communist Party, and in 2004 he co-edited with Karl Hack *Dialogues with Chin Peng: New Light on the Malayan Communist Party* (Singapore University Press). ccchincc@singnet.com.sg

CHUA AI LIN teaches at the Department of History, National University of Singapore, and received her Ph.D. in History from Cambridge University, UK in 2008. Her undergraduate degree from Oxford University was followed by an M.A. from the National University of Singapore on national identity and Anglophone Asians in inter-war Singapore. Her current research interests continue to focus on Anglophone Asians in 20th century colonial Singapore, particularly on the themes of modernity, cosmopolitanism, as well as popular and consumer culture. hiscal@nus.edu.sg

MICHAEL FERNANDEZ was born in India in 1934 and at age 12 was exported to Malaya, where he lived on a rubber estate in Klang. He studied at Singapore's Teachers' Training College and later in the University of Singapore. In the early 1960s, he was involved in the student and trade union activities and was detained without trial in Changi Prison for nine years and again briefly in 1977. Later, he was actively involved in civic organizations, was a school teacher and eventually worked in a publishing company. He wrote a number of short biographical pieces on Singapore and Malaysian historical figures such as James Puthucheary (2000), the family-plight of Said Zahari 'The Scars of Detention' (2001), and G. Sarangapani, the founder and publisher of *Tamil Murasu* daily in Singapore (2002). He travels frequently to India as an education counsellor to the Catholic Community in Kerala. Presently, with Loh Kah Seng, Lim Cheng Tju and Seng Guo Quan, he is working on a book project on the history of the University Socialist Club in Singapore and Malaysia.

CHERIAN GEORGE is an Assistant Professor at the Wee Kim Wee School of Communication and Information at Singapore's Nanyang Technological University, where he heads the journalism and publishing division. He is a research associate at Murdoch University's Asia Research Centre. He holds a doctorate in communication from Stanford University, and graduated from the Journalism School, Columbia University, and Cambridge University. His main research interests are in press and politics, and alternative media. He is the author of *Contentious Journalism and the Internet: Towards Democratic Discourse in Malaysia and Singapore* (Singapore University Press and University of Washington Press, 2006) and *Singapore: The Air-Conditioned Nation: Essays on the Politics of Comfort and Control* (Landmark Books, 2000). He is the editor of a website on Singapore press issues, www.journalism.sg. cherian@ntu.edu.sg

KAY GILLIS holds a Ph.D. in Politics and History from Murdoch University in Perth and is a Research Associate of the Asia Research Centre in Perth, Western Australia. She authored *Singapore Civil Society and British Power* (Talisman, 2005), which traces the ebb and flow of civil society in Singapore during the British period. In 2006, she co-authored *The Book of Singapore's Firsts* for the Singapore Heritage Society. She has been living in Singapore for 15 years and works as an independent scholar. Her current project is a study of British and Straits Chinese co-operation in fund-raising for fighter planes during World War I in Singapore. rkgillis@hotmail.com

HUANG JIANLI is an Associate Professor in the History Department of the National University of Singapore. His primary area of research and publication is on the history of student politics and local self-government in Republican China from the 1920s to 1940s. He also maintains an academic interest on the intellectual and business elites in postwar Singapore Chinese community, especially their relations vis-à-vis China and the Chinese diaspora. He authored *Politics of Depoliticization in Republican China: Guomindang Policy towards Student Political Activism, 1927–1949* (Peter Lang, 1996), co-authored *The Scripting of a National History: Singapore and its Pasts* (NUS Press, 2008), and his articles were published in *Modern Asian Studies, Journal of Oriental Studies, East Asian History, Journal of Southeast Asian Studies* and *Journal of Chinese Overseas*. hishjl@nus.edu.sg

LOH KAH SENG is a Ph.D. candidate in History at the Asia Research Centre, Murdoch University. He is working on a social history of the 1961 Kampong Bukit Ho Swee Fire. Loh has a keen research interest in Singapore history, particularly the official use of history, the Great Depression, leprosy, the student movement, and oral history and memory. Loh received his BA (Hons) and MA degrees from the Department of History, National University of Singapore, in 1996 and 2005 respectively. In between those years, he was a History teacher in a junior college, and still teaches and gives lectures to school students. lkshis@gmail.com

LENORE LYONS is Director of the Centre for Asia-Pacific Social Transformation Studies (CAPSTRANS), an Australian Research Council Key Centre for Teaching and Research, at the University of Wollongong. Recognised as the leading scholar on the feminist movement in Singapore, she was awarded her Ph.D. in Gender Studies from Griffith University, Australia in 1999. She has published widely on the women's movement in Singapore, and on cross-cultural feminist methodology. Her recent publications include *A State of Ambivalence: The Feminist Movement in Singapore* (Brill Academic Publishers, 2004) and a collection titled "Democracy and Civil Society: NGO Politics in Singapore" in *Sojourn* (October 2005). In 2005 she was awarded two grants by the Australian Research Council: one examines the intersection between citizenship, nationality and identity in the Riau Islands which form the borderlands between Singapore and Indonesia (with Dr Michele Ford, University of Sydney); and the other is a study of migrant worker activism in Malaysia and Singapore. lenorel@uow.edu.au

LILY ZUBAIDAH RAHIM is a Senior Lecturer in Government and International Relations at the University of Sydney, Australia. She lectures on the comparative politics and development of Southeast Asia and is the author of *The Singapore Dilemma* (Oxford University Press, 1998, 2001). Her multidisciplinary research interests have been published in numerous international journals. She has taught and carried out research in Australia, Malaysia, Singapore and The Netherlands. She has been commissioned by United Nations agencies to prepare papers on indigenous minorities in Southeast Asia. Her publications reflect a broad range of research interests ranging from governance in authoritarian states, ethnicity, education, and regionalism to political Islam. Lily Zubaidah is completing a book on the mercurial nature of Singapore-Malaysia relations. l.rahim@usyd.edu.au

CARL A. TROCKI is an Professor of Asian Studies in the School of Humanities and Human Services at Queensland University of Technology in Brisbane, Australia. He has a Ph.D. in Southeast Asian History from Cornell University. He has lived and worked as a teacher and researcher in Malaysia, Singapore, Thailand and the United States as well as in Australia. He has published on the history and politics of Singapore, Malaysia, Thailand, the Chinese diaspora, and the drug trade in Asia. His recent books include *Opium, Empire and the Global Political Economy: A Study of the Asian Opium Trade, 1750–1950* (1999) and *Singapore: Wealth, Power and the Culture of Control* (2006) both by Routledge. c.trocki@qut.edu.au

JAN VAN DER PUTTEN is Assistant Professor at the Department of Malay Studies of the National University of Singapore, where he teaches Malay Literature. His research interests lie in traditional Malay writing, especially writings that originate from Riau. He also researches popular forms of expression, such as magazines, comics and films. His recent publications include the article 'Abdullah Munsyi and the missionaries', in *Bijdragen tot de Taal-, Land- en Volkenkunde* 162–4 (2006), and he co-authored with Hans Stravers and Chris van Fraassen *Ridjali Historie van Hitu* (Landelijk Steunpunt Educatie Molukkers, 2004). mlsjvdp@nus.edu.sg

SIKKO VISSCHER is a Lecturer in Asian History at the University of Amsterdam and coordinates both the Minor Asian Studies and the Masters in Contemporary Asian Studies. He is also Project Manager of Asian Studies in Amsterdam (ASiA) at the International Institute of Asian Studies, which organizes and supports research and outreach activities on Asia. His main topics of interest are ethnic Chinese entrepreneurs and their social and political behaviour, as well as local processes of social and economic development and their interaction with globalization. His current research includes knowledge production and management in ethnic Chinese family businesses in a comparative perspective, and alternative histories of social and political development in Singapore. His work has been published in edited volumes and refereed journals, and his main monograph is *The Business of Politics and Ethnicity: A History of the Singapore Chinese Chamber of Commerce and Industry* (NUS Press, 2007). S.Visscher@uva.nl

YAO SOUCHOU is a Senior Lecturer at the Department of Anthropology, the University of Sydney, Australia. He has written widely on the cultural politics of Southeast Asia and the Chinese diaspora generally. He is the author of *Confucian Capitalism: Discourse, Practice and the Myth of Chinese Enterprise* (RoutledgeCurzon, 2002) and *Singapore: The State and the Culture of Excess* (Routledge, 2007). souchou. yao@usyd.edu.au

Introduction

Carl A. Trocki and Michael D. Barr

The Research Project

'Reclamation' is a very familiar concept to Singaporeans. The sea is continually being 'reclaimed' and the coastline smoothed to allow for new housing and industrial estates. The term 'reclamation' also means retrieving something that has been lost. The chapters in this book contribute towards both kinds of reclamation. On the one hand, we intend to construct new, refreshing and sometimes challenging histories of Singapore. On the other hand, we want to reclaim for future generations the memory of a period extending from late colonial days into the 1960s when Singapore was host to a dynamic and idealistic culture of political contestation and pluralism.

When we say these histories are 'new', we simply mean that they have not been written into the history of Singapore as it is usually told. They are 'new' histories based on old memories and archives that have, for the most part, been neglected or forgotten — and so are 'paths' that have not been taken. The result, we hope, is an upgraded conception of Singaporean history — not one that replaces the standard 'Singapore Story' sponsored by the regime,[1] but one that complements it, allowing the histories of those

1

unrecognised contributors to the construction of Singapore to be told alongside those who have claimed sole responsibility.

Most of the papers in this book were first presented in 2005 at an international symposium hosted in Singapore by the National University of Singapore's Asia Research Institute (ARI) under the direction of Professor Anthony Reid[2] and opened by Mrs Jean Marshall, the widow of Singapore's first Chief Minister, David Marshall.

The Symposium

The symposium was planned as an academic conference for about three dozen scholars who could sit around a table and discuss each others' research papers. When registrations from the public passed the 200 mark we realised that it was going to be much more than this. For many locals it offered a rare opportunity to open windows into their society's past that were usually shuttered — for them the 'paths not taken' were not primarily histories to be upgraded, but societal memories to be reclaimed, and — sometimes — reputations to be redeemed. One member of the audience, a Singapore lawyer and mother of teenagers, bemoaned the fact that her children had no inkling of the events, situations and personalities that we were discussing. Their Singapore history lessons at school were completely silent on the topics we were covering. It was as if they had never existed.

This book has thus become an archaeological experience. We found ourselves forced to clear away the overburden of the 'Singapore Story' in order to recall the worlds of the past that existed now only in myth and in the memories of the few who could not forget. Except for these and those few historians who had bothered to dip into the archives and consult the survivors, many of the events of the 1940s, 1950s and 1960s, even the 1970s and 1980s, had become *terra incognita*. So successful has the current regime been in obliterating the unresolved past, that the 'Singapore Story' of Lee Kuan Yew and the People's Action Party (PAP) was all that remained visible. There was only the account of their struggle for 'survival' against colonialism, communism, large and unpredictable neighbours, and uncertain economic circumstances. This was followed by the triumphal story of rapid economic development. In this history, even the contributions of Lee's colleagues tended to be swamped by the Lee Kuan Yew story, thus narrowing the story even further.[3]

Although elements of these alternate histories still existed in some accounts, most scholars treated these perspectives in a rather negative fashion.[4] The pre-PAP age was portrayed as a chaotic and uncertain time before the events of 'real' history took place. And yet, for those who know the era, it was one of dynamism, great political movements, and high aspirations. This was true, we argue here, not only for the rest of Asia, but also for Singapore itself.

The age was one of revolution and hope, a hope that, many will argue, has yet to be fully realised, even today. In remarks addressed to the symposium, Professor Wang Gungwu, who not only lived through most of the events covered in this book, but was also an active participant, portrayed some of the sentiments being expressed as a kind of 'nostalgia' for a bygone era and unachieved dreams. Professor Chua Beng Huat suggested that much of the interest in the panels was from Singaporeans who 'love to hear others tell them how bad they had it'. Perhaps parts of both are true, but whatever the case, it is clear that the presentations touched a nerve that many felt was long in need of stimulating. It is in that spirit that we offer these papers.

The book is the final output of a research project funded in its pilot phase by the Queensland University of Technology (QUT) and the Australian Technological Network of Universities in 2001, and later by the Australian Research Council (ARC).[5] The project's founders, Carl A. Trocki and Michael D. Barr, were both based in QUT at the beginning of the project, but it soon became a multi-institutional project as Barr moved to the University of Queensland and then Flinders University, and Yao Souchou and Lily Rahim of Sydney University joined. By this stage it had also become an international project, as several colleagues from the National University of Singapore — notably Huang Jianli, Tim Barnard and Kevin Tan — came on board. The international status of the project was cemented when ARI agreed to host the project's symposium in Singapore and Professor Chua Beng Huat from ARI joined Trocki and Barr as a symposium co-ordinator.

Our aim was to recast Singapore's post-war history through accounts of the civil and political movements that operated outside the parameters of imagination created by the ruling PAP. It was largely intended to present a 'not-the-PAP' version of Singapore's recent past and to focus on the positive contributions and efforts of those alternative movements. The work was never intended to present an anti-PAP or anti-Lee Kuan Yew approach to the study of Singapore's social and political order. Unfortunately, that disclaimer has become slightly tendentious, despite our best intentions. In a number of cases, it has been impossible to provide a satisfactory account of a particular movement without noting the manner in which it met its demise or was destroyed. The fact that these paths were not taken was often the result of forceful action by those in power. One does not make an omelette without breaking eggs, and the recent history of Singapore is littered with its share of eggshells.

Although both the editors are historians, many of the contributors are not. The project draws from disciplines as diverse as history, political science, cultural studies, anthropology, sociology and media studies. The book has no underlying theoretical structure other than to look with a sceptical eye at current assumptions and to present the evidence of our research and our thoughts on how these stories were lost, and what it can mean to Singaporeans to find them.

The Age

Our starting point is six decades ago. In the years immediately following World War II, Asia was shaken by a wave of popular movements. Most were nationalistic, anti-colonial and to some extent motivated by a Marxist vision of a reformed social and international order. Virtually all of them were anti-colonial and demanded national independence and freedom from European domination. Even those that were not overtly political indicated the emergence of a vibrant civil society that felt little hesitation in laying its concerns before the public and the white colonial rulers.

They were especially important in what T. N. Harper has styled the 'Indian Ocean Port Cities', particularly places like Singapore.[6] These cities hosted great confluences of people and ideas that were extremely vibrant and cosmopolitan. Such places had always been modern, and they fuelled what would become the great social movements of the post-war era. Although few Asians had the physical weapons to combat colonialism, the ideas were already being formulated. It took only 40-odd chaotic months of the Japanese invasion and occupation of Southeast Asia to totally shift the balance of power.

After 1945, the colonialists found themselves confronted by new and demanding aspirations from their Asiatic subjects. Where once there were only dissatisfied intellectuals, oppressed peasants and downtrodden coolies, now there were mobilised armies of trained and armed troops, angry students, militant labour unions and organised political parties. They raised the banners of revolution and sought to bring an end to the European empires either by negotiation, intimidation or violent overthrow — whatever the situation seemed to demand.

By the 1960s, colonialism had been defeated in most of Asia, yet the anti-colonialist movements and the rhetoric of revolution persisted even in the newly victorious regimes. There were new ideas and new projects, and the aim was to create a brave new world on the ashes of the colonial order. President Sukarno of Indonesia called them the NEFO — the New Emerging Forces — and sought to line them up against the OLDEFO — the Old Established Forces, the colonial and neo-colonial powers. A new age seemed to open when he convened a conference of non-aligned nations at Bandung in 1955. It was a heady time for the new countries. Everywhere, it seemed that colonialism and the West were in retreat, and that power and prosperity would soon fall into the hands of the proud new peoples.

Then, in one country after another, the dreams were gradually frustrated. In most countries, one or another of the local 'contenders' grabbed the brass ring of power and scooped up all the marbles of state control. A jealous nationalism soured the dreams of third world unity. The new leaders demanded international recognition from the great powers and turned around to bring the revolution to a halt. This was true even of Sukarno. Everywhere, censorship was re-introduced and dissent was stifled. Opposition or alternative political parties were suppressed as one group or party took control of each state. Labour unions were emasculated and the political aspirations of the minorities, particularly the Chinese in Southeast Asia, were quashed. In many cases the state became barely distinguishable from the personality or the party of the political leadership.

Singapore

Before 1942, Malaya was merely a geographical expression that included Singapore. Singapore was grouped together with Melaka and Penang as the Straits Settlements, while the Peninsular states were divided among the Federated Malay States and the Unfederated Malay States. There were also the Borneo territories of Sarawak, North Borneo (now Sabah) and Brunei, each with its own unique status. Despite these administrative divisions, goods, services, people and information moved quite freely throughout the various sectors. Some people, whether they lived on the Peninsula or in Singapore, began to think of themselves as 'Malayans'. The post-war era saw Singapore abruptly separated from the rest of 'Malaya' and left to seek independence very much on its own.

Singapore thus entered this world of political ferment and social revolution with an ambiguous status. Immediately after the war, there was a first burst of political activity, led by the Malayan Democratic Union (MDU), but this was rapidly suppressed with the outbreak of armed resistance on the Malayan Peninsula by the Malayan Communist Party (MCP). In 1948, the British declared an 'Emergency' (the word that has stuck to the guerrilla war which was fought in the Malayan jungles). It lasted for the next decade or so. Meanwhile, in an attempt to anticipate the post-colonial environment, British planners tried to set up the Malayan Union on the Peninsula in 1946, leaving Singapore as a separate Crown colony. The Malayan Union scheme failed, but the Federation of Malaya was created and granted self-government in 1955, which was quickly followed by independence in 1957. Singapore, however, remained a Crown Colony. Singapore, along with the Borneo states of Sabah and Sarawak, joined the Federation in 1963 to form the Federation of Malaysia. Malaysia continues as a nation-state to this day, but Singapore separated from Malaysia in 1965 and began life as an independent republic.

The three decades from 1945 to the mid-1970s in Singapore were characterised by extraordinary cultural, intellectual and political dynamism, and those years are the primary focus of this book. Students, labour unions, ambitious political contenders and representatives of the various ethnic communities all stepped forward to offer alternative visions of Singapore's future. They came from across the entire political spectrum, and between them generated a ferment of ideologies, priorities, perspectives and social visions such as mainstream 'official' Singapore politics had never known before, and has not seen since.

For approximately three decades, politics in Singapore was pluralistic and relatively open, but by the end of the 1960s pluralism was fighting a rearguard action against the monopolisation of all public discourse — not just politics — by the state. The PAP had won the 1959 elections as a radical socialist party with strong left-wing backing. Once in government, however, the right wing of the party under Lee Kuan Yew embarked on a more conservative and authoritarian course. In 1963 the Singapore government arrested most of the leading leftists in a security operation called Operation Cold Store, and then systematically began to dismantle and marginalise all forms of civil society in the country — from the labour and student unions to the clan associations and the Chinese Chamber of Commerce. By the beginning of the 1970s, it was clear that all paths were closed except for the one being built by the ruling party. This was a path of elitism, meritocracy, ethnic essentialism, state-directed industrialisation, and — a radical departure from reigning political orthodoxy among post-war nationalist movements — integration with global capitalism. By the mid-1970s, the ruling party's hegemony was so complete and its rule so successful — at least by its own measures — that it had become difficult to conceive of the earlier alternatives having ever had merit. Public discourse now contemplated with horror the possibility that the nation-building project could have had any form other than that which emerged. Alternatives were seen as options for failure, if not chaos and anarchy. Yet the studies presented here suggest that this was not necessarily true. Alternative outcomes to the current state of affairs used to be well within the imagination of Singaporeans, and some of these alternatives may have even contained viable seeds for a different kind of social development than that which Singapore experienced. The present did not just happen. It was crafted. Whether by design or by accident, intended or not, it was made by the actions of specific people at specific times. It is also true that people were caught, as it were, in the more imponderable and impersonal blind forces of history over which they had no real control. There were global economic, environmental, political and social trends at work, and those in Singapore could only hope to shield themselves from them or to take advantage of them.

The Book

The book is divided into four thematic sections. The first two papers, grouped under the heading, 'Opening New Paths', introduce the age and the ideas. The second group of papers deals with party politics during the 1950s and 1960s, and the third group focuses on broader social, cultural and popular movements within Singapore between the late 1940s and the mid-1970s. The final section, containing only three papers, discusses the 1980s and 1990s, with some consideration of what sort of civil society activity is currently possible in Singapore.

Part 1: Opening New Paths

The first chapter, by Chua Ai Lin, deals with the pre-war period and gives us some idea of the social and intellectual atmosphere of Asian Singapore in the 1920s and 1930s. It does not launch straight into the paths that were not taken, but describes the social and political milieu that produced the post-war and post-independence political elite: the 'English-speaking domiciled community' of Singapore and Malaya. This group was made up of those Asians who were educated in English-language schools and who worked for the government, in the professions and in the international companies that made their bases in Singapore. She shows how they were already developing a political and civic consciousness as early as the 1920s and 1930s. This was bolstered by the English-language *Malaya Tribune*, which for a time had the largest circulation of any newspaper in Malaya. This group of middle-class Asians would form the social and cultural base for the next generation of Singapore's leaders.

In the post-war years, Singapore's anti-colonial activists continued to see Singapore as part of something bigger. They understood their place in the wider world of newly-emerging nations. They were part of a global movement that was breaking the chains of colonialism and embracing socialism and communism and redefining itself as the 'third world', an expression which gained currency in the Bandung conference of non-aligned nations convened by President Sukarno of Indonesia in 1955. Sunil Amrith, who comes to Singapore studies from a South Asian perspective, looks at Singapore's internationalist connections during the 1950s and early 1960s, and places Singapore within a global and regional context. He discusses Singapore's participation at the Bandung conference and explores the connections to the Afro-Asian non-aligned movement of that age. At least for a while, Singaporeans sought solidarity with the global struggles for liberation and the search for an alternative to the Cold War alignments of the great powers. He also reviews the growth of nationalist sentiments and the process whereby more rigid boundaries were erected between the newly emerging states.

Part 2: Party Politics

The second set of papers pays attention to party politics in Singapore during the early independence period. In most cases these political movements, as varied as the MCP, the Singapore Chinese Chamber of Commerce (SCCC) and the Malay parties, all played a role in bringing the PAP to power. Their story is also that of the decline of civil society and an organised political opposition in Singapore. The chapter by C. C. Chin is an important re-examination of the role of the MCP in Singapore's political life during the 1950s and 1960s. Chin, focusing on the strengths and weaknesses of the party as an organisation, argues that it was more a follower than a leader in the late 1950s and early 1960s. Those were the days of the so-called United Front. While it could offer moral and spiritual leadership, the party on the ground in Singapore had little influence over everyday events. Student and labour movements, strikes and demonstrations were often the result of spontaneous actions by the individuals directly involved. Chin's account provides new and valuable information on the inner workings of the party and also directly challenges the idea that it posed a serious threat to Singapore's established order.

Sikko Visscher explores the rise and fall of political action by some of the politically ambitious leaders of the SCCC. This group that constituted an important faction of the Chamber contested only the 1955 election.

Nevertheless, the SCCC represented a key structure within Singapore's civil society. Like the Malay Education Council (MEC) it was most influential during the last days of colonialism. It fought to achieve greater citizenship rights for Singapore's Chinese and worked to get out the vote during these early elections. It also played an important role in the support of Chinese education and culture as well as in the social welfare of the masses of ordinary Chinese because it supported and led temple committees, cemetery committees and the vast number of clan, place-of-origin, surname and occupational groups among Singapore's Chinese. Despite this activism, it remained an intensely conservative force and could not escape its roots in the colonial system.

Lily Rahim concentrates in the main on the rise and fall of Malay political activism in Singapore and on Malay involvement in the rise of the PAP. Focusing on much the same group of Malay writers and activists that Barnard and van der Putten studied (see the next section of this chapter), she reviews their role within the PAP and explores the progress of the relationship between the Lee Kuan Yew faction of the party and the Malays of Singapore. Support from Malay activists and journalists such as A. Samad Ismail and Said Zahari was crucial to the PAP's credibility as a multiracial party. Once Singapore had achieved independence through its separation from Malaysia, however, Malay support ceased to be a necessity for the party.

Carl Trocki examines the career of David Marshall in the years after his short tenure as Chief Minister, when he devoted himself to acting as the 'loyal opposition' in Singapore as it came under PAP domination. As a member of the Legislative Assembly he fought to oppose the misuse of the Preservation of Public Security Ordinance and later the Internal Security Act by the government. He agitated publicly to ensure the rights of detainees and to preserve the jury system in Singapore. Later, Marshall returned to private life and his career as a barrister, but he continued to work through the courts to defend the civil and human rights of many who were victimised by the regime. He was also a key figure in the fight to preserve press freedom in Singapore and established links with international left-liberal and humanitarian movements such as Amnesty International.

Part 3: Activists and Popular Movements

The third set of papers focuses on a number of popular movements in Singapore, especially those of the artists, writers, students and labour unions. Although they were not formal political parties, these movements demonstrate the active civil society that characterised Singapore in these years. They reflect some of the most important social movements of the 1950s and 1960s.

Tim Barnard and Jan van der Putten's chapter on Malay political and cultural life in Singapore during the post-war years breaks new ground in bringing to light the vibrant alternative political paths pursued by Singapore's Malays. Men such as Yusuf Ishak, A. Samad Ismail and Said Zahari, together with scores of other young Malay activists, were galvanising Singapore's Malay community in the middle decades of the twentieth century. Not only did they play important parts in the rise of the PAP, they also exercised significant influence across the Causeway through the *Utusan Melayu*, which was founded and based in Singapore from the 1920s and into the 1950s.

Malay writers and activists in Singapore played roles in a number of political movements, including the Kesatuan Melayu Muda and the Partai Rakyat Singapura, not to mention the United Malays National Organisation (UMNO) and later its local branch, the Singapore Malay National Organisation. At the same time, there were Malays who embraced a much broader vision of their political and cultural universe. This was the idea of *Melayu Raya*, or *Indonesia Raya*. These were concepts that saw a grand unity among all of the peoples of the Malay World, a region that, at its broadest, might have included everything that today makes up the countries of Indonesia, Malaysia, Singapore, Brunei and much, if not all, of the Philippines. Other Malay activists besides journalists and politicians also played an important part in the vibrant civil society of the age.

E. Kay Gillis's chapter focuses on the Malay Education Council which, for a time, managed to develop patterns of political activism that gave them influence on government policies during the 1950s and 1960s. Understanding the role that a pressure group can play in a plural democracy, the MEC was able to promote its own educational agenda in the face of bureaucratic inertia.

Yao Souchou tells the story of the rise and fall of Nanyang University, or Nantah, in the 'immigrant imaginary' of Singapore's Chinese-educated communities. The establishment of Southeast Asia's only Chinese-medium tertiary institution was seen as a great step for the vast masses of Singapore's Chinese, whose many small contributions were essential to its realisation. It is worth stressing the words of the Eurasian writer, Han Suyin, quoted by Yao, to the effect that the student radicals' relation to communism was '… not a pattern to imitate exactly, but a frame of reference'. Yao argues that in many ways this was true of the entire Chinese-educated community.

The chapter by Huang Jianli addresses some of the issues raised by the student movements that were so important in the early politics of Singapore. He takes issue with the common conception that the student movement was the exclusive province of the Chinese-educated. He shows that students from all streams and mediums were actively involved in the anti-colonial struggle and the move to open up political life in Singapore. It was not only the Chinese-educated students that flexed their political muscle in Singapore, but students from the English-medium universities as well. Moreover, in several cases students from both language streams collaborated in their activities.

Michael Fernandez and Loh Kah Seng examine the important role played by the left-wing trade unions in Singapore during the period between 1954 and 1965. They, too, take issue with the charge that the left was dominated by communist infiltrators. They marshal considerable evidence to show that union activity was largely focused on economic issues: wages, hours and working conditions. The most effective personalities were the natural leaders who rose from the ranks and responded to the aspirations of the workers. Their account is supported by Chin's discussion of the MCP that shows that student and labour activity was largely spontaneous and beyond the control of the party.

Part 4: Walking Narrow Paths

The final three chapters are set in the 1980s and 1990s and demonstrate the conditions of political life in these more recent decades. This was the period when the system of out-of-bounds (OB) markers was laid down by the national leadership, whereby the exercise of political control was achieved principally through self-censorship, rather than outright oppression. Civil society, the press and other public associations are now so disciplined that they police themselves, rather than step over the line and risk censure by the government.

Michael Barr's chapter looks at the rise and demise of a Catholic social action movement that emerged in the 1980s. He shows how they fell afoul of the authorities and found themselves accused of engaging in a 'Marxist conspiracy', hence suffering arbitrary and abrupt suppression. With its typically ruthless approach, the government confronted the Catholic hierarchy in Singapore and forced the bishop to accept the spurious charge that they were followers of liberation theology and were part of a subversive conspiracy to overthrow the social order. The offending clerics were forced out of the country while their lay associates were detained for periods varying from a few months to several years.

Lenore Lyons's chapter on the Association of Women for Action and Research (AWARE) concentrates on one of the survivors of Singapore's civil society. AWARE arose in the period leading up to the demise of the Catholic activists, but has managed to find a path for survival, and like the media, has learned to play the game within the OB markers. Nonetheless, she makes it clear that there are areas of action that have been closed to activists. A kind of civil society manages to survive in Singapore, but only just, and it is constantly looking over its shoulder.

Finally, Cherian George reviews the role of the press in Singapore which, like AWARE, also looks over its shoulder. He challenges the myth that the press has been the docile handmaid of authority in the past or even in the early independence period. Rather, he shows that even the Asian press has strongly asserted its right to an independent voice, often criticising authority, throughout Singapore's history. He also assesses the PAP's methods of controlling the press today, noting that effective censorship has been achieved without the heavy hand of government intervention. Rather, commercial concerns and government influence now guide the press to such an extent that it willingly accepts the blinkers which the state has fitted on it.

Together, this last set of papers shows the limited options for citizen participation in Singapore's political life. Political activity has been closed off to all who are not officially designated as politicians. Other organised social bodies are prohibited from engaging in political action. This has meant the elimination of civil society as it is understood elsewhere. It has left a situation where the continued threat of the Internal Security Act and the tight regulations on organised groups prevent the emergence of any challenge from below.

The Gaps

We have not covered all, or even the most important of the movements of this era. There is much more work to be done, and we see this effort as only a beginning. We have not, for instance, systematically covered those that chose the path of formal opposition to the government in Parliament, although we made two gestures in that direction: Carl A. Trocki's chapter is devoted to one such figure (David Marshall), and Michael D. Barr published an article in an academic journal on another (J. B. Jeyaretnam).[7]

Beyond these two personalities, there remain major issues that still beg attention from future scholars. First, there is the question of the period of Singapore's membership in Malaysia, perhaps as seen from the Malaysian perspective, or at least from the view of the Malays in Singapore. Second, we have no chapter devoted entirely to Barisan Sosialis (the Socialist Front). Its members were among the founders of the PAP and represented some of the more militant activists in Singapore. After 1961, these men and women split from the PAP and, as the Barisan, comprised the most credible opposition to the PAP until the party's self-destruction in the late 1960s.

Though mutually opposed at the time, the Barisan and the Malaysian experiment each represented for Singapore a more pluralist alternative which has since been abandoned. Albert Lau's book, *A Moment of Anguish*, offers a good account of the official negotiations and the public and diplomatic story of Singapore's membership in Malaysia and the events that subsequently led to Singapore's expulsion from the Federation, but it does so from very much an official Singaporean perspective.[8] There is little there that the PAP would find objectionable. Nor is there any discussion about those who favoured Malaysia or what sort of social forces were affecting Singapore as a member of Malaysia, or vice versa. Much less is there any thought given to what Singapore and the Federation would have been like if separation had never happened. What were the possibilities?

The left-wing opposition represented in the Barisan, had it survived, would certainly have meant a much stronger labour movement and a more solid presence of the Chinese-educated groups within Singapore. Had Dr Lee Siew Choh maintained a credible opposition presence, both in Parliament and in Singapore's civil society, the monolithic shutdown of public discourse might not have been possible. Counterfactual situations aside, however, even though parts of the story of the rise and fall of the Barisan are woven into some of our chapters, the full story is untold, and is certainly an area that deserves further study.

The symposium where these papers were read generated considerable excitement in Singapore. The response to the papers and to the overall project of resurrecting these aspects of Singapore's past was very positive, even enthusiastic. Clearly many Singaporeans were interested in learning more about their recent but forgotten past. We hope that this book can fill a real need, and perhaps generate further research into these areas.

NOTES

1   See, for instance, Archives and Oral History Department, *Road to Nationhood: Singapore 1819–1980* (Singapore: Singapore News and Publications, 1984); National Heritage Board, *Singapore: Journey into Nationhood* (Singapore: National Heritage Board and Landmark Books, 1998); Ministry of Information and the Arts, *The Singapore Story: Overcoming the Odds. An Interactive Media*, CD-ROM, a National Education Project by the Ministry of Information and

the Arts, 1999; Lee Kuan Yew, *The Singapore Story: Memoirs of Lee Kuan Yew* (Singapore: Prentice Hall, 1998); and *From Third World to First: The Singapore Story 1965–2000. Memoirs of Lee Kuan Yew* (Singapore: Singapore Press Holdings and Times Editions, 2000).

2   See the symposium website at http://www.ari.nus.edu.sg/conf2005/postwar.htm.

3   For the first book-length attempt to broaden the focus of Singapore's historiography away from Lee Kuan Yew, see Kevin Y. L. Tan and Lam Peng Er, eds., *Lee's Lieutenants: Singapore's Old Guard* (St Leonards: Allen & Unwin, 1999).

4   See, for example, C. M. Turnbull, *A History of Singapore, 1819–1988* (Singapore; New York: Oxford University Press, 1989); John Drysdale, *Singapore: The Struggle for Success* (Sydney: Allen & Unwin, 1984); Alex Josey, *Lee Kuan Yew: The Crucial Years* (Singapore: Times Books, 1980); Ernest C. T. Chew and Edwin Lee, eds., *A History of Singapore* (Singapore; New York: Oxford University Press, 1991); Dennis Bloodworth, *The Tiger and the Trojan Horse* (Singapore: Times Books International, 1986) and Lee, *The Singapore Story*, volumes 1 and 2.

5   See the project's website at http://www.pathsnottaken.qut.edu.au.

6   T. N. Harper, 'Communists, Leftists and Populists: The Social and Ideological Roots of Post-war Left-wing Politics', Paths Not Taken Symposium, http://www.pathsnottaken.qut.edu.au/.

7   Michael D. Barr, 'J. B. Jeyaretnam: Three Decades as Lee Kuan Yew's *Bête Noir*', *Journal of Contemporary Asia* 33, 3 (2003): 299–317. This article, also available at the project's website at http://www.pathsnottaken.qut.edu.au, was researched and written during the pilot phase of the Paths Not Taken project, with funding from QUT and the Australian Technological Network of Universities.

8   Albert Lau, *A Moment of Anguish: Singapore in Malaysia and the Politics of Disengagement* (Singapore: Times Academic Press, 1998).

PART 1

Opening New Paths

1

Imperial Subjects, Straits Citizens: Anglophone Asians and the Struggle for Political Rights in Inter-War Singapore

Chua Ai Lin

Political awareness was not alien to the Asian population in colonial Malaya, even before World War II and the Japanese Occupation; neither was it limited to the communist-inspired working classes and Chinese radicals. English-educated white-collar workers, professionals and prominent local figures were also enthusiastic in their political expression, with Anglophone Asians of varied ethnic backgrounds standing as compatriots in the struggle for greater political rights. In this transnational public sphere, political identity and an embryonic sense of shared Malayan identity brought these groups together, assisted by the lingua franca of English — the language in which their proficiency helped them to engage with the state.[1] The political pluralism of the post-war period was, in fact, a direct derivative of a pre-war culture that saw Anglophone Asians exercising their public voices as advocates of local, Asian interests — usually to no avail.

Their pre-war political debates and the firmness of their conception of their rights laid the foundations for the English-educated political parties of the post-war era; both conservative, such as the Progressive Party, as well as leftist groups, namely the Malayan Democratic Union, the Singapore Labour Front and the People's Action Party. In the formative years during the 1930s, members of these post-war groups were constantly exposed to public debates on political rights, citizenship and national identity. The Progressive Party, in particular, was founded by figures who had been prominent public voices before the war, most notably John Laycock and N. A. Mallal.[2] Even more importantly, the shared political identity emphasised by Anglophone Asians of varied ethnic backgrounds was the precursor to the multi-ethnic, non-communal parties of post-war Singapore.

Political Development in the Straits Settlements

On the scale of formal political advancement, India led the way among the British colonies, while the Straits Settlements ranked near the bottom. In the Straits Settlements, there was a colour bar that prevented non-Europeans from being appointed to higher civil service posts, as well as a lack of Asian and non-governmental representation in public representative bodies. In 1924, the Straits Settlements Legislative Council was expanded to include more non-government members, known as Unofficials, and in 1932, the Executive Council was also reformed to include one Asian member.[3] Despite these reforms, the Straits Settlements and Hong Kong were the only Crown Colonies without an Unofficial majority in their Legislative Councils — a fact that agitators for change in the Straits Settlements did not fail to point out. Civil administration in the Straits Settlements was also more back-ward than other colonies such as Ceylon, where locals reached top levels in government service. In the Straits Settlements, all non-Europeans were excluded from senior posts in the civil service. Even the Federated Malay States had the Malay Administrative Service, which allowed Malays to hold civil service offices of responsibility.[4] In 1933, the Straits Settlements Civil Service was formed to redress this problem,[5] but public opinion in the Straits noted that the very highest levels of government were still blocked by the colour bar. These political inequalities roused the ire of educated Asians in the Straits who saw themselves as excluded from the rights due to them.

Anglophone Asians' political consciousness was raised further by other contemporary events, such as nationalism in China and India, the Great Depression,[6] and Sir Cecil Clementi's 'Decentralisation' policy, which proposed wide-reaching administrative changes across British Malaya. In particular, the Straits Chinese community had become increasingly critical of the colonial administration because of policies which were perceived as being racially discriminatory. As part of the decentralisation plans for Malaya, grants-in-aid to Chinese and Tamil schools were removed in 1932, with only Malay primary education being provided free by the government.

The Legislative Council's Chinese member for Penang, Lim Cheng Ean, was so incensed by this that he withdrew from the Legislative Council, becoming the first and only person to do so.[7] The following year, 1933, an Aliens Ordinance was introduced aimed at preventing the entry of individuals suspected of seditious or disorderly behaviour. In particular, this referred to Chinese nationals from both the Kuomintang and communist camps, rather than political activists from India who were natural-born British subjects.[8] Legislative councillor Tan Cheng Lock summed up Straits Chinese frustrations when he stated in council that the Aliens Ordinance could be seen as 'part and parcel of an anti-Chinese policy, probably with a political objective, based on distrust and fear, which the Chinese on the whole as a community have done nothing and have given absolutely no cause to merit'.[9] In what was formerly known as 'A Land Without Politics',[10] the people of Malaya had clearly begun to raise their political voices.

The Public Sphere and a 'Repertoire of Activism'

As in other parts of the British Empire, the 1920s was a period of many changes in the colony of the Straits Settlements. An increasingly well-educated population was able to take advantage of developments in the legislative machinery, community organisations and the press in order to express opinions on social and political issues.

Following the expansion of the Legislative Council in 1924 to include more non-governmental as well as Asian voices, the rigour and scope of its debates improved. Whereas the earlier composition of the council had included only six Unofficials — including one token Straits Chinese — out of 17 members,[11] the new constitution provided for 27 members, comprising the Governor and equal numbers of Officials and Unofficials. Of the Unofficials, seven were European, three Chinese, and one each from the Malay, Indian and Eurasian communities.[12]

Many organisations were formed in the first two decades of the twentieth century; not only social and community groups but also those with an interest in politics and public affairs. Of the latter, the most prominent was the Straits Chinese British Association (SCBA), which was formed in 1900 to defend the interests of the Straits Chinese community. Other quasi-political organisations were formed by English-educated community leaders around the 1920s, such as the Eurasian Association in 1919, the Singapore Indian Association in 1923, and the Singapore Malay Union (Kesatuan Melayu Singapura) in 1926.[13] There were also debating societies and reading clubs, such as the Straits Chinese Reading Club and the Chinese Students' Literary Association, which took an active interest in current affairs, as well as interest groups such as the Clerical Union and the Singapore Ratepayers' Association, which spoke out on public issues.

English-educated Asians in the Straits Settlements were familiarised with Empire-wide events and Western political concepts of democracy, citizenship and social justice in the Christian mission schools they attended. The history of the British Empire was an important component of the curriculum and students were trained in public speaking through literary and debating societies, especially in the American mission-run Anglo-Chinese Secondary School, which had a separate debating society in each class to promote American values of democracy.[14] Those who progressed to university in Britain would have personally experienced the political ideas and developments there. After the opening of Raffles College in Singapore in 1928, even students who received a local tertiary education were trained to have a greater understanding of politics. In the Arts stream at Raffles College, students were required to choose one major and two minors from history, economics, English language and literature, and geography.[15] The second-year history syllabus concentrated on the history of the British Empire, and third-year compulsory courses included the political and constitutional history of England, and the history of political thought. Required reading for those majoring in history included not only several textbooks on constitutional history and political thought, but also an account of the French Revolution, and seminal texts such as *The Republic of Plato*, Aristotle's *Politics*, Hobbes' *Leviathan*, *Two Treatises of Civil Government* by Locke, and Mill's *On Liberty*.[16]

Newspapers were the key source of up-to-date information, and Anglophone Asians read them keenly. Well-established daily papers by this time were the *Singapore Free Press* (founded 1835), the *Pinang Gazette* (1838), the *Straits Times* (Singapore, 1845) and the *Malay Mail* (Kuala Lumpur, 1896).[17] Of the many new journals that emerged in the early years of the century, the more successful daily titles included the *Straits Echo* (Penang, 1903), the *Times of Malaya* (Ipoh, 1904) and the *Malaya Tribune* (Singapore, 1914). In Singapore, the 1931 census recorded 57,251 non-Europeans as literate in English; a year later, the circulation of the Malaya Tribune newspaper came to 4,800 copies, which was comparable to that of the *Straits Times*. Although the *Malaya Tribune* closed down in 1951, it was extremely important during the pre-war period, chalking up sales of 13,000 in 1937, a 'circulation over the whole country far larger than that of all the other afternoon English papers in the country put together'.[18]

Most crucial to our story was the political agenda of the *Malaya Tribune*. It was founded in Singapore in 1914 to defend the interests of the Asian 'domiciled communities' — comprising both local-born and those permanently settled in Malaya — and called itself the 'People's Paper'. It was priced at five cents, compared to the *Straits Times* and *Singapore Free Press*, which were aimed at the elite European reader and cost ten cents each.[19] The financial backers at the *Tribune's* founding were prominent Asians and Eurasians: Straits Chinese Lim Boon Keng, Koh San Hin, Ong Boon Tat, See Tiong Wah, S. Q. Wong, Lee Chim Tuan and Tan Cheng Lock; Indians M. V. Pillai and A. M. S. Angullia; a Eurasian, Alexander Westerhout; and a Jew, Ezra Aaron Elias.[20] Only Asians (including Eurasians) were allowed onto the board of directors or to hold shares. Europeans on the staff could only do so at the discretion of the board of directors and were subject to a limit of 15 per cent of the total number of shares.[21] Although editorial leadership came from 'seasoned journalists from world-famed Fleet Street',[22] as far as possible, Asian journalists and sub-editors were hired and groomed for top positions in the paper — a radical aim at the time.[23]

These simultaneous developments increased the volume and level of public debate on political and social issues because they provided multiple forums for discussion. For example, through newspapers, readers were apprised of public events, debates in the Legislative Council, ideas raised at lectures organised by societies such as the Rotary Club and Hu Yew Seah, resolutions passed by the Straits Chinese British Association or Straits Settlements Association, complaints lodged by the Clerical Union, comments from newspapers and societies elsewhere in Malaya as well as the views of newspaper editors and readers. The contents of each day's papers formed the topics of informal conversation in the coffee shops or organised discussions in reading clubs, and inspired further lectures and formal debates by various societies.[24]

Citizens and Subjects in the Straits Settlements

When it came to the issue of nationality, well over one-third of Singapore residents were British subjects by birth, with a significant number of them Anglophone Asians active in the public sphere. Hence, discussions of citizenship rights were relevant to more than just an insignificant minority of the population. The 1931 *Census of British Malaya* reveals that 38.9 per cent of those living in Singapore were born in Malaya; moreover, 96.7 per cent of the Malaya-born Singapore population were born in the Straits Settlements.[25] The significance of being born in the colony was that this conferred British nationality by birth. On the other hand, those born in the Federated Malay States or Unfederated Malay States would only have the status of British protected persons and subjects of the sultan in whose state they had been born. Since nationality formed one of the criteria for the distribution of political rights, this distinction was significant.

During the inter-war years, there were shifts in the definition of the terms 'nationality' and 'citizenship'. Under British law, holding British nationality made one a British 'subject', while 'citizenship' was a political rather than legal concept which conferred on worthy individuals of a particular state the status of 'citizen', entitling them to rights and privileges as well as placing them under certain obligations to the state.[26] However, popular usage of this period treated the words 'nationality' and 'citizenship' as synonymous. The roots of this understanding lay in the advent of nation-states in Europe in the late 18th century, when states legislated to determine who qualified for the status and rights of a citizen. One of the qualifying criteria was holding the legal status of that state's nationality.[27] The principles of democratic government spread even to Britain, where the legal term 'subject' was still used but began to incorporate more qualities of citizenship, represented by the four Reform Acts from 1832 to 1918, which progressively extended the franchise.[28] When it came to changes in language being reflected in the constitution, it was not until the promulgation of the British Nationality Act of 1948 that the term 'Commonwealth citizen' was introduced as an alternative to 'British subject'.[29]

The key difference between 'citizenship' and 'subjectship' was the role of democratic participation in the governing of the community as one of a citizen's duties, whereas a subject's duty was, above all, allegiance, which implied his or her unquestioning loyalty to the arbitrary power of the king. While citizens could expect the state to provide education so that the people would be well-informed enough to participate in democratic government, subjectship assumed the inability of the ignorant, governed masses to decide their own affairs, much less those of the state.[30]

Given their education, access to news and information, and the vibrancy of the public sphere, it is unsurprising that domiciled, Anglophone opinion in the inter-war years demonstrated a strong consciousness of themselves as 'citizens', with the rights and responsibilities of citizens. In 1923, Song Ong Siang published his *One Hundred Years' History of the Chinese in Singapore*, in which he profiled prominent Chinese personalities. These included Ong Boon Tat, 'one of the group of young Straits Chinese who are taking a practical interest in public affairs, having realised the *duties of citizenship* [emphasis mine] which devolve more especially on the men of education and standing in our community'.[31] Similarly, R. B. Krishnan, the editor of the Singapore Indian Association's organ, *The Indian*, and regular contributor to the *Malaya Tribune*,[32] in 1925 described the mission of *The Indian* as being to remind the public of the 'rights and privileges of the Indians in Malaya' as well as 'their responsibilities and duty': 'in short we have to exist so that the Malayan Indian shall become a better type of *citizen* [emphasis mine] than what he is now'.[33] By the 1930s, the growing sense of these sentiments led to calls for citizenship training in schools to be further strengthened. For example, Heah Joo Seang,[34] writing in the *Malayan Chinese Review* in 1932, criticised the lack of political education in the Malayan educational system and recommended that secondary students be 'equipped with a knowledge of the principles of good citizenship and civic duties'.[35] Similarly, the principal of Raffles Institution, Mr. D. W. McLeod, at the school's speech day in 1937, 'urged that the curriculum of the school must be extended to include direct study of public affairs' such that 'students of to-day, before leaving school, must be given a general knowledge of the duties of true citizenship'.[36]

The early 1930s also saw more widespread use and explicit discussions of political rights. In letters to the English language press, domiciled Asians confidently and consistently referred to the principle of citizenship and to themselves as citizens when arguing for their rights, even though these were not in the terminology of British nationality law. For example, a letter to the *Malaya Tribune* from a reader in Singapore calling himself 'Citizen' suggested that the term 'Empire' be replaced with 'British Commonwealth of Nations', as the latter better reflected political developments in the Dominions, India and other colonies.[37] Furthermore, while writers to the press were conscious of the differences in nomenclature, the words 'subject' and 'citizen' were taken as synonymous in popular usage. A letter to the *Malaya Tribune* referred to 'we British subjects' and immediately clarified, 'citizens is a more euphonious term, but then asked, "What's in a name?"'.[38] No matter which term was used, however, it seemed that domiciled Asians saw themselves very much in line with the political concept of citizenship rather than as subjects. For example, one *Malaya Tribune* reader wrote, 'What constitutes a British subject? In civic times to give civic dues and enjoy civic rights — in martial times to be prepared to lay down his life for his country and home.'[39] The writer in this case demonstrated a formal understanding of political theory — perhaps acquired at school or college — as his phrasing was reminiscent of the Roman ideal of 'civic virtue' which also included a military element.

In tandem with the interchangeability of the terms 'subject' and 'citizen', another form of etymological looseness was common: the use of 'citizenship' to refer to legal nationality status. When Heah Joo Seang, the President of the SCBA in Penang, spoke at the association's annual general meeting in 1931, he referred to 'Chinese in Penang who claim, either by birth or through naturalisation, British citizenship'.[40] Similarly, the *Malay Mail*, in questioning the position of non-Malay domiciled communities in the Federated Malay States (FMS), mentioned the 'absence of any Malayan citizenship' and that 'local Courts [have] held that there is no F.M.S. citizenship as such', but rather, different legal nationalities for each Malay State.[41] Colonial officials themselves contributed to the confusion; for example, in the Legislative Council, Mr A. S. Haynes referred to 'citizens of Malaya' when he appealed to the local inhabitants 'not to allow themselves to be split up into different camps on racial lines irrespective of citizenship'.[42]

Given that democratic privileges were inherent in the concept of citizenship, the conflation of the terms 'nationality' and 'citizenship' became an easy shorthand for local public opinion to express the idea that nationality status (even as British *subjects*) conferred political rights. As a letter writer to the *Malaya Tribune*, going by the pen name 'British Subject', expressed: 'we are by birth *ipso facto* British subjects, and will always continue to be so, and therefore claim greater political franchise'.[43] The demand for political rights could even be seen as a willingness to take on the duties of a citizen. 'The more insistent we are in asking for political privileges the more effectively shall we demonstrate our loyalty, as it is our loyalty and sense of citizenship which instil in our hearts a desire to take a greater share in and shoulder greater responsibilities of the administration of this Colony,' wrote a 'Chinese British Subject' to the *Malaya Tribune*.[44] However, the colonial administration did not share this viewpoint and continued 'withholding the legitimate rights from its citizens',[45] in the words of the disenfranchised Asian community.

Official Attempts to Assess Allegiance

Following the logic of citizenship, Straits British subjects believed that their political loyalty to the British legitimised their entitlement to greater political rights. The domiciled communities therefore expended great effort in trying to prove their allegiance. Even within the concept of subjectship, loyalty was the most important duty of a subject, and British administrative policies emphasised the role of allegiance as a necessary criterion for the distribution of rights. The colonial government developed administrative methods of assessing an individual's allegiance based on two criteria: nationality status and domiciled status.

The political rights demanded by the domiciled communities were based on the assumption that one was a British subject by birth in the first place. Only British subjects could serve in official representative bodies like the Legislative Council and the Executive Council, become Justices of the Peace, and join the Straits Settlements Civil Service and Straits Settlements Legal Service. British subjects also could not be banished from the colony.[46] While this may seem straightforward enough, there was actually a significant degree of confusion as to the precise nationality status accorded to people in 'British Malaya'. Many people, including prominent community leaders, did not understand the complexities of nationality status in Malaya. J. S. M. Rennie, a European British subject and member of the Straits Settlements (Singapore) Association (SS(S)A), asked at a meeting of that association for clarification of what constituted a British subject; he knew only what was popular knowledge — that 'Chinese born in this Colony *ipso facto* became British subjects'.[47] In 1933, Federal Councillor San Ah Wing asked for clarification of the nationality status of Chinese born in the Federated Malay States.[48] The *Malaya Tribune* added that 'it is the most natural thing in the world for any Chinese in the F.M.S., wherever he comes from, to believe that his children who are born there are automatically British subjects, just the same as in the Straits Settlements'.[49]

To answer these questions, one needed to realise that 'British Malaya' did not exist in law. The fact that this was a popular misconception might have been the motivation for prominent Singapore lawyer Roland Braddell to publish his book, *The Legal Status of the Malay States*, in September 1931.[50] He pointed out that 'no map [used] the word "Malaya"' and that neither 'Malaya' nor 'British Malaya' were official titles. Nevertheless, these terms were commonly used as a matter of convenience to refer to: '(1) the Straits Settlements, a Crown Colony belonging to Britain; (2) the Federated Malay States of Perak, Selangor, Negri Sembilan and Pahang, under the protection of Great Britain; (3) the State of Johore, under the protection of Great Britain; and (4) the States of Kedah, Kelantan, Trengganu and Perlis, under the suzerainty of Great Britain'.[51] The only true colony was that of the Straits Settlements, comprising Singapore, Penang and Malacca. The 'Malay States', on the other hand (referring to the Federated Malay States as well as the Unfederated Malay States of Johore, Kedah, Kelantan, Trengganu and Perlis) remained as technically sovereign sultanates, whose populations were subjects of the respective Malay rulers. Administratively, the idea of 'British Malaya' was held together by the Governor of the Straits Settlements colony, who was also High Commissioner in the Malay States, as well as the Peninsula-wide Malayan Civil Service, to which the most senior government posts belonged.[52]

One also needed knowledge of British nationality law. Natural-born British subjects were divided into those who acquired their nationality *jure soli* (by place of birth, that is, being born in British territory) and those who held it *jure sanguinis* (by descent). An example of the latter case would be children of British subjects born in the Malay States. British nationals *jure sanguinis*, whose fathers were British subjects by naturalisation, were subject to a number of procedural requirements before they could obtain their British nationality and retain it after the age of 21. It is quite possible that many would have lost their British nationality through sheer ignorance of the correct procedures. One could also become a British subject by naturalisation, but such people could have their British nationality revoked, and if they had been granted only 'local', rather than 'Imperial', naturalisation, they would have been treated as aliens in Britain. To complicate matters further, there were many long-standing residents in the Straits Settlements who were not British subjects at all because they had been born in the British protected territories of the Malay States, and this granted them only the status of British protected persons, not that of British subjects.

Yet British officials realised that nationality status alone was not an accurate indication of political allegiance. Therefore, in determining who was eligible to join the Straits Settlements Civil Service, they included a second criterion: the length of an individual's family's domicile in the Straits Settlements. Not only did applicants have to be natural-born (rather than naturalised) British subjects, not hold dual nationality and be domiciled in the Colony, but they also had to have at least one parent who was a naturalised or natural-born British subject, and both parents had to have been domiciled in the Straits Settlements at least since the birth of the candidate.[53] By including length of domicile and parents' status in the requirements to join the Straits Settlements Civil Service, officialdom acknowledged the assertions of the domiciled community that their long family history in Malaya had resulted in a deep attachment to Malaya and British rule in the territory. Decades of agitation for recognition of domiciled identity had finally been recognised because it now fitted in with Governor Clementi's new policy of 'Malayanisation' aimed at integrating non-Malay domiciled communities into Malayan society and the political community.

Expressions of Imperial Loyalty

Despite the fact that the Anglophone, domiciled communities mostly held British nationality and had long family histories in the Straits Settlements, the government continued to find them politically suspect. Firstly, this was because many Malayan Chinese and Indians took a keen interest in the nationalist political happenings in China and India at the time, and secondly, because all ethnic Chinese automatically held nationality from China *jure sanguinis*, resulting in the fact that all Straits British subjects of Chinese descent held dual nationality, whether they wanted to or not. These factors made it even more difficult for the colonial government to accurately distinguish the differing levels of political loyalty within the large and diverse Chinese and Indian populations as a whole.

In response, the domiciled communities emphatically expressed their loyalty throughout the period. In 1935, the Colony's Legislative Council voted, for the second year running, a gift of $500,000 for defence of the Empire, over and above the annual Defence Contribution of $4,000,000 and the cost of local forces which amounted to $500,000 a year. The response of the English-speaking domiciled communities to the imperial defence contribution was very positive: 'In this Colony we recognise fully that we are lightly taxed and a duty devolves upon us to share to the utmost of our power in the responsibilities as well as the assets of the Empire.'[54] Once again, the language and ideas of citizenship lay behind such views. Another important example was the celebration in Singapore of the coronation of King George VI in 1936. One Indian correspondent expressed in the *Malaya Tribune* that 'surely this [was] the best opportunity for the Indian community in Malaya to show their loyalty to His Majesty and to the Colony itself', and during the coronation celebrations, the 'citizens of this city' from each of the different communities participated enthusiastically.[55] As part of the festivities, the Indian and Ceylonese communities gave an address on Loyalty to His Majesty the King in English, Tamil and Hindustani.[56] Other occasions when the locally domiciled communities were able to express their loyalty to the British were the 1935 King's Jubilee celebrations and the annual charity collections on Poppy Day. In addition, representatives of the various communities often made assertions such as: 'the Chinese British subjects of this Colony are zealously loyal British subjects, and [attach] great value to their status',[57] or, in the case of Eurasians, 'in spite of the fact that a number are descended from Portuguese and Dutch ancestors, they are British by birth and British in outlook'.[58]

Military service was an even more direct way of expressing loyalty. Indians in Singapore encouraged the formation of an Indian volunteer company, promising that 'when the time for enrolment [came], the Government [would] be astonished to see the rush, and this in itself [would] prove the loyalty and devotion of the rising generations of the Indians for King and country'.[59] Domiciled Indians wanted to be on an equal footing with the Chinese and Eurasians, who already had the privilege of having their own companies in the Singapore Volunteer Force. From the mid-1930s onwards, the Eurasian community was even calling for the creation of a regular Eurasian battalion.[60] The Straits Chinese British Association also unsuccessfully petitioned the government in 1940 for the creation of a colony regiment of local-born youths as a means of making 'British subjectship and its privileges and responsibilities more real and vital to our people'.[61] In the face of external threats to the Empire with the onset of World War II, the action of the English-speaking domiciled communities proved that their loyalty could not be doubted.[62]

Limitations of Subjectship

In general, those pushing for political progress felt that only by pursuing reasonable demands did they have a chance of succeeding. Moderate demands would prove their good intentions and loyalty, which would then engender British confidence in them, and result in the subsequent liberalisation of rights. Even British failure to concede on 'unchallengeable rights'[63] did not alter their approach, and in 1940, a *Malaya Tribune* editorial stressed that:

> nobody in Malaya has ever advocated reform in this country on the hurried lines of that adopted for Ceylon ... we ask for something quite different and more moderate — A SIMPLE EXTENSION OF THE COUNCIL TO SECURE AN UNOFFICIAL MAJORITY AND MORE DIRECT REPRESENTATION OF THE DIFFERENT COMMUNITIES THROUGH THEIR OWN ASSOCIATIONS.[64]

The basis of this moderate approach was a strong belief in the reciprocity of the relationship between the government and the people. It was seen as 'the duty of every paternal Government to show this friendly gesture gracefully, to guide its citizens wisely along the constitutional lines'.[65]

The importance of fulfilling the citizen's duty of loyalty, and proving this to the colonial government, was clear to the English-speaking domiciled communities — it was one half of the reciprocal relationship between citizens and the state; and it was the principle of reciprocity that justified their claim to political participation, itself one of the fundamentals of democratic citizenship. Over and over again, local Asian leaders emphasised that 'duty must of necessity breed privileges'.[66] The domiciled community founded their relationship with the government on the basis of trust and a gentleman's honour — the British ideals they had learnt in English-medium schools, and as such, expected the colonial administration to reciprocate correspondingly. In the words of a 'prominent resident', commenting on the continued restriction of the Malayan Civil Service to candidates of pure European descent:

> We in Malaya have always had a deep regard for the traditional John Bull, who typifies both justice and fairplay. Can this gentleman have changed so considerably as to institute a regulation that is fundamentally at variance with that attribute?[67]

The same 'prominent resident' declared that the domiciled community were still being 'denied a right that is theirs by birth, nationality and the deep-rooted ties of patriotism'.[68]

Public opinion and officialdom may have agreed on the criteria on which the distribution of rights was based, but what was under dispute was the level of rights that the population could lay claim to. Local leaders failed to realise that there was a limit to the rights available to subjects, such that no matter how loyal a subject was, he would not be accorded the same status as a citizen. Moreover, race continued to weigh on many European minds despite the inclusive spirit of imperial policy during this period, and as pragmatic considerations of law and order, as well as military security, grew more urgent towards the end of the 1930s.

Other Constraints: Race and Imperial Security

British imperial theories and government proclamations portrayed a misleading picture of the political situation in the colonies. For example, the party programme of the British Labour Party (which formed the British government from 1929–31) published in 1918 advocated a 'great Commonwealth of all races, all colours, all religions and all degrees of civilisation that we can call the British Empire'.[69] A *Malaya Tribune* editorial of 18 March 1931 quoted the *Spectator* of London proclaiming that 'the only possible motto for a world Commonwealth such as ours to adopt is "Equal rights and equal treatment for every civilised man, whatever his colour"'.[70] In addition, the doctrine of trusteeship had been one of the cornerstones of imperial theory since the late 19th century.[71] The theory had its roots in the idea first expressed by Edmund Burke in 1783, with reference to India, that all political power was to be exercised for the benefit of mankind at large, and such rights were a trust and therefore to be rendered accountable. Later this developed to include the guidance of subject populations towards self-government, as embodied in Queen Victoria's 1858 proclamation that British subjects of 'whatever race or creed, be freely and impartially admitted' to government posts as long as they qualified.[72] The impetus for political progress in the colonies was given a further push in the 1930s with the development of the Commonwealth idea. Originally a strategy of colonial economic development, this concept evolved into a moderate political ideal by the late 1930s, and was put into practice by giving greater autonomy to the Dominion territories and moving India towards self-rule.[73] A *Malaya Tribune* editorial from 1933 summarised these two theories, stating that there was 'a recognised Imperial duty to develop the Colonies commercially, politically and culturally, so that they may become conscious supporters of British ideals, actual self-governing parts of the British Commonwealth of Nations'.[74]

Despite the existence of these progressive policies and the rising numbers of well-educated Asians in the Straits, in reality, Europeans remained disdainful of the ability of Asians to manage their own affairs. In 1904, a colour bar in the Malayan Civil Service was introduced at the request of Sir John Anderson, the newly-appointed Governor of the Straits Settlements and High Commissioner for the Malay States, who argued that the majority of Asians were prejudiced against non-European officials.[75] Similarly, Europeans in government as well as in the private sector felt that Asians in general could not be trusted and would not command the necessary respect that senior civil service posts required. They objected in particular to the introduction of the Straits Settlements Civil Service in 1933 and the Straits Settlements Legal Service in 1938, which were formed to allow non-Europeans in the colony to hold more senior civil service positions.[76] In addition, the formation of the European Association of Malaya by a breakaway group from the Straits Settlements (Singapore) Association was an indicator of European objections to Asians taking up leadership roles in the SS(S)A, previously a European-dominated organisation. Official racism in the Empire reared its head most concretely in discrimination against non-white immigrants, primarily Indians, in the legislation of white settler Dominions.[77]

European objections to Asians in the civil service came despite the fact that the more prestigious Malayan Civil Service (MCS), whose officers staffed all the top government posts, continued to be closed to non-Malay

Asians. This was not simply because of the colour bar, but because of the anomalous constitutional structure of the different components of British Malaya. MCS officers could be transferred anywhere in the Peninsula, and thus had to be acceptable to the sovereign sultans in the Malay states, in addition to the British government of the Straits Settlements colony. Non-Malay Asians were seen as aliens in a Malay land and thus not accepted by the Malay rulers. Hence, the MCS was staffed almost entirely by British officials, along with a few Malay members.[78] When the Straits Chinese British Association petitioned Sir Samuel Wilson, the Permanent Under-Secretary of State at the Colonial Office, in 1932, one of their demands was for the removal of this racial discrimination in the civil service. Given the political and constitutional status of the Malay states, the best solution was for a service limited to the colony of the Straits Settlements alone, and at a more junior level to the MCS.[79]

Besides racial considerations, there were other factors contributing to the Straits government's unwillingness to concede to political demands. Firstly, the Colonial Office was wary of repeating the Ceylon experience where the introduction of an unofficial majority had reduced the government to impotence. The Straits Settlements governor, Sir Cecil Clementi, had been Colonial Secretary in Ceylon from 1922–25, where he had witnessed the potential instability resulting from council reform.[80] Another threat to stability was unrest organised by the Malayan Communist Party, especially in the form of labour strikes during the periods 1936–37 and 1939–40. The strikes spread from Singapore to other parts of Malaya and grew in militancy. After the outbreak of the Sino-Japanese war in 1937, the communists were able to draw more support by participating in the Chinese National Salvation Movement.[81] Maintaining stability in Malaya was especially important because of the naval base situated in Singapore. Singapore played a critical role in imperial defence in the East. The impending threat of war, and the subsequent outbreak of hostilities in Europe in 1939, made it even more vital for the British to keep a close grip on Singapore.

With these larger concerns at stake — the preservation of British power in Malaya as well as the defence of the entire empire in the East — the persistent calls for political rights by the English-speaking domiciled communities were not a priority for the government. The domiciled communities based their claims for rights on the strength of their loyalty to the British, so they were not likely to disturb law and order or threaten the position of the British in Malaya. In any case, their livelihoods depended on the stability provided by the colonial government. Following the outbreak of war in Europe in 1939, the domiciled communities were even less likely to make demands on the government and instead focused their energies on supporting the British war effort. As the *Malaya Tribune* commented:

> Forming the bulk of the population of Malaya, Asiatics have given wholehearted support to Britain's case, realising that on the result of the war depends the freedom and other benefits they have enjoyed under British rule.[82]

Conclusion

English-educated post-war politicians regardless of party affiliation — whether the Progressive Party on the right, or the Singapore Labour Front, Malayan Democratic Union or People's Action Party on the left — grew up in this atmosphere of vocal public opinion. While their commitment to achieving decolonisation and independence may have been specific to the post-World War II era, their self-confidence and ability to think politically were not. The long and successful history of the *Malaya Tribune* newspaper, as well as organised political petitions and campaigns, were testimony to this. With the structural limitations on democratic participation within a colonial society, it is no wonder that from a distance, it appears as if pre-war political activity in Singapore was limited to left-wing radicals, and political change was imperceptible. But qualitatively, the Anglophone public sphere was vibrant and critical, and once broader political circumstances changed, as they did after the war, the energy and ability of local, English-language political activism was able to make real progress. By considering pre-war Anglophone political activity, we are reminded that committed political engagement can influence society and leave a legacy, even if fundamental constitutional change is not achieved.

The other social legacy of the Asian Anglophone public sphere was the fluid and natural interaction between individuals of different ethnic backgrounds. It was a multi-ethnic zone, whose parts were bonded together by a lingua franca, common educational experiences (and hence cultural references), the fabric of everyday life in Singapore, as well as a shared political identity and predicament. The Anglophone sphere deserves more critical attention as the arena where 'boundary-crossers', whose interests straddled ethnic and linguistic lines, could be found even before the nationalist period of the 1950s, when powerful anti-colonial sentiments were shared by locals of varied ethnic backgrounds.

Furthermore, the category of 'English-educated' has typically been posited in opposition to 'Chinese-educated', with Malay as a third group. Yet while the latter two refer to ethnic categories, 'English-educated' is not.

'English-educated' and 'Chinese-educated' only make sense as a comparative binary when referring to the Chinese community. A more meaningful
approach is to use the term 'Anglophone', which opens the category to all
those who could engage and interact in the English language, and does not
obscure the possibility of multiple educational backgrounds and linguistic
faculties, as was often the case with English-speaking Asians. By escaping
the inference of conservative political orientation (i.e. uncritical and pro-
British) and the restrictive social elitism in the term 'English-educated',
the Anglophone sphere opens up the fascinating possibilities of a cosmopolitan, hybrid community that in many ways pre-figures the Singaporean
of today.

NOTES

1   I am grateful to the participants of the Paths Not Taken: Political Pluralisms of
    Post-war Singapore Symposium, 14–15 July 2005, who were kind enough to
    read and comment on earlier drafts of this paper: Sunil Amrith, Tim Harper,
    Lim Cheng Tju, Loh Kah Seng and Carl Trocki.
2   See Yeo Kim Wah, *Political Development in Singapore, 1945–55* (Singapore:
    Singapore University Press, 1973).
3   Kevin Y. L. Tan, ed., *The Singapore Legal System*, second edition (Singapore:
    Singapore University Press, 1999), p. 38; Looi Wun-Kion, 'The Straits Settlements
    Government: A Study of the Straits Settlements Executive Council (1867–1941)',
    Academic Exercise, National University of Singapore, 1995, p. 17.
4   Khasnor Johan, *The Emergence of the Modern Malay Administrative Elite*
    (Singapore: Oxford University Press, 1984), p. 1. The Malay Service was intro-
    duced in 1910 but the term 'Malay Administrative Service' only came into use
    in the 1920s.
5   CO 273/584/92144, Clementi to Cunliffe-Lister, 14 October 1932.
6   Loh Kah Seng, 'Beyond "Rubber Prices" History: Life in Singapore during
    the Great Depression Years', M.A. Dissertation, Department of History,
    National University of Singapore, 2004. Loh argues that the economic crisis,
    in intensifying the debate on the local-born and foreign-born, helped to frame
    public preference for the principle of *jus soli* in nationality law in the Straits
    Settlements. Furthermore, the Depression contributed to a more local and
    family-oriented labour force, and presumably the same happened to the white-
    collar and professional classes. See also Leong Yee Fong, 'The Emergence and
    Demise of the Chinese Labour Movement in Colonial Malaya, 1920–1960',
    in *The Chinese in Malaysia*, ed. Lee Kam Hing and Tan Chee Beng (New York:
    Oxford University Press, 1999).
7   Harold E. Wilson, *Social Engineering in Singapore: Educational Policies and
    Social Change, 1819–1972* (Singapore: Singapore University Press, 1978),
    pp. 39–41.

8   Kok Pin Loong, 'Aliens Ordinance 1933', Academic Exercise, Department of History, University of Singapore, 1972.

9   Ibid., p. 29.

10 *Malaya Tribune*, 18 November 1932.

11 Kevin Y. L. Tan, ed., *The Singapore Legal System*, p. 36.

12 Rupert Emerson, *Malaysia: A Study in Direct and Indirect Rule* (New York: Macmillan, 1937; reprint, Kuala Lumpur: University of Malaya Press, 1964), pp. 276–9.

13 Myrna Braga-Blake, ed., *Singapore Eurasians: Memories and Hopes* (Singapore: The Eurasian Association, 1992), p. 18; Suresh Kumar, 'Singapore Indian Association, 1923–1941', Academic Exercise, National University of Singapore, 1995, p.1; William R. Roff, *The Origins of Malay Nationalism*, second edition (New Haven: Yale University Press, 1994), p. 190.

14 Ong Yed Deed, 'The Development of the History Curriculum in the English-Medium Schools in Singapore from 1899 to 1991', M.A. Thesis, Columbia Pacific University, 1992, p. 26; Herbert Henry Peterson, 'The Development of English Education in British Malaya', M.A. Thesis, University of Denver, 1942, p. 138.

15 CO 273/ 593/13164, 'Annual Report on Education in the Straits Settlements for the Year 1932', p. 32.

16 *Raffles College Calendar* 1932–33, pp. 26–9.

17 C. M. Turnbull, *Dateline Singapore: 150 Years of the Straits Times* (Singapore: Times Editions for Singapore Press Holdings, 1995), pp. 6, 8, 17, 51, 66.

18 *Malaya Tribune*, 16 July 1937. In a commemorative history of *The Straits Times*, Turnbull confirms that the *Malaya Tribune*'s circulation in 1937 was 'far in excess of the *Straits Times*'; see Turnbull, *Dateline Singapore: 150 Years of the Straits Times*, p. 96. From May 1934 onward, the daily slogan underneath the newspaper's masthead read, 'Largest Circulation of Any Daily Newspaper in Malaya'. Circulation figures for the paper were professionally audited by chartered accountants Messrs. Derrick and Co., and the figures open to inspection by the public. *Malaya Tribune* Special Supplement, 18 January 1935; *Malaya Tribune,* 3 February 1937.

19 *Malaya Tribune* Special Supplement, 18 January 1935; *Malaya Tribune* Silver Jubilee Supplement, 16 January 1939; Peter Laurie Burns, 'The English Language Newspapers of Singapore, 1915–1951', Academic Exercise, Department of History, University of Malaya, 1957, p. 31.

20 *Malaya Tribune* Silver Jubilee Supplement, 16 January 1939.

21 Burns, 'The English Language Newspapers of Singapore, 1915–1951', p. 28.

22 *Malaya Tribune* Silver Jubilee Supplement, 16 January 1939. The chief editors of the paper were Chesney Duncan (1914–16), Frank Neville Piggott (1916–17), George Bogaars (1917–19, concurrently working as managing director of the paper from 1916–33), W. A. Wilson (1919–23; 1928–34), Stanley Jones (1923–26), Granville Roberts (1926–28), H. L. Hopkins (1934–39) and G. S. Hammond (1939–42). When Bogaars retired, E. M. Glover took over as Managing Director. Ibid., pp. 32–54.

23 *Malaya Tribune* Silver Jubilee Supplement, 16 January 1939; ibid., pp. 52–53. For example, Lim Keng Hor, who joined the *Malaya Tribune* in 1933, became editor and general manager of the paper after World War II.

24 There are numerous examples of the interwoven nature of the public sphere. For example, the campaign for Raffles College to be made a university was hotly pursued in 1937 in speeches at alumni dinners of the Old Rafflesians' Association, Raffles College and the King Edward VII College of Medicine, at the Anglo-Chinese School's annual prize-giving, in Legislative Council speeches, resolutions by the Straits Chinese British Association, the Clerical Union and the Straits Settlements (Singapore) Association, editorials and correspondence in the *Malaya Tribune* and in magazines of Raffles College and the College of Medicine, and by an official commission.

25 C. A. Vlieland, *British Malaya (the Colony of the Straits Settlements and the Malay States Under British Protection, Namely the Federated States of Perak, Selangor, Negri Sembilan and Pahang and the States of Johore, Kedah, Kelantan, Trengganu, Perlis and Brunei): A Report on the 1931 Census and on Certain Problems of Vital Statistics* (London: Crown Agents for the Colonies, 1932), tables 88 ('Straits Settlements: The European Population by Birthplace'), 92 ('Straits Settlements: The Eurasian Population by Birthplace'), 96 ('Straits Settlements: The Malaysian Population by Birthplace'), 100 ('Straits Settlements: The Chinese Population by Birthplace'), 104 ('Straits Settlements: The Indian Population by Birthplace'), and 108 ('Straits Settlements: Other Population by Birthplace').

26 Dawn Oliver and Derek Benjamin Heater, *The Foundations of Citizenship* (New York and London: Harvester Wheatsheaf, 1994), p. 10.

27 Ibid., p. 21.

28 Ibid., p. 17.

29 Ibid., p. 58

30 Ibid., pp. 58–60.

31 Song Ong Siang, *One Hundred Years' History of the Chinese in Singapore*, reprint edition (Singapore: Oxford University Press, 1984), p. 99.

32 Colonial intelligence described Krishnan as 'a writer of objectionable articles in the *Malaya Tribune*'; CO 537/911/24384, *Malayan Bulletin of Political Intelligence*, April 1923.

33 *The Indian* (Singapore), May 1925, p. 2.

34 Heah Joo Seang (b. 2 November 1899, Penang) was a prominent Penang merchant, who served as a member of the Chinese Advisory Board, Penang (1931) and as a Municipal Commissioner, Georgetown (1931–32), in addition to being the editor and proprietor of the *Malayan Chinese Review* (1931–33). Information from *Who's Who in Malaya 1939: A Biographical Record of Prominent Members of Malaya's Community in Official, Professional and Commercial Circles* (Singapore: Compiled and published by Fishers in conjunction with Printers, 1939).

35 *Malaya Tribune*, 21 June 1932.

36 *Malaya Tribune*, 8 June 1937.

37 *Malaya Tribune*, 26 May 1931.

38 *Malaya Tribune*, 17 February 1931.
39 *Malaya Tribune*, 11 February 1931. See Oliver and Heater, *The Foundations of Citizenship*, p. 13.
40 *Malaya Tribune*, 16 February 1931.
41 Article reproduced in *Malaya Tribune*, 14 March 1932.
42 *Proceedings of the Legislative Council of the Straits Settlements*, 4 December 1933, B218.
43 *Malaya Tribune*, 16 February 1931.
44 *Malaya Tribune*, 13 February 1931.
45 *Malayan Chinese Review*, 18 June 1932; reprinted in *Malaya Tribune*, 21 June 1932.
46 CO 273/571/82049/1, *MRCA* 7 (March 1931), 16–17, CO273/584/92144, encl. 3 Clementi to Cunliffe-Lister, 14 October 1932; *Malaya Tribune*, 21 September 1940.
47 *Malaya Tribune*, 20 May 1931.
48 *Malaya Tribune*, 31 October 1933.
49 *Malaya Tribune*, 31 October 1933.
50 Roland St John Braddell, *The Legal Status of the Malay States* (Singapore: Malaya Publishing House, 1931).
51 Ibid., pp. 5–6.
52 Emerson, *Malaysia: A Study in Direct and Indirect Rule*, p. 25.
53 CO 273/584/92144, Clementi to Cunliffe-Lister, 14 October 1932, and encl. 3 to the same.
54 *Malaya Tribune*, 19 February 1935.
55 *Malaya Tribune*, 22 January 1937.
56 *Malaya Tribune*, 10 May 1937.
57 *Malaya Tribune*, 12 February 1931.
58 *Malaya Tribune*, 4 December 1940.
59 *Malaya Tribune*, 29 May 1937.
60 *Malaya Tribune*, 28 April 1937.
61 *Malaya Tribune*, 7 October 1940.
62 *Malaya Tribune*, 2 November 1940.
63 *Malaya Tribune*, 12 May 1932.
64 *Malaya Tribune*, 29 February 1940. Capitals present in the original text.
65 Editorial by Heah Joo Seang in *Malayan Chinese Review*, 18 June 1932; reprinted in *Malaya Tribune*, 21 June 1932.
66 *Malaya Tribune*, 31 December 1940.
67 *Malaya Tribune*, 21 September 1938.
68 Ibid.
69 Paul B. Rich, *Race and Empire in British Politics*, second edition (Cambridge [England] and New York: Cambridge University Press, 1990), p. 77.
70 *Malaya Tribune*, 18 March 1931.
71 See W. D. McIntyre, *Colonies into Commonwealth* (London: Blandford Press, 1966), pp. 145–75; Ronald Hyam, 'Bureaucracy and "Trusteeship" in the Colonial Empire', in *The Oxford History of the British Empire, vol. IV: The*

Twentieth Century, ed. Judith M. Brown (Oxford: Oxford University Press, 1999), pp. 255–79.

72 *Malaya Tribune*, 16 January 1931.

73 Rich, *Race and Empire in British Politics*, pp. 68–9.

74 *Malaya Tribune*, 27 October 1933.

75 John G. Butcher, *The British in Malaya 1880–1941: The Social History of a European Community in Colonial South-East Asia* (Kuala Lumpur: Oxford University Press, 1979), pp. 107–9. Butcher lists J. O. Anthonisz, a Ceylonese, P. J. Sproule, a Eurasian from Ceylon, and E. T. Talma, a Negro from the West Indies, as examples of non-Europeans who had entered the Malayan Civil Service in the late 19th century, prior to the introduction of the colour bar.

76 CO 273/584/92144, Clementi to Cunliffe-Lister, encl. 4 by A. P. Robinson, 14 October 1932; CO 273/649/50576, Small to MacDonald, encl. 1 by P. A. McElwaine, Chief Justice, Straits Settlements, 19 October 1938.

77 D. George Boyce, *Decolonisation and the British Empire, 1775–1997* (New York: St. Martin's Press, 1999), p. 239.

78 Yeo Kim Wah, *The Politics of Decentralization: Colonial Controversy in Malaya 1920–1929* (Kuala Lumpur: Oxford University Press, 1982), pp. 33–4.

79 Lee Yong Hock, 'A History of the Straits Chinese British Association, 1900–1959', Academic Exercise, University of Malaya, 1960, p. 54.

80 Yeo Kim Wah, 'British Policy Towards the Malays in the Federated Malay States, 1920-40', Ph.D. Dissertation, Australian National University, 1971, pp. 137–8.

81 C. F. Yong, *The Origins of Malayan Communism* (Singapore: South Seas Society, 1997), pp. 210–70; 'Leong Yee Fong, Labour and Trade Unionism in Colonial Malaya: A Study of the Socio-Economic and Political Bases of the Malayan Labour Movement, 1930–1957', Ph.D. Dissertation, Universiti Malaya, 1990, pp. 89–138.

82 *Malaya Tribune*, 2 November 1940.

2

Internationalism and Political Pluralism in Singapore, 1950–1963

Sunil S. Amrith

The narratives of Singapore's political discourse in the 1950s flowed from a diverse range of histories and experiences that drew sustenance from events and ideas across Asia and beyond, invigorating the radical political imagination that flourished in late-colonial Singapore. The narrowing of the bounds of political debate by the 1960s relied, in part, on the dominant power casting aspersions on the cosmopolitanism of its leftist and liberal opponents; a natural, lived sense of internationalism came to be branded as 'anti-national'. The historical narrative underpinning the explosion of popular protest in the 1950s was part of a global wave of anti-colonial struggle, but by the 1960s the only acceptable story in Singapore (and beyond) was that of the rise of state sovereignty as the ultimate end of Asian politics. This chapter is concerned with the original, internationalist impulse.[1] I argue that for a few years after the decline of transnational political projects, the Singapore left drew nourishment and inspiration from the examples and stories of their counterparts in the broader Afro-Asian arena.

The starting point for this story lies in the myths and meanings of the 1955 Asian-African Conference in Bandung, which coincided, almost to the week, with the inauguration of democratic politics — of a constrained sort — in Singapore. I argue that the most important manifestation of internationalism in Singapore's political discourse was in creating a space wherein diverse groups could transcend the racialised public sphere and forge a range of interactions and common political projects. This produced something very different from the officially sanctioned 'multi-racialism', which was deployed by the state as a tool of government.[2] The People's Action Party's (PAP) defeat of political pluralism involved stripping Singapore's public sphere of its cosmopolitan imagination. And they succeeded, in part, by using the language of absolute state sovereignty and non-interference enshrined at Bandung. My underlying assumption is that Singapore's political history has had smallness thrust upon it; and that one way to capture the rich pluralism of Singapore's political discourse before the consolidation of PAP dominance is to rediscover its cosmopolitanism. The enduring relevance of the earlier cosmopolitanism of Singapore's progressive left can be seen, perhaps, in the strength that various civil society groups in Singapore continue to derive from their counterparts elsewhere in the region — in the fields of human rights activism, the consumer movement and radical theatre, amongst many others.

A Brave New World

The Asian-African conference was held in the cool hills of Bandung, Indonesia in April 1955; it was a time of political upheaval in the colony of Singapore. The Rendel Constitution had been inaugurated on 1 April, just weeks before the Bandung conference was held. David Marshall's Labour Front government had assumed office, and the fledgling PAP had been given its first taste of electoral victory, winning three of the four seats it contested and making Assemblymen of Lee Kuan Yew and Lim Chin Siong. Notwithstanding the colonialist attempt to 'quarantine' Singapore from outside influences, international influences impinged on the everyday language of Singapore politics.[3] In the words of a memorandum by the Council for Joint Action, a grouping led by Lee, which would feed into the establishment of the PAP:

> [Malaya could not but be influenced] by the decisive, and at times turbu-
> lent political development in surrounding countries. We, the people of
> this colony, are not deaf to the waves of political passions, ambitions and
> hopes that surge and spread over the shores of Malaya.[4]

The questions of Bandung informed Singapore politics. There was, firstly, the issue of 'neutralism' versus militarism, a debate that came to a head over the question of national service in Singapore.[5] Secondly, there was the vexed question of international communism and its relationship to nationalist aspirations: the debates between aligned and non-aligned countries in Bandung were reflected in the range of political positions taken in Singapore, and even within the PAP itself.[6] Above all, the spirit of anti-colonialism expressed at Bandung found a ready echo in Singapore. A submission by the Singapore Factory and Shop Workers' Union, led by Lim Chin Siong, reveals the melding of these different elements of Singaporean and Afro-Asian politics. The memorandum demanded an end to emergency regulations in Malaya and the abolition of the National Service Ordinance; it also demanded non-alignment, opposed the establishment of a SEATO base in Singapore, and called for immediate self-government.[7]

In this context, the Bandung conference evoked a sense of great possibilities. Beyond the spectacle of Asian and African leaders meeting to stake their claims on the world stage, itself an unprecedented occurrence, the political language of Bandung resonated in Singapore politics for a long time afterwards. Bandung lent new life, and a new language, to the anti-colonialism of the Singapore left. The words of Indonesian President Sukarno rang out most clearly. 'This is the first intercontinental conference of coloured peoples in the history of mankind,' he declared boldly, united 'by a common detestation of colonialism in whatever form it appears, by a common detestation of racialism and a common determination to preserve and to stabilise peace in the world.' Colonialism was far from dead, he reminded his audience, a fact felt acutely in Singapore. 'Afro-Asia,' he concluded, 'far more than half the human population, can mobilise what I have called the moral voice of nations in favour of peace.'[8] One of the most astute observers of the conference, the liberal African-American writer Richard Wright, was convinced that the anti-colonial solidarities invoked by Sukarno went 'beyond left and right'; 'ideology was not needed to define [Asian-African] relations … racial realities have a strange logic of their own'.[9]

The Singapore press eagerly covered the Bandung meeting.[10] A *Singapore Standard* editorial, "Voices of Asia and Africa", declared that 'for too long have the Asian and African worlds suffered from the colour blight introduced by Western nations into … their lives'.[11] The new forces of Asia alone could bring about peace, the *Standard* declared, because the great powers were too 'permeated with the militant spirit of the "right hook to the jaw"'. Sukarno was seen to epitomise Afro-Asia's 'voice of reason'.[12] The PAP declared Bandung to be a 'milestone on the road to self-respect for millions of Asians and Africans', and sent the radical Malay journalist Abdul

Samad Ismail as their observer.[13] For his part, David Marshall despatched C. H. Koh to Bandung on behalf of the Labour Front, declaring that 'we are an integral part of Asia and it is my hope that we will take up a rightful place'. Marshall also expressed the hope that the 'next Bandung' might take place in Singapore.[14] Spurred by the spirit of the conference, the Labour Front and PAP observers submitted a joint memorandum to the conference denouncing Singapore's emergency regulations.[15]

Bandung raised great hopes in Singapore, as in the rest of Asia. Students of Singapore's Chinese middle schools, fresh from their struggle with the government over the National Service Ordinance, placed their faith in the moral economy of Afro-Asianism as a means of redress. Chinese middle school students' associations asked the Afro-Asian conference to 'intercede on their behalf ... to give them freedom of organization'.[16]

A few months later, however, it was David Marshall who seemed to have gleaned the real, and much less romantic, significance of Bandung. If the heroes of the 'Bandung story' were clear to all — Sukarno, Nasser, Zhou En Lai, and (perhaps) Nehru — the plot was more open to contestation. In an interview with student representatives from Singapore Chinese High School and Nanyang Girls' School, Marshall declared:

> I want you to try and understand it is not Singapore alone that allows arrests and detentions without trial, but free countries like the great Republic of India, the great socialist country of Burma also find it necessary in these troubled times to have such powers.[17]

Asian states, it appeared, shared one overwhelming problem in common: the problem of dissent. In the year following Bandung, almost all Asian leaders began to make references to 'anti-national' forces — Nehru in connection with the demand for linguistic states in southern and western India, and Sukarno with regard to a plethora of conspiracies, real, manufactured and imagined. Lee Kuan Yew would learn this lesson well.

Nevertheless, the energies unleashed by Bandung swept across the political arena in Singapore, and they did so in a way that complicated the language of race. In Singapore's fertile soil, the myths and memories of Bandung took root. A myriad of voices invoked the spirit of Bandung in the context of debates on questions of language, culture and autonomy. The Final Communiqué of the Bandung conference had reaffirmed the UN Charter's commitment to the 'principle of self-determination of peoples and nations', and the right of nations to 'freely choose their own political and economic systems and their own way of life'.[18] Champions of Chinese education in Singapore immediately made the link between the rights of nations to self-determination, and the rights of their constituent peoples to the same. In one of his first speeches in the legislative assembly, Lim Chin Siong, only days after the Bandung conference, made his defence of Chinese education in terms that were at once multiracial (in the Singapore context), and more broadly international:

> What is the Government's policy towards vernacular education? Do we accept the principles of the United Nations charter that the right of every community to develop its own language and culture must be respected ...? [A] democratic education policy ... will respect and encourage the full development of the mother tongues of people which are Malay, Chinese, and Tamil.[19]

The language of Bandung, itself invoking the UN Charter, legitimised Lim's call for a 'democratic education policy' in Singapore, one that allowed for a multiplicity of linguistic and cultural aspirations, seeing them as complementary rather than mutually antagonistic. Here, Lim might have taken his cue from Sukarno's sentiments at Bandung, his insistence that 'it is possible to live together, to meet together, speak to each other, without losing one's individual identity ... all men and all countries have their place under the sun'.[20] In the context of a global movement against colonialism, Lim could defend the beleaguered Chinese middle schools whilst at the same time exhibiting 'a deeper commitment to Malay as a national language than many more moderate, and more Anglophone, leaders'.[21]

It was the world of youth, whence Lim Chin Siong emerged, which most enthusiastically embraced the possibilities of Bandung, seeing in the language of Afro-Asianism a reflection of their own local concerns. These aspirations found an outlet the following year with the organisation of an Afro-Asian Students' Conference, again in Bandung. The official delegation from Singapore, largely from the University of Malaya, was conspicuously multiracial; they were accompanied by an unofficial 'observation party' consisting of representatives from Nanyang University (Nantah), the Middle Schools Students Union, and the Pan-Malayan Students Federation.[22] The Nantah observation party delegates declared, on the eve of their departure, that 'Asian and African students will be united like a giant'. The spirit of Bandung, they suggested, was at one with their aspirations for Chinese education in Singapore:

> The example of the founding of the Nanyang University being obstructed explains the discrimination against community education which suffers man-made and unreasonable treatment under the colonial power.[23]

Local concerns melded into Afro-Asian ones in unlikely ways. Fu Sun Min, the leader of the observation party from the Middle Schools Students Union, related the aspiration for Afro-Asian unity to the question of multi-racialism in Singapore:

> In the past there was little or no contact between students of Chinese schools, English schools and Malay schools, not to mention of contact between students of Asia and Africa. When we get to Bandung, we must learn to build up true friendship.[24]

The potential conflict between the claims of Chinese, Malay or English education was thus blunted by looking outwards; Chinese and Malay education were conjoined by the language of anti-colonialism, each seen as an expression of Singapore's democratic right to self-determination. Indeed, despite the strong presence of Nantah and Chinese Middle School students amongst the delegation headed for Bandung, the students' conference gained the support of *Utusan Melayu*. Dismissing fears that the students' conference might become an instrument of communist subversion, an *Utusan Melayu* opinion piece predicted that it would 'promote goodwill, understanding and unity amongst students of Africa and Asia'.[25]

Anti-colonial struggles elsewhere in the world galvanised diverse groups in Singapore. Solidarity with, for example, Algerian or South African freedom fighters allowed groups that disagreed on much else to come together and share a discursive space. Algeria featured particularly prominently in the political imagination of Singapore in the 1950s. It was an issue to which *Utusan Melayu* devoted many column inches. 'Mass Murder in Algeria!' cried one fairly representative headline; 'Algeria is now hell for the French people and French colonialism ... large-scale murders are committed daily on the people of Algeria who are defending their rights'.[26] Said Zahari recalled in his memoirs that 'the *Utusan Melayu* sided with Asian and African peoples struggling against the colonialists and imperialists bent on perpetuating their power'.[27] Han Suyin made the point rather cuttingly in her own memoirs:

> Despite the sedulous repetition of the 'loyal Malay' theme (loyal to what?), none knew better than the British that the Malays were also nationalists, sharing a common culture, language and script with Indonesia and that the Islamic world, from Algeria to the Philippines, was effervescent. There were fears of pan-Arab, pan-Islamic movements affecting Malaya. *Utusan Melayu*, the Malay newspaper, reported favourably on upsurges against colonial domination in Iraq, Syria and Algeria, and Egypt's Nasser was immensely popular.[28]

Yet, Han's comment notwithstanding, solidarity with Algeria was also an issue that *united* Malay, Chinese and Anglophone radicals in Singapore.[29] In his rousing Hokkien (and later Mandarin) oratory, Lim Chin Siong repeatedly related political struggles in Singapore to events in Algeria, South Africa, Turkey and South Korea.[30]

Singapore's university students, too, came together on several occasions across the divide between Nantah and the University of Singapore to condemn French atrocities in Algeria. A petition submitted to the French consul by a delegation of Nantah and University of Singapore students was characteristic in its combination of local and international concerns. The petition condemned the 'persistence of the French Government in carrying on the war and all the inhuman measures it resorts to', and associated itself with the 'overwhelming desire of the nations of the world as expressed by them at the recent General Assembly of the UNO, to help colonial countries achieve freedom and eliminate the evils of colonialism'.[31] Revelations of the French use of torture in Algeria were immediately carried in lurid detail in the Singapore student press, with the information coming from pamphlets smuggled out of Algeria for circulation among radicals around the world.[32] A representative of the FLN (National Liberation Front) visited Nantah and the University of Singapore to thank the students for their support and solidarity.[33]

There was much scope in this political world for outward-looking practices of cultural coexistence and synthesis that were, at the same time, rooted in local experience. 'Race' in Singapore could function as an immutable identity ascribed to discrete groups, an amalgam of skin colour, language and economic position. From this view, 'multiracialism' was something to be managed from on high. Race became an official category in the management of citizens, first among 'multiple, cross-cutting and shifting classifications of the population as the targets of multiple policies'.[34] But the language of race was fluid. As well as dividing discrete communities into targets of policy, race could express political solidarity. There was no contradiction in the Singapore branch of Ahmad Boestamam's Partai Rakyat demanding that the question of South Africa be raised in Singapore's Internal Security Council (in the aftermath of the Sharpeville massacre), and following that with a complaint that 'The Government has not made good their promises to help Malays in the Alsagoff Estate Area'.[35] Here a language of sympathy and identification with distant black South Africans overlaps with a more inward-looking language of ethnicity as a claim on resources. If the latter prevailed in post-colonial Singapore, it was after a protracted political struggle over the meaning of race, Singapore's place in the world, and the nature of Singapore's integration with Malaya, rather than as an inexorable process rooted in the pervasive power of the colonial and post-colonial states.[36]

Lumumba in Singapore

Historians can sometimes see in dramatic moments, from riots to epidemics, a window into more quotidian social experience. Such was the case with a (relatively) minor incident that occurred on 26 February 1961, an incident that highlighted the many levels of everyday cosmopolitanism in Singapore's political discourse.

The episode was connected to the death of Patrice Lumumba, the first Prime Minister of the Democratic Republic of Congo, who was killed on 17 January 1961 at the hands of secessionist forces in Katanga province, backed by the departing Belgians and with the support of the Central Intelligence Agency. When pictures of Lumumba's assassination were flashed around the world, they provoked mass protest in Singapore.[37] A rally was held at Victoria Memorial Hall, attended by over a thousand unionists, members of rural associations, and student bodies. Of particular concern to the colonial authorities was the fact that a special issue of *Fajar*, the magazine of the University of Singapore Socialist Club, which had survived the government's charge of subversion in 1954, was 'on sale at the entrance of the meeting, which was printed in English, Chinese and Romanised Malay'. Lim Chin Siong and Fong Swee Suan were among the speakers at the conference, with Lim urging the crowd to unite their sympathy with the Congolese and 'hatred of the Belgians' with an opposition to 'colonialism within their own state'.[38]

The climax of the protest against Lumumba's assassination was a mass rally held by the PAP at Singapore's Happy World Stadium, on 26 February 1961. The colonial authorities estimated that perhaps 12,000 people attended the rally. It was reported that 'a large number' of the crowd 'came from trade unions and rural associations',[39] suggesting that the initiative was very much from the left of the PAP, which continued to have an almost unassailable base within both these groups. The Singapore General Employees' Union led a march through Singapore to the stadium, 'bearing a coffin and a skeleton representing the remains of Dag Hammerskjold and 2 effigies representing Mobutu and Tshombe hanging from scaffolds'.[40] The international solidarity expressed was not purely imaginative; at the head of the procession stood Lim Chin Siong and Fong Swee Suan with their guests, two anti-apartheid activists from South Africa. The group, of around

4,000 people, then marched down Middle Road to the US Embassy on Cecil Street, chanting 'Long Live Lumumba' and 'I Love Malaya'.[41]

What is particularly striking about the Lumumba rally is its window into the everyday, lived, cosmopolitanism of Singapore's political discourse. It was a world in which it was natural for thousands to take to the streets in support of their imagined brethren who were engaged in an anti-colonial struggle on the distant shores of Africa. This is a testament to the power of anti-colonial narratives; the story of self-realisation and the progression of freedom that the Bandung myth encapsulated.

Dockworkers, for example, played a leading role in the protest.[42] Many of them were recent migrants from Kerala. They brought with them a political culture of activism, inspired by the rising power of the Kerala Communist Party, one that took root in the cosmopolitan neighbourhood of Sembawang.[43] Malayalee workers — ironically dependent on the British naval base for employment — clustered in Sembawang, a neighbourhood in equal parts Tamil, Chinese and with 'lots of whites'; a world of inter-action in countless bars, and in the food stalls selling everything from *vadai* and *murukku* to spiced *sarabat* tea. In this world, many cells of the Kerala Communist Party galvanised dockworkers, painters and fitters with literature and regular study sessions, at times reaching well beyond the Malayalee community. With the Malayalee press providing regular coverage of international events, it was not a surprise that Keralan workers featured substantially in the Lumumba rally.

Singapore's itinerant food hawkers, too, participated in the rally, and they, too, found the language of Afro-Asian solidarity a meaningful one within which to situate their own struggles: after the murder of Lumumba, the Itinerant Hawkers and Stall-holders Association 'appealed to Singaporeans to support the Congolese in their righteous struggle until victory is achieved'.[44] After the mass rally at the Happy World Stadium, the state's security agents reported that '1,000 from rural and hawkers' asso-ciations marched to Kallang Park where they burnt an effigy representing "American Imperialism."'[45] In the early 1950s, thousands of hawkers had expressed their Chinese ethnic patriotism by contributing their meagre resources to the Nantah fund — 'how many oyster omelettes, sliced crab, noodles of all kinds', Han Suyin mused, 'went into Nanyang University?'[46] In the early 1960s, the same group of people looked towards broader Afro-Asian solidarities to express their political aspirations. To see their rhetoric of Afro-Asian solidarity as merely a mask for more parochial interests, I think, would be to miss the point, and to underestimate the power of the anti-colonial imagination. The question to ask is why internationalism provided such a widely shared language of political protest in Singapore, and the answer, I believe, is that it offered diverse groups in Singapore a way of situating their struggles in a broader frame, while providing hope of a solution (a global anti-colonial revolution), however unrealistic this may appear, with hindsight.

Internationalism and Anti-Nationalism

By the time of the Lumumba rally in February 1961, political struggles within the PAP were coming to a head. The debate over Singapore's place in the world reached its endgame in the so-called Battle for Merger. The tortuous political negotiations surrounding merger are now widely known, thanks to recent work by British imperial historians using newly released documents.[47] Briefly: the increasing restiveness of the PAP's left wing, and Ong Eng Guan's humiliating defeat of the PAP in the April 1961 Hong Lim by-election, convinced Lee Kuan Yew and the PAP leadership that only a speedy merger with the Federation (and consequent action against the Singapore left) would allow the PAP to remain in control. The turning point came when Malaya's Tunku Abdul Rahman, alarmed by the possibility of Lee Kuan Yew falling from power, dramatically reversed his opposition to merger in a speech to the Southeast Asian Foreign Correspondents' Association in Singapore, on 27 May 1961. The UMNO leadership saw the dangers of integration with Singapore as being outweighed by the prospect of 'another Cuba' across the Causeway. The strategy, in short, was to cut the Singapore left loose of its global anti-colonial connections by consolidating Singapore's position within the firm walls of a Malaysian national federation, secured by a round of internal repression that could now be carried out in the name of national integration.

What followed, in the Battle for Merger, was a struggle over the very definition of the 'national' (and its dark side, the 'anti-national'), with both sides invoking the moral authority of international norms to validate their claims. This struggle over the meaning of *merdeka* raged from mid-1961 to the end of 1962, in arenas ranging from the Singapore press and the legislative assembly to the United Nations Special Committee on Colonialism in New York. Where the left stressed the universalist anti-colonialism of their stance, the PAP leadership stressed the post-colonialism of theirs. The left emphasised the struggle for freedom from the exercise of arbitrary power by colonial (or neo-colonial) powers standing in the shadows; the PAP focused on their claim to hold legitimate authority in the state that they controlled. Both sides drew on the legitimating force of UN General

Assembly Resolution 1514 calling for an end to colonialism: for the PAP, merger signified the realisation of the resolution's aspirations; the PAP's opponents argued that the nature of the merger violated the spirit and substance of the resolution.[48]

Drawing on the notion of neo-colonialism,[49] the Singapore left criticised the plans for merger as a British and Malayan plot to perpetuate imperial interests in Southeast Asia.[50] Lim Chin Siong stressed repeatedly that 'the pro-West, pro-British and pro-US policy of the present government … makes us a pawn of the western imperialist powers'.[51] Whilst not against genuine merger, on a basis of equality, the Barisan Sosialis argued that the proposed referendum on merger — with no option to reject it outright, and with blank votes counted as an endorsement of the government position — was a denial of the 'democratic right of dissent'. Singapore, they argued, risked becoming a colony of Malaya, in direct opposition to UN Resolution 1514.[52]

In response, the PAP leadership branded the left as not anti-colonial so much as 'anti-national'. In an assured and combative speech before the UN Committee, Lee declared that the issue was no longer about colonialism, but about national integration: 'I am, constitutionally and legally, the rightful authority of Singapore,' Lee declared. Whilst he was happy to put his case to the UN, Lee argued that he did not, in fact, have to do so: the question of merger was 'a matter of internal politics', between a self-governing state, Singapore,[53] and a sovereign nation-state, Malaya. Lee was in New York simply as 'a necessary aspect of the battle for men's minds'. In Lee's view, it was the left who wanted to perpetuate colonial control, for:

> … if Singapore becomes independent, in the Federation of Malaya, then the constitutional struggle against the imperialists, so far as the political plane is concerned, will be over and it will no longer be a straightforward battle against the British.[54]

The left would then find itself fighting 'a popularly elected government on what it should do with the political independence it has won for itself'. At a single stroke, the opposition to the PAP could then be branded anti-national, committed to destabilising and undermining a sovereign state.

Inevitably, the debate came to focus on the question of race and multiracialism. The PAP leadership developed their claim that the left was anti-national by implying a link between the Barisan and a subversive internationalism; but they also made a contrary insinuation: the left was anti-national because it was sectional and communal, and the spectre of

Chinese chauvinism arose once more. As Goh Keng Swee put it to the UN, the anti-merger movement was 'dangerous to the racial harmony of which Singapore is justly proud'. He told the committee that 'the majority of Singapore's population, about 70 per cent, is Chinese, a thrifty and hard-working people'. The anti-nationalist left, he claimed, exploited this fact: 'their propaganda, through word of mouth at the ground level, represented merger to the Chinese as domination over them.' Goh went further, accusing the left of resorting to 'blatant racist propaganda in a desperate attempt to frustrate the merger'.[55]

The PAP argument (then, as now) was that only a strong state could manage the potentially explosive racial tension in a plural society. But the left, too, focused on the question of race, and multiracialism. In their view, the management of ethnicity through elite compromise would only serve to perpetuate divisions between people. Indeed, they argued that the 'colonial-cum-feudal economic and social set-up', which Malaysia would perpetuate, lay at the root of racial division.[56] Lim Chin Siong addressed the question of race directly, and in doing so, tried to reclaim the mantle of nationalism:

> The problem of uniting the various races is also important. Everyone
> says we must fight the racialist and warns against the evils of racialism.
> But lately, we were told that there are the "national left" and the "anti-
> national left". The anti-national left is supposed to be un-Malayan and
> does not like a Malayan consciousness and is disloyal to the country.
> The use of these epithets are intended to arouse fear and suspicion
> between the different communities, especially between the Chinese and
> the Malays. ... I would like now to say a few words about Nationalism.
> Nationalism is the political consciousness manifested in the colonial
> people's struggle against their common enemies — the colonialists.
> Therefore one's attitude towards colonialism should form the criterion by
> which one may be judged to be anti-national or otherwise.[57]

In effect, the PAP and its leftist and liberal opponents appealed to different visions of the international order, and Singapore's place within it. The left continued to invoke an international order of Afro-Asian solidarity, the spirit of Bandung that resonated so widely in Singapore's public sphere in the 1950s and early 1960s. Lim Chin Siong articulated his aspirations for a genuinely democratic Malaysia (as opposed to what he called 'phoney merger') with his hopes for 'moral pressure ... to see that Africans are treated like human beings'; with inspiration from the 'untold sacrifices' of Algerians; and solidarity and admiration for Cuba's success in shaking off the 'yoke of US imperialism'.[58]

The PAP leadership, by contrast, used the debate on Malaysia to signal its arrival on the world stage of nation-states. Lee Kuan Yew stated that he appeared at the UN Committee on Colonialism because 'I am seeking and have sought and will continue to seek the support of the non-aligned Afro-Asian countries, whose history is akin to us, whose problems are also akin to us'.[59] Lee's appearance at the UN in July 1962 followed months of intensive diplomacy, and a trip that took him to Rangoon, New Delhi, Cairo and Belgrade, seeking support for Malaysia.[60]

It was Lee Kuan Yew's 'moment of arrival' on the international stage.[61] He spoke in the unambiguous voice of state power; he could speak the language of order in a way which allowed for his acceptance in a concert of nation-states. He played on the principle of non-interference enshrined at Bandung (merger was an internal matter for the Malaysian nation-state), *and* on the fact that peaceful coexistence had in fact begun to fragment ('the Indians considered [Malaysia] a sound development because it would help to keep China's influence out of Southeast Asia'). Lee remembers that 'Nasser spent an hour listening to me on the dangers of Singapore going it alone and becoming … a Chinese entity in the midst of a Malay archipelago'.[62] Only an increasingly isolated Sukarno stood aside from the Afro-Asian support for Malaysia — indeed, Sukarno's move towards *Konfrontasi* would only strengthen the Singapore leadership's arguments about the dangers of internal and external subversion. Lee spoke the language of sovereignty and subversion effectively. When the Singapore left came out in support of the December 1962 Brunei revolt as a 'popular nationalist movement for national independence and freedom from British colonial domination',[63] Lee found his 'heaven-sent' opportunity to move against his opponents, once and for all.[64]

Conclusion

The literary scholar Philip Holden suggests in a recent essay on nationalist biography that the Bandung spirit was sustained because it was able to construct a powerful 'social imaginary'; 'storytelling played a key part in the production and dissemination of the spirit of Bandung'.[65] Singapore in the 1950s was awash with stories. The language and the promise of Bandung were interpreted within a cultural world that was deeply cosmopolitan. The Chinese middle schools, which lay at the heart of the youthful political dynamism of the 1950s, gave their students a strikingly broad range of cultural referents. Tan Jing Quee writes of the Chinese-educated students of Lim Chin Siong's generation, that:

Like most Chinese high school students of that era, they were introduced
— through easily available translations — to the world of Russian literature of Pushkin, Gogol, Turgenev, Tolstoi, and Western writers like Jack
London, Henrik Ibsen, Romain Rolland, Goethe — an eclectic mix of
romantic, naturalist and realist writers who wrote of oppression, struggle
and freedom. It was a heady literary diet, quite different from the staple
fare most English educated students were exposed or accustomed to.[66]

This was a generation that had its political vision shaped by the astonishing cosmopolitan sweep of Jawaharlal Nehru's *Glimpses of World History*
and by the ecumenical thought of Gandhi and Tagore.[67]

Similarly, Yao Souchou writes of growing up in Kuala Lumpur, in a
world in which a sense of Chinese identity — a 'fusion of ethnic attachment,
cultural memory and literary pleasure' — was often sustained and cultivated
through the enjoyment of translated Russian literature, available in cheap
translations from the Foreign Languages Press of Beijing. The same names
resound: Chekhov, Tolstoy, Ibsen, Flaubert, Zola.[68] One might go so far as
to suggest that, among this generation, a particular canon of taste united
secondary school students and autodidacts alike, from Djakarta to Rangoon
to Calcutta. This stemmed from a commitment to a universal 'literature', a
commitment that had a greater hold outside Europe than within it. [69]

In Singapore, as elsewhere in Asia, there was a 'refusal to be beaten
into parochialism'[70] on the part of the Chinese-educated, despite being
repeatedly denigrated as 'communal' by the colonial elite. The values underpinning the literature that was so widely consumed in Singapore's middle
schools (as Yao puts it 'something "progressive" and which at the same time
satisfied our nascent literary taste')[71] were often deemed 'humanist'. This
rather ambiguous label has been used equally to characterise the language
of Bandung.[72] This 'cultural matrix'[73] — the repertoire of references and
narratives — shared by a generation of youth in the late-colonial, and
newly post-colonial world, made it meaningful for Sukarno, in his Bandung
speech, to begin his 'journey' with Paul Revere, and to invoke the words
of Longfellow.

Singapore's world of Malay literature and journalism was also outward-
looking, in its own fashion. Though committed to 'art for society', and to
upholding Malay language and literature as a tool of nation-building,[74]
Singapore Malay writing never completely shed the early influence of the
'universal humanism' of the Indonesian *Angkatan* 45 — Generation of 45
— spearheaded by the poet Chairil Anwar. There remained in Malay writing
something of the spirit of Chairil Anwar's universalist call to arms:

Hopplaa! Jump! Fire the pure fire the brotherhood of nations, that will not be extinguished.

Hopplaa! Up, my generation, toward the flawless Indonesia, the flawless world.[75]

In his 1961 review of Malay literature, A. Samad Said argued that this strand of universalism in Singapore-based Malay literature had been neglected unjustly. He wrote that 'while ASAS 50 was content to affirm that literature should be used as a means of developing awareness within society in a rather general way, this statement is surely in accordance with universal humanism'. Malay poetry, he argued, citing many examples, was 'concerned not just with Malaya and Indonesia, but also with Africa and Algeria'.[76] Such poems, by Usman Awang and Kassim Ahmad, among others, appeared in *Utusan Zaman* on a regular basis, alongside translations of Chekhov and Rabindranath Tagore.[77]

Lim Chin Siong did not leave a memoir. But in an interview with Melanie Chew not long before his death, Lim situated his own political commitments in the context of the international struggle of which he was a part:

> The 1950s was a very exciting period throughout Afro-Asia and Latin America. It witnessed the collapse of the colonial empires and the emergence of many independent states!"
>
> Was it my mistake or was it the mistake of history that I had become a member of the ABL at that time?[78]

The Singapore Story is unequivocal: it was Lim Chin Siong and his allies who were 'mistaken' and who ended up on the wrong side of history. The Singapore state has tried particularly hard to forget the paths not taken of the 1950s, investing much into 'naturalising' the official story. A good part of this effort depended on crushing the 'subversive' sense of vernacular cosmopolitanism that I have tried to capture in this essay, in favour of a managed, state-directed production of 'multiculturalism'.[79]

In beginning to explore the history of Singapore's paths not taken, we must remember that in the minds of so many Singaporeans in the 1950s, Singapore's paths were entwined with those of near and distant others.

NOTES

1   I am grateful to participants of the Paths Not Taken symposium held at the National University of Singapore, 14–15 July 2005, for their comments on an earlier version of this paper; I am particularly grateful to the organisers and to Tim Harper, Mark Frost and Chua Ai Lin. Earlier versions of some of these

arguments appeared in my article, 'Asian Internationalism: Bandung's Echo in a Colonial Metropolis', *Inter-Asia Cultural Studies*, December 2005. I am solely responsible for any mistakes or misunderstandings that remain.

2   Chua Beng Huat, 'Multiculturalism as Instrument of Social Control in Singapore', *Race and Class*, 44, 3 (2003): 58–77.

3   T. N. Harper, 'Lim Chin Siong and the "Singapore Story"', in *Comet in Our Sky: Lim Chin Siong in History*, ed. Tan Jing Quee and Jomo K. S. (Kuala Lumpur: Insan, 2001).

4   Cited in Yeo Kim Wah, *Political Development in Singapore, 1945–55* (Singapore: Singapore University Press, 1973), p. 120.

5   On opposition to national service in the Chinese Middle Schools, see The National Archives of the United Kingdom, Public Record Office (henceforth, TNA, PRO), CO 1030/360, 'Trouble in Chinese Schools — Singapore'.

6   On 'pro-Communists' and 'non-Communists' within the PAP, see Thomas J. Bellows, *The People's Action Party of Singapore: Emergence of a Dominant Party System* (New Haven: Yale University Southeast Asia Series, No. 14, 1970), Chapter 2.

7   Yeo, *Political Development*, p. 247.

8   Text of speech by President Sukarno at the Opening of the Asian-African Conference in Bandung, Indonesia, on 18 April 1955, *Selected Documents of the Bandung Conference: Texts of Selected Speeches and Final Communiqué of the Asian-African Conference, Bandung, Indonesia, April 18–24* (New York: Institute of Pacific Relation, 1955), pp. 2–6.

9   Richard Wright, *The Colour Curtain: A Report on the Bandung Conference* (Cleveland: World Publishing, 1955), pp. 175–6.

10   See, for example: *Utusan Melayu*, 17–20 April 1955; *Tamil Murasu*, 17 April 1955.

11   *Singapore Standard*, 18 April 1955.

12   *Singapore Standard*, 19 April 1955.

13   *Singapore Standard*, 16 April 1955.

14   *Singapore Standard*, 20 April 1955.

15   Lee Khoon Choy, *On the Beat to the Hustings: An Autobiography* (Singapore: Times, 1988), p. 34. Lee covered the conference as a reporter for *Nanyang Siang Pau*.

16   *Singapore Standard*, 19 April 1955.

17   'Transcript of Interview Given by the Chief Minister, Mr David Marshall to 14 Student Representatives From Singapore Chinese High School and Nanyang Girls Schools on August 4th, 1955, at 1645 hours', TNA, PRO, CO 1030/360.

18   See Jansen, *Afro-Asia*, Appendix A.4.

19   *Singapore Legislative Assembly Debates* (hereafter *SLAD*), 1, 3, 27 April 1955, col. 111; also cited in C. J. W.-L. Wee, 'The Vanquished: Lim Chin Siong and a Progressivist National Narrative', in *Lee's Lieutenants: Singapore's Old Guard*,

ed. Lam Peng Er and Kevin Y. L. Tan (Sydney: Allen & Unwin, 1999), pp. 169–90.

20 Speech by President Sukarno, *Selected Documents of the Bandung Conference*, pp. 2–6.

21 Harper, 'Lim Chin Siong', p. 19.

22 *Sin Chew Jit Poh*, 23 May 1956.

23 Ibid.

24 *Nanyang Siang Pau*, 23 May 1956.

25 *Utusan Melayu*, 23 May 1956.

26 *Utusan Melayu*, 9 April 1956.

27 Said Zahari, *Dark Clouds at Dawn: A Memoir* (Kuala Lumpur: Insan, 2001), p. 68.

28 Han Suyin, *My House Has Two Doors* (London: Jonathan Cape, 1981).

29 Zahari, *Dark Clouds*, Chapter 26; Tan Jing Quee, 'Lim Chin Siong: A Political Life', in *Comet in Our Sky*, ed. Tan and Jomo, pp. 56–97.

30 See, for example, the accounts of Lim's speeches in TNA, PRO, FO 1091/107, Internal Security — Special Branch Reports.

31 *Malayan Undergrad* 12, 2 (November 1960).

32 *Malayan Undergrad* 12, 8 (May 1961).

33 *Malayan Undergrad* 12, 5 (February 1961). The historian Matthew Connelly has argued that such examples of international solidarity with the Algerian cause were important to its final outcome. The Algerian revolution, in Connelly's view, was won as much in the international arena as at home. Matthew Connelly, *A Diplomatic Revolution: Algeria's Fight for Independence and the Origins of the Post-Cold War Era* (New York: Oxford University Press, 2002).

34 Partha Chatterjee, 'Populations and Political Society', in *The Politics of the Governed: Reflections on Popular Politics in Most of the World* (New York: Columbia University Press, 2004), p. 36. On the ways this official multira-cialism developed in Singapore, see Chua, 'Multiculturalism'.

35 TNA, PRO, FO 1091/107 Internal Security — Special Branch Reports.

36 Cf. Chatterjee, 'Populations and Political Society', who sees it as a straight-forward shift: He argues that in the twentieth century, 'ideas of participatory citizenship … have fast retreated before the triumphant advance of govern-mental technologies', p. 34.

37 A. Mahadeva, 'Remembering Lim Chin Siong', in *Comet in Our Sky*, ed. Tan and Jomo, p. 153.

38 TNA, PRO, FO 1091/107, Internal Security — Special Branch Reports; *Fajar*, Lumumba Special Issue, 21 February 1961. "Lumumba is Dead — Murdered!" the headline screamed. The editorial, entirely in capital letters, declared that 'AFRICA AND ASIA ARE CRYING ALOUD AND THE COLONIALISTS MUST EVERYWHERE BE ANNIHILATED'.

39 TNA, PRO, FO 1091/107 Internal Security — Special Branch Reports.

40 TNA, PRO, FO 1091/107 Internal Security — Special Branch Reports.

41 Ibid. The account in the colonial archive is, interestingly, corroborated by the

memories of the journalist A. Mahadeva, who participated in the rally. Although he remembers the date of the rally incorrectly (putting it in 1960 rather than 1961), his account is very similar to that quoted above. See Mahadeva, 'Lim Chin Siong'.

42 Dominic Puthucheary and Tan Jing Quee: personal communications.

43 The following description is based on these interviews held by the Oral History Department, National Archives of Singapore: No. 764, Alikunju, Salleh (reel 1); No. 1236, Ramachandran, Padmanabhan (reel 13); No. 1177, Nair, Karunakaran (reel 13).

44 TNA, PRO, FO 1091/107 Internal Security — Special Branch Reports.

45 Ibid.

46 Han Suyin, *My House Has Two Doors*.

47 Matthew Jones, *Conflict and Confrontation in South East Asia, 1961–65: Britain, the United States, and the Creation of Malaysia* (Cambridge: Cambridge University Press, 2002); S. J. Ball, 'Selkirk in Singapore', *Twentieth Century British History* 10, 2 (1999): 162–91. For an account of these events more closely attuned to the nuances of Singapore, rather than imperial politics, see Harper, 'Lim Chin Siong'.

48 UN Resolution on the Ending of Colonialism (1514 (XV), of 14 December 1960): 'Recognizing that the people of the world ardently desire the end of colonialism in all its manifestations ... Convinced that the process of liberation is irresistible and irreversible ... Convinced that all people have an inalienable right to complete freedom, the exercise of their sovereignty and the integrity of their national territory ... Solemnly proclaims the necessity of putting an end rapidly and unconditionally to colonialism in all its forms and manifestations'.

49 Robert Young dates the use of the term 'neo-colonialism' from 1961: Robert J. C. Young, *Postcolonialism: An Historical Introduction* (Oxford: Blackwell, 2001), p. 46.

50 *Plebian: Fortnightly Paper for the Common Man*, 15 May 1962.

51 Lim Chin Siong, 'Malaya Must Adopt Non-Aligned Position', *Plebian,* 20 November 1962.

52 Cambridge University Library, United Nations papers (hereafter, UN), Special Committee on the Situation With Regard to the Implementation of the Declaration on the Granting of Independence to Colonial Countries and Peoples, Verbatim Record of the 86th meeting, 26 July 1962, A/AC.109/PV.86 [restricted].

53 The left's retort, of course, was that Lee did not even control internal security.

54 UN, Committee on Colonialism, Verbatim Record of the 86th meeting, 26 July 1962, A/AC.109/PV.86.

55 UN, Committee on Colonialism, Verbatim Record of the 86th Meeting, A/AC.109/PV/87.

56 Said Zahari, 'Malaysia — Colonial Conspiracy', *Fajar*, December 1961.

57 Lim Chin Siong, 'The Constitutional Struggle Ahead' (Speech to SGEU), *Fajar*, August–September 1961.

58 Lim Chin Siong, 'Malaya Must Adopt Non-Aligned Position', *Plebian*, 20 November 1962.

59 UN, A/AC.109/PV.87

60 Lee Kuan Yew, *The Singapore Story: Memoirs of Lee Kuan Yew* (Singapore: Times Editions, 1998) p. 421.

61 Here I am adapting the phrase of Partha Chatterjee, *Nationalist Thought and the Colonial World: A Derivative Discourse?* (London: Zed Books, 1986).

62 Lee, *Singapore Story*, p. 422.

63 *Plebian*, 14 December 1962.

64 On the Brunei revolt and its aftermath, see Jones, *Creation of Malaysia*.

65 Philip Holden, 'Imagined Individuals: National Autobiography and Postcolonial Self-Fashioning', Asia Research Institute, Working Paper Series, No. 13 (Singapore, 2003), p. 2.

66 Tan Jing Quee, 'Lim Chin Siong: A Political Life', in *Comet in Our Sky*, ed. Tan and Jomo, p. 61.

67 Tan Jing Quee, personal communication.

68 Yao Souchou, 'Books from Heaven: Literary Pleasure, Chinese Cultural Text and the "Struggle against Forgetting"', *Australian Journal of Anthropology* 8, 2 (1997): 204–5.

69 Amitav Ghosh, 'The March of the Novel through History: The Testimony of my Grandfather's Bookcase', in *The Imam and the Indian* (Delhi: Permanent Black, 2002), pp. 287–304.

70 Ibid.

71 Yao, 'Books from Heaven', p. 205.

72 Itty Abraham, for example, writes that for Nehru, 'peaceful co-existence meant the recognition of difference, and the ability to live with it. It was a deeply humanist idea …', Abraham, 'State, Place, Identity: Two Stories in the Making of Region', in K. Sivaramakrishnan and A. Agrawal, *Regional Modernities: The Cultural Politics of Development in India* (Delhi: Oxford University Press, 2003), p. 413. Cf. Amitav Ghosh's attractive characterisation of 'universal literature' as 'a form of artistic expression that embodies differences in place and culture, emotion and aspiration, but in such a way as to render them communicable'. Ghosh, 'March of the Novel', p. 292.

73 The phrase is from Nadine Gordimer, *Living in Hope and History: Notes from Our Century* (London: Bloomsbury, 1999), p. 41.

74 On ASAS 50, see Virginia Matheson, 'Usman Awang, Keris Mas and Hamzah: Individual Expressions of Social Commitment in Malay Literature', *Review of Indonesian and Malaysian Affairs* (1987): 108–31, and T. N. Harper, *The End of Empire and the Making of Malaya* (Cambridge: Cambridge University Press, 1998), pp. 296–307.

75 Rudolf Mrazek, 'Bridges of Hope: Senior Citizens' Memories', *Indonesia* 70 (October 2000), pp. 40–41; Liaw Yock Fang, ed., trans., *The Complete Poems*

of Chairil Anwar (Singapore: University Education Press, 1974).

76 A. Samad Said, '1948: Dawn of a New Literary Era' [1961], in *Between Art and Reality: Selected Essays* (Kuala Lumpur: Dewan Bahasa Dan Pustaka, 1994).

77 Ibid.

78 Lim Chin Siong, interview with Melanie Chew: cited in C. J. W.-L. Wee, 'The Vanquished'.

79 See Carl A. Trocki, *Singapore: Wealth, Power and the Culture of Control* (London and New York: Routledge, 2006), Chapter 5.

PART 2

Party Politics

3

The United Front Strategy of the Malayan Communist Party in Singapore, 1950s–1960s

C. C. Chin

Pre-1948: MCP United Front Strategy before the Emergency

The Malayan Communist Party (MCP) began its struggle to lead the Singapore workers' movement in the 1930s[1] and tried from the beginning to build up a strong political organisation. Yet its first successful attempt to institute a united front strategy came only in the late 1930s, and only as a direct result of the Japanese invasion of China. The MCP capitalised on the anti-Japanese sentiment among the Chinese in Malaya and successfully brought workers, peasants, shopkeepers, petty merchants, students, and men and women belonging to other trades and professions under its umbrella. It joined forces with both the so-called progressive nationalists and the local bourgeois organisations such as the Chinese Chamber of Commerce and the clan associations.

At this point, the MCP's united front strategy was fundamentally premised on local Chinese loyalty to China and was China-centric.[2] It was modelled explicitly on the united front strategy that the Chinese Communist Party (CCP) had adopted in 1937, which resulted in a united front with the ruling Nationalist Party Guomindang (GMD). The Japanese aggression in China had stirred a tremendous emotional response among the Chinese in Southeast Asia that in turn provided a golden opportunity for the MCP to expand. As a consequence, it built up such strength that it became the main mobilising agent for the Chinese masses, and succeeded in creating a pan-Malayan anti-Japanese movement.

The MCP's anti-Japanese united front strategy underwent a fundamental change of character after the Japanese occupied Malaya and Singapore. This became the period of the Nine-Point Anti-Japanese Program which was designed to transform the anti-Japanese fight (and the united front) into a multiracial struggle that included Malays and Indians.[3] While the united front strategy before 1942 was fundamentally China-centric, the Party's proposal to join the British against the Japanese occupiers was a fundamentally Malaya-centric nationalist response to invasion, as well as an attempt to capitalise on that sentiment in order to pursue the ideological struggle for the Party's version of an ideal Malayan nation. The shift in the focus of the Party and the united front to Malaya was substantially achieved, but the attempt to reach out to the other communities was less successful, and the Party and the united front remained mainly concentrated on Chinese affairs.

The united front strategy implemented during the Peace Period (from the end of the war in August 1945 to the beginning of the Emergency in June 1948) was in a way an important continuation of the Japanese occupation period, though carried out through legal and constitutional means rather than by armed insurrection. The sudden surrender of the Japanese in August 1945 caught the British off guard, but the MCP's treacherous Secretary-General, Lai Teck (a British agent), successfully thwarted the MCP's plans to seize the opportunity to declare and fight for independence at the moment of victory.[4] During the ensuing Peace Period, the MCP enjoyed the status of a legal party, but it was also put on the defensive by the British and branded as an agitator of social unrest. The MCP tried various strategies to capitalise on its legal status, working to build a constitutional and legal united front. It announced the Malayan Democratic Program[5] and then initiated the formation of a multiracial anti-British alliance between all the progressive parties of Malaya. The establishment of the Pan-Malayan Council of Joint Action-Pusat Tenaga Ra'ayat Alliance (PMCJA-PUTERA) was a tangible sign of the short-term success of this strategy.[6] Another was the formation of the Malayan Democratic Union (MDU) from among the progressive English-speaking circles, as well as Indians and Malays. But the key MCP members in the operation were Chinese (Wu Tian Wang and

Quok Peng Cheng), and the united front never fully succeeded in breaking away from its Chinese character.[7] During these years, the MCP was very successful in promoting its programmes and in attacking British policies through the MDU. The MCP was a formidable force behind the movement against the Malayan Union and the Federation of Malaya Proposal and in drafting the People's Constitution.[8] Had the MCP's united front strategy been successful in bringing about a truly multiracial opposition to British rule, the political picture in Malaya and Singapore today might have been very different; possibly even leaving it free of much of the overt racial politics and tensions that were bequeathed by the British colonial government's divide-and-rule strategy and perpetuated subsequently by post-colonial governments.

June 1948 to December 1953: The MCP Singapore Town Committee

With the imposition of Emergency Regulations in June 1948, the MCP became once more an illegal organisation, and was forced to reorganise its operations in Singapore. The MCP Singapore Town Committee (STC),[9] established during the Japanese Occupation, was active during the Peace Period. Though the STC still existed after the declaration of the Emergency, it underwent a drastic reorganisation to cope with the new situation. Most of the MCP members were evacuated, went underground or were mobilised to join the Malayan People's Anti-British Army (MPABA) in the jungles of Peninsular Malaya. The MCP's front organisations under the direction of the STC were banned or made defunct due to the implementation of the new Societies Ordinance and Trade Union Ordinance as well as the mass arrests that took place during 18–20 June 1948. These included the powerful Singapore Federation of Trade Unions (SFTU) and the Pan-Malayan Federation of Trade Unions (PMFTU), the Neo-Democratic Youth League, the Women's Organisation and the MPAJA Old Comrade Association. The STC then divided the island geographically into four operational districts:

- The Bukit Timah District
- The Sembawang and Naval Base District
- Xiao-Po (The North of Singapore River) District
- Da-Po (The South of Singapore River) District[10]

Four district committees were formed as the organising bodies charged with carrying out underground activities in the districts. Under the district committees were area branches that conducted organisational tasks and directed the activities of the party cells, such as the newly formed Anti-British League (ABL) and sympathiser cells.[11] In addition, there were functional committees formed to tackle specific tasks. The main functional committees were the Student Movement Committee, the Workers Movement Committee, the United Front Committee and the Propaganda Committee.

From the organisational structure, one can see that the MCP continued to emphasise the importance of the united front strategy, with a committee formed specifically to pursue this project. In fact, the United Front Committee was formed explicitly to ensure the perpetuation of the Party's contacts with the radical English-educated circle, a task previously performed by the now-deregistered MDU.[12] The direct recruitment of English-speaking candidates into the Party was thought to be unwise, but the Party, through the United Front Committee, sought to maintain and expand contact with English-speaking circles through the ABL. Singapore Town Committee Vice Secretary Ah Har (Ah Xia) established an English-speaking ABL in late 1948, soon after the declaration of the Emergency. In March 1949, Eu Chooi Yip was selected as a candidate for membership and given the task of gathering the central committee members of the MDU and forming the ABL English-speaking section under the direction of STC member Ho Seng. P. V. Sharma, Dr Joseph K. M. Tan and Lim Chan Yong were persuaded to become ABL activists. By late 1949, Lim Kean Chye was also introduced into the Party and Eu Chooi Yip was inducted as a full MCP member in March 1950. Subsequently, these pioneering English-speaking ABL leaders were all inducted into the MCP as full members and, together with Eu Chooi Yip, soon became MCP District Committee members.[13] The United Front Committee was then converted into the MCP English-speaking Branch.[14] Eu Chooi Yip was put in charge of editing and publishing the Chinese edition of the STC organ, *Freedom News,* working under Ho Seng, while P. V. Sharma was made editor of the English edition.

In December 1949 the Special Branch obtained the full list of the STC through a planted informer, and conducted a raid on 1 May 1950. Singapore Town Committee Vice Secretary Ah Har and three other committee members were arrested while meeting in a hut at Lorong 33 Geylang. Later that month, 20 more MCP and ABL members were arrested. Seven months later, on 5 December, because of an alert Special Branch officer, STC Secretary Ah Chin and his assistant, Ho Seng, were caught during a rendezvous at a bus stop in front of Tong Chai Medical Hall.[15] Even though the mass arrests caused the near collapse of the MCP's operations in Singapore, the Party was still able to install a temporary Deputy Secretary (Liu Cheng Yong), who maintained skeletal operations for eight months until Ah Hua, the wife of Ah Chin, arrived from Johore to take over as STC Secretary. Unfortunately, Ah Hua was soon arrested as well, and from then on, the STC was left with only the Student Movement Committee and the Workers Movement Committee in operation. They were linked through a cumbersome courier system with South Malayan Politburo Secretary Ho Lung, leaving the STC and its two remaining committees substantially to their own devices in terms of day-to-day operations.

In support of the MCP's armed struggle in Peninsular Malaya, the STC was ordered to establish Urban Armed Working Units (武工队). Ah Chin organised a unit in early 1950 and Wong Fook Kwang (黄福光 aka Tie-Feng 铁锋), Secretary of MCP 'E' Branch of 'O' District, was put in charge and led a team of ten members with two hand guns between them. The Unit began a programme of assassinations and violence straight away, but then in October 1951 the MCP issued a new directive aimed at restraining the Urban Armed Unit from engaging in what it viewed as excessive and counter-productive violence.[16] It is not clear, however, if this directive had much effect. Certainly the Unit continued carrying out assassinations until Wong was arrested and banished to China in June 1954.[17] It played an important historical role by intimidating and killing blacklegs (strike-breakers) in the unions, which in turn helped the ABL and MCP cadres in their political activities among the workers.

It should be noted at this point that even though the operational integrity of the STC suffered serious damage during the period June 1948 to December 1953 because of the arrest of the entire committee, the newly created ABL continued expanding rapidly. By 1954, the ABL's total membership had reached more than 2,000. ABL members were able to organise effectively and efficiently in the workers' front and in the student movement. They proved particularly effective in mobilising the Chinese middle school students to fight against the National Service Ordinance, which resulted in a violent riot on 13 May 1954. The strength of the ABL's organising power was demonstrated again during the Hock Lee Bus riot of May 1955.

1954–1957: The United Front with the PAP

The left in Singapore grew tremendously in size and power in 1954, thanks largely to the levels of economic exploitation and social injustice and the liberalisation that accompanied moves towards self-government and democracy. Trade unionism was revitalised as workers sought organisational protection in this new environment. Coinciding with this social discontent, overall anti-British, anti-colonial sentiment became overwhelming and widespread. These responses were natural and even predictable, but the colonial authorities looked upon them simplistically as the result of MCP agitation.

The Rendel Constitutional Commission Report of 22 February 1954 provided Singapore with a new political prospect and a number of new political parties formed, including the People's Action Party (PAP). The MCP continued building mass movements through its Student Movement Committee and Workers Movement Committee,[18] with the most important open organisations being the Singapore Chinese Middle School Students' Union (SCMSSU), and trade union fronts like the Singapore Factory and Shop Workers' Union (SFSWU) and Singapore Trade Union Congress (STUC), along with numerous rural resident associations, hawker associations, and cultural organisations and old-boys' associations. The PAP's formation was in fact the direct result of the cooperation between the Fabian socialists represented by Lee Kuan Yew and his team, and the left wing represented by Lim Chin Siong with the backing of the ABL and MCP STC, and was evidence of the success of the MCP's united front strategy. The Partai Rakyat Singapore (PRS) and the Workers' Party (WP) were also infiltrated.

These mass movements took place substantially without the direction of the MCP, except for the support for the PAP's formation. The success of these largely spontaneous activities was a surprise to both the MCP and the British. The MCP had not planned for this degree of success and had no specific instructions from the South Malayan Politburo on how to operate in this environment. The Party's achievements during this period rested on the unity of the left-wing forces against the British that had been generated by a common hatred of exploitation, British rule and the declaration of the Emergency. Moreover, it offered a vision of an ideal society as its ultimate goal. These factors gained the support of intellectuals from both the English and Chinese educational streams, including students, workers and peasants of different races. Instead of asserting that the MCP was consciously building up united fronts during this period, it should be understood that the trained cadres of the MCP were recruited as natural leaders and organisers of the struggle. Yet passions among the masses were running so high that these leaders could not successfully impose any sense of restraint, let alone strategy, over the crowds that they had brought together.

The 13 May 1954 Chinese student demonstration-turned-riot against the National Service Ordinance was a case of a match thrown into explosives. It was followed by the Hock Lee Bus strike that also turned into a riot in May 1955. The government ban on the SCMSSU in October 1956 brought the people's anger to a new height. The MCP had placed its cadres and associates in leading positions in these movements, but they were unable to control the development of events. Untrained, undisciplined enthusiasts simply took over in the heat of the demonstrations, turning aroused crowds into violent ones. The result was that every 'success' systematically weakened the MCP, because every conflict was followed by the arrest of ABL members and MCP cadres who were correctly identified as organisers of the demonstrations and therefore blamed for the violence.

A number of great names came to the fore during this period, the key figures being Lim Chin Siong and Lee Kuan Yew representing the communist camp and the non-communist camp, respectively, though it should be remembered that they were both considered left-wing leaders at the time. The true united front was seen in the formation of the PAP, when the two camps finally came to terms. The MCP had accepted that there was never likely to be a legal left-wing party in Singapore with which it would be satisfied. There were no illusions that the group represented by Lee was pro-communist, and yet Lee had been closely associated with the unions and students as their legal adviser and advocate. The progressive attitude of Lee and his group made them satisfactory 'comrades', at least for the anti-British struggle. As the key MCP cadre in Singapore in charge of the overall operation, Wong Meng Keong (黄民强 aka Ng Meng Chian and Zhang Jian) told one of his subordinates:

> … in Singapore history, there had never been a true leftwing political party. The present PAP could represent Singapore's 'Anti-Colonialism' political party and although the characteristics of the leaders of the PAP were of the petty bourgeoisie type, we should still help them to function in order that our Party could realise our objective.[19]

Yet because anti-colonialism was the only substantial element binding the two groups, the united front with the PAP did not go smoothly. The Lee faction was continually seeking to differentiate itself from the leftists in the eyes of the British,[20] and the leftists were continually frustrated that the price of maintaining the united front appeared to be that they could not take leadership positions in the PAP. Finally, in 1957, the left decided to push for dominance of the Central Executive Committee (CEC) of the PAP.[21] It took half the CEC seats, giving it more power than it had ever exercised to date, and offered to let Lee and his group continue as the senior office-bearers. When Lee refused — tacitly breaking the united front and exposing the leftists to the likelihood of being arrested — the leftists had to take those positions as well. On 22 August, the government duly arrested five of the six leftist CEC members, whereupon the Lee group resumed full control of the CEC.

At this point, it is important to note that even though some leftist members of the CEC were associated with the MCP, their actions were not directed by the Party. Their aggressive push for power grew from local frustrations and not from any sort of strategic planning or instructions. Indeed, the end result was that it set back the programme of the left by destroying the united front with the PAP. It seems that even at this senior level, the Party was unable to keep control of events — or even its own associates — with grassroots passions generating counter-productive activity. In fact, since 1956, the MCP had considered the Singapore operations as a whole to be overly 'left' and too militant and had criticised the 13 May 1954 riot and the May 1955 Hock Lee Bus riot as overly 'left'. A directive from Yeung Kwo through Ho Lung reached Singapore in late 1956 urging moderation, but the political situation in Singapore was moving faster than the courier communication system. Isolated directives arriving months after the events on which it was passing judgement had little impact on the ground. The Singapore political situation was shifting so rapidly that even the STC was unable to remain properly appraised of developments. Neither Lim Chin Siong and other union leaders, nor the underground MCP cadres, were able to control events, with the rank and file on the ground taking the initiative time and again and moving without 'proper direction and control'. The left-wing leaders and MCP cadres lit a match and the masses turned the blaze into an inferno, resulting in the movement being directed from below rather than being controlled rationally or centrally from above.

Further confirmation of the disconnection between the higher levels of the Party and the actions of their cadres, associates and followers on the ground came in April 1957 with the release of an MCP document titled, 'A Summing Up of Experience in the Struggle against Persecution' (反迫害斗争的经验总结).[22] This MCP review of the policy pursued in Singapore remarked that the Singapore movement had wrongly focused its attacks on Chief Minister Lim Yew Hock instead of the British, and that it was inflexible in its tactics. It singled out Lim Chin Siong for specific criticism and branded the MCP cadres and leftists in Singapore as left-wing adventurists.

Following this chastisement, the South Malayan Politburo made extraordinary efforts to rein in its supporters in Singapore and give some strategic direction to their activities. Its overhaul of the Singapore operation was thorough and can be summarised as follows:

- The cessation of *Freedom News*; open publications to be used for propaganda.
- The disbandment of the ABL; its members to be absorbed as full members of the MCP or kept as sympathisers.
- The infiltration of MCP cadres into legal and open organisations, particularly the political parties, trade unions, peasant organisations, cultural associations and old-boys' associations.
- Full support to be given to the PAP.

As well as these directives from the South Malayan Politburo, the Party's lines of authority and communication were also overhauled under the direction of Xiao Zhang (小张 aka Zhang Lin Yun 章凌云), the MCP Beijing delegation leader and Secretary of the External Politburo.[23] Eu visited Beijing in the summer of 1957 to meet with Xiao Zhang and he was instructed to establish a Singapore Branch Committee at Jakarta with Eu Chooi Yip, Wong Meng Keong and Chiam Chong Chian as committee members. As we see below, even before the end of 1957 the Indonesia committee had entrusted a young cadre called Fang Chuang-Pi (aka 'The Plen', as Lee Kuan Yew acknowledged him) with full authority for all operations on the ground in Singapore[24] and a brief to rebuild the united front with the PAP.

The post-1957 strategy of the MCP was thus set. It was to be underpinned by a broadening of the concept of the united front so that it reflected a much more catholic and less sectarian impulse. It was announced that 'all party members shall try to infiltrate into legal associations or organisations irrespective of whether it be right or leftwing, feudalistic or otherwise'[25] and to make this effective it closed down the open front organisations that were overtly associated with the Party.

1957–1966: 'The Plen' and the Death of the United Front

Introduced by Eu Chooi Yip, Fang Chuang-Pi began engaging in Party activities sometime in late 1948 as an ABL member while working as a journalist with the *Nan Chiau Jit Pau*. After the *Nan Chiau Jit Pau* was banned, Fang worked under Eu Chooi Yip as the member of the Propaganda Committee responsible for the printing and distribution of the Chinese edition of *Freedom News*. By this time, the entire STC had collapsed and both Eu and Fang were struggling to revitalise the Party's connections.

Fortunately, the Student Movement Committee was still intact and re-establishment was possible. Fang applied to join the Party at Eu's recommendation in late 1950 and was inducted as a full member in early 1951. He went underground in mid-1951 and was almost caught the following year when the printing house was raided by the police, but managed to escape by jumping into the pond of a pigsty.[26] He continued to write, print and distribute *Freedom News* through the Student Committee. In 1952 and early 1953, when Wong Meng Keong, Chiam Chong Chian (詹忠谦) and Eu Chooi Yip were evacuated to Indonesia, Fang was put in charge of some of the MCP operations in Singapore. He liaised with Eu, Wong and Chiam in Indonesia, but was not properly in charge of MCP activities in Singapore since Wong and Chiam continued to direct the student and worker movements from Indonesia.[27] Then in late 1957, Fang was asked to sit in on a Party meeting at Moro Island, three hours by speed boat to the south of Singapore, where a thorough review of past events was to be conducted and new policy formulated based upon both the directive from Ho Lung and the instructions Eu had received from Xiao Zhang in Beijing. When Fang arrived, he was told a three-man Singapore Working Committee was to be formed for the proper direction and control of the Singapore MCP operation, which had grown too big and unwieldy to be controlled from the Peninsula. The Party was especially concerned that some members had tried to seize power in the PAP at their own initiative, with disastrous consequences for the united front, but this was just a particularly serious manifestation of a general lack of unified leadership that also afflicted the worker and student movements. The Party was concerned that the lack of discipline risked undermining the collective effort in the struggle against British colonial rule. At the meeting Fang was inducted as a member of the team as a subordinate to Eu and Wong (who was then using the alias Zhang Jian).[28] Even though he was notionally junior, Fang was put in charge of the Singapore operation on the ground — now with full authority over all operations. His primary task was to remedy the damage done to the united front with the PAP through the adventurism of Tan Chong Kin (陈从今) and Goh Boon Toh (吴文斗). This young, relatively inexperienced man was thus given full authority to negotiate with Lee Kuan Yew to remedy the damage done by the incident of August 1957, and if possible to win better treatment and placement of leftist and MCP underground members in the PAP structure, both in the party and in any future government. It was perhaps an early sign of his naivety that Fang did not consider this to be a difficult task because he understood that Lee recognised the importance of mass support and did not want its strength to be diluted through internal divisions and divergent tactics. He also took solace in the fact that Lee had grossly overestimated the Party's control over the mass movements.[29]

Decades later, Fang realised that he had completely misread his adversary — indeed, he appears not to have even realised that he was an adversary. 'It was a total mistake!' he told me in interview. 'We were whole-heartedly and genuinely supporting him and believed that he was a real anti-colonial fighter who we regarded as a friend and close member of the united front.' Fang considered that he was approaching Lee with an honest and honourable proposition to share political leadership. The MCP had no intention of taking over the government in Singapore, both because the imperialists would never have allowed a communist regime to be established in such a strategic position as Singapore and because the MCP itself considered that it was not possible to control British-trained civil servants so as to be effective in government. [30]

Fang, however, was interested in establishing a left-wing presence in the government in Singapore because this would be advantageous to the MCP struggle on the Peninsula. In retrospect, he realised the invidious position which he was proposing to place himself in, even if Lee had played along. What then was the 'united front' he was proposing?

> It was a united front under colonial rule; it was a united front hand-cuffed by the Emergency Regulations; it was a united front whereby the left were in prison and the right acted as bureaucrats; it was a united front in which the Chinese-educated were petty officials and the English-educated were in power ... it was an odd and lopsided united front relationship.[31]

Yet he still stood by his decision to place the MCP's future in the hands of Lee Kuan Yew and the PAP because there were no other options: 'It was merely the choice in selecting a "bad" from "the worst".'[32]

His big mistake, he now concedes, was in surrendering all his winning cards in the first hand, just to establish his good faith (and perhaps to reinforce Lee's misconceptions of the power of the Party). At the opening of the negotiations, Fang agreed to order the MCP's Chang Yuen Tong to resign from the City Council and the Executive Committee of the Workers' Party, effectively abandoning the Party's work in the WP. He also ordered the withdrawal of Party support from the Partai Rakyat Singapore, burning yet another bridge. Both acts were designed to establish Fang's credentials and goodwill, but they also removed the only other political options open to the MCP. Finally, he also withdrew the Party's support from David Marshall in his bid for re-election in 1959.

Fang believed that he would still have the upper hand because of Lee's weakness at the grassroots, even in his own party, since most of the PAP branches were in the hands of either MCP cadres or leftists who were heavily influenced by the MCP.[33] He thought that Lee would still need all the left's support, and so would be malleable. 'I should have taken a much stronger position and taken the initiative instead of giving concessions and compromising ourselves,' he has since conceded.[34]

The mistake was made based mainly on the consideration to provide full support to the PAP and the purpose was to create a stabilised political environment and thus strengthen the PAP in its position in the negotiations with the British.[35]

For some reason Fang did not seem to have considered, even to this day, that until he burnt his bridges at Lee's behest, there were other options for a united front of political parties: namely the WP and PRS. The MCP had already infiltrated each of these organisations at the highest levels. Chang Yuan Tong and Pang Toon Tin were key office-bearers in the WP and the PRS, respectively. Why the MCP did not consider these options, but continued to stick to the PAP, has yet to be examined. Fang had no answer to this question. Perhaps Fang could not trust David Marshall and considered that:

> … the PRS was too leftist and would create confusion and commotion.
> Only the PAP was basically leftist, and it was the objective we could
> strive to co-operate at present. Therefore, we should give our whole-
> hearted support to the PAP

as Fang was reported to have explained to one of his subordinates.[36] Or perhaps he just did not consider it his job to think outside the parameters of his instructions. He was told to rebuild the united front with the PAP and to avoid leftist adventurism and that was what he was doing. After all, he was appointed precisely to bring the loose cannons under control and impose Party discipline on the cadres. Initiative had not been appreciated by the Party before 1958 and would probably earn a rebuke now.

In March 1957, only a few months before his negotiations with Fang, Lee had taken a leading role in the drafting of a new constitution for Singapore, and had pushed for the creation of the Internal Security Council, whose prime purpose was to allow the British to continue suppressing the MCP. In effect, Lee had already formed a united front with the British Government against the MCP, so there should have been no illusions about his intent.

Unsurprisingly, the MCP's second united front with the PAP began withering as soon as the party won power in the 1959 general election.[37]

Political detainees were released and Lim Chin Siong, Fong Swee Suan, C. V. Devan Nair and S. Woodhull were hailed as heroes, but all leftists — even those not associated with the MCP — were excluded from important portfolios in the newly formed government. Lee's faction held on to all the key positions and a series of legislative actions were taken to neutralise the communist influence, especially in the trade unions.[38]

After the party had been in government for a little over a year, there began a series of public confrontations that destroyed even the pretence of unity. The ultimate points of contention were the existence of the Internal Security Council (ISC), and the issue of merger between Singapore and Malaya, Sarawak and Sabah to form Malaysia. The MCP considered (correctly) that the ISC was nothing more than a weapon aimed directly at them, and they denounced the Malaysia plan as a neo-colonial construction designed to profit British economic interests and assist British and American Cold War strategies. Lee and his group were committed to maintaining the ISC and to pushing for merger. The differences between Lee's group and the MCP first became public in April 1961 during the Hong Lim by-election, which pitted Lee's former Minister for National Development, Ong Eng Guan, against a novice candidate from the PAP.[39] The MCP dismissed Ong as an opportunist and continued to support the PAP, but they used the opportunity to bring pressure to bear on Lee to request the abolition of the Internal Security Council and to demand full independence for Singapore instead of merger with Malaya. Despite MCP support for the PAP, Ong won the election comfortably to retain his seat.

The next flashpoint came only a month later, when the Malayan Prime Minister, Tunku Abdul Rahman, announced his Malaysia Plan. Fang and Lee had met earlier that month on 11 May and discussed the prospect of Singapore self-government and the possibility of abolishing the ISC. They had also discussed the likelihood of a merger with Malaya but Lee had assured him that there was little likelihood of the Tunku agreeing. He also made no reference to Sarawak and Sabah. When the Tunku announced the Malaysia Plan on 27 May, Fang was shocked. He became convinced that Lee had deceived him. Six days later, on 2 June, Lim Chin Siong, together with five other STUC leaders, issued a statement calling upon the government to strive for full self-government for Singapore (as opposed to independence through merger in Malaysia) and the abolition of the ISC in the coming constitutional meeting with the British in 1963.[40] The PAP responded by reiterating its support for the Malaysia Plan. Lim repeated his call on 12 June, and on 13 June, eight PAP Assemblymen[41] led by Dr Lee Siew Choh and 43 trade unions issued a separate statement in support of

Lim. As if this were not public enough, Singapore happened to be holding another by-election at that time, and the MCP decided to send Lee another message by not only withdrawing their support from the PAP candidate, but supporting David Marshall, the opposition candidate, who went on to win by a small margin.[42]

The MCP then planned to escalate its pressure on Lee both by using its dominance of the PAP branches,[43] and through a motion of no confidence in the Legislative Assembly. There were 51 members in the Legislative Assembly and it needed only 26 to overthrow Lee. Lee thwarted the revolt in the party branches by refusing to hold the party conference, and he pre-empted the attack in the Legislative Assembly by moving a motion of confidence in his own government. He survived by two votes, one of which came from an independent. Thirteen members of the government abstained from the confidence vote. Immediately after the showdown, Lee expelled the 13 from the party, formalising the split in the united front. The split quickly spread through all mass organisations, including the trade unions, student and cultural organisations, and even the People's Association and its community centres and Work Brigades.[44] There was now a clear line between the left (now regrouping under the banner of the Barisan Sosialis [Socialist Front]) and the 'turned right' PAP, as the MCP labelled it.

In 1961, Eu again was in Beijing reporting to Chin Peng, who had taken over from Xiao Zhang (aka Zhang Lin Yun) as the Secretary of the MCP's External Politburo. In view of the setbacks that had been suffered in the armed struggle on the Peninsula, Chin Peng was in fact seeking direction from the CCP on whether to carry on the struggle or suspend it. He arrived in Beijing full of doubts and despondency, but he received nothing but encouragement from the Chinese Party. The CCP told him to revitalise the armed struggle rather than disband the guerrilla units, and it promised financial support. Chin Peng was immensely encouraged and subsequently the MCP policy was completely reoriented towards a more aggressive line.[45] In southern Thailand, the base of the MCP armed units, a New Policy was implemented to recruit and train new fighters. The External Politburo also enlarged its functions to facilitate a more aggressive participation in international communist affairs with specific emphasis on the Sino-Soviet dispute and for more aggressive underground activities in Malaya (including Singapore). Eu was told to dissolve the Singapore Branch which had been established in 1957 and to form a new South Malayan Politburo, superseding the defunct South Malayan Politburo under Ho Lung, who had surrendered to the Malayan government in April 1958. Wong Meng Keong was elected Secretary, and Eu, Chiam and Fang were committee members. Eu and Wong had already (in late 1959) been elected to the MCP Central Executive Committee.[46] Later in 1963, Eu replaced Wong as the Secretary of the Politburo.

Yet, despite the optimism that had spread from Beijing to Jakarta, this was a dreadful time for grand initiatives involving Singapore. The underground cadres were desperately trying to escape from the tightening grip of the Special Branch, and in the wake of the split with the PAP, most MCP cadres operating in the PAP and the mass movements had shown their hands for all to see, making them utterly vulnerable to arrest and either imprisonment or deportation. That was the price paid for the 'full support' given to the PAP in 1957. Far from launching new initiatives in Singapore, Chin Peng had to order the evacuation of all exposed MCP cadres in Singapore to safe places. From late 1961 till early 1964, some 60 key MCP members were smuggled out of Singapore to various points in Indonesia and elsewhere. Those rescued included Chan Sun Wing, Lee's former Parliamentary Secretary, and Wong Soon Fong, the MP of Toa Payoh and the Director of the Work Brigade. Yet many MCP cadres were left to fend for themselves. Operation Cold Store on 2 February 1963 netted most of those cadres who remained in Singapore, along with many of the left-wing leaders who had no direct connection with the MCP.

This all but ended the operation of the MCP in Singapore. The creation of the Barisan Sosialis was never a viable alternative to the united front with the PAP because it was too narrow, weak, vulnerable and disunited. In this last, pale manifestation of the united front, the Party was reduced to the role of supporting actor to Dr Lee Siew Choh as he led the Barisan through a series of highly principled gestures that cost dearly and achieved little. The main points of contention were over a new boycott on registration for national service, the adoption of a 'Crush Malaysia' slogan, the recognition of Singapore's independence after its separation from Malaysia, and a boycott of Parliament. On all of these issues the Party was urging moderation and Dr Lee was (successfully) urging the more extreme option, but it was always the MCP cadres and supporters who suffered when the arrest warrants were issued. By 1966, there was simply no one left to carry on the fight in Singapore.

APPENDIX 1

MCP Central Committee and Politburo
Chin Peng

Central/South Malayan Bureau
Yeung Kwo/Ho Lung

Singapore Town committee
Liu Kwang (till Feb 1949)
Ah Chin (till Dec 1950)
Liu Cheng Yong (till Aug 1951)
Ah Hua (till Nov 1951)

Singapore Town Working Committee

Student Movement Committee
Wong Meng Keong (till 1954)

Workers Movement Committee
Wong Meng Keong (till 1954)

United Front Committee
Chiam Chong Chian (till 1957)

Propaganda Committee
Ho Seng (till Dec 1949)
Eu Chooi Yip (till early1953)
Fang Chuang-Pi (till 1957)

**English Speaking ABL
(Branch — by end-1949)**
Ah Har (till May 1950)
Eu Chooi Yip (till 1953)

Four District Committees
Bukit Timah District
Sembawang and Naval Base District
Da-Po District
Xiao-Po District

NOTES

1   The Nanyang General Labour Union (NGLU) was formed in May 1926 as a branch of the China General Labour Union in Canton. When the Nanyang Provisional Committee of the Communist Party of China was established in 1928, the NGLU thus became the key front organisation for communist propaganda. One of its key aims was the unification of workers in trade and industry, particularly the seamen and harbour workers. The NGLU was renamed the Malayan General Labour Union and came under the direction of the MCP after its formation in April 1930.

2   In early September 1936, the MCP's Fifth Enlarged Plenum of Party Central passed a motion to form a Singapore national salvation organisation in support of the anti-Japanese movement in China. Subsequently, the MCP-controlled Singapore Overseas Chinese Anti-Japanese National Salvation Association (SOCANSA) was established in February 1937. In December 1937, the MCP formed the Singapore Overseas Chinese All Circles Anti-Enemy Backing-Up Society (AEBUS) to replace SOCANSA. The AEBUS set up sub-divisions such as the Student AEBUS, Shop-Keepers AEBUS, Women AEBUS, Writers AEBUS, Workers AEBUS, Peasants AEBUS, etc., in support of the Singapore China Relief Fund Union and the South Seas China Relief Fund Union which were led by Tan Kah Kee, the Chairman of the Chinese Chamber of Commerce, Singapore. The AEBUS was effective in organising the masses in all kinds of fund-raising and anti-Japanese propaganda campaigns during the period.

3   The Nine-Point Anti-Japanese Program called for the formation of an all-races anti-Japanese united front. It tuned down its aggressiveness by proclaiming to strive for the establishment of a Republic of Democratic Malaya instead of the Workers and Peasants' Soviet Republic of Malaya.

4   In December 1943, the representatives of SEA Command led by John L. H. Davis, with Frederick Spencer Chapman, Richard Broome and Lim Bo Seng (under the assumed name of Tan Chong Lim), negotiated with the MCP led by Secretary-General Lai Teck (under the assumed name of Zhang Hong) and one other member, Chin Peng, at Blandan, Perak. They reached the so-called Bidor Agreement, whereby the MCP agreed to accept the military leadership of the SEA Command, with the agreement to be enforced till social order was restored with the return of the Alliance forces. During the Japanese Occupation, Lai Teck assisted the Japanese Military Administration to capture and kill almost all the MCP Central Committee members and some senior cadres, which culminated in the 1 September 1942 Incident where 18 high-ranking MCP Central Committee members and top MPAJA commanders, along with several soldiers, were killed at Batu Caves. Following the surrender of the Japanese, on 25 August 1945 Lai Teck issued the 'Eight-Point Proposition' in the name of the MCP Central Committee in which the establishment of the Republic of Democratic Malaya stated in the Nine-Point Anti-Japanese Program was abolished. The MPAJA was soon ordered to disband and surrender its weapons. Chin Peng and Ian Ward, *My Side of History* (Singapore: Media Masters, 2003), pp. 14–27;

C. C. Chin, 'The Plight of the Chinese during Japanese Occupation', *Journal of the South Seas Society* 52 (1998): 161–88.

5   The MCP was recognised as a legal political party in Malaya since it was engaging in constitutional struggle according to the Nine-Point Democratic Programme of 1 February 1946. This Programme was designed to further the Party's national democratic united front strategy, which was established to achieve autonomy for Malaya from the British colonial government. See C. C. Chin, 'The Revolutionary Programmes and their Effect on the Struggle of the Malayan Communist Party', in *Dialogues with Chin Peng: New Light on the Malayan Communist Party*, ed. C. C. Chin and Karl Hack (Singapore: Singapore University Press, 2004), p. 266.

6   Yeo Kim Wah, *Political Development in Singapore 1945–55* (Singapore: Singapore University Press, 1973), pp. 22–44.

7   Ibid., p. 93.

8   Ibid., p. 95.

9   See Appendix 1, 'MCP Town Committee organisation chart'.

10 Interview with Wang Guo Xing, STC District member, 1950–52, 20 March 2004.

11 The ABL was a semi-underground front organisation of the MCP for mobilising the masses and was formed in the style and format of the Anti-Japanese League (AJL) during the Japanese Occupation period. Its full name was the Malayan People's Anti-British League, and in Singapore, the Singapore People's Anti-British League. ABL members were considered sympathisers of the MCP and on probation to become full MCP members should they be considered up to the mark.

12 By the time of the outbreak of the Emergency, the ABL in Singapore had successfully recruited a substantial number of the English-educated into communist activities, particularly from the MDU. See Yeo Kim Wah, 'Joining the Communist Underground: The Conversion of English-Educated Radicals to Communism in Singapore, June 1948–January 1951', *Journal of the Malaysian Branch of the Royal Asiatic Society* 67, 1 (June 1994): 37–9.

13 Eu Chooi Yip was the first to be enrolled as an MCP member and was entrusted with full responsibility to recruit MDU members into the ABL or MCP. See ibid.

14 Ibid., p. 42. See also Eu Chooi Yip's Oral History Record reel 12, Singapore National Archives 001359/23, 1992.

15 Interview with Wang Guo Xing, STC District member 1950–52, 20 March 2004, and interview with Ho Seng, STC Head of Propaganda Department, 20 September 2006.

16 A document issued by the MCP dated 1 October 1951 on the current situation and directives, sometimes referred to as the October Resolution (十月决议). It was meant for the rectification of the strategy and tactics for the struggle against the British, and explicitly condemned the wrongdoings of the MPABA or later the MNLA in their intimidation and terrorist acts, such as the burning of public buses, derailing of passenger trains, slashing of rubber trees, and confiscation and destruction of identity cards, which caused the deaths of innocent civilians

and indirectly brought about hardship to plantation workers and also provoked harassment of ordinary people by the British; C. C. Chin, 'The Revolutionary Programmes', p. 272.

17 Memoir of Huangfuguang: 'Twice Imprisonment in Singapore during the British Colonial Rule' in *The Passionate Years*, ed. Luo Wu and Chen Jian (Hong Kong: Witness Publishing House, 2005), pp. 103–32.

18 The Student Movement Committee and the Workers Movement Committee were under the direction of Wong Meng Keong and were most effective in mobilising the masses to stage strikes.

19 See Lee Ting Hui, *The Open United Front: The Communist Struggle in Singapore, 1954–1966* (Singapore: South Seas Society, 1996), p. 54.

20 People's Action Party, *6th Anniversary Celebration Souvenir 1960* (Singapore: People's Action Party, 1960), p. 16; People's Action Party, *Our First Ten Years, 1964* (Singapore: People's Action Party, 1964), p. 206; People's Action Party, *15th Anniversary Celebration Souvenir, 1969* (Singapore: People's Action Party, 1969), p. 127. See also Fong Sip Chee, *The PAP Story: The Pioneering Years (November 1954–April 1968) A Diary of Events of the People's Action Party: Reminiscences of an Old Comrade* (Singapore: Times Periodicals, 1979), p. 38.

21 Ibid., pp. 56–61, 265–6.

22 See Lee, *The Open United Front*, pp. 132–5, 175.

23 Eu Chooi Yip travelled to Beijing to meet Xiao Zhang in June 1957. The author's interview with Fang Chuang-Pi, 12–15 February 1995; and a brief interview with Eu Chooi Yip 30 April 1965. See also Eu Chooi Yip's Oral History Record reel 16, Singapore National Archives, 001359/23, 1992; Fang Chuang-Pi, *Response to Said Zahari's Criticism in his Memoir 'Dark Clouds at Dawn'*, cyclostyled statement dated 19 March 2001, pp. 2–3.

24 Ibid., p. 175; and the author's interview with Fang Chuang-Pi, 12–15 February 1995.

25 Lee, *The Open United Front*, p. 175.

26 The author's interview with Fang Chuang-Pi, 12–15 February 1995.

27 Fang Chuang-Pi, *Response to Said Zahari's Criticism*, p. 2.

28 Fang Chuang-Pi, *Response to Said Zahari's Criticism*, p. 3; and the author's interview with Fang Chuang-Pi, 12–15 February 1995.

29 Fang Chuang-Pi, *Response to Said Zahari's Criticism*, p. 3.

30 Ibid., p. 4.

31 Ibid.

32 Ibid., pp. 3, 4.

33 Ibid.

34 Ibid.

35 Ibid.

36 Lee, *The Open United Front*, pp. 157–8, 182 note 213.

37 Fong, *The PAP Story*, p. 75.

38 Ibid., pp. 79, 80.

39 Ibid., pp. 84–92.

40 Lee, *The Open United Front*, pp. 202, 203.

41 The eight assemblymen were: Dr. Lee Siew Choh, S. T. Bani, Lim You Eng, Fong Ying Ching, Teo Hock Guan, Tee Kim Leng, Wong Soon Fong and Tan Cheng Tong.

42 David Marshall of the Workers' Party won by a slight margin (3,598 votes against 3,052) over PAP candidate Mohamud Awang, President of the newly formed Trade Union Congress (TUC).

43 Ibid., p. 204.

44 People's Association, *The First Twenty Years of the People's Association* (Singapore: [People's Association], 1980), pp. 24, 48–65.

45 Author's interview with Chin Peng, 10–12 February 1999, in Canberra.

46 Author's interview with Fang Chuang-Pi, 15 February 1995.

4

Chinese Merchants in Politics: The Democratic Party in the 1955 Legislative Assembly Election

Sikko Visscher

In the canon of Singapore political history, the 1959 Legislative Assembly election is habitually presented as the key electoral event on Singapore's road to independence. The fact that the People's Action Party (PAP) came to power in 1959 contributes greatly to this historical selectivity. On the occasions that it is mentioned, the 1955 election is most often regarded as limited in scope because of a smaller electorate, and as a transitional election more important for which party did not win. Indeed, the colonial overlords and the English-educated elite had expected that the Progressive Party (PP) would secure a majority. The failure of the latter to do so is attributed largely to the participation of the Democratic Party (DP). The common analysis then concludes that the DP split the conservative vote, thereby preventing a PP majority and opening the door for the Labour Front (LF) government of David Marshall, Singapore's first Chief Minister. This chapter revisits the 1955 election and the role of the DP. A framework of civil society analysis is used to illustrate the DP's societal foundations in the Singapore Chinese Chamber of Commerce (SCCC) and to underline the importance of the ongoing political contribution of the Chamber during Singapore's last years as a self-governing colony.[1]

Politics in Singapore, 1945–55

When the British returned with their pride dented after World War II, it was soon clear that a transfer of power to a form of local government would eventually end colonial rule in Singapore. As a result, various groups contemplated what their reactions should be and what role they wanted to play in the process. Naturally, the elite institutions that played the role of societal representatives in the indirect rule system of the British figured prominently. As the primary representative of the Chinese majority under colonial rule, the SCCC and its leadership realised that they must adapt to the new circumstances. The SCCC was founded in 1906 as a lobby organisation of the Chinese business elite towards both the Imperial Chinese court and the British colonial government. At the same time, its election structure and the nature of its membership immediately positioned it as the natural apex of a pyramid comprising Chinese associations, clan groups (*huiguan*) and dialect groups (*bang*), of which wealthy merchants were presidents or chairmen. In this capacity, the Chamber played a social, cultural and political role from its inception as a guardian and leader of the Chinese community. Reflecting the general pattern in the Chinese community, most of the Chamber members and leaders were China-born or Chinese-educated, with a minority representation being local-born, English-educated or Straits Chinese.

As awareness of the political and economic stakes of decolonisation rose among the Chamber leadership, it went through a process of what I have defined elsewhere as 'localisation'.[2] This localisation entailed a shift in orientation towards Singapore as a permanent home instead of a temporary sojourn, towards the emerging Singapore political arena instead of the cauldron of ideological conflict in China, and towards becoming locally grounded actors instead of migrants.

In the late-colonial power equation, despite the stated goal of a transfer of power to local actors, British colonial forces kept control of the early stages of the decolonisation process. Their roadmap was to slowly increase the number of local representatives in the existing Municipal, Legislative and Executive Councils, first by appointment and later by popular election. They saw this as a prerequisite for the development of a local polity that would eventually lead to a fully locally elected assembly and a form of self-government. During this process, only those Singapore residents possessing British nationality or British-protected status would have the right to vote or stand for election. These realities made the Chamber leadership look towards its English-speaking minority for suitable actors in the political

game. The four men from within the SCCC leadership who were successfully projected into politics over the next decade all bridged the worlds of
the China-born and local-born, and had strong networks among both the
Chinese and European communities.[3]

The Chamber's political strategy was based on pragmatism and aimed
to influence the inevitable changes to the system from within. Meanwhile,
internal political discussions within its leadership centred on identifying
the main political goals. Three were identified: (1) enfranchisement of
first-generation migrants through the implementation of local citizenship;
(2) introduction of all local languages in the developing parliamentary
system; and (3) equal treatment and importance of all language streams
in education. Over the succeeding years, it petitioned the Governor, the
British Prime Minister and eventually the Queen on these issues, raising
local awareness of the stakes of decolonisation among its Chinese constituency in the process. At first this was done through its English-speaking
representatives inside the colonial political system, but after 1950–51, the
Chinese-speaking leaders became more ambitious and assertive in their
political actions.

This change was due partly to the process of localisation described above,
but it was also influenced greatly by the fact that the China-born had more
at stake because they would be left without any political rights or influence
if the British roadmap prevailed. A supporting factor was that a number of
China-born business leaders had amassed considerable fortunes, especially
during the rubber boom caused by the Korean War. This gave them the
means to champion their own political, cultural and educational agendas,
of which the Nanyang University was only one example. I have dubbed this
group of leaders as 'the Ambitious'.[4] They were assertive and not afraid to
put their demands on the table or to finance alternative policies out of their
own pockets. Above all, they believed that the Chinese business elite, and
its main vehicle, the SCCC, had a major role to play in Singapore politics.

Yet even as the confidence and political assertiveness of the Chinese business community grew, new rival forces were beginning to emerge from within
the community. Faced with low wages, high unemployment and falling
living standards, the working class of Singapore was restless and looking for
agents and institutions of their own to improve their situation. These were
ideal circumstances for the rise of a strong labour movement and indeed, in
the early 1950s, many workers' organisations were established. Strikes were
the order of the day and caused major disruption to the Singapore economy.
It was the first indication that politics was moving from being an exclusively
elite arena to an expansive, populist field of endeavour.

Chinese education proved to be the spark for the politicisation of Singapore society. To the China-born immigrants of Singapore, the issue of Chinese education tied together culture, identity and politics in a manner that Singapore had not witnessed before. A number of incidents concerning this issue were to become defining events in the political development of the territory. As their class consciousness was awakened, the issue of Chinese education became a symbol of the struggle of the Chinese-speaking working class against the English-speaking colonial and local elites. Because anti-colonial feelings were linked to issues of Chinese culture and identity, both left-wing unions and parties, as well as the Chinese elite, were obliged to enter the arena of Chinese education. The Chamber leaders were deeply committed to the issue because of their role as leaders of dialect organisations and *huiguan*, which were the very organisations that ran or supported private Chinese-language schools. Chinese education was not only part of their own identity, it was also part of the institutional structure from which they derived their status and power.

In the years leading up to the 1955 election, education issues and political actions by Chinese students provided the setting for a number of heated political battles as well as riots, student strikes and coordinated union actions. In the midst of this, Singapore prepared to take a big step towards self-rule.

In order to guide this transformation, a new constitution for the colony of Singapore had to be prepared which would set out the parameters for such a transfer of power. The Rendel Commission was created in 1953 to draft this constitution and elections were scheduled to take place in April 1955. The colonial Legislative Council with its ex-officio and appointed Unofficial members was to be replaced by a Legislative Assembly with members elected from 25 electoral constituencies, three ex-officio ministers and four nominated Unofficials. The party gaining the majority in the elections would assemble a government consisting of a cabinet of nine ministers led by a Chief Minister. Three ex-officio ministers, the colonial Financial Secretary, the Attorney General and the Chief Secretary (the former Colonial Secretary) would control the crucial ministries of finance, justice and foreign affairs/defence. The remaining six ministers were to be in charge of commerce, industry, labour, immigration, social welfare, education, housing, communication, public works and health.[5] By including in the new constitution the automatic registration of eligible voters, the Rendel Commission made electoral participation easier and generally added to the heightened awareness of political opportunities among the population.[6]

With so much at stake, a major regrouping of political forces started to take place in 1954. There was no shortage of parties with alternative power bases and policy platforms. First there was the Progressive Party led by local lawyer C. C. Tan, which was expected to dominate the election. It ran on a conservative platform that did not include a definite date for, or road to, independence for the colony. Three parties, the Singapore branch of the United Malays National Organisation, the Singapore Malay Union and the Singapore branch of the Malayan Chinese Association, prepared an alliance. This initiative originated at the headquarters of these parties in Peninsular Malaya, where the Alliance, led by Tunku Abdul Rahman, was the dominant political force. Because many political parties viewed the eventual independence of Singapore within the framework of a merger between Singapore and the Federation of Malaya, the political strategies and positions of the parties in Peninsular Malaya had a bearing on the scene in Singapore.

While the Chamber, in the period 1951–53, was unsuccessful in forcing the British to give in to its appeal for the enfranchisement of all local China-born Chinese, it did manage to make the general public aware of the importance of this issue. Partly because of these efforts, other actors in the political arena, such as David Marshall's Labour Front and Lee Kuan Yew's PAP, included demands for increased political rights for local residents in their party platforms.

The Voter Registration Campaign

The SCCC leaders were not satisfied with merely influencing the policy platforms of the political parties. They believed that the Chamber should itself be active in politics and thereby assure itself of a leading role in the new political system under the Rendel Constitution. The fact that appointed seats for business sector representatives in the legislature were to be discontinued under the new constitution only strengthened their resolve. The Chamber had protested against this development, arguing that 'a situation might well arise in which trade would be seriously affected by uninformed legislation, and both businessmen and workers would suffer'.[7] It was particularly concerned that the trading port heritage of Singapore would be squandered away through popular politics. It also wanted to secure political rights for the China-born and a place for the Chinese language commensurate with the demographic dominance of the Chinese.

Its programme began with a change of personnel in 1954 that gave pre-eminence to those who were most enthusiastic about the Chamber's political agenda. In March that year, the SCCC held its bi-annual election, where it was the Hokkien community's turn to put forward a candidate for the presidency. On this occasion, the politically adventurous Ko Teck Kin was elected with widespread support from among the Hokien Huay Kuan. In light of the forthcoming Singapore elections the following year, Ko presented a six-point plan at the installation ceremony. Two strategies were laid out: firstly, to ensure a high Chinese participation rate in the elections by making the voters aware of the main issues and their rights; and secondly, to continue lobbying for the retention of the appointed Chamber of Commerce seats in the Legislative Assembly,[8] a strategy that indicated that the Chamber was hedging its bets, and that the campaign of direct intervention in politics did not have the confidence of all members.[9]

As awareness of the upcoming election increased, aided no doubt by all the political attention given to the Chinese education issue, the Chamber stepped up its involvement in politics. In November 1954, an election and electoral registration committee was formed to devise a strategy. The committee decided to stage a voter information campaign to explain the issues in mass rallies across the island. As a result, a speech-cum-variety show toured the island from 15 January until 1 March. Representatives from the different ethnic groups took the floor, addressing the Chinese population in several Chinese dialects, while dance and music groups provided entertainment. The first rally was held on 15 January in the Tanjong Pagar district, with all the Ambitious Chamber leaders — Tan Lark Sye, Ko Teck Kin, Ng Aik Huan, Lam Thian and Colonel Chuang Hui Tsuan — lined up as speakers, while a lion dance troupe intermittently entertained the crowd.[10]

A rally was even held in Changi, then a remote and isolated rural district.[11] By this time the Chinese press had hopped on the bandwagon and strongly endorsed the goals of the campaign, saying that 'the Chamber was trying to make the Chinese voice heard'.[12] At the Changi rally, 10,000 people were present to hear speeches by Tan Lark Sye, Ko Teck Kin, Lim Cher Keng, the Chamber Management Council member in charge of the Changi district, and the Malay chairman of a local electoral committee. The speakers placed their main emphasis on the need for Singaporeans of all ethnic groups to vote, but almost all the speakers also touched on the issue of safeguarding vernacular education in Chinese, Malay and Tamil.[13] The English language press also reported on the rally, with a large picture of the lion dance gracing the front page of *The Straits Times*. It quoted Tan Lark Sye instructing the crowd 'not to vote blindly if they wanted a truly democratic government'. He emphasised that it was well-known that the Chamber has been a 'bridge of understanding' between the government and the people.[14]

The pitch was clear. The Chamber had been a long-trusted connection of the common people, and by creating a multi-ethnic platform and raising issues that embraced all Singaporeans, it was attempting to avoid being labelled as a force for the advancement of Chinese issues alone. The British appreciated the Chamber's efforts and the Governor expressed his gratitude for the voting drive in informal talks with Ko Teck Kin, Tan Lark Sye and Lee Kong Chian.[15] In total, seven 'use your vote' rallies were held at a cost of only S$858 to the Chamber coffers. Undoubtedly, individual Chamber leaders had picked up the bill rather than have it deplete the Chamber budget.[16]

The Democratic Party

After a few weeks of persistent rumours that the Chamber would set up a party, *The Straits Times* reported on 8 February that a new body, the Democratic Party, had entered the fray on the very day the Rendel Constitution came into force. The paper said that the SCCC would finance the party to carry on its battle for multilingualism within the Legislative Assembly and noted that until recently the Chamber had denied that it would actively participate in politics.[17] Three days later, the paper reported on the identity of the sponsors of the party, declaring they were all millionaires or near-millionaires. Secretary Tan Ek Khoo, a Teochew who was an SCCC Management Council member and the party spokesman, said that nine sponsors had made the party financially stable. Of the nine, three were Chamber Management Council members, and the others ordinary members.[18] Dr. S. Y. Wang, executive secretary of the Chamber, reiterated that the party had no official connection with the Chamber, a statement confirmed by her husband, DP President Tan Eng Joo. The party had its headquarters at the Ee Hoe Hean Club at Bukit Pasoh.[19] Immediately afterwards, the 'biggest ever' voter registration event was announced for 13 February, at the Great Eastern Trade Fair in Geylang Serai. Modern Malay dancing and lion dance performances would be staged and Tan Lark Sye, Colonel Chuang Hui Tsuan, Ko Teck Kin and two Malay leaders would deliver speeches.[20]

Despite the repeated statements by the SCCC that the DP was not a Chamber party, the connections with the SCCC were unmistakable. All its financial sponsors were involved in the Chamber and its headquarters was located at the club where Tan Lark Sye was president, while his nephew, Tan Eng Joo, was DP president. In the following weeks, the connection would be made even clearer as the DP's constituency organisations were exposed to scrutiny. Many of the Chamber's voter registration committee members in charge of electoral districts now stepped forward as DP candidates for the election, and the party fielded candidates in 20 districts. In reality, the DP was entirely made up of and funded by Chinese merchants from within the Chamber leadership, with the lone exception of the intriguing figure of Murray Brash, a Scottish lawyer on retainer to a number of large Chinese businesses and a Singapore resident of 20 years, who stood for the DP in Queenstown.[21]

Devoid of any regular members, the DP was composed of only its governing committee and the candidates it had nominated and, according to one source, its manifesto was 'composed in three hours over a convivial dinner'.[22] Trusting their traditional position at the top of the Chinese pyramid of organisations, the DP leadership leaned heavily on these social power structures and networks to lure and secure votes. This was achieved through the clan, district and *bang* organisations of which these Chamber leaders were the presidents and financiers. Tan Eng Joo explained later that by 'leashing' the liberal Progressives and checking the potentially 'dangerous' Labour Front, they could win communal votes without becoming involved in savage ideological disputes.[23]

It is clear, however, that this ambitious political initiative did not have the support of all in the Chamber leadership. When Tan Lark Sye finally sought formal Chamber endorsement for the DP on 28 February 1955 (the day by which all parties had to nominate their candidates) he found himself facing a divided Management Council. In the end, Ko Teck Kin, as Chamber President and chairman of the meeting, took the middle ground, saying that some members had already joined parties on an individual basis — this despite the fact that (according to a former DP election candidate in an interview) Ko had been directly involved in the idea of setting up the DP, together with Tan Lark Sye and Lee Kong Chian.[24] This interpretation is sustained by another decision taken at the same meeting: to discontinue the voter registration campaign.[25]

Despite the lack of official connections with the Chamber, and the Chamber's official ambivalence towards politics *per se*, the DP was clearly a creature of the SCCC and was known as such, with popular epithets including the 'Chamber Party' or the 'Millionaire's Party'.[26] Other parties deliberately attacked the DP on its pedigree. David Marshall of the Labour Front jibed in an interview that the DP consisted of 'potbellied millionaires', with Brash retorting on the DP's behalf that 'while a number may answer to the adjective, I know of very few that answer to the noun'. Labour candidate Lee Yong Min said that the DP had introduced a new kind of democracy: 'the millionaire democracy and now they want the power to go with it'. Independent candidate Mr Raj said that if the DP were to come to power, Singapore would be turned into a 'slave camp as their aim was not to better the people's lives but that of free trade'.[27]

The DP saw Singapore as a crossroad in Asia where people of all races and creeds had set up their homes and businesses and aspired to live in prosperity and harmony. In line with their own immigrant background, the DP leaders stressed that Singapore society should remain open, multiracial and focused on the equality of all races so that Singapore could perform its role as a regional centre of business, communication and learning. They referred to this vision as Singapore becoming the 'New York of Southeast Asia'.

Echoing the SCCC campaigns of previous years, the DP viewed Singapore citizenship, accessible to all who had made Singapore their home, as a first priority, as well as the introduction of a bill to implement the use of all four major languages in the Legislative Assembly. Equally important was giving all language streams parity in terms of allocation and funding for education. Free trade, the lifeblood of Singapore for almost 150 years, was the vital ingredient of the DP's economic and regional policy. It vowed to keep taxation on trade to a minimum and envisioned sending out official trade missions throughout Southeast Asia and beyond to let it be known that Singapore would remain the premier free trade harbour of Asia.[28] Yet not all the motives were as honourable. One academic observer argues that Tan Lark Sye and Lee Kong Chian 'did not commit their persons to the various parties but sought to exercise their control indirectly through the medium of patronage whilst they themselves remained in the shadows. It was the substance, not the appearance of power that they wanted'.[29] Governor Nicoll divulged later that Tan Lark Sye blamed the Progressive Party for the dropping of nominated Chamber of Commerce seats in the Legislative Assembly and for blocking multilingualism, and therefore 'cordially hated the Progressives'.[30] Mr Rajah of the PP even accused Tan of setting up the DP with the deliberate intention of 'ditching' the PP, which he thought otherwise must win.[31]

The 1955 Election

In an indication that the political demands of Singapore citizenship and multilingualism, championed by the SCCC, had made a great impact on the political arena, the makeup of the list of candidates for the 1955 election differed considerably from that of the 1951 Legislative Council election. In 1951 only four Chinese candidates had run, compared to 56 in 1955. There was also a large number (24) of bilingual candidates, due mainly to the DP. Of the total number of candidates, 45 were businessmen, 20 professionals, ten office workers and four others. Forty-three (43) were Singapore born, ten were from the Federation with 22 others.[32] The DP fielded 20 candidates who were all described as businessmen or merchants in the constituency-by-constituency discussion of candidates provided by the *Singapore Free Press* in the run up to the elections. With one exception they were in their 30s and 40s, and many had graduated from Chinese High School.

Campaigning was lively and sometimes fierce. On 24 March, Radio Malaya held an election forum live on air with Lee Kuan Yew of the PAP, David Marshall of the LF and Murray Brash for the DP. During the debate, Brash tried desperately to ward off the suggestion that the DP was a party of the rich but he failed miserably. The transcript of the discussion shows that Lee Kuan Yew made his customary reference to the millionaires of the DP who stayed at the Ee Hoe Hean club in Bukit Pasoh.

> Brash: Where is this club? I have never seen it.
> LKY: But the address is on your own manifesto.
> Brash: I said I hadn't seen it.
> LKY: Good Lord, that's terrible. How will we know where to find the man?
> Marshall: Perhaps they have shifted to the Chinese Chamber of Commerce.[33]

In all likelihood these allegations would stick in the voters' minds, but perhaps because of the large amount of enthusiasm at voter registration meetings and the popular support for multilingualism, the DP had high expectations of the election. *The Straits Times* on the morning of polling day reported Tan Eng Joo crowing: 'I have every confidence that the Democratic Party will win an overwhelming majority.'[34]

Alas, the DP — along with the Progressive Party — was to be disappointed. The anticipated victory for the PP, to which end the Rendel Constitution seemed to have been tailored by the British, did not materialise. The PP only managed to win four seats due to the change in political atmosphere during 1954–55. It was now seen as a pro-British party in an increasingly anti-colonial Singapore. To the great disappointment of its leadership, the DP did even worse, winning only two seats. To add to its frustration, the DP came in second in eight constituencies, with a total of 32,115 votes. All that was required was an average swing of 4.5 per cent in eight of the 25 constituencies (a total swing of only 2,274 votes) for a DP-led government to become fact (see Appendix 1). But it was not to be. David Marshall's party emerged the great victor, securing ten seats.

With the support of the ex-officio ministers, the three Singapore Alliance members and two of the nominated Unofficials, the LF formed a left-wing minority government.

The political adventurism of the SCCC leadership had been inspired by the liberating idea of self-determination that swept through the colonised world after World War II, and they believed that their traditional status and position in the hierarchy of Chinese clan and dialect organisations would automatically qualify them as leaders on the road to Singapore's independence. Aided by the great wealth acquired during the rubber boom of 1950–51, they unfolded ambitious initiatives in politics and education such as the Democratic Party and Nanyang University. But in this success also lay the seeds of their defeat. There existed an inherent contradiction in the political position of these men. On the one hand, they wanted to be seen as modern, populist, democratic and enlightened. On the other hand, they still depended for their elite status and power on a paternalist, hierarchically-based communal structure in which ethnicity and tradition were key elements. The self-image of being modern popular leaders inspired them to campaign vigorously for political rights for the Chinese community. The success of this ambition meant that the electorate was greatly enlarged and that the nature of politics changed. Paradoxically, the Chamber could not play a central role in the populist electoral political game controlled by democratic socialist parties because, contrary to the self-image of the SCCC leaders, the voting public considered it an elite organisation with an elite agenda. Ironically the Chamber was instrumental in changing the political landscape but its would-be politicians at the same time failed to adjust to the consequences of these very changes. The DP was seen as a conservative, elite party and therefore could not do well with an electorate awakened to social issues.[35] The days of elite politics of the late colonial system were over.

Despite being viewed as a millionaire's party, the DP, with its championing of Chinese culture, language, education and citizenship, did pull off two feats. Firstly, it split the PP vote by attracting 20 per cent of the votes. Secondly, it heightened awareness of citizenship and education issues in the elections. Partly due to these pressures, the Labour Front also gave these issues prominence in their policy platform.[36]

However, after all the effort and the apparent success of the voter registration campaign, the initiators of the DP must have been surprised at the poor showing. They learned that popular electoral politics was a different arena to the pyramid of clan and dialect organisations which had hitherto exemplified the politics of the Chinese community. With the benefit of many years of hindsight, the individuals involved said that they were not disappointed with the DP's defeat because the issues it raised had become central to the political debate and because, in the end, a party with a similar policy platform was returned to power.[37] This is an extraordinary revision of history because it overlooks the fact that their political aspirations and strategies had patently failed.

Continued Importance of Elite Chinese Mercantilism

The path that Singapore did not take in 1955 was made up of two elements: firstly, an elite leadership style based on wealth and status and grounded in a coalition of Chinese dialect and *huiguan* organisations; and secondly, a local merchant perspective based on a free trade ideology and focused on existing regional and worldwide commercial networks. Both these elements provided an impetus — albeit a negative one — that drove the creation of an opposing left-wing movement connected with labour unions, and the commensurate awakening of the working classes to the stakes of the political game. Changes in society, and to the make-up and rules of the political arena in Singapore, had already made the elite-based aspirations of the Chinese merchants a non-starter. Viewed in the context of worldwide decolonisation, this development away from local colonial-era elites and towards those parties and institutions that could rally a broad electorate is not at all surprising.

Yet the fact that the DP lost the 1955 election did not mean that this worldview and political outlook ceased to be an important force in the political landscape. In fact, in the decade immediately following, the leaders of the SCCC at times held the key to important developments and decisions concerning Singapore's course towards independence. The most potent example of the way the Chamber could influence the political balance came in the early 1960s, when independence through merger into a new Federation of Malaysia became the central issue in Singapore politics. The PAP, which had come to power in 1959, had always advocated independence through a Singapore-Malaya merger. From the moment the Prime Minister of the Federation of Malaya, Tunku Abdul Rahman, acknowledged the possibility of merger on 27 May 1961, the issue dominated Singapore politics and eventually led to a crisis within the PAP. Its left wing opposed the idea of a Federation of Malaysia, to include the Borneo territories, Brunei and Singapore, on ideological grounds and an untenable political situation developed. From an economic and political point of view the conservative technocrats within the PAP felt that Singapore as a

completely independent unit would not be feasible. Lee Kuan Yew decided
to bring the conflict into the open and after a long debate on the issue in
the Legislative Assembly, a vote of confidence was put forth on 21 July
1961, in which all 13 left-wing PAP members abstained.[38] The next day,
the PAP Central Executive Committee, which Lee Kuan Yew controlled,
expelled the 13 Assemblymen and on 26 July the left formed a new party,
the Barisan Sosialis.[39]

With the establishment of the Barisan Sosialis, an important political
shift took place. It became clear the left wing controlled the PAP local
party branches and the government-run People's Association, and through
them, the party's grassroots links with the community. The PAP was crip-
pled because of the defection of the left wing, but it needed working class
votes to survive the merger referendum. The technocratic PAP elite had
to find a conduit to reach the Chinese-speaking part of the population
and looked to the Chamber because it still had great influence in the
Chinese community through its domination of the pyramid of Chinese
organisations. The local business community and the SCCC supported
Lee's argument for a common market with Malaya and were impressed by
the Malayan leadership's promise to retain Singapore's free port status and
allow it autonomy over educational and labour issues — all issues close to
its heart. Despite its image as a rich man's club, the Chamber became a
key force in convincing the Chinese community of the political and social
logic of the PAP's arguments, capitalising on its traditional leadership
role at the head of the hierarchy of *bang* and *huiguan*. Initially it merely
organised information meetings across the island, but part way through the
campaign, the Management Council dropped all pretext of impartiality and
decided to unanimously endorse the government's preferred option. It then
placed advertisements in all the major newspapers in which it appealed to
'all public institutions, its affiliated trade associations and its members to
awake their friends and relatives who possess the voting right to the duty
of voting for Alternative 'A' [the government's preferred option] ... and by
dissuading voters from casting blank votes to the detriment of the rights
and interests of the people of Singapore'.[40] The merger referendum resulted
in a victory for the PAP — 70.8 per cent of the electorate cast their votes
in favour of option 'A'.

In a contemporary interview, Lee Kuan Yew described the Chamber's
advertising campaign as one of the two key factors that 'carried the day'
in the referendum, the other being his success in convincing the Tunku to
remove all ambiguity about Singaporeans' status as full Malaysian citizens.[41]
The Chamber had done Lee Kuan Yew and the PAP a great favour. Aware

of this, Lee met the Chamber leaders immediately after the referendum results were out — even before going on his victory parade through his own constituency — and thanked them for their support.[42]

The Storm Before the Calm

Yet Lee Kuan Yew's gratitude proved a very transient reward. Merger did not last and neither did the newfound pivotal role of the Chamber. The influence of left-wing political actors was drastically reduced by Operation Cold Store even before merger was enacted, reducing the PAP's need for allies on the right. Over the next few years the technocratic elite of the PAP took all political matters firmly in its grip and there was no place for an independent, activist SCCC — or anyone else, for that matter. The government's vision was global and heavily geared towards foreign direct investment, industrialisation and later services, and it had little time for the old-fashioned and traditionalist merchants of the SCCC. The Chamber continued to lobby for free trade and regional economic networks, as well as for Chinese education and culture, but for the next decade and a half its efforts on these issues met with implacable hostility from the government, which systematically worked to marginalise the Chamber and limit its political influence. Only with the resurrection of Chinese education, language and culture as central elements in Singapore society in the late 1970s was there any solace at all for Chinese conservatives, and even then it was pretty poor fare. They could cheer the government or complain (very quietly) as they chose, but they could no longer exercise much influence. That path had long since been closed.

APPENDIX

Election results for the 1955 election and hypothetical swing scenario for a Democratic Party victory

Although the table is only hypothetical, it shows that the Labour Front victory was really gained by a very slim margin and that shifts of only 200 or 300 votes in several key constituencies could have swung the election to the Democratic Party.

Party	Real result	Paya Lebar	Farrer Park	Whampoa	Seletar	Telok Ayer	Tanglin	Cairnhill	Rochore	Hypothetical result
		Change	Change	Change	Change	Change	Change	Change	Change	
LF	10		−1	−1				−1	−1	6
DP	2	+1			+1	+1	+1		+1	7
PP	4	−1		+1			−1	+1		4
PAP	3		+1							4

Swing constituency										Total swing
Positional swing between	1(PP) and 2(DP)	1(LF) and 2(PAP)	1(LF) and 2(PP)	1(Ind) and 3(DP)	1(Ind) and 2(DP)	1(PP) and 2(DP)	1(LF) and 2(PP)	1(LF) and 2(DP)		
Needed vote change	133	184	199	261	235	357	388	517		2,274
Total votes cast	6,494	6,803	6,523	5,620	4,951	7,125	7,011	6,414		50,941
Percentage change	2.1	2.7	3.1	4.7	4.8	5.1	5.6	8.1		4.5

Sources: www.singapore-elections.com/ and www.elections.gov.sg/past_parliamentary1955.htm

NOTES

1   This chapter focuses on one particular event in the long history of political, social and cultural activities by the Chinese merchant elite of Singapore. The author deals with this history more extensively in his dissertation on the Singapore Chinese Chamber of Commerce, and his book based on the thesis: S. Visscher, 'Business, Ethnicity and State: The Representational Relationship of the Singapore Chinese Chamber of Commerce and the State, 1945–1997', Ph.D. Thesis, Free University, Amsterdam, 2002, and in S. Visscher, *The Business of Politics and Ethnicity: A History of the Singapore Chinese Chamber of Commerce and Industry* (Singapore: NUS Press, 2007).

2   Visscher, 'Business, Ethnicity and State', Chapter 1.

3   The four were: Lee Kong Chian, Lien Ying Chow, Tan Chin Tuan and Yap Pheng Geck.

4   Visscher, 'Business, Ethnicity and State', Chapter 2.

5   *Report of the Constitutional Commission, 1954* (Singapore: Singapore Government Printer, 1954).

6   Yeo Kim Wah, *Political Development in Singapore 1945–1955* (Singapore: Singapore University Press, 1973), p. 255.

7   Singapore Chinese Chamber of Commerce, *Fifty-Eight Years of Enterprise: Souvenir Volume of the New Building of the Singapore Chinese Chamber of Commerce — 1964* (Singapore: L.M. Creative Publicity, 1964), p. 128.

8   *The Straits Times*, 16 March 1954.

9   In fact the Council was seriously divided over the issue of direct engagement in the political arena, but that is not the concern of this chapter. See Visscher, *The Business of Politics and Ethnicity*, for a more complete picture of the political divisions within the SCCC.

10 *The Straits Times*, 14 January 1955.

11 *Nanyang Siang Pau*, 7 February 1955.

12 Ibid.

13 Ibid.

14 *The Straits Times*, 8 February 1955.

15 *The Straits Times*, 1 March 1955.

16 Ibid.

17 *The Straits Times*, 8 February 1955.

18 *The Straits Times*, 11 February 1955.

19 Ibid.

20 *The Straits Times*, 12 February 1955.

21 *Singapore Free Press*, 22 March 1955.

22 George Sweeney, 'Political Parties in Singapore, 1945–1955', MA Thesis, University of Hull, 1973, p. 292 quoting Elegant, p. 164.

23 Rene Peritz, 'The Evolving Politics of Singapore: A Study of Trends and Issues', Ph.D. Dissertation, University of Pennsylvania, 1964, interview with Tan Eng Joo, September 1962, p. 111.

24 Interview with Lim Cher Kheng, 5 July 1996.

25 *The Straits Times*, 1 March 1955.
26 Thomas J. Bellows, 'The Singapore Party System: The First Two Decades', Ph.D. Dissertation, Yale University, 1968, p. 128.
27 S. R. Pugalenthi, *Elections in Singapore* (Singapore: VJ Times International, 1996), pp. 11, 12.
28 For the DP campaign platform, see *The Straits Times,* 2 April 1955.
29 Sweeney, *Political Parties in Singapore*, p. 216.
30 Ibid., interview with Nicoll on p. 295.
31 Ibid., interview with Rajah on p. 295.
32 Yeo, *Political Development in Singapore*, pp. 268–70.
33 Radio Malaya transcript quoted in Pugalenthi, *Elections in Singapore*, p. 14.
34 *The Straits Times*, 4 April 1955.
35 Robert E. Gamer, *The Politics of Urban Development in Singapore* (London: Cornell University Press, 1972), pp. 21–2.
36 Yeo Kim Wah and Albert Lau, 'From Colonialism to Independence, 1945–1965', in *A History of Singapore*, ed. Ernest C. T. Chew and Edwin Lee (Singapore: Oxford University Press, 1996), p. 134.
37 Interview with Lim Cher Keng, 5 July 1996.
38 Yeo and Lau, 'From Colonialism to Independence', pp. 141–2.
39 Richard Clutterbuck, *Conflict and Violence in Singapore and Malaysia 1945–1983*, revised edition (Singapore: Graham Brash Ltd, 1984), p. 154.
40 *The Straits Times*, 30 August 1962.
41 Ministry of Information and the Arts documentary, *Riding the Tiger*, DVD (Singapore: MITA, 2001).
42 *The Straits Times*, 6 September 1962.

5

Winning and Losing Malay Support: PAP-Malay Community Relations, 1950s and 1960s

Lily Zubaidah Rahim

Singapura in the *Nusantara*

In the decades preceding and following World War II, Singapore was not only the region's cosmopolitan financial hub and entrepot but had attained a reputation as a mecca for scholars, artists, intellectuals and political exiles, and as a veritable hotbed of left-wing anti-colonial activity. The island's leftist political orientation was buttressed further when, after the declaration of the 1948 Malayan Emergency, a steady stream of leftist political activists relocated from the Peninsula, believing it to be less stringently affected by the draconian Emergency Laws. Among the stream of émigrés were leaders and supporters of left organisations suppressed or banned by the British, such as the Malay Nationalist Party (MNP) and API (*Angkatan Pemuda Insaf* or Generation of Aware Youth). Journalists and writers were also attracted to the island's reputation as a literary, publishing and theatrical centre in the *Nusantara* (Malay World).[1]

Left Malay nationalists were strongly influenced by the Indonesian anti-colonial nationalist movements and supportive of the *Melayu* and *Indonesia Raya* (or Greater Indonesia) ideal. This ideal was premised on the political union of Indonesia with Malaya in accordance with the expansive territorial reach of pre-colonial and pre-Islamic kingdoms such as Sri Vijaya and Majapahit.[2] Concerned by the numerical and economic clout of the non-Malay immigrant communities and disillusioned with the collusion of the Malay aristocratic elite with the British colonial apparatus, the *Melayu* and *Indonesia Raya* ideals inspired left Malay nationalists to work towards a post-colonial republican pan-Malay nation-state cemented by the intimate bonds of language and religion. Farish Noor insightfully comments on the significance of the *Melayu* and *Indonesia Raya* ideal as representing not only a nostalgic return to the past, but just as importantly encapsulating 'the traumatic manner in which the Indo-Malay world had been torn apart by treaties and pacts agreed upon by foreign powers that had descended upon Malay people and their homeland'.[3] Not surprisingly, in the 'European-ruled Chinese city'[4] of Singapore, where Malay insecurity was amplified by its rapidly declining numerical and socio-economic status, the *Melayu* and *Indonesia Raya* ideals were appealing.

Fired up by the *Melayu* and *Indonesia Raya* ideals, hundreds of Malay youths were alleged to have been recruited to serve in the Republican Army in Sumatra and Java. Other well-known local personalities supportive of the republican struggle included Saadon bin Jubir, a member of the Singapore Legislative Council, and *Utusan Melayu's* deputy editor Samad Ismail. Their pro-republican activities involved smuggling arms and foodstuffs to Indonesia. Chinese traders from Singapore were also readily drawn into the lucrative smuggling trade with Indonesian nationalists. Indeed, Singapore's multifaceted role in the republican struggle contributed to its reputation as the 'third front' in the Indonesian revolution.[5]

This chapter examines the ideological cross-fertilisation across the Straits of Malacca and its impact on the political orientation of the Singapore Malay community. It highlights the role of *Utusan Melayu* and radical Malay nationalists in the anti-colonial movement and the political ascendancy of the People's Action Party (PAP). Malay activists were eagerly sought out by the PAP leadership to enhance the electoral standing of the fledgling party and to promote the PAP's image as a genuinely multiracial party. Just as importantly, the 'Malay-isation' of the PAP and the larger Singaporean polity was expected to enhance the PAP's prospects for eventual inclusion into the Alliance coalition. Finally, the chapter considers the systematic containment of the Malay community's electoral and political clout when they were no longer vital to the political calculations of the PAP government after separation from Malaysia.

Samad Ismail, *Utusan Melayu* and the Political Ascendancy of the PAP

Numerous literary personalities and political activists associated with left-wing Malay political organisations were employed or closely associated with the staunchly anti-colonial Malay daily, *Utusan Melayu* (henceforth, *Utusan*). Founded by Singapore's first President, Yusuf Ishak, in 1939, *Utusan* was the first Malay-owned and managed nationalist newspaper that reflected the aspirations and concerns of the *raayat* (masses). Headquartered in Singapore, *Utusan's* motto of upholding religion, people and country, ideals which the paper promised to 'live for and fight to the death', reflected the anti-colonial nationalist ideals of the paper's editors.[6] Positioned at the forefront of the nationalist struggle for independence, *Utusan* developed a formidable reputation as the 'mouthpiece of an ascendant Malay nationalism'.[7] Not surprisingly, *Utusan's* anti-colonial stance struck a chord with the Malay masses and, by 1957, it was the highest circulating Malay newspaper in the British colony.[8]

Utusan's analysis of the plight of urban and rural Malays, rooted in a historical and political economy perspective, helped raise the political consciousness of non-Malay political activists and left intellectuals who were inclined to empathise and identify with the problems confronting the Malay masses. They called for the elevation of Malay as the common language and, according to R. Rajakumar, 'exploded with rage at the fashionable explanation for poverty that the Malay peasants were lazy'.[9] Left-wing Chinese school students demanded that Malay replace the study of English in their Chinese medium schools. Left nationalists such as Lim Chin Siong had apparently shown deep concern for Malay problems in Singapore and the Federation and was in favour of recognising the Malay language as the national language'.[10]

An acknowledged intellectual doyen and political tactician, Samad Ismail was much sought after, with political activists, student leaders, trade unionists, literary and cultural figures and educationists routinely congregating at the *Utusan* office in Cecil Street to discuss politics with him. Regular *Utusan* visitors included Lee Kuan Yew, Lim Chin Siong, Devan Nair, James Puthucheary, UMNO leaders such as Jaafar Albar and Hamid Jumat, and left Malay nationalist Dr Burhanuddin al-Helmy. In addition to serving as a 'bridge' between the Chinese, Malay and Indian nationalists, workers and students, and left and right nationalists, Samad and *Utusan* were pivotal in creating greater awareness among left intellectuals and activists of the challenges confronting the Malay masses.

Samad's contribution to the political ascendancy of Lee Kuan Yew and the PAP in the mid-1950s has been consistently downplayed in mainstream and official historiography in Singapore. Instructively, Samad's inclusion in the tightly knit inner core of the embryonic PAP was acknowledged by Lee in an almost cavalier way. Lee wrote:

> Our small group ... decided to invite Samad to join us to discuss the prospects for waging a constitutional struggle for independence without finding ourselves sucked into the communist movement. We also wanted him in because he could give us access to the Malay speaking world and get our views across to the Malay masses through the *Utusan Melayu*. After two meetings, he asked if he could bring his friend Devan Nair along because he could make a useful contribution.[11]

Not acknowledged in Lee's memoirs was the pivotal role Samad played in providing him with the initial contacts to forge close links with both the Chinese and Malay left. These contacts were used to promote his standing as a lawyer who was sympathetic to the nationalist left and to build mass support for the PAP. Indeed, when Chinese middle-school students required legal representation, they purportedly sought the advice of Samad, who in turn suggested Lee Kuan Yew.[12]

As a major recruiter of Malays into the PAP, Samad persuaded many *Utusan* journalists, trade unionists and former Singapore Malay National Organisation (SMNO) activists to throw their lot in with the party.[13] This has been acknowledged by former *Utusan* journalist and PAP cabinet minister Othman Wok, who noted that Samad enthusiastically distributed PAP membership forms at the *Utusan* office.[14] Yaacob Mohamed, who had established a formidable reputation as a veteran of the Malayan People's Anti-Japanese Army, the MNP, and API and as head of an SMNO branch in Bukit Panjang, had been actively encouraged by Samad to join the PAP since 1954. When Yaacob finally left the SMNO shortly after *Merdeka*, more than 30 SMNO members followed him into the PAP.[15] Other SMNO defectors, similarly disillusioned with the conservative feudal orientation of the senior SMNO leadership and attracted to the leftist political orientation of the PAP, were to become leading PAP politicians. They included veteran trade unionists Rahmat Kenap, Buang Omar Junid and Ariff Suradi. Without doubt, the entry of these seasoned former SMNO activists and trade unionists with considerable mass support boosted the PAP's credentials as a multiracial party.

To be sure, Samad's contacts ensured that Tunku Abdul Rahman and other Alliance leaders were in attendance at the PAP's inauguration in Singapore in November 1954.[16] His PAP affiliation did not inhibit SMNO politician Hamid Jumat, then a minister in David Marshall's Labour Front coalition government, from requesting Samad to enlist *Utusan*'s support for Singapore's exclusion from the plans for an independent Malaya. Samad had in fact proposed to Hamid, prior to his departure for the 1956 constitutional talks in London,[17] that a clause be included in the Singapore constitution to promote the political, economic and cultural interests of the Malays.[18] In the event, a clause protecting Malay interests was accepted by delegates at the constitutional talks and is currently enshrined in Section 152 of the Singapore Constitution.[19]

Lee and Samad's Cat-and-Mouse Machinations

Lee Kuan Yew's deft manipulation of Malay nationalist circles in Singapore became more apparent shortly after Samad resigned from the PAP in 1956. A comprehensive analysis of his resignation has yet to be undertaken but it appears that the major considerations included disagreements centring on the political operations of the PAP, the integrity of Lee's nationalist credentials and his opportunistic manipulation of left-wing political connections. Samad also believed that Lee would eventually betray the left wing in the PAP.[20] Without doubt, Samad's political manoeuvrings beyond the political ambit of the PAP were of great concern to the PAP leadership, who were intent on winning government in the 1959 elections. In particular, Samad's departure represented a severe setback to Lee's plan of maintaining cordial relations with senior UMNO politicians with a view to paving the way for the PAP's entry into the Alliance coalition. It is worth noting that in the lead up to the 1959 election, UMNO and PAP leaders were engaged in negotiations to contest under a coalition umbrella. However, these discussions came unstuck when the PAP refused to comply with UMNO's insistence on fielding ten candidates.[21]

As the English-educated PAP leadership did not command a mass following within the Chinese or Malay communities, the footloose Samad now represented a direct threat to their short- and long-term political ambitions. Naturally, Samad's links with radical nationalists and his influence among trade unionists alarmed the colonial authorities, who were in the throes of granting independence to Malaya. Dominic Puthucheary poignantly captures the fear and envy generated by Samad's astute political wheeling and dealing:

> Lee realised he had met his match, an intellectual who could rival him
> for the leadership of Singapore. Samad's standing with the Left and the
> Malay nationalist movement gave him a stature which had far reaching

potential. From then on, Samad's survival was a cat and mouse game with Lee and the British.[22]

There are grounds to believe that following Samad's departure from the PAP, Lee may have instigated *Utusan*'s boss, Yusuf Ishak, to 're-assign' Samad to Jakarta. Former *Utusan* Editor Said Zahari and Solicitor-General of Singapore Francis Seow[23] highlighted the plausibility of Lee's hand in Samad's 'reassignment' to Jakarta. Said postulates that the PAP leadership was determined to win the 1959 elections but did not want Samad in Singapore in the lead up to or after the elections because he remained a respected political force within left-wing circles and the general Malay community.[24] Samad's continued presence in Singapore was thus a stumbling block to the PAP's goal of winning government in the 1959 election and eventual inclusion into the Alliance coalition.

Samad's return from a brief 'reassignment' in Jakarta, where he rekindled relations with Indonesian nationalists who by then held senior positions in the Sukarno government,[25] his 1958 appointment as editor of *Berita Harian* (part of the Straits Times Group) in Kuala Lumpur, and his position as Permanent Chairman of the SMNO no doubt ruffled feathers in the PAP. Lee's fear that Samad would now use his influence on public opinion and contacts within UMNO to subvert the PAP may explain his determination to get Samad arrested.

In a series of public talks over the radio in 1961, entitled 'The Battle for Merger', Lee repeatedly alleged that Samad (using his MNP code name Zainal backwards), was a communist and connected to the Malayan Communist Party.[26] The then general manager of the Straits Times Press in Kuala Lumpur, A. C. Simmons, also confirmed that he was under pressure from 'certain Singaporeans' to sack Samad from *Berita Harian*.[27] Much to Lee's annoyance, the campaign to tarnish Samad proved ineffectual. This was demonstrated by Samad's rapid rise within the ranks of the Straits Times in Kuala Lumpur, and his growing influence within leftist UMNO circles close to Tunku's successor, Tun Razak. Indeed, Samad and other former PAP stalwarts who had relocated to Kuala Lumpur, such as James Puthucheary, were advising the Alliance leadership on rehabilitating Malaya's pro-Western image within the Afro-Asian bloc. Samad and Puthucheary were regularly included in Malayan delegations to Afro-Asian solidarity conferences in the mid-1960s.[28] However, Samad's insider status within UMNO circles was short-circuited by the 1976 'confession' of ISA detainee Hussein Jahidin, a Singaporean *Berita Harian* editor and former *Utusan* journalist. Inter alia, Hussein had 'confessed' that Samad and other senior Malaysian newspapermen were communists. Shortly after, Samad and other supposed communists were detained under the ISA in Malaysia. Satisfied by the Malaysian government's swift clampdown against Samad and other 'communists', Lee noted in his memoirs that "Hussein Onn has the courage to act against a pro-communist Malaysian intelligentsia".[29]

Courting the Singapore Malays: The 1959 Elections

While courting the Chinese left, the PAP also wooed the Malay community before and after the 1959 elections. Importantly, Malay support was required to convince the British colonial authorities and the UMNO leadership that the PAP was a genuine multiracial party supported by the various ethnic communities. To this end, the PAP's pre-election manifesto categorically recognised the Malays as indigenous people who were 'the oldest race in Malaya' and promised to foster Malay as the national language. As the Malays were economically behind the other races, the PAP assured the community that 'We will always give them priority and special help to catch up with the others'.[30]

Despite forming government after winning 53 per cent of the votes cast and 43 of the 51 seats in the 1959 Legislative Assembly elections, the PAP was defeated by the SMNO in the Malay electoral strongholds of the Southern Islands, Geylang Serai and Kampong Kembangan. This suggests that many Malays remained uncertain about the PAP's genuine commitment towards them. Even though the line up of seven PAP Malay candidates from the trade union movement, former SMNO stalwarts and *Utusan* journalists, must have appealed to the left-oriented Singapore Malay community, the SMNO's standing as the guardian of Malay interests and its direct association with UMNO still held considerable sway. Additionally, warnings by the respected left-wing Malay nationalist and leader of the Partai Raayat Singapura (PRS), Ahmad Boestamam, about the dubious sincerity of the PAP, at a public rally in Geylang Serai, probably aroused Malay insecurities.[31] Recounting his experience of Malay hostility, the PAP candidate in Kampong Kembangan, Othman Wok, noted in his memoirs that he was told to '*balik kampong*' (go back to where you came from), chastised for '*masuk parti Cina*' (joining a Chinese party) and claimed that some of his posters were smeared with excreta.[32]

Notwithstanding the PAP's failure to convincingly win over the Malays, its leadership must have been heartened by the less-than-resounding electoral support for the SMNO in Malay strongholds such as Kampong Kembangan. This realisation no doubt fuelled expectations that the PAP had a realistic chance of success in Kampong Kembangan and other Malay strongholds in future elections, particularly as the PAP was now in government and in control of the state apparatus.

Promises to recognise the special status of the Malays and rectify the imbalance between the Malay and non-Malay communities, principally through educational assistance, were regularly issued by the PAP leadership after the 1959 elections. A Malay Education Advisory Committee was formed to assist the Minister of Education in formulating education policies sensitive to the needs of the Malay community.[33] In February 1960, the PAP government issued a statement noting:

> While the process of strengthening the economic position of the Malays will take some time to complete, immediate steps should be taken to strengthen their competitive position in society in general and in the economic sphere in particular.[34]

In an attempt 'to cloak the infant state in the swaddling clothes of Malay-ness',[35] Yusuf Ishak was installed as the island's *Yang di-Pertuan Negara* (Head of State), a national anthem (*Majulah Singapura*) was composed by a Malay (Jubir Said) in the Malay language, and the state crest depicted a Singapore lion with a Malayan tiger. The latter was symbolic of closer future collaboration between Singapore and Malaya. Moreover, the state flag, which included the Islamic insignia of crescent and moon, was akin to the insignia on the Malayan flag.

To deepen the social integration of the predominantly Chinese island with the mainland, Singaporean students were required to study Malay as a second language. From 1959, all teachers had to pass at least Standard 1 Malay before their confirmation as teachers.[36] In addition to retaining the British policy of free education for the Malays, the community was promised bursaries and scholarships to improve their representation in tertiary institutions. In 1961, the first Malay secondary school (*Sang Nila Utama*) was established and by 1965, 13 Malay secondary schools had been built.[37] It is worth reiterating that these assurances, policies and initiatives were undertaken not only to court the island's Malay community but, just as importantly, to impress and appease the UMNO leadership in Kuala Lumpur.[38]

Winning Conditional Malay Support: The 1963 Elections

Much has been made by the PAP leadership of Malay electoral support for the PAP and rejection of the SMNO in the 1963 elections,[39] but a discerning analysis of the 1963 electoral trends suggests that the Malay community did not solidly support the PAP even though it had defeated the SMNO in the three Malay strongholds of Geylang, Kampong Kembangan and the Southern Islands. The PAP's narrow margin of victory, particularly in the Southern Islands and Geylang Serai, suggests that there were many variables contributing to its success. Put simply, Malay support for the PAP in these three constituencies was at best conditional and cautious. Bedlington argues that the three Malay electoral strongholds were won not as a result of resounding support from the Malays but largely due to the strong backing the PAP received from an insecure Chinese electorate in these wards. The latter's support for the PAP is likely to have been motivated by a fear of Malay-based parties in the face of Singapore's merger into a Malay-dominated Federation.[40] Furthermore, MacDougall believes that the PAP's narrow electoral successes in the traditional Malay strongholds were aided by its urban resettlement policies, which had eroded the Malay numerical dominance and electoral clout in these seats.[41] Defeated SMNO candidate for Geylang Serai, Ahmad Taff, attributed the PAP's success in the seat to Malay vote-splitting arising from their disapproval of the SMNO participating in the elections under the tarnished Singapore People's Alliance umbrella. In contrast, the Chinese vote in Geylang Serai tended to be strongly weighted in the PAP's favour.[42] Of related interest is Said Zahari's belief that the SMNO's electoral defeat was largely a consequence of the flawed presumption of its leadership that the bulk of the Malays could be relied on to vote along communal lines and support the SMNO.[43]

Of the several reasons that explain the relative success of the PAP among the Malays in 1963, a number of them were related to the weakness of the opposition forces vying for the Malay vote. For instance, it must be remembered that the predominantly working class Singapore Malays had never strongly identified with the feudal-oriented Malayan society and were only weakly connected to the 'old boy' feudal network inherent in the UMNO and SMNO. In particular, the feudal mindset and aloofness of senior SMNO leaders towards the rank-and-file membership was a source of tension within the republican-oriented Singapore Malay community, which was inspired by the leftist ideals of radical Malayan and Indonesian nationalists.[44] SMNO's problems were complicated further by limited funds, weak leadership and internal policy divisions.[45] Tunku's appointment of Hamid Jumat as head of the SMNO was a major source of party in-fighting, particularly after he was implicated in a corruption scandal during his tenure as a minister in the David Marshall government. In 1960, 1,000 SMNO members resigned from the party, claiming they no longer had confidence in Hamid's leadership and that the SMNO no longer had the solid support of the Malays in Singapore. To appease the SMNO's rebellious rank and file and prevent the party from imploding, particularly after the suspension of several SMNO branches and the expulsion of many party members, Kuala Lumpur UMNO replaced Hamid with Ahmad Taff in 1961.[46]

In contrast to the SMNO's chronic intra-party divisions, the PAP government had steadily built up a reputation for efficiency after its election in 1959. The defection of leading SMNO members to the PAP, some apparently enticed by the offer of attractive positions,[47] had elevated its multiracial image. Kuala Lumpur's ill-advised decision for the SMNO to join Lim Yew Hock's tarnished Singapore Alliance Party coalition in the 1963 election further enhanced the good governance image of the incumbent PAP government. *Inter alia*, it had in a short period of time built many new schools, constructed 24,000 low-cost public flats and established the Jurong industrial estate whilst ensuring that the state treasury was in surplus.[48] As Singapore's impending merger into the Federation would further strengthen their political clout, many Singapore Malays saw themselves as the providential beneficiaries of both worlds and tended to discount the SMNO's barrage of criticisms against the PAP.

An alternative political party also with the potential to galvanise the Singapore Malay community and make more problematic the PAP's success in Malay strongholds was the multiracial-oriented PRS, headed by former *Utusan* editor Said Zahari. A protégé of Samad Ismail, Said's credentials were enhanced further when he was dismissed from *Utusan* after rejecting the UMNO leadership's insistence that the paper end its editorial independence. His pivotal role in the six-month strike by *Utusan* workers and the Printing Workers Union in 1961 prompted the Federal government to deny him re-entry into Malaya after lending moral support to striking *Utusan* workers in Singapore.[49] Disillusioned with the PAP leadership for failing to support *Utusan* strikers but heartened by the support received from left-wing trade unionists, students and political activists, Said decided to throw his lot in with the left-wing PRS. He believed that the PRS was the only party with the potential to unite the Singapore Malays whilst collaborating with genuinely left parties for the island's independence.[50]

Prior to Said's decision to lead the PRS, the PAP leadership had attempted to coax him into their ambit (to thwart Lim Chin Siong's overtures to join the Barisan Sosialis). S. Rajaratnam had apparently warned Said against fraternising too closely with Lim, whom he ridiculed for being little more than a Chinese chauvinist.[51] Of considerable anxiety to the PAP leadership was the effect that Said's reputation as a left nationalist would have on enhancing the electoral standing of the PRS within the left-oriented Malay community. They were only too aware that even though the Malays were disillusioned with the SMNO's feudal conservatism, the community was not strongly aligned to the PAP despite the influx of former SMNO politicians into the PAP. Confirming the PAP's fears, Said noted in his memoirs that the Singapore Malays in the early 1960s were not particularly attracted to the PAP and tended to be 'sitting on the fence'.[52]

To add to the PAP's angst, Said not only hoped to work closely with Barisan Sosialis, but also drew up plans for the PRS to 'look for points of political agreement with UMNO and the PMU (Peninsula Malay Union), two right-wing political parties, to unite the Malays in Singapore' and to 'represent the Malays of Singapore in negotiations on the future of the country with the other political parties and with the British colonial authorities'.[53] Without doubt, Said's ambitious plans for the PRS represented a serious threat to the support base of the PAP. Failure to strengthen its Malay support base would have been potentially disastrous for the party, particularly after the 1961 mass defection of left-wing elements from the PAP to the Barisan Sosialis. This exodus had left the PAP with only a razor-thin majority in a legislature deluged by opposition party-sponsored motions of no confidence against it.

At any rate, Said's bold plans for the PRS and the Singapore Malays were effectively short-circuited by his detention only hours after he assumed the position of party president on 1 February 1963. He was detained together with Barisan Sosialis leaders and more than 100 left-wing political activists in a joint assault undertaken by the PAP and the Alliance government in cooperation with the British authorities, in the infamous operation code-named Operation Cold Store.

Initially accused of being a leading member of the communist united front, then as an agent of a foreign power, Said was eventually denounced as a communist by the PAP leadership without having to prove their allegations. The communist tag was eventually relied on to justify Said's incarceration without trial for 17 years. Said and fellow detainee Chia Thye Poh were the longest-serving political prisoners in Singapore, and were among the longest-serving political detainees in the world.

Losing Malay Support: The 1964 Riots

Singapore's merger into the larger Malaysian federation elevated the clout of the Malays, who were now part of a politically potent ethnic majority. Even though the 1963 Malaysian Agreement stipulated that the special privileges accorded to the Malays in the Federation would not be extended to the Malays in Singapore, Article 152 of the Singapore Constitution did recognise their special claims on the state. After the 1963 elections, the Singapore Malays expected the PAP government to make good its constitutional responsibilities and pledges to narrow the socio-economic gap between the Malay and non-Malay communities. What they did not expect was to find themselves caught in the political cross-fire between the PAP and SMNO in Singapore and the PAP and the Federal government.

Buoyed by the PAP's success in the island's Legislative Assembly election, held just days after the merger, Lee signalled the PAP's desire to be included in the Alliance coalition by proposing that some PAP leaders be invited into the Federal Cabinet.[54] Determined to prove to UMNO leaders that the PAP was more of an electoral asset than the MCA, and intent on pre-empting the expected avalanche of anti-MCA protest votes to the Socialist Front, the PAP breached the gentleman's agreement with Tunku Abdul Rahman that it would not participate in Federal politics. In a risky political gamble, it decided to contest 11 Federal and 15 Assembly seats in predominantly urban-based Chinese constituencies in the 1964 elections. However, far from trouncing the MCA, the PAP performed disastrously, winning only one Federal seat from the Socialist Front, and was soundly defeated by the MCA in six constituencies.[55] The PAP's failed political gamble only served to dissipate what little remained of the political goodwill between the Alliance and PAP leadership and eliminated once and for all any possibility of the PAP's inclusion in the Alliance coalition.

Disheartened by the increasingly cantankerous relations between Kuala Lumpur and Singapore, Singapore Malay insecurities were aggravated by the SMNO's determination to regain Malay support after its humiliating performance in the 1963 elections. At its July convention, attended by 150 Malay organisations, UMNO leaders such as Jaafar Albar accused the PAP government of deliberately breaking the political, economic and cultural backbone of the Malay community by resettling Malays away from traditional Malay residential enclaves.[56] Jaafar's focus on the resettlement policy was astute as it was one of the most serious Malay grievances against the PAP government, together with the Malay community's persisting relative socio-economic marginality.

In an attempt to placate the Malay community and counter the impact of the SMNO-sponsored convention, the PAP sponsored a rival convention, also in July, inviting 114 'non-political' Malay organisations to discuss their views on improving Malay educational and living standards.[57] To tackle the problem of workplace discrimination against the Malays, particularly in the private sector,[58] delegates suggested that the government implement job quotas for Malays and establish a Malay Affairs Department. Both suggestions were rejected by Lee.[59] The failure to adopt concrete policies to address Malay perceptions of discrimination in the workplace only served to lend credence to the allegations by the SMNO and the UMNO-controlled *Utusan Melayu* that the PAP was not genuinely committed to improving the relative socio-economic status of the Malay community.[60]

Shortly after these politically charged conventions, racial riots erupted in late July and September, culminating in 33 dead and more than 600 injured. One of the most serious areas of rioting was in the economically depressed Malay residential enclave of Kampong Kembangan, where Malay frustrations were stoked by allegations of discrimination by Chinese factory owners in the area who were reluctant to employ Malays.[61] It is beyond the scope of this chapter to identify the instigators of the riots and the veracity of divergent interpretations of the causes of the riots by the UMNO and PAP leadership.[62] Whether the prime instigators were Indonesian agent provocateurs, irresponsible journalists, or politicians wantonly advancing their partisan interests, what is certain is that without the existence of genuine Malay grievances, the provocative actions of these myriad forces would never have been effective. What is also clear is that after the riots, the acutely insecure Singapore Malays turned to the SMNO and UMNO for support and leadership. This was frankly acknowledged by former PAP minister Othman Wok more than three decades after the event:

> When Lee Kuan Yew and I went to Kampong Kembangan, to see
> the Malays — you know — it was one day after the riot. Khir Johari
> followed us ... There was one big gathering of Malays. And they just
> ignored me and Lee Kuan Yew. They spoke to Khir Johari. Not us. As if
> we were not there ... And we went to Changi. Same thing.[63]

Not beyond using the riots to advance the PAP's larger political game plan, Lee is alleged to have appealed to Tunku to accept the PAP into the Federal government following each racial riot.[64] Having been repeatedly rebuffed by the UMNO leadership, the PAP leadership now boldly challenged the Federal government through its leadership of the Malaysia Solidarity Convention (MSC), made up of predominantly non-Malay parties in East Malaysia and Chinese-based parties from the Peninsula. This rival federation, which would include Sabah, Sarawak and possibly Penang and Malacca, had Singapore as its political centre.[65] In this politically charged environment, the MSC aggressively championed the Malaysian

Malaysia concept, which overtly challenged the *bumiputera* (indigenous) status and privileges of the Malays. In doing so, communal tensions in Malaysia and Singapore became perilously volatile.[66]

Not Needing Malay Support: Separation and Beyond

While the brief pre-merger and merger years had elevated the status and political clout of Singapore Malays in the Malaysian Federation, separation precipitated severe insecurity and an identity crisis. Simply put, Singapore Malays now felt insecure and uncertain about their fate and destiny in a predominantly Chinese society run by a Chinese-dominated PAP government.[67] This insecurity and uncertainty was strongly fuelled by the perception that the PAP had not honoured many of its pre-merger and merger promises, particularly its pledge to assist in narrowing the socio-economic gap between the Malay and non-Malay communities. While the policy of expanding Malay education resulted in a marked increase in Malays educated in the Malay language stream, employment prospects were poor because English remained the language of administration and English and Chinese the languages of commerce. Negligible usage of Malay in both the public and private sectors rendered the educational credentials of Malay-stream students of limited economic value, thereby reinforcing Malay economic insecurity and frustration.[68]

Efforts by community leaders and grassroots organisations to persuade the PAP government to adopt 'a more concerted and sustained effort' to address the relative socio-economic and educational marginality of the Malays[69] were not taken seriously. Indeed, the urgings of PAP Malay MP Shaari Tadin, at a high-profile seminar organised by the multi-ethnic-based Community Study Centre and Central Council of Malay Cultural Organisations in 1970, which argued that 'the problems of the Malays must not be looked upon as a communal problem to be tackled by the Malays alone ... Malays' problems must be looked upon in a national perspective involving different groups', reinforced suspicions that the Malays in the PAP were marginal, particularly in policy formulation.[70] Shaari's farsighted proposal of establishing a secretariat with research facilities and staffed by officers with appropriate expertise who were able to work closely with Malay organisations[71] (paradoxically akin to the latter-day Mendaki) was disregarded. As Chan Heng Chee perceptively observed, the PAP government's equivocal commitment to systematically addressing the Malay community's persisting socio-economic marginalisation contributed to the Malays feeling that they were engulfed by crisis and 'doomed never to succeed in catching up with the other communities'.[72]

The Malay community's political alienation was demonstrated by its weak participation in the various community-based organisations and facilities promoted by the PAP government, such as the Citizens' Consultative Committees (CCC) and Community Centres (CC). Bedlington's survey of Malay attendance at CCCs and CCs in the early 1970s found that they were rarely involved in or attended activities organised by these bodies, particularly in areas where the Malays were not a substantial numerical force. Malays were also disinclined to attend meet-the-people sessions in areas where they were weakly represented, suggesting that they distrusted the government authorities to resolve their problems.[73]

The electoral re-apportionment initiatives of 1967 and 1971, which largely affected Malay electoral strongholds and ensured that ethnic-based parties such as the SMNO would face major difficulties in getting candidates elected, reinforced Malay suspicions that the PAP government was attempting to systematically erode their political clout. In particular, re-apportionment led to the abolition of the largely Malay Southern Islands constituency and divided Geylang Serai into two, with both sections then merged with other constituencies containing large numbers of non-Malay voters.[74] The redrawing of Kampong Kembangan and the creation of an adjacent new constituency had the desired effect of splitting the one-time Malay electoral stronghold. Another boundary-delineation in 1971 purposefully counteracted the rising numerical Malay representation in Kampong Kembangan.[75] In addition to these electoral engineering initiatives, the government's urban resettlement programmes, which effectively dispersed the Malay community throughout the island, reduced them to a numerical minority in all constituencies. The Malays now became less important to the electoral clout of the PAP.

To counter the influence of dissenting clerics, the Administration of Muslim Law Act of 1966, which helped establish the state's highest religious authority, the *Majlis Ugama Islam Singapura* (MUIS or Islamic Religious Council of Singapore) in 1968, ensured that the body comprised an equal number of appointed and elected members. The SMNO's objection to this numerical calibration, on the grounds that it would allow the PAP government undue influence on MUIS, was dismissed.[76] As the president of MUIS would be appointed by the president of Singapore on the recommendation of the prime minister, the possibility that MUIS would be headed by someone critical of the PAP was diminished. Not surprisingly, MUIS has been commonly perceived as a religious bureaucracy that is unduly influenced by the PAP rather than the *ulama* (clerics).[77]

Singapore's separation from Malaysia, Indonesia's *Konfrontasi* campaign and the 1964 riots left an indelible psychological mark on the PAP leadership. This is manifested by their generally suspicious attitude towards the Malays in Singapore and neighbouring countries.[78] This paranoia was demonstrated in the policy of reducing Malay representation in the security forces, implemented shortly after separation. The policy was not publicly acknowledged until the late 1980s because it contradicted the rhetoric of Singapore's supposedly meritocratic and multiracial society. Just as importantly, the policy appears to violate articles 12 and 16 of the Singapore Constitution, which do not allow for discrimination on the basis of religion, race, descent or place of birth.[79] Thus, when compulsory national service was introduced in 1967, ironically to foster a Singaporean national identity and improve inter-ethnic relations, young Malay men were excluded from this nation-building exercise for more than a decade.[80] Malays already serving in the armed forces were not appointed to combat positions.[81]

As the military had long been a traditional avenue of employment during the colonial era and a vehicle for social mobility,[82] the PAP government's covert policy of institutional discrimination undermined further the Malay community's marginal socio-economic standing. Young Malay men excluded from national service were not issued exemption certificates and therefore faced severe difficulties in the labour market.[83] Significantly, this policy of institutionalised discrimination rendered farcical the PAP's professed commitment to multiracialism and meritocracy. Malay exclusion from national service and discrimination in the armed forces also exposed the limited ability of PAP Malay leaders to effectively represent Malay concerns and shape government policy. Those who attempted to assertively articulate Malay concerns on sensitive issues had their political careers prematurely terminated, or failed to climb far up the PAP hierarchy.[84] In this catch-22 situation of balancing the often-conflicting roles of a PAP and a Malay leader, their credibility as Malay leaders suffered a battering.

Conclusion

Mainstream and official narratives of the 'Singapore Story' in the 1950s and 1960s tend to focus on the PAP's tryst with communists and radical Chinese students without according commensurate attention to left-wing Malay nationalists, organisations and newspapers in the struggle for independence. This truncated perspective of Singapore's history downplays the pivotal role of progressive Malay nationalists and trade unionists in the PAP's rise to prominence. Also misunderstood is the significance of conditional Malay electoral support for the PAP in the 1963 elections.

Malay support was crucial to the political ambitions of the PAP during the tumultuous pre-merger and merger period, when its own political fortunes hung precariously in the balance. Expediently, the Malay community was offered cultural goods, constitutional guarantees on the special position and rights of the Malays and promises to strengthen their relative socio-economic status. However, when the Malays were no longer as politically important to the political calculations of the PAP leadership after separation, they became less sensitive to the concerns of the community. In the event, the PAP government's obligations under Section 152 of the Singapore Constitution have been disregarded in the rhetorical fanfare of building a multiracial and meritocratic society.

When placed in the context of the Cold War, Samad Ismail's incarceration, his involvement with the MNP, PAP, SMNO and UMNO and his meandering political journey from Singapore to Jakarta and finally Kuala Lumpur is all the more fascinating. He symbolises in many respects the meandering political journey and nuanced ideological orientation of the Singapore Malays. Like many Singapore Malays of that era, Samad was more strongly inspired by the left-wing nationalist currents in Indonesia. It was thus not altogether surprising that he was attracted to the PAP and, in the context of the party's larger Malayan game plan, was briefly one of its star players. Yet Samad's support for the PAP was conditional, as was the PAP's broader base of Malay support. Both Samad's political capital and that of the Malay community stemmed from their extensive linkages with progressive nationalists from the Malay World. In the context of Malaysia this was a powerful asset, but with the separation of Singapore from Malaysia in 1965, this asset was suddenly transformed into a source of official concern. Overnight it became an option that could not be countenanced; a path never to be taken again.

NOTES

1   See Timothy Barnard and Jan van der Putten's chapter in this volume.
2   Left Malay nationalist Ibrahim Yaacob extolled that 'The aim of Melayu Raya is the same as Indonesia Raya which is the aspiration of the Malay nationalist movement, that is to revive again the heritage of Srivijaya, which is the common unity of the bangsa'. See Ibrahim Yaacob, *Nusa dan Bangsa Melayu* (Jakarta: N.V. Alma'ariff, 1951), p. 65.
3   Farish Noor, 'Fine Young Calibans: Broken Dreams of Melayu Raya', in www.Malaysiakini.com/. Accessed 13 January 2002.

4   C. M. Turnbull, *A History of Singapore, 1819–1875* (Kuala Lumpur: Oxford University Press, 1977), p. 100.

5   Yong Mun Cheong, *The Indonesian Revolution and the Singapore Connection* (Leiden: KITLV Press, 2003).

6   Cited in Said Zahari, *Dark Clouds at Dawn: A Political Memoir* (Petaling Jaya: INSAN, 2001), p. 53.

7   A. Samad Ismail, 'Our James', in *No Cowardly Past: Writings, Poems, Commentaries*, ed. Dominic Puthucheary and Jomo K. S. (Petaling Jaya: INSAN, 1998), p. 55.

8   Melanie Chew, *Biography of President Yusuf bin Ishak* (Singapore: SNP Publishing, 1999), p. 77.

9   R. Rajakumar, 'Malaysia's Jean-Paul Sartre' in *A. Samad Ismail: Journalism and Politics*, ed. Cheah Boon Kheng (Kuala Lumpur: Singamal, 1987), p. 40.

10 A. Samad Ismail, 'Lim Chin Siong: Some Memories', in *Comet in Our Sky: Lim Chin Siong in History*, ed. Tan Jing Quee and Jomo K. S. (Kuala Lumpur: INSAN, 2001), p. 166.

11 Lee Kuan Yew, *The Singapore Story: Memoirs of Lee Kuan Yew* (Singapore: Prentice Hall, 1998), p. 160.

12 Puthucheary and Jomo, *No Cowardly Past*, p. 14.

13 Said Zahari, *Dark Clouds at Dawn*, p. 81.

14 Othman Wok, *Never in My Wildest Dreams* (Singapore: SNP Editions, 2000), p. 124.

15 Zuraidah Ibrahim, 'Malay Mobilisers', in *Lee's Lieutenants: Singapore's Old Guard*, ed. Lam Peng Er and Kevin Y. L. Tan (Sydney: Allen & Unwin, 1999), p. 125.

16 The PAP Malay convenors were Samad Ismail, Ismail Rahim and Mofradi Haji Mohamed Nor. Ismail and Mofradi were unionists.

17 The Singapore delegation was led by Chief Minister David Marshall. The PAP was represented by Lee Kuan Yew and Lim Chin Siong.

18 A. Samad Ismail, 'Lim Chin Siong: Some Memories', p. 166.

19 'It shall be a deliberate and conscious policy of the Government of Singapore at all times to recognise the special position of the Malays who are the indigenous people of the island and who are in most need of assistance and accordingly, it shall be the responsibility of the Government of Singapore to protect, support, foster, and promote their political, educational, religious, economic, social, and cultural interests, and the Malay language' (Section 152, Singapore Constitution).

20 The last point was advanced by James Minchin, *No Man is an Island: A Study of Lee Kuan Yew's Singapore* (Sydney: Allen & Unwin, 1986), p. 56.

21 Lee Khoon Choy, *On the Beat to the Hustings: An Autobiography* (Singapore: Times Books, 1988), p. 53.

22 Dominic Puthucheary, 'James Puthucheary: His Friends and His Times', in *No Cowardly Past*, ed. Dominic Puthucheary and Jomo K. S., p. 34.

23 Francis Seow, *The Media Enthralled: Singapore Revisited* (Boulder: Lynne Rienner Publishers, 1998), p. 29.

24 Said Zahari, *Dark Clouds at Dawn*, p. 81.
25 Indonesian Foreign Minister Adam Malik provided Samad with an office in Jakarta at the Antara news agency.
26 Lee Kuan Yew, *The Battle for Merger* (Singapore: Government Printing Press, 1961), p. 54.
27 Said Zahari, *Dark Clouds at Dawn*, pp. 82–3.
28 Dominic Puthucheary, 'James Puthucheary', p. 29.
29 Cited in Khoo Boo Teik, *Beyond Mahathir: Malaysian Politics and Its Discontents* (London: Zed Books, 2003), p. 272.
30 Cited in Stanley Bedlington, 'The Singapore Malay Community: The Politics of State Integration', Ph.D. Thesis, Cornell University, 1974, p. 126.
31 Said Zahari, *Dark Clouds at Dawn*, p. 132.
32 Othman Wok, *Never in My Wildest Dreams*, p. 127.
33 Sharom Ahmat, 'Singapore Malays, Education and National Development', in *Malay Participation in the National Development of Singapore*, ed. Sharom Ahmat and James Wong (Singapore: Eurasia Press, 1971), p. 8.
34 Bedlington, 'The Singapore Malay Community', p. 289.
35 Ibid., pp. 134–5.
36 Lily Zubaidah Rahim, *The Singapore Dilemma: The Political and Educational Marginality of the Malay Community* (Kuala Lumpur: Oxford University Press, 1998), p. 189.
37 Ibid.
38 Chan Heng Chee, *The Dynamics of One Party Dominance: The PAP at the Grassroots* (Singapore: Institute of Southeast Asian Studies, 1976), p. 76.
39 For example, PAP stalwart Lee Khoon Choy claims that 'The most significant victories for the PAP in the 1963 General Elections were three Malay dominated constituencies of Geylang Serai, Kampong Kembangan and the Southern Islands, all originally UMNO strongholds ... The PAP had succeeded in winning over the Malays in Singapore where the MCP had failed, for Malay voters had indicated their support of a multi-racial party'. See Lee Khoon Choy, *On the Beat to the Hustings*, p. 75.
40 Bedlington, 'The Singapore Malay Community', p. 190.
41 John Arthur MacDougall, 'Shared Burdens: A Study of Communal Discrimination by the Political Parties of Malaysia and Singapore', Ph.D. Thesis, Harvard University, 1968.
42 Bedlington, 'The Singapore Malay Community', p. 143.
43 Interview with Said Zahari at his residence in Subang Jaya, Malaysia on 3 February 2005.
44 Bedlington, 'The Singapore Malay Community', p. 123.
45 Ibid., p. 124.
46 Ibid., p. 118.
47 Ibid., p. 122.
48 K. J. Ratnam and R. S. Milne, *The Malayan Parliamentary Election of 1964* (Singapore: University of Malaya Press, 1967), p. 337.

49 Said Zahari, *Dark Clouds at Dawn*, p. 74.

50 Ibid., p. 123.

51 Ibid., p. 117.

52 Ibid., p. 135.

53 Ibid., p. 134.

54 Thomas Bellows, *The People's Action Party of Singapore* (Yale: Yale University, Southeast Asian Studies No. 14, 1970), p. 53.

55 V. Suryanarayan, 'Singapore in Malaysia', *International Studies* 11 (July 1969): 117.

56 Ibid., p. 148.

57 Ibid.

58 Chan, *The Dynamics of One Party Dominance*, p. 72.

59 Bedlington, 'The Singapore Malay Community', p. 148.

60 Ibid., p. 151.

61 Chan, *The Dynamics of One Party Dominance*, p. 72.

62 See Michael Leifer, 'Communal Violence in Singapore', *Asian Survey* 10, 4 (1964).

63 Cited in Melanie Chew, *Biography of President Yusuf bin Ishak*, p. 124.

64 T. J. S. George, *Lee Kuan Yew's Singapore* (London: Andre Deutch, 1974), p. 184.

65 Lee stated publicly, '… those states that want a Malaysian Malaysia can come together. I can think of three straight away — Sabah, Sarawak, Singapore. I can think of a few others like Penang and Malacca. I can even believe that Johore would be one … '. Cited in T. J. S. George, *Lee Kuan Yew's Singapore*, p. 85.

66 Hua Wu Yin, *Class and Communalism in Malaysia: Politics in a Dependent Capitalistic State* (London: Zed Press, 1983), p. 142.

67 Ashfaq Hussain, 'The Post-Separation Effect on the Malays and their Response', *Journal of the Historical Society* (July 1970): 67.

68 Sharom Ahmat, 'Singapore Malays', p. 9.

69 Ibid., pp. 10–11.

70 Opening Address by Shaari Tadin, Parliamentary Secretary to the Minister of Culture, in Sharom Ahmat and Wong, *Malay Participation in the National Development of Singapore*, pp. 3–5.

71 Ibid.

72 Chan, *The Dynamics of One Party Dominance*, p. 76.

73 Bedlington, 'The Singapore Malay Community', pp. 215–22.

74 Ibid., pp. 183–5.

75 Chan, *The Dynamics of One Party Dominance*, pp. 71, 72.

76 Bedlington, 'The Singapore Malay Community', pp. 179–80.

77 Suzaina Kadir, 'Islam, State and Society in Singapore', *Inter-Asia Cultural Studies* 5, 3 (2004): 369.

78 Lily Zubaidah Rahim, *The Singapore Dilemma*, p. 104.

79 Refer to Kevin Y. L. Tan, 'The Legal and Institutional Framework and Issues of Multiracialism in Singapore', in *Beyond Rituals and Riots: Ethnic Pluralism and Social Cohesion in Singapore*, ed. Lai Ah Eng (Singapore: Eastern University Press, 2004), p. 101.

80 This policy was not acknowledged by the government until 1987 and the details of its operation have never been made public.

81 Bedlington, 'The Singapore Malay Community', p. 242.

82 Prior to 1959, Malays formed approximately 80 per cent of the armed forces and police force in Singapore. Ibid., p. 241.

83 Refer to Tania Li, *Malays in Singapore: Culture, Economy and Ideology* (Singapore: Oxford University Press, 1989), p. 109.

84 Lily Zubaidah Rahim, *The Singapore Dilemma*, p. 90.

6

David Marshall and the Struggle
for Civil Rights in Singapore

Carl A. Trocki

Anyone familiar with the hapless opposition figures who presented themselves to the Singapore electorate in the 1980s or 1990s would not believe
that a viable and critical tradition of parliamentary and public opposition
had ever existed in Singapore. Indeed, the generation of Singaporeans who
were then coming of age had not experienced a time when it was possible
to voice real opposition. Only people of their parents' generation could
have remembered a period when an opponent of the PAP and the then
Prime Minister Lee Kuan Yew had the freedom to present a cogent alternative view of political life to Singaporeans. There was, for a time at least,
one opposition voice that championed the causes of political plurality, the
rule of law, administrative transparency, human and civil rights, and the
basic principles of democratic government. That was David Marshall. He
defended these practices at the very time that the government was busily
eliminating them.[1]

The Singapore government, according to political scientist Chan
Heng Chee, accused such figures, especially people like David Marshall,
of perpetuating an 'alien tradition born of Western liberal thought'. Chan,
once a critic of the government herself, responded to Lee Kuan Yew's claim

that Singapore needed to emphasise 'Asian values' in its political discourse. She argued:

> ... I find it hard to believe that the urge to speak up and to criticise ruling power is only a Western tradition. I cannot think of a Chinese philosopher, an Indian, Malay or Japanese philosopher who said to posterity, 'Don't tell the truth, be afraid to speak up against injustices and wrongdoings' and there are many Chinese scholar-officials who have lost their heads criticising the emperor. Every age has its critics of power. The intellectual, if he is a real intellectual, may have no role accorded to him by those in power but he still has a role if he keeps his integrity for by his example he may infuse into society a moral and spiritual quality without which no state becomes a nation.[2]

Chan is certainly correct in pointing out that the West has no monopoly on the right to dissent and to speak truth to power. On the other hand, it is probably true that Marshall, in his role as an opposition member of the Legislative Assembly and a barrister, saw himself acting in what he regarded as the Western political tradition. It is no great secret that the practices of tolerance for dissent, public debate, and criticism of those in power, are among the paths not taken in modern Singapore. These were the principles that Marshall supported. So, too, were adherence to the rule of law, respect for political plurality, freedom of speech, freedom of assembly, a right to a trial by a jury of one's peers, and the right of *habeas corpus*. All of these are clearly in the Western legal and political tradition and these are the principles that Marshall endeavoured to defend when he went into opposition.

Marshall was one of the key opposition figures of the 1960s and early 1970s. He had been the first elected Chief Minister of Singapore in 1955. Prior to that, Marshall was one of Singapore's leading barristers. He was also a committed democratic socialist. His brief administration was constrained, on the one hand, by the limited range of self-government then available, and on the other, by the strength of a determined and divisive opposition. During those years, Singapore was still under colonial rule, and would remain so for almost another decade.

Chan Heng Chee and James Low both wrote extensive accounts of Marshall's political career.[3] Alex Josey published an earlier and less authoritative account of his administration.[4] Chan's account also covers (although less comprehensively) his years in opposition, in her chapter, 'The Peripheral Politician'. Chan argues, not without reason, that because he was an English-educated Jew in a Chinese city, Marshall's chances of ever enjoying a long-term career as a popular politician in Singapore were poor. Moreover, his 'mercurial temperament' did not suit a political existence.

There is little in her account to conclude that she saw Marshall's political career as anything but a failure.

Low demonstrates that Marshall's appeal to the masses of Singaporeans was really much more deeply rooted than one would have thought from reading the English-language press. Low's examination of previously untapped accounts in the vernacular press of the 1950s shows that there was considerable appreciation for Marshall and his message in the Chinese-language press. He was more genuinely respected in the vernacular press than he was in the English-language press, which regularly treated Marshall with scorn.

In view of these divergences in the popular versus the 'official' estimations of the man, we may ask if the vernacular press saw something the English press and the official critics missed. It may be that they represented what most of the population actually thought of Marshall. The man may have been mercurial and unpredictable. He may not have been a capable administrator or even a savvy politician, but he did stir the people, and he did appeal to them. Perhaps he fooled them, since they only saw a public persona, but on the other hand, perhaps they sensed in him his sincerity, his idealism, and his commitment to justice. Western or Asian, these were values that both communities understood.

Low did not deal with Marshall's career as an opposition politician or examine Marshall's career as a human rights activist. In late 1956, Marshall, failing to achieve greater self-government for Singapore during constitutional talks in London, somewhat rashly promised to resign. He thus turned the chief ministership over to his one-time ally and deputy, Lim Yew Hock.[5] Once out of power, Marshall found himself marginalised in the Labour Front and in disagreement with the general direction of politics in Singapore. He resigned from the Legislative Assembly in April 1957, vowing to stay out of politics. Despite this, he founded the Workers' Party in October 1957, and ran for election for the seat of Cairnhill in 1959. Unsuccessful in this attempt, he again resigned from politics. Later, however, he contested the seat of Anson in a by-election in 1961, and was elected and remained in the Legislative Assembly until 1963, when he left active politics for good.

After political power passed into the hands of the PAP and Lee Kuan Yew, Marshall became one of the most formidable and, at least for a time, one of the most untouchable opponents that Singapore had to offer. He saw his role in politics after 1956 as being part of the 'loyal opposition'. He was there not necessarily to replace the ruling party, but to keep it honest and to protect the minority from the tyranny of the majority.

In this chapter, I focus on three particular issues where Marshall stood in opposition either as a legislator or as a private barrister. These include the government's misuse of the Internal Security Act (ISA) and the rights of detainees under it; the jury system; and freedom of the press. Marshall was, of course, active across a range of issues, but I believe these best exemplify his commitment to Western liberal principles. Moreover, all represent issues touching on the rule of law, a value which Marshall, as a barrister, held most tenaciously.

Throughout the 1960s and into the early 1970s, Marshall championed the causes of freedom of speech, freedom of the press and freedom of conscience in Singapore, while the increasing wealth and power of the PAP government worked to systematically stifle all voices of opposition. He worked conscientiously within the law to ensure basic human and civil rights for detainees and prisoners in Singapore's penal system. In taking this course in his public life, Marshall walked a path that has been virtually abandoned today. Until his brief suspension from the Bar in 1972, Marshall remained one of the few voices of liberal dissent within Singapore.

Detainees and Arbitrary Arrest

One of the first major confrontations came in 1958, when Marshall clashed with the Lim Yew Hock government over the acceptance of the so-called Gangster Law, or the Preservation of Public Security Ordinance (PPSO). Marshall had grudgingly agreed to the extension of emergency powers at the request of the colonial executives while he was Chief Minister in order to deal with the disorder accompanying the Hock Lee Bus strike. He disapproved, however, of the way in which Lim Yew Hock subsequently misused the law and he now opposed the further extension of the measure. He claimed that the law gave virtually unchecked power to the colonial government to detain anyone it chose.

> ... this gang law authorises the Chief Secretary in his complete discretion with the consent of the Attorney-General, without any inquiry to detain any person whom he believes to be associated with activities of a criminal nature whose detention he believes is in the interests of public safety, peace and good order.[6]

Marshall, in his letter to the editor of *The Straits Times*, noted that although the law was ostensibly aimed at Chinese secret societies or triads, there was no mention of such organisations in the act. Also, although there already was a Societies Ordinance, this law was not made a part of it.

It is our humble opinion that the Lim Yew Hock Government has broken faith with the people of Singapore. It has broken faith, firstly, by using against our people the repressive laws of colonialism which it should be the sacred duty of a Government which seeks Merdeka to remove. It has broken faith, secondly, by a vicious campaign of slander and vilification of popular anti-colonial forces instead of further strengthening these forces in order to ensure the success of the Merdeka Movement.[7]

At the time, the PAP also opposed the law, because the power to apply it, Lee later said, was not vested in the elected government, but was in the hands of colonial officials (for example, the Chief Secretary, the Attorney-General and the Financial Secretary) who were not responsible to the people of Singapore. By 1959, however, as it began to appear the PAP would take power in the impending election, they were reluctant to take it off the books. Lee Kuan Yew, then a member of the Legislative Assembly, voiced his approval of the continuation of the PPSO for another year. Once elected in 1959, the PAP took the opportunity to extend the measures of the PPSO for another five years by replacing it with the ISA. Since then, the PAP has never ceased to rule without this or some similar ordinance.

This was one of the first in a long series of battles, most of which Marshall lost, as an opposition figure in Singapore. Whether as a politician or as a barrister, he now found himself as one of a decreasing number of voices calling for effective checks on the government's use of its authority. The major difference was that after 1959, the government was an elected one. The colonial rulers now faded into the background and were replaced by leaders who proved to be even more authoritarian than the British.

In 1961, the seat of Anson opened up and Marshall decided to stand for it. Having won the seat with support from the left wing of the PAP, Marshall took his fight against the ISA and the PAP's terms for merger with Malaya into the Legislative Assembly. Marshall must have felt somewhat uncomfortable finding himself in an alliance with those whom he considered to be communists or communist sympathisers. Nevertheless, he may also have realised that despite his distrust of them, they were now in a less powerful position. Future events would prove that the balance of power had clearly shifted. Armed with a strengthened ISA and with British and Malayan forces at his back, Lee now moved to eliminate his rivals.

Marshall scored a minor coup against the government following its sweeping move to crush the left with Operation Cold Store, but in the end, he lost the battle. In the early morning hours of 2 February 1963, police detained over 100 left-wing activists. These were the leaders of the Barisan Sosialis and the Partai Rakyat Singapura as well as student and labour union leaders. Most were thrown into the Outram Road prison where they were subjected to particularly harsh conditions.

Utilising a little-known statute that had been passed by the colonial government, Marshall discovered that he was able, as an Assemblyman, to demand access to the prison. The warden and the Solicitor-General, despite their reluctance, were finally forced to allow Marshall to visit the detainees, interview them and to report on their conditions to the Legislative Assembly:

> In Singapore, as you will see from my report on the conditions I person-
> ally witnessed on the 23rd March 1963, male detainees are in small
> rooms in solitary confinement behind locked doors with a chamber pot
> in their own room, are not allowed out to visit the lavatory, have no
> chair, no table, a small 40-watt bulb high up in the ceiling, no writing
> material and not allowed to receive any newspapers or books from
> outside. The prison books are mostly infantile in character. Detainees
> arrested on 2nd February 1963 were not allowed to see a lawyer till
> 5th March.[8]

The government was embarrassed by this exposure of their mistreatment of the prisoners,[9] particularly when Marshall publicised the fact that those detainees who had been Malayan citizens and who had been sent to Kuala Lumpur for detention enjoyed far more comfortable situations:

> I may add, for your information, that in the Federation of Malaya not
> only have detainees sent by the Singapore Government for custody there
> been allowed unimpeded access to counsel from the date of their arrival
> many weeks before their counterparts in Singapore, but they may have
> all the reading material available in the Federation for which they can
> pay, and every facility to read and write, and generous opportunities to
> meet their relatives.[10]

In a response from the government a PAP spokesman heaped scorn on Marshall's report, explaining that the conditions of the Outram Road prison were a result of its having been built a century before, and that if he were concerned with the welfare of the prisoners, Marshall should have attended to the building when he was Chief Minister. The response also defended holding the prisoners incommunicado by saying that they were still being interrogated.[11] Nevertheless, the government was clearly stung by Marshall's comment that even the colonial government had never detained prisoners under such conditions. Following Marshall's report, it quickly moved the detainees to much more comfortable quarters at Changi, allowed them more time to exercise and socialise, and gave them access to reading matter and writing materials.

From this time forward, Marshall remained in contact with Peter Berenson, the founder of Amnesty International. Singaporeans being detained under the PPSO and later the ISA were thus among the earliest of the political prisoners to be defended by that organisation. Marshall continued his fight against the manner in which the government exercised its powers under the ISA and the PPSO. Despite his efforts, these laws or similar measures remain on the books to this day.

The Jury System

It was, in fact, over the judicial process itself that Marshall came into conflict with the government on another front. In 1959, soon after it first came to power, the PAP introduced legislation to abolish the jury system in all but capital cases. Here again, as a barrister, David Marshall, with support from the Law Society of Singapore, opposed the government's attempt to eliminate the jury system. At the time, Lee Kuan Yew argued that since jury trials were only used for capital offences in the Federation, he was only bringing Singapore's legal system into line with Malaya's, a move which would facilitate the anticipated merger of Singapore and Malaya. Lee entirely ignored Marshall's opposition in his autobiography, suggesting that Marshall had supported the move, but noting that Marshall, as a barrister, was only interested in defending his clients and not in their guilt or innocence.

> Soon after I became prime minister in 1959, I abolished the jury system for all cases except murder. I retained this exception to keep in line with the law in Malaya at that time. In 1969, after separation, I asked Eddie Barker as minister for law to move a bill in Parliament abolishing the jury system for murder trials. During a parliamentary select committee meeting, David Marshall, then our most successful criminal lawyer, claimed he had 99 acquittals out of the 100 cases he defended for murder. When I asked if he believed the 99 acquitted had been wrongly charged, Marshall replied his duty was to defend them, not judge them.[12]

Marshall criticised Lee and the government for their attacks on the jury system in 1959 and he resumed his opposition in 1969. By then, however, Marshall was finding himself more isolated in his protests. Andrew Phang, who has written extensively on the abolition of jury trials in Singapore, asks '… why the decline and fall of a major legal institution aroused so little public debate let alone outcry'.[13] Marshall, however, did attempt to raise the issue publicly. Phang identifies him as the 'staunchest defender of the jury system in Singapore'.[14] Marshall put forward some of the traditional arguments used to defend the jury system:

The reason for its success in all democracies is simple. The community is deeply interested in its own protection against evildoers and through its ordinary members it can be relied upon to convict the evildoer because his acts have been proved a danger to the community. At the same time the jury can be relied upon to block the tyranny of kings and governments in resisting pressure to convict against conscience. It is impossible to punish 12 anonymous people whereas it is not impossible to get at a judge appointed by the government. Let us remember that in Singapore the Prime Minister appoints the judges and there is nothing to stop him from appointing reliable 'yes-men' to the Bench.[15]

Marshall's objections received very little press attention at the time and were repeated to the media only through Lee Kuan Yew's reference to them. Marshall had convened a meeting of Singapore lawyers on 24 April 1969. The Council of the Bar Society passed a resolution condemning the government's attempt to end the jury system and warned against possible pressures that might be placed on judges and argued that the abolition of the jury system would deprive citizens of the protection of the law. They argued that there was no valid reason for the abolition of the jury system, and that the alternative was inappropriate and unworkable, and asked that the jury system be restored. Initially, no notice was taken of this resolution by a single Singapore newspaper, or by any of Singapore's radio or TV stations. For several months Marshall was refused permission by police to hold a public meeting. Finally, on 26 September, he was given permission.[16]

The government argued that the jury system was unsatisfactory for Singapore. To Marshall, this meant that the government felt that the people of Singapore were not fit to be jurors.

Does it occur to Members of Parliament that if we are not fit to be jurors then are we fit to be voters? Jurors get all the facts that are known, with skilled assistance from Bench and Bar — if after all that we are not fit to return a verdict on one man, then are we fit to return a verdict in general elections in respect of matters affecting the welfare of the country as a whole? Do Members of Parliament really believe that the people of the large number of countries which have juries are more fit than we are to be jurors? [17]

Despite protests from Marshall and other members of the Bar, Lee was able to pass his anti-jury measure with ease. In 1969, a new Supreme Court of Judicature Act was enacted for Singapore and jury trials for murder cases were also abolished. Judges have always been appointed by the president with the advice of the prime minister, and tenure is constitutionally protected to age 65, after which judges can remain on the Bench on a contractual basis.[18]

The *Nanyang Siang Pau* and the End of Press Freedom

In 1971, one of the last-remaining arenas of open public discourse and possible opposition to the government was the press. Although the government had long dominated the major English-language paper, *The Straits Times*, its influence over the Chinese press was less powerful. During that year, a couple of new English-language papers appeared which ventured to criticise government actions. They did not last long. *The Singapore Herald* was forced to shut down due to government pressure. The other independent English-language newspaper, *The Eastern Sun*, also closed down after being accused of receiving funding from foreign sources.[19]

At the same time, the government detained a number of reporters for the *Nanyang Siang Pau* on charges of spreading communist propaganda and making statements favourable to communist China. Marshall agreed to take their case. On 25 May 1971, Keck Loong Sing, Ly Singko, Shun Tung Tao and Lee Mau Seng instructed their lawyers to protest when the government claimed that the four had confessed to 'promoting the newspaper's policy of sympathy for the People's Republic of China'. Each of the detainees issued a deposition denying the government's accusations.[20]

At the same time, Marshall was in contact with Amnesty International. As it happened, representatives from Amnesty were attending the Annual Conference of the International Press Institute in Helsinki, and on 7 June 1971, the conference was to be addressed by Singapore Prime Minister Lee Kuan Yew. Marshall, who was representing both the detainees and the newspaper itself, was instructed to use the opportunity to pressure Lee into releasing the men. They would provide the representatives at the meeting with copies of the detainees' depositions. They would thus be able to confront Lee with the evidence of his own government's violation of press freedom. The move turned out to be Marshall's undoing.

At the International Press Institute meeting, Lee defended his actions against the press in Singapore claiming that there was a

> ... sinister and for the most part covert assault of communism —
> Chinese communism, using Hongkong as a vantage point ... And there
> was the western world which offered some necessary imports like science
> and technology but which nowadays peddled as well an undesirable ethos
> against which Singapore must stand on guard.[21]

Marshall's attempt to embarrass Lee in Helsinki seems to have provoked a reprisal. The information provided to the conference was contained in the detainees' depositions to the High Court, which were scheduled to be placed before the court on 7 June 1971. As court documents, they should not have been made public before being submitted in court. Marshall was alleged to have violated an agreement he had made with the Solicitor-General not to release information to the press before the 7 June hearing. Against Marshall's instructions, the Amnesty International representative in Helsinki distributed copies to the conference delegates on 6 June, the day before the hearing in Singapore. Marshall was ultimately deemed to have violated his undertaking to the Attorney-General. He denied he had acted improperly and pointed out that although they were distributed before 7 June, they were not made public in the press until 8 June. It was clear from the government's conduct of the case, however, that the real issue was not the technicality of the timing, but the embarrassment of the Prime Minister in an international forum.[22]

It is of interest that the Attorney-General, who initially accused Marshall of impropriety in a letter dated 1 June, actually withdrew the accusation.[23] Only several weeks later did he file a complaint with the Law Society, which led to Marshall's suspension from practising law for six months. Marshall decided to leave Singapore for a time and travelled to London to take a number of refresher courses there.

Marshall, who had married in 1961, had four young children, two of whom were in school in Singapore. The family now found that former friends no longer called and they began to hear 'rumours' about the possibility that Marshall himself might be detained on his return to Singapore. Marshall was being warned that further expressions of dissent would not be tolerated in the 'rugged society'. Realising that he was now quite isolated, as far as life in Singapore was concerned, it seems that Marshall decided to keep a low profile and find a *modus vivendi* with the regime in return for their permission to let him come home. At the time, he wrote to a friend expressing his relief at coming back to Singapore.

> It is good to be back. There is a curious emotional attachment to one's
> country and one's home which my brother calls adolescent but which
> to me is very real. And despite the wonderful welcome I received from
> many fine human beings in London whose respect stems from the day I
> struggled against them for Singapore's independence, I nevertheless felt a
> zombie away from Singapore which is very much a part of me.[24]

Although he now became less active in domestic political issues in Singapore, Marshall continued to express himself in the area of human rights. The following year, he wrote to the editor of the *Far Eastern Economic Review* calling for more extensive coverage of human rights issues in Asia.

> It seems to me that the major tragedy of Asian countries today is the
> drive to fill the belly and forget the spirit, so that we are producing
> humanity that is 'cribbed, cabined and confined' and transformed into
> anthood. A few years back, I was asked by the International Institute
> of Human Rights to present the case for countries in the Far East at a
> symposium in Uppsala, and the little I learnt then turned my stomach —
> we seem to have so little respect for human values.[25]

Although the issues for which he had come to stand had indeed been
pushed to the margins in Singapore, Marshall lasted longer than most in
attempting to defend them. While he was able, Marshall continued to
defend the rule of law in Singapore and opposed the ISA and its use against
political opponents. He continued to stand for the principles of freedom
of speech and freedom of the press and struggled to maintain a society in
which openness and plurality could survive and flourish.

Finally, Marshall's ultimate, though grudging, acceptance of the PAP
system of governance needs some attention. Following his return to Singapore
in 1973, Marshall remained within the out-of-bounds markers in public and
did little to openly antagonise the powers that ruled Singapore. In 1981, he
was tapped to be Singapore's ambassador to France. This could be seen as
both a reward for good behaviour as well as the regime's way of removing
articulate and intelligent critics from the day-to-day life of Singapore. He was
not the first, or the last, to accept such a compromise with the government.
As a man of honour, Marshall accepted his role as a diplomat, and that it
was his job to defend Singapore in international fora. He also considered
it an honour to be given the opportunity to serve his country. Despite its
ruthlessness, Marshall was willing to acknowledge the many achievements
of the PAP government. Nevertheless, in private, he continued to offer
his frank views to individuals, both in the government and otherwise.

Although Marshall himself remained a committed democratic socialist,
and even though he later developed a clear appreciation for individuals
such as Lim Chin Siong, it is clear from his writings and his experience
that he always harboured uneasiness with the Chinese-educated left in
Singapore. In the 1950s and early 1960s, he saw Lim and Fong Swee Suan
as 'Chinese chauvinists', if not as communists or communist sympathisers.
It is also probable that many other English-educated and English-speaking
Singaporeans shared his suspicions of the Chinese left.

Even though he was occasionally allied with them, particularly in the
years after 1961 when the Barisan Sosialis and the PAP split, he remained
suspicious, nonetheless. In his later years, when interviewed by Lily Tan of
the Singapore National Archives in the 1980s, he described Lim and Fong

as 'Chinese chauvinists'. Of Fong, whom Marshall had arrested in 1955 at the time of the Hock Lee Bus riots, he said:

> Well he was a Chinese-speaking Chinese. So to start with communication between us was difficult. But I got the impression of a man ... who just intended to use me for his own ends. Totally immoral in his tactics, totally contemptuous of European ways. Not only Europeans, he just wanted to smash us ... without smashing himself.[26]

Marshall later offered a more positive appraisal of Lim Chin Siong, but it was clear that there was a cultural gap between the two:

> I would say that he was a well-meaning, a totally sincere person who was brought up within the context of Chinese chauvinism and saw the rest of the world as being inimical, as being unfriendly, as having to fight them. He was first and foremost, a Chinese chauvinist.[27]

Marshall also held similar feelings about the Chinese students[28] with whom he came into contact during the 1950s and 1960s, and it was perhaps this mutual suspicion that weakened the position of both the English-educated liberals and the Chinese leftists, and thus helped to open the way for Lee Kuan Yew and the PAP to out-manoeuvre both groups. While one may find fault with Marshall's uneasiness with the Chinese-educated, it seems clear that they understood and trusted him. As a Western-educated person, schooled in the values of British law and constitutionalism, he continued to promote those values throughout his life. He made a choice between power and principle and chose the latter.

NOTES

1   This paper was researched and written with support from the Australian Research Council, Queensland University of Technology, the Institute of Southeast Asian Studies (ISEAS), Singapore, and the History Department and the Asia Research Institute of the National University of Singapore. I am grateful to Mrs Jean Marshall and ISEAS for permission to consult the David Marshall Papers. I am also grateful to Mrs Marshall and Dr Michael Barr and Dr Kevin Tan for reading and commenting on earlier versions of this paper. I also wish to thank Mr. Ho Chi Tim for his assistance in gathering materials from the David Marshall Papers.

2   Chan Heng Chee, *The Role of Intellectuals in Singapore Politics*, Occasional Paper Series No. 26 (Singapore: Department of Political Science, University of Singapore, 1976).

3   Chan Heng Chee, *A Sensation of Independence: David Marshall: A Political Biography*, re-issue of 1984 edition with a new acknowledgement (Singapore: Times Books International, 2001); James Choon Sai Low, 'Kept in Position:

The Labour Front-Alliance Government of Chief Minister David Marshall in Singapore, April 1955–June 1956', MA Thesis, National University of Singapore, 2000. Also, James Choon Sai Low, 'Kept in Position: The Labour Front-Alliance Government of Chief Minister David Marshall in Singapore, April 1955–June 1956', *Journal of Southeast Asian Studies* 35, 1 (2004): 41.

4   Alex Josey, *David Marshall's Political Interlude* (Singapore: Eastern Universities Press, 1982).

5   John Drysdale, *Singapore: Struggle for Success* (North Sydney and Hemel Hempstead: George Allen & Unwin, 1984).

6   DM.45.56, 1 October 1956 — David Marshall's open letter to the Singapore Legislative Assembly sent to *The Straits Times*.

7   Ibid.

8   DM.326.43, undated — presumably during the week of 25 March 1963, 'Report to Anson'.

9   These are some of the key circumstances of Marshall's report:

I saw a total of 86 detainees, nine of whom are women …

The men are detained in individual cells, 11 ft. long × 5ft. wide × 11ft. high, with a 1½ ft. high barred window at the very top of one side, and a 12" barred window on the other, very thick walls and a 2½ inch thick steel door painted white; an iron bed cemented to the floor, with springs, a thin grass mattress, two blankets, one aluminium chamber pot with cover, one aluminium beaker for water, one electric bulb (40 watts) right against the ceiling. Those were the only prison articles in each cell.

The heat in each cell was oppressive, and I understand that this is particularly so when the cell door is locked and remains locked for 23 hours and 15 minutes in every day. The detainees are not allowed to receive any newspapers whatsoever 'not even the Straits Times or Sin Chew'. They are not allowed to receive any books from outside, not even dictionaries and engineering or medical books, whether from their own homes or reputable stores.

A few copies of the Bible and some paper-backs and tattered infantile reading matter from the prison stores are available to the detainees. The detainees are not allowed any writing materials, not even a pencil, but recently they have been allowed once a fortnight to have pen and paper to write one letter.

All meals must be taken in the cells. All calls of nature must take place in the chamber-pot in the cell because the detainee is not allowed to leave his cell except for a period of 45 minutes a day (originally 20 minutes) when seven detainees at a time (originally two) are allowed to file out to the showers and to run about the cement courtyard by way of exercise under supervision to prevent any conversation.

The Chamber-pots are removed fairly regularly and only three of the cells smelt of urine, but these chamber-pots cannot be removed between the hours of midnight and 6 a.m. and they must also act as slop basins for the morning toilet at 6 a.m. (DM.326.9, 23 March 1963, 'Report on P.P.S.O. detainees and detention conditions')

10 DM.326.5, 14 March 1963 — Letter to Solicitor General.

11 DM.326.12, 25 March 1963 — Singapore Government Press Statement.

12 Lee Kuan Yew, *From Third World to First: The Singapore Story: 1965–2000: Memoirs of Lee Kuan Yew* (Singapore: Times Media, 2000), pp. 241–2.

13 Andrew Boon Leong Phang, 'Jury Trial in Singapore and Malaysia: The Unmaking of a Legal Institution', *Singapore Journal of Legal Studies* 25 (1983): 50. I am grateful to Kevin Tan for bringing this article to my attention.

14 Ibid., p. 53, fn 29.

15 DM.326.54, undated – circa 1969, 'The Jury'.

16 DM 38.5, 16 December 1969, 'Why Abolish the Jury'.

17 Ibid.

18 I am grateful to Kevin Tan for information on the status of the judiciary in Singapore.

19 Marvin L. Rogers, 'Malaysia and Singapore: 1971 Developments', *Asian Survey* 2 (1972): 175–6.

20 DM.298.4, 'Instructions of Mr Keck Loong Sing to his lawyers on 25 May 1971'; DM.298.5, 'Instructions of Mr. Ly Singko to his lawyers on 25 May 1971; DM.298.6, 'Instructions of Mr. Shun Tung Tao to his lawyers on 25 May 1971; DM.298.7. 'Instructions of Mr. Lee Mau Seng to his lawyers on 25 May 1971'.

21 *The Times*, 10 June 1971.

22 DM298.13, 9 October 1971 — Letter from David Marshall to the Secretary of the Law Society.

23 DM298.29, 19 May 1972, Statement by David Marshall at the Law Society Hearing. 3 June 1971 telephone conversation:

> I was furious when I received the AG's letter because of the implication that I had acted improperly. In my view, rightly or wrongly, there was no question of my giving the affidavits or the instructions in respect of affidavits for publication in the sense understood on the 26th May. I was sending these documents for legitimate purposes in pursuance of the interests and on the instructions of clients, and I am quite certain that the AG repeatedly said 'I do not intend to make any charge against you in the letter, it is not a charge.' Or words indicating that he was not imputing any improper conduct on my part because he refused my suggestion that he should report me to the Law Society and instead agreed to withdraw the letter.

24 DM.225.22, 9 May 1973, David Marshall's letter to Mr Justice Irving Hill.

25 DM.225.87, 3 October 1974, David Marshall's letter (requested not to be published) to the *Far Eastern Economic Review*.

26 DM 512, 24 September 1984, National Archives of Singapore, Interview by Lily Tan with David Marshall, 'Political Developments in Singapore, 1945–65', volume 1, p. 89.

27 DM 512, 24 September 1984, volume 1, p. 65.
28 DM 512, 24 September 1984, volume 1, pp. 40–1:

> And the curious thing is I found them delightful individually and totally
> deaf collectively. They had a curious deafness. They would listen and
> you'd feel your words weren't sinking in at all. And then they would
> have a little confabulation together and then they would have something
> totally different from what you'd been saying and sometimes they left
> you just in the air, wondering what the hell this was all about, whether
> it was worth your coming along to advise them, because they really did
> not seem to respect your advice … I never really seemed to get through
> to them in reality. And I never got the impression I was influencing their
> conduct. They were getting information from me, factual, legal or other-
> wise. But we were not on the same wave length.

PART 3

Activists and Popular Movements

7

Malay Cosmopolitan Activism
in Post-War Singapore

*Timothy P. Barnard and
Jan van der Putten*

Shortly after the establishment of colonial Singapore in 1819, Malays became a minority community in the British-controlled port. Despite this minority status — the percentage of Malays in the population has remained at a relatively stable level of around 15 per cent since the mid-nineteenth century — Singapore has played an important role in the development of Malay intellectual debates and activism. As William Roff pointed out in his seminal 1967 work, *The Origins of Malay Nationalism*, Singapore — within the colonial framework as part of the Straits Settlements — was home to vigorous intellectual activity that was unimaginable in the *negeri* (states) of the Malay Peninsula.[1] Acting as the key entrepot for technology, education and publishing in the region, Singapore existed outside of traditional restrictions that were placed on alternative ideas in the Malay courts, while also being open to the radical ideas and changes emanating from Indonesia.

The cornerstone of activism in the Malay community was journalism. Various shop houses along the streets running through Kampong Glam had been home to printing presses that had been publishing newspapers and magazines since the 1870s. These newspapers were the focus of a number of key pre-war debates in the Malay community, ranging from the role of Islam in, and the composition of, the Malay community to the status of Chinese and Indian immigrants in the Peninsula.[2] Important pre-war Malay leaders, such as Syed Sheikh al-Hadi and Abdul Rahim Kajai, were active in the publishing industry and were influential in the development of nascent political movements that were beyond the control of the British authorities or the traditional Malay leadership. These leaders learned their trade in a number of publishing centres in the Archipelago, ranging from Penang to Bukittinggi to Makassar. Penang was one of the primary publishing centres buzzing with activity in the 1930s. The complement of printers, publishers and writers extended to nearby Medan in Sumatra, which was another node in this network that churned out a welter of magazines and other serials with stories driven by Islam, socialism and a call for political freedom.

Although quite diverse and individualistic, post-war Malay political, journalistic and artistic networks,[3] with roots in the Malay Peninsula as well as in Indonesia, intersected to such an extent that every journalist was potentially a politician, an author of fiction, a publisher, a graphic designer or cartoonist, or an actor in a theatrical troupe or on film. These networks converged in Singapore, and surfaced in public debates, publications and other artistic expressions, and were often the result of long meetings in coffee shops and homes. Although these discussions touched upon a variety of socio-political topics — with the primary focus on the pending independence of Malaya — the issue of language unified all participants. *Bahasa Melayu* (Malay language) was glorified as a tool in the fight against the 'feudalism' of the traditional elite, the colonial overlords, and a majority of foreign elements in society, as well as a means to connect with the masses in the Peninsula and Indonesia. Malay was to become the language of independent Malaya. People who wanted to join that nation should learn it, including Malays themselves, and the language should be modernised to meet the demands of modern life on the stage of world politics. A cultural industry comprising newspapers, magazines, books, theatres and films was considered of the utmost importance to modernise the language, boost nationalistic feelings and prepare the masses for independence.

This chapter will examine the role of the diverse groups that originated in the world of journalism and spread to other fields and that were united in a belief that the Malay language and arts were vital components of independence. While many of the figures discussed went on to important political roles in both Singapore and Malaysia, their focus on language and culture reverberated for decades in the region. The legacy of these debates between journalists from Indonesia, the Peninsula and Singapore over the Malay language was far-reaching, leaving its mark on the nation 'like a thunderbolt awakening Malay consciousness that had lain dormant for centuries'.[4]

Indonesia, Malay Literature, Singapore

The Malay literary and nationalist movement that arose in Singapore in the 1950s had its origins in developments in Indonesia and pan-Malayan politics before World War II and shortly thereafter. In Indonesia, a simmering anti-colonial movement linked to the literary scene began to emerge in the 1930s. A voice for this movement was *Pujangga Baru* (New Poets), a literary magazine led by a group of young writers — such as Sutan Takdir Alisjahbana, Armijn Pane and Amir Hamzah — who came to be known collectively by the name of the magazine they edited and wrote for. Initially, the magazine concentrated completely on literature, but after it came fully under Alisjahbana's influence in 1935, it became more political in tone and more influential. *Pujangga Baru* was a forum for new forms of literature in the Western mould, which taught readers to develop a critical stance towards the changes that were taking place in late colonial Indonesia. In broad terms, the proponents strove to develop a national culture that would be on par with the 'modern' Western cultures and possess the same genres, but in its own language. These writers also organised the first National Language Congress in Indonesia in 1938, which as a matter of course was highly politically charged as political parties had been curtailed following the capture and exile of their leaders.[5]

Although well-versed in Dutch, *Pujangga Baru* authors consciously wrote in *Bahasa Indonesia*, since they believed that local languages and their written traditions represented the mode of thinking that had led to division in the Archipelago, making European colonial rule possible. These Indonesian activists advocated an embrace of Western ideals, along with modern forms of literary expression as a tool for emancipation. Ultimately, literature would have a utilitarian role in society, acting as a guide in the independence movement and the larger modernisation project. Socialist realism, which had developed during the first decades of the twentieth century, and which was being enforced in Stalin's Soviet Union, clearly influenced Alisjahbana's writings. His idea of the writer as *insinjoer pembentoek djiwa* ('engineer shaping human souls') was also not too far distant from the concept of the writer as (moral) educator of his readers, which is still a fundamental concept in writing in the Malay World, with its profound religious slant.[6]

The writings and ideologies of the *Pujangga Baru* authors, who worked in close contact with colonial institutions, were attractive to writers in the Malay Peninsula. In the 1920s, the example of Balai Pustaka, the colonial Indies publishing house that provided 'good-quality' (i.e. Dutch-sanctioned) reading materials for Indonesian youths, was influential at the Sultan Idris Training College (SITC), where it was emulated in the college's translation bureau and teaching materials. Many of the schoolteachers who became political-cultural activists in Singapore between the 1930s and 1950s were trained at the SITC, where they were exposed to the writings of the *Pujangga Baru* exponents, which subsequently influenced literary works published in the Peninsula during the 1930s.[7] Combined with the forces of nationalism, members of the *Pujangga Baru* movement influenced the development of pride in the Malay language and its proper use among 'the older generation' of post-war writers in the Malay Peninsula.

The literary movements from Indonesia that moved across the Melaka Straits in the 1930s also found a receptive audience among Malay nationalist politicians. The main political movement in pre-war Malaya was the KMM (*Kesatuan Melayu Muda*), led by Ibrahim Yaakob, Ishak Haji Muhammad and Burhanuddin al-Helmy. They viewed island Southeast Asia as a vast Malay world, *Melayu Raya*, which they considered to be a nation that had been divided through British and Dutch colonialism. In the late 1930s, Ibrahim Yaakob gained control of *Warta Malaya*, a newspaper that he used to promote his goal of removing the British from Malaya.[8] When the Japanese invaded, Ibrahim was among those most receptive to their presence. Along with Burhanuddin, he hoped that the unification of Indonesia and Malaya could be continued in the Great Malay Nation that would be free of the colonial powers and would bring welfare to the poor population that had been dominated by 'foreign' powers for so long.

Just as the political aspirations of the KMM leaders were undermined due to their co-operation with the Japanese, so, too, were the *Pujangga Baru* writers, who came to be perceived as backward since they had failed to criticise fascism and had co-operated with the Japanese during the war. At this time, *Pujangga Baru* proponents began to clash with a new group of writers known as *Angkatan 45* (Generation of 45). This new group called for a more nationalistic consciousness in literature, combined with an overwhelming focus on the modern.[9] As soon as the physical struggle for independence ended in Indonesia in 1949, however, a debate over a presumed ideological crisis started in the periodicals that had appeared since the beginning of the Indonesian Revolution. These new literary writings were imbued with universal realism, although in principle they were not that much different from their predecessors. The various authors called for literature to guide the masses into modern life, which became an increasingly dominant point of discussion in periodicals and meetings throughout Indonesia.[10]

The *Pujangga Baru* and *Angkatan 45* movements had a substantial influence on the development of the literary scene in the Peninsula, and more precisely Singapore, through the steady flow of Indonesian materials and the periodic visits of writers. Singapore had always been an important port for Indonesians since it operated as a key node for trade or as the starting point for the *hajj* (pilgrimage). After World War II, Singapore became a site from which goods, including arms and other provisions, were obtained for the Revolution. The Indonesian government also established an office in Singapore during this period, which existed next to other organisations active in the political and social fields, all with the goal of mobilising support for the Revolution and its principles. Many politicians, journalists and other cultural activists from the Peninsula were receptive to such ideas, particularly after their freedoms were curtailed due to the Emergency laws of 1948.[11]

Singapore, the most modern city in the Malay Peninsula, with its thriving printing industry and developing entertainment industry, functioned as a magnet for these cultural and political adventurers. As described by one Malay writer:

> Singapore was the hub of politics, the centre for trade, economic and industrial growth and consequently, the focal point of cultural and social activities. Singapore too was the communication centre for both the government and the people and subsequently the centre for broadcasting, information, publishing, printing, filming and so on, thus attracting artistically inclined individuals and professionals such as journalists, writers, singers, musicians, actors and film stars.[12]

The 'artistically inclined' who arrived in Singapore after 1945 searched for work in the renowned journalistic community. These young writers had been followers of, or at least sympathetic to, Ibrahim Yaakob, who moved to Indonesia where he became a voice for pan-Malayan unity, and Burhanuddin, who became president of Partai Kebangsaan Melayu Malaya (PKMM).

Indonesian literature, as well as tales of the Revolution, influenced the political understanding of many of these young Malay writers, who were tiring of traditional conventions within Malay literature (such as the predominance given to the traditional poetic forms of *gurindam* and *syair*) as well as the role of the traditional elites and colonial rulers. They believed that a new society could be created through activist-oriented literature.

Using their writing as a means to educate the people, they wrote in a more radical tone, tackling problems that previously had been taboo, such as poverty. The goal of their short stories and poems was to point out the flaws of colonial society and traditional Malay understanding of their role in it. As Keris Mas wrote in his biography:

> I did not believe that individuals who were intellectually and spiritually dead would be able to bring about change. Feudalism, religious fanaticism and colonialism would never be changed by people who still left everything to fate, to the *keramat*, and the spirits, still backward, still small minded. Thus saw the proliferation of short stories and poems that looked at society in a critical light in addition to playing up the theme of the independence struggle.[13]

Journalists saw their duty in this context as one in which they could actively fight for the independence of the nation in terms that were not only political but also in relation to issues of modernity.

Activists/Journalists

The journalistic world of post-war Singapore was divided into several groups centring on relatively big publishers. The first, and most often discussed, was the *Utusan Melayu* group that published the newspaper of that name as well as the periodicals *Mastika* and *Utusan Zaman*. The group had been established in 1939 by Yusuf Ishak and was the first all-Malay publishing company owned by Malay shareholders from all layers of society. The editorial board through time consisted of nationalist heavyweights such as Abdul Rahim Kajai, A. Samad Ismail, Ahmad Boestamam, Ishak Haji Muhammad, Said Zahari and several others. Almost inevitably, the editors imbued the newspaper with a distinct nationalist purport. As Said Zahari put it:

> They created a motto based on three causes to be upheld (religion, people and country) and made a sacred pledge in the *Utusan Melayu*'s maiden issue: 'These three causes are what the *Utusan Melayu* stands for, and these *Utusan Melayu* will live for and will fight to the death for'.[14]

The newspaper was a publication owned by and written for Malays, especially in Singapore, where it reached its biggest readership through street sales, and took pride in its openness to the needs and desires of the Malay populace.

Another group of publications was under the influence of Harun Aminurrashid, who had taught at the SITC but was banished to Brunei for his nationalist teachings. After World War II he entered the publishing industry in Singapore, where he became chief editor of an astonishing number of publications, mostly produced at Royal Press on North Bridge Road, of which the magazines *Hiburan, Mutiara, Filem Raya, Fashion* and *Belia* were the most popular. Harun also led the radical newspaper *Melayu Raya* that was temporarily banned after the Maria Hertogh Riots in 1950.[15] Being an 'old' schoolteacher, he was associated with the Singapore Malay Teachers' Union (KGMS), which was a branch of the larger Malay Teachers' Association of Malaya (KPGMS), and later became involved in many of the discussions over the official status of the Malay language.[16]

The third force in the Malay language publishing industry in Singapore after the war was Syed Abdullah bin Abdul Hamid al-Edrus (Edrus), who started out as a journalist with *Utusan Melayu*, but came into conflict with the editors and staff because of his religious fervour and inflexibility. He set up his own publishing company, Qalam, which published an Islamic periodical of the same name as well as religious and political books. He financed these less popular publications by publishing a range of self-authored popular (and rather risqué) novels under his pen name, Ahmad Lutfi, and popular magazines such as *Aneka Warna* and *Filem*. Edrus was a highly controversial figure whose books were once banned by a *fatwa* (religious edict) from the *mufti* (Islamic legal expert) of Johor, and whose periodicals *Warta Masyarakat* and *Qalam* UMNO members in Johor — led by Tunku Abdul Rahman — publicly burned for publishing controversial content that was critical of their party.[17]

These journalists-writers knew one another and met regularly at coffee shops in the Malay quarters of the town. Although generally friendly — as all were working for a common goal — there were also tensions between the different centres, which sometimes caused unhealthy competition between the publishing companies. Through the meetings, and the hothouse atmosphere of such a small group of intellectuals, which also consisted of Malay teachers who gathered at the Royal Press premises, a variety of political beliefs and influences permeated their dialogues.

The PKMM was still influential among many of these young writers, and this often resulted in their arrest and questioning by British authorities, who were also suspicious of any discussions that smacked of communism.[18] Ahmad Boestamam, one of the founders of PKMM and a journalist, for example, served a seven-year sentence in prison (1948–55), and Samad Ismail became well-known for his frequent appearances at the police station and periods spent in gaol. Many also admired the Angkatan 45 authors, whose works were increasingly difficult to acquire since the British wanted to limit their distribution because they appealed to PKMM followers. They began to copy the Indonesian literary style that promoted cultural and political awareness, and followed debates in major publications in Indonesia.

A serious literary magazine — such as the *Pujangga Baru* or one reflecting the work of Angkatan 45 — was not yet viable in Singapore in the late 1940s, as the evolution of *Mastika* exemplifies. This magazine had originally been a forum for didactic editorials and serious short stories. By 1948 its declining popularity forced Yusuf Ishak — before his departure for study in England — to challenge Keris Mas and Samad Ismail to increase its popularity. They quickly turned it into a film magazine with a glossy cover photograph often featuring female Malay stars of the era. When the first cover of the new edition featured famous 'good girl' Kasma Booty, sales took off. Once its fan base was secured, Samad Ismail began to infuse the magazine with more serious literature, transforming it into an opportunity for presenting locally written short stories, as well as translations of writers such as Chekov. *Mastika* eventually became an eclectic journal featuring entertainment news, poetry and even detective stories, and an example of how the lines between serious Malay journalism and entertainment blurred.[19] Be that as it may, *Mastika* retained its reputation for publishing good-quality short stories and poems written by the leading authors of that period. Even more important were *Hiburan* and *Mutiara*, magazines edited by Harun Aminurrashid, which were the channels most of these cultural activists used to gain reputations as authors. *Hiburan* also provided a young activist named Jimmy Asmara with a special column for his network of Pen Pals (*Sahabat Pena*), which would become an important incubator for talented young writers, and the base for membership roles in activist organisations of the 1950s.

By 1950, this diverse young group of writers had grown increasingly vocal in their desire to modernise Malay literature in terms of both language and content. One of the reasons for this was the fact that they were deprived of a left-wing party that could promote Malay interests.[20] Among the most determined in this new stance, often filled with the vigour of possible change and modernity, were such figures as Asraf, Rohaizad, S. Roomai Noor and Jamil Sulong, all of whom had contributed to *Melayu Raya* or *Utusan Melayu*. They were 'young men who were religiously inclined but modern in outlook',[21] and felt that the colonial authorities had victimised and oppressed Malays. Believing that 'old school' writers focused too much on the superficial and on stereotypes, Mohd Arif Mas (aka MAS), a graduate of the SITC, put forward a proposal for a meeting at which a writer's association could be formed. The initial proposal was generally accepted at a meeting of the Singapore Malay Teachers' Union in March 1950, even by those from the 'old school'. It was believed that any differences in their approach were simply due to the style of writing. Eventually, however, the proposal failed due to it being lost within the Byzantine bureaucratic structure of the Teachers' Union.

When the initial proposal for a writer's association fell apart, young scribes at *Hiburan* — especially Hamzah Hussin, Jimmy Asmara and Rosmera — began to consider organising a literary society on their own. MAS now approached Keris Mas, who was a bit older than the other young writers, about forming their own independent group. For membership they tapped into the content of Jimmy Asmara's extensive list of names in the *Sahabat Pena* organisation he managed. The first meeting was held at MAS's house on Henderson Road on 6 August 1950, at which time it was decided to form ASAS 50 (*Angkatan Sasterawan* 50 [ASAS 50], Generation of the Writers of the 1950s). The name was taken following an off-hand comment Hamzah had made, in an attempt to compare them to Angkatan 45, in April of that year when introducing the young writers to a visiting Indonesian scholar. The initial meeting in August 1950 simply set the foundation for ASAS 50, while a subsequent meeting at Hamzah's house in Geylang allowed for the establishment of a more formal structure for the organisation. The Singapore Malay Teachers' Union also developed its own literary association, *Lembaga Bahasa Melayu* (LBM), which was labelled 'old school', on 1 October 1950.

Following the second meeting of ASAS 50, the members began to support activities that would highlight the role that Malay language and literature could play in developing modernity in Singapore, and to reach out to all aspects of society. One of their first activities was a special night market, to promote Malay culture as well as Indonesian and Malay books, which was held at New World Amusement Park on 8 October 1950. These activities, and much of the initial vigour, came from Asraf, who began to oversee an organisation that spread out beyond newspapers and magazines as the members began to find jobs to supplement their meagre income in journalism. From this position, they influenced and pushed their activism and promotion of the modern into schools, the newly developing genre of film, labour activism, and ultimately nationalism. The branching out of membership represented the diversity of views that had originated in the world of journalism and had been influenced by Indonesian literary movements. Their earliest successes were achieved through a series of language congresses, which resulted in the establishment of institutions and policies that still play a role in Singaporean and Malaysian society.

Writing Clearly with Diverse Voices

At the First Malay Language and Literature Congress in 1952, one of the main areas of discussion was the need for a style of writing that would reflect the percolating modern desire to use politics, society and culture as themes to promote self-sufficiency and nationalism. Among the methods to accomplish such goals was a proposal to write in *Rumi*, or Romanised Malay, put forward by the young writers of ASAS 50. The proposal and earlier adoption of this script by the Malay Teachers' Association on the Peninsula had met with strong resistance from the more traditional Singapore teachers of LBM and, as was to be expected, from conservative Islamic parties that emphasised the strong identification of *Jawi*, the Perso-Arabic derived script, with a Muslim-Malay identity. The proposal itself seems rather paradoxical as it came from people who wrote and published in a thriving print industry that predominantly made use of *Jawi*. As the centre of this print industry, 65 per cent of the output of the 14 publishers who were active in Singapore in the 1950s was in *Jawi*, while most of the other 35 per cent consisted of textbooks in *Rumi*. These textbooks were used at schools controlled by the colonial authorities, who promoted *Rumi* to counter an Islamic-inspired definition of Malay identity. Ironically, the nationalistic members of ASAS 50 embraced the propagation of *Rumi*, but based on quite different considerations. Time and again, they showed in their publications a great admiration for the developments in modern culture and literature that were occurring in Indonesia, but their brothers across the Straits could not follow the developments in the Peninsula because they could not read the *Jawi* script, since *Rumi* was the norm in the Indies. Malays, it was argued, should open up to groups within the nation-to-be, but more importantly to the outside world, so that Malay could become a recognised modern language as well as a tool for independence and nationalism.[22]

The emphasis on the modernisation of the Malay language had its own specific relevance in Singapore. Although it is situated at the heart of the Malay World, Singapore is a Chinese city where English was the most important language in public life. The colonial government considered Malay appropriate for primary education, and only allowed English to be used for secondary and tertiary education. This meant that English was important for the development of a career, but was also regarded as the language of the oppressor by Malay nationalist politicians. English was even more important in Singapore, where the Malay population was a minority and public life was in the hands of the Chinese and English. It is therefore no surprise to learn that many Malay political activists sat for their senior

Cambridge examinations, including Ismail Haji Muhammad, A. Samad Ismail and Said Zahari; or that during A. Samad Ismail's detention in the early 1950s Yusuf Ishak wrote his editorials for *Utusan Melayu* in English, which were then translated into Malay; or to read how A. Samad Ismail had to be ordered by his father to read the Malay newspaper instead of the English detective stories that he bought every week; or that the renowned short story writer and journalist Kajai spoke English rather than Malay, except perhaps when he was in debate with someone and would shower the opponent with a flood of abuse. As A. Samad Ismail writes about his language use in the early 1940s:

> A rather important change took place in me. English was the language for daily conversation with my friends. Even Kajai normally would use English with me. Maybe because my Malay at that time was still the bazaar type, the language used at home and the kampung. My English was not so good either, because I only used that language at school. But since I started at *Utusan* and Kajai sent me to attend press conferences, watch film previews and such, I was forced to use English. Actually I was not confident in using the two languages.[23]

Keris Mas was an exception to the rule because he had studied in West Sumatra, so it must have been quite awkward for him when he visited Singapore for the first time in the early 1940s. The influx of Indonesians and people from the Peninsula after the war made Singaporean Malays aware that they were part of the Malay world and that language was an important tool in the struggle for independence. As Keris Mas states in his autobiography, 'English as the official language … was clearly undermining sovereignty'.[24]

While Malays — albeit with some difficulty — began to rally around language and its form of writing as a key issue, frictions began to arise in the community. Although ASAS 50 remained a force, not all young writers accepted it as a representative organisation. For example, although Samad Ismail had no major objections to the formation of such a group, a stance he made even before the initial meeting at the Singapore Malay Teachers' Union, he believed that such an association was unnecessary as long as writers took their job seriously.[25] The greatest opposition, however, came from Hamzah Hussin, one of the founding members. He believed that the phrase 'Art for Society' — which became a popular catchphrase for the organisation soon after its founding — was propaganda masquerading as art, since it seemed to satisfy the artist only. During this period the short stories that were being produced, while extremely nationalistic, were simply too didactic for the audience. In addition, he believed that the writings had taken on an anti-Islamic tone. This conflict seems to have started with a discussion of the Indonesian novel *Atheis* (1949) by Achdiat Karta Mihardja, and was further exacerbated by a poem (*Syurga*) by Asraf in *Mastika* that questioned the existence of heaven. This controversy led to accusations that *Utusan Melayu* was anti-religious, an argument taken up by ex-students of Al-Junaid Secondary School and fanned by Edrus in *Qalam*.[26] Within the literary scene this controversy was the start of a rift between writers proposing the guiding function of literature and others who were more inclined to write in a universal humanist mode. In addition, Hamzah was tiring of the leadership of ASAS 50 — at this time led by Asraf — whom he perceived as being too autocratic and arrogant. In response, Hamzah began promoting 'Art for Art's Sake', believing that ASAS 50 was leading people astray.[27]

Despite such debates, the young nationalistic writers did retain the core belief that the Malay language was the key to a modern, independent nation. By 1955 one of their main goals was accomplished when the Legislative Assembly of the Federation of Malaya adopted Malay as the national language. In the two years after the first Congress, a Department of Malay Studies at the University of Malaya in Singapore was established under the leadership of Za'ba (Zainal Abidin) with the goal of promoting the new national language.[28] While the English-educated Malay students at the university often clashed with the young writers over language use and educational policies, leading Keris Mas to label them as 'arrogant' and 'snobbish',[29] the students' activities reflected the importance of these language and literature groups when they organised themselves as the *Persekutuan Bahasa Melayu Universiti Malaya* (Malay Language Association of the University of Malaya). These students, as well as Hamzah, had opposed many of the basic statements of ASAS 50, and it is true that the diversity of the Malay response to issues surrounding independence was remarkable. At the core, however, was a desire for modernity and independence.

Amid this rising cacophony of voices, a pivotal Malay language conference — the Third Language Congress — was held in April 1956. Here it was proposed that a language institute be established, leading to the development of the Dewan Bahasa dan Pustaka (DBP), which was modelled on Indonesia's Balai Pustaka organisation, led by a group of authors who tried to counter the Institute of People's Culture (LEKRA), which had become closely affiliated with the Indonesian Communist Party after 1949. Within the context of developing a multiracial Malaya and Singapore, the attendees at the conference believed that Malay was the logical choice for a national language, but more importantly, that it could act as a unifier beyond the colonial-tinted English that many of the other ethnic groups preferred.

At this crucial congress, one of the speakers representing the diverse voices of Malay activists was S. Roomai Noor, who made a passionate plea for Malays to gain control over the content of Malay films so that they would reflect the cultural values and proper language of Malays.[30] Roomai Noor was not just a young activist advocating the use of standardised Malay in film; he was the leading romantic star of the early 1950s. Originating from Pahang, he had been an itinerant actor in Indonesia during World War II. Arriving in Singapore in the late 1940s as part of a PKMM youth theatre group, Roomai Noor quickly became a star for MFP (Shaw Brothers' Malay Film Productions), before moving to Cathay Keris in 1954. His activism eventually pushed him behind the camera, where he became one of the first Malay directors in the 1950s, and a studio executive for Cathay in the early 1960s.[31] Throughout his film career, he championed films that would promote both modernity as well as an appreciation of the common man in Malaya. Such an approach was not unique. The film industry was one of the main avenues for the ideas of these young Malay activists, ideas which would come to dominate not only the stories on the screen but also the activities of employees. Much like the earlier push for the romanisation of written Malay, as well as the founding of language institutes, it would have a long-term effect on how Malays perceived themselves in society, reflecting not only language use but also the interconnected networks between language, activism and politics — both cultural and labour — among Malays in the Singapore of the 1950s.

Entertaining Activism

Among the earliest writers to find employment in the film industry were Jamil Sulong and Omar Rojik, who began working as a script writer and common labourer, respectively, in 1950 at MFP, the dominant film studio in Singapore. While films in Singapore — particularly those from the 1950s — were produced to enhance the profit margins of Chinese theatre owners, and were often quite innocuous, many of the Malay intelligentsia understood that they were an avenue for reaching a mass audience. The film industry was thus seen as an extension of the writings published in magazines. Both media enhanced their popularity through the publication of very popular film magazines that also contained short stories. While Roomai Noor used to hang out with writers such as Jamil Sulong and Asraf at the *Utusan Melayu* offices in the late 1940s, these meetings soon shifted to the MFP film studios, which were located near Balestier Road.

Each of these figures made their biggest contribution by promoting modern, nationalistic ideals through the entertainment industry. From this position, they influenced and pushed for the activism their literature promoted into the newly developing genre of film, and in the process they received the support of the biggest stars of the era, who began to infuse many of their films with the ideals of modernity, proper language use and individualism. As the audience for Malay film grew, these young writers began to use its popularity as a conduit for promoting their ideals. For example, P. Ramlee — the biggest star of the era — published his own film magazine, *Bintang* (Star), and the address for the magazine was the same as the office for ASAS 50. P. Ramlee, of course, spent little time writing for the magazine. This task was left to Fatimah Murad, Asraf's wife, who oversaw a staff of activist writers, such as Jamil Sulong and Abdullah Hussain, who paid the bills with innocuous articles about movie stars.[32]

It is easier to understand the issues these activist writers felt were important through the art they produced. Such values are poignantly shown in the film *Penarek Bechak* (The Trishaw Driver, 1955), which P. Ramlee wrote and directed with the support of Jamil Sulong and Abdullah Hussain. The film tells the tale of a trishaw driver named Amran, played by P. Ramlee, who helps a rich young woman named Azizah, played by Sa'adiah, when she is being harassed by a group of spoiled urban youths. To repay him for his kindness, Azizah hires Amran as transportation to her daily lessons at a school named *Wanita Harapan* (Ideal Women), which trains women to be modern housewives by introducing them to appliances such as stoves and sewing machines. Seeing the nobility of his character, Azizah falls in love with Amran. Within the context of a simple drama, P. Ramlee is able to raise a number of issues that reflect the goals of many of the Malay activists who worked in the film community. For example, the film focuses on the conflict between modernity and tradition. Throughout the film, the character Ramlee plays discusses his fate, while Azizah constantly challenges him to stand up as an individual. That she embraces such a poor man is also part of the ideal of overlooking class differences to forge a new union, an independent nation that is not dependent on old traditions.[33]

The popularity of such films allowed Malay activists to push for a greater role in the film-making process, leading to their acceptance as directors and screenwriters, jobs previously dominated by Indians who had been imported from Calcutta and Bombay. By the late 1950s almost all Malay films, whether produced by Cathay Keris or MFP, were written and directed by people who had first found a place in Singapore through their commitment to journalism. Among these activists were Jamil Sulong and Omar

Rojik at MFP, and S. Roomai Noor and Hamzah Hussin at Cathay Keris. As Malayan independence grew closer, the new approaches to understanding society that they advocated grew more apparent in the language used and stories being told on screens throughout the region. Beyond entertaining the audience, their approach to issues such as labour also became representative of many of the tensions in Singapore society during the 1950s.

One of the earliest manifestations of the influence of these activists in the film industry beyond writing and performing was the founding of a film workers union, PERSAMA (*Persatuan Artis Malaya* or Malayan Artists Union), in 1954, with P. Ramlee as the first president and Salleh Ghani and Jamil Sulong as the other main officers. The goals of PERSAMA were common to most trade unions at the time, such as improving the wages of members and acting as a representative for negotiations between employers and employees. By February 1957 PERSAMA was organised well enough to approach the Shaw Brothers to ask for an increase in wages, as well as a new structure for contracts. Most of the employees were hired on a film-to-film basis, and their wages were 'less than street sweepers and janitors'.[34] Only the biggest stars, such as P. Ramlee, were under contract. While these MFP employees received bonuses for each film they completed, and many lived in the Shaw Brothers-owned housing complex on Boon Teck Road, they chaffed at 'good conduct' clauses as well as the time periods, often up to five years, of these contracts. Under these circumstances, PERSAMA representatives made four basic demands: an agreed salary scale for all MFP employees; bigger bonuses for each completed picture; prompt payment of overtime; and one half day off on Saturdays and a full day off on Sundays.[35]

The reply to these demands was received on 3 March: three PERSAMA members were fired from MFP. They were Musalmah, Omar Rojik and H. M. Rohaizad. Musalmah was an actress whose home on Tembeling Road served as PERSAMA's headquarters. Omar Rojik, originally a journalist at *Utusan Melayu*, had worked his way up to assistant director and supporting actor since joining MFP in 1950. In the early 1960s he became one of the leading directors of dramatic political films at MFP. During the strike, Omar was described as a villain in Malay films. The third person fired, Rohaizad, was an assistant director and prominent PERSAMA member. When the protests continued, two of the most vocal agitators, S. Kadarisman and Syed Hassan Safi, who worked as assistant directors, were also fired on 5 March.[36]

The firings shifted the focus of the dispute. PERSAMA members approached leading Malay politicians and cultural figures asking them to issue statements of support. Shortly thereafter, the Malay rulers announced that they would not take sides in the dispute, which further infuriated the workers since the rulers refused to back those they supposedly represented. Protests were planned. With Shaw Brothers declining to negotiate, claiming that the five were fired due to 'non-cooperation and lackness', a strike began on 16 March 1957. Over 120 MFP employees picketed the front of the Jalan Ampas studios, and film production was shuttered. In addition, film stars such as Ahmad Mahmud were seen picketing Queens Cinema in Geylang, where his own film was being shown. The strikers were showered with goods, such as rice and sugar, from sympathetic workers throughout Singapore, which made the area in front of the studio take on the atmosphere of a *pasar malam* (night market). Among the people who provided provisions were Cathay Keris executives who attempted to lure some of the strikers over to their rival studio. In an attempt to gain further support, mass protests occurred — at Happy World amusement park, Pulau Berani and Al-Islamiah Madrasah on Pasir Panjang Road — all public places that were popular gathering places for the Malay community.[37]

Such strikes and protests were not limited to the film industry. Both workers and employees throughout the Peninsula and Singapore were in a state of anxiety over the form of the new nation that was to be created. With the final details of the structure of an independent Malaya being negotiated in London in the first few months of the year, trade union strikes were rampant amidst fears that foreign employers would leave once the security provided by the British presence was removed, and anxiety over the status of Chinese and Indian immigrants in the new nation.[38] Against a background of strong trade union activism, the Malay film industry reflected the larger anxieties of the time.

The convergence of labour issues, activism and the arts was coming to a head. As the protests outside Shaw Brothers' cinemas continued throughout March 1957, the future financial stability of the Singapore studio became increasingly shaky, leading finally to the involvement of Malay politicians. Tunku Abdul Rahman, who five months later was to become the first prime minister of the Federation, sent one of his senior aides, Senu Abdul Rahman, to act as a mediator between the two parties after a delegation including P. Ramlee, Jamil Sulong and Abdullah Hussain travelled to Kuala Lumpur to plead for his intervention. Following two days of negotiations, the strike was resolved on 7 April 1957. Run Run Shaw, who was 'very cooperative and sincere', rehired the five fired employees and the PERSAMA representatives agreed to drop demands for payment of overtime. How the other issues were resolved was not mentioned.[39]

A not-so-subtle artistic critique of the Shaw Brothers' management during the strike, reflecting how Malay activists could spread their message and influence over a variety of mediums, appeared on screen later that year in the film *Mogok* (Strike). Written by former *Utusan Melayu* employee Jamil Sulong, the film tells the story of factory workers who are exploited by a manager — ironically played by S. Kadarisman — who is working with the greedy daughter of their kind, but distant, employer. The film intersperses the day-to-day toils of the factory workers with monologues in which Omar Rojik and several other workers discuss the importance of union representation for a stable nation. After a series of accidents, including the factory owner's daughter hitting an employee with a car, the manager burns down the house of a suffering female employee. Just as the workers are about to riot, the kindly factory owner arrives. He fires the manager, disowns his daughter, and embraces the workers and their union as vital components of a prosperous future for all.

By mid-1957, the excitement over the future an independent Malaya held for the region, including the politically, socially and economically interlinked city-port of Singapore, made such hopes seem possible. Labour and the arts were worth fighting for. Debates were raging on the future make-up of the nation, and a sense of the possibilities that modernity and independence held permeated the air with a vibrancy that excited and invigorated the populace of the region. Much of this debate, as had been advocated since the late-1940s, was in the Malay language.

Conclusion: *Majulah Singapura*

The Third Malay Language Congress in 1956 solidified many of the goals and aspirations of Malay activists. The Congress focused on how the Malay language could enrich the nationalist experience, and the methods by which it could be infused into society through literature, film and the arts. Among the participants at the conference was Zubir Said, a composer of music and *bangsawan* (theatre) performer who had migrated to Singapore from West Sumatra in 1947. In his speech before the delegates he proclaimed that music could be more than entertainment, and could serve as a way to express nationalist feelings throughout the land. His stance impressed many in the audience, and in July the following year, 1957, he introduced a number of patriotic songs to the public at a specially arranged concert at Victoria Theatre to celebrate the pending independence of Malaya. The songs composed for this concert, while in the Malay language, were not meant to be exclusive. They were a conduit for the entire population of the Peninsula and Singapore to celebrate in a language that was not tied to colonialism. Such songs were to represent a new beginning for a new nation.[40]

Following the triumphant concert at Victoria Theatre, Zubir Said became established as a nationalist, not just a Malay, musician. In 1958, Syed Ali Redha, a member of the Legislative Assembly, approached the composer to write a song specifically about Singapore that would capture the hopes of many for the city-port and its place in the region. The song was *Majulah Singapura* (Onward Singapore), whose simple lyrics are still sung by school children every day in Singapore, and at all official events. The song was first performed at the Victoria Theatre in September 1958. The next year, it was adopted as the official anthem of Singapore, and was first performed in this capacity on 3 December 1959, when Yusuf Ishak was installed as the head of state, the *Yang Dipertuan Negara*.[41] The symbolism of various ethnic groups in Singapore singing a Malay song to celebrate the installation of the founder of *Utusan Melayu* as the head of state represented a culmination of many of the goals of activist-journalists in the 1950s.

Although Malay activists had been united in the idea of an independent nation, and the role of the Malay language within it, the differences among them, as well as shifts in politics, economics and society, began to pull them apart. The film industry, for example, was moribund by the early 1960s. Film, now beginning to compete with television, began to move away from many of the goals of earlier activist-influenced films, such as *Penarek Bechak*. In addition, important figures such as Jamil Sulong were shunted to the side. The 1957 strike had been a turning point for the film industry, as well as for many of the artists and activists who had been promoting the Malay language and modernity. Their attempts to tap all of the resources at the Shaw Brothers' disposal seemed to lead to further anxieties and tensions among the Malay staff. In addition, resentment over labour issues remained at MFP. Over the next five years there were numerous strikes, work slowdowns and protests. However, within the union there was little unity. The financial situation was unstable, and considerable tension existed between the technicians and artists over the role of culture and politics in Malay film, resulting in a stark decline in the quality of the films. While there was a brief period of nationalistic films made at Cathay Keris in the early 1960s, under the influence of S. Roomai Noor and the young firebrand director Hussain Haniff, MFP's main rival also went into decline. At MFP labour issues and the economics of film undermined any activism, while at Cathay Keris the employees began to chafe under the leadership of Tom Hodge, an Englishman who was best remembered for his attempts to cut film budgets and his dislike of activist cinema.[42] By 1961 Run Run Shaw had reached the limit of his patience with the loss-making studio and its labour problems. He purchased Merdeka Studios in an attempt to transfer production to Kuala Lumpur, where costs would be less than in the volatile labour market of Singapore. In 1963 Shaw Brothers transferred most of their Malay language film production to Kuala Lumpur; Cathay Keris sputtered along until the mid-1960s with minuscule budgets.[43] Many of the Malay language activists who worked in the film industry — including Jamil Sulong, S. Roomai Noor and P. Ramlee — made the move to the Malaysian capital at about this time.

The decline of the Malay film industry in Singapore was mirrored in developments in the lives of almost all of these activists/journalists, who fell from power or left the port city. By the late 1950s Keris Mas was busy developing the Dewan Bahasa dan Pustaka, which moved to Kuala Lumpur after a brief period in Johor Baru. *Utusan Melayu*'s reputation as a leftist newspaper also gradually diminished following British restrictions when A. Samad Ismail was arrested in the early 1950s, and his banishment to the Jakarta office in 1957. The newspaper was finally shut down after it came into open conflict with Tunku Abdul Rahman and UMNO in 1961.[44] A. Samad Ismail became the editor of *Berita Harian*, the Malay version of the English *Straits Times*, and moved to Kuala Lumpur, where in the early 1960s he eventually switched to UMNO from an earlier allegiance to the PAP, which he felt had relinquished its left-leaning policies and ideology.

Still, many of the goals of these activists/journalists had been achieved. Malay was the official national language, and people were learning it in schools and singing it as their national anthem. The ability to create a truly independent mindset through the arts seemed possible in the 1950s and Singapore had been the focus of many of these activities.

NOTES

1   William R. Roff, *The Origins of Malay Nationalism* (Kuala Lumpur: Oxford University Press, 1967).

2   The nature of these debates and how they influenced the development of the community is the subject of a number of studies, including a recent doctoral thesis by Mark Emmanuel. Also see Roff, *The Origins of Malay Nationalism*; and Ariffin Omar, *Bangsa Melayu: Malay Concepts of Democracy and Community, 1945–1950* (Kuala Lumpur: Oxford University Press, 1993).

3   While described as 'Malay', these networks were perhaps more accurately described as Muslim, since they comprised people of Indian and Arabic descent, and also included 'Indonesians' who visited Singapore for longer or shorter periods.

4   Arena Wati, *Memoir Arena Wati: Enda Gulingku* (Bangi: Penerbit Universiti Kebangsaan Malaysia, 1991), p. 358.

5   Keith Foulcher, *'Pujangga Baru': Literature and Nationalism in Indonesia, 1933–1942* (Bedford Park: Flinders University, 1980); Henk Maier, *We Are*

Playing Relatives: A Survey of Malay Writing (Leiden: KITLV, 2004), p. 279.

6   Maier, *We Are Playing Relatives*, pp. 186–92.

7   Ibid., pp. 219–24.

8   This takeover financed with Japanese funds alienated him from other activists, such as A. Samad Ismail and Ishak Haji Muhammad. A. Samad Ismail, *Memoir A. Samad Ismail di Singapura* (Bangi: Penerbit Universiti Kebangsaan Malaysia, 1993), p. 93.

9   Keith Foulcher, 'Literature, Cultural Politics, and the Indonesian Revolution', in *Text/Politics in Island Southeast Asia*, ed. D. M. Roskies (Athens, Ohio: Ohio University Center for International Studies, 1993), pp. 230–1.

10 Maier, *We Are Playing Relatives*, pp. 284–90; A. Teeuw, *Modern Indonesian Literature* (The Hague: Martinus Nijhoff, 1979), pp. 114–42.

11 Firdaus Haji Abdullah, *Radical Malay Politics: Its Origin and Early Development* (Petaling Jaya: Pelanduk Publications, 1985), pp. 52–6; Ibrahim Chik, *Memoir Ibrahim Chik: Dari API ke Rejimen ke-10* (Bangi: Penerbit Universiti Kebangsaan Malaysia, 2004), pp. 37, 61.

12 Keris Mas, *The Memoirs of Keris Mas: Spanning 30 Years of Literary Development*, tr. Shah Rezad Ibrahim and Nor Azizah Abu Bakar (Kuala Lumpur: Dewan Bahasa dan Pustaka, 2004), p. 59.

13 Ibid., p. 55.

14 Said Zahari, *Dark Clouds at Dawn: A Political Memoir* (Kuala Lumpur: Insan, 2001), p. 53.

15 Firdaus Haji Abdullah, *Radical Malay Politics*, pp. 125–40.

16 He was also involved in political parties such as PKMM and Parti Rakyat Singapura, which he led until the elections of 1959. Abdullah Hussain, *Harun Aminurrashid Pembangkit Semangat Kebangsaan* (Kuala Lumpur: Dewan Bahasa dan Pustaka, 1982), p. 211.

17 Talib Samat, *Ahmad Lutfi: Penulis, Penerbit dan Pendakwah* (Kuala Lumpur: Dewan Bahasa dan Pustaka, 2002), pp. 10–11.

18 Syed Hussin Ali, 'Pertubuan-pertubuan Bahasa dan Sastera Melayu di Singapura selepas Perang Dunia II (Khasnya Asas 50)', Honours Thesis, University of Malaya, 1959, p. 20.

19 Keris Mas, *The Memoirs of Keris Mas*, pp. 70–3, 99. In the mid-1950s, Othman Wok wrote a series of highly popular ghost stories for the magazine which succeeded in boosting its sales; Othman Wok, *Never in My Wildest Dreams* (Singapore: SNP Editions, 2000), pp. 133–4.

20 Firdaus Haji Abdullah, *Radical Malay Politics*, pp. 118–22.

21 Keris Mas, *The Memoirs of Keris Mas*, p. 85.

22 Apart from these ideological considerations, economic ones also seem to have played an important role, since the adoption of *Rumi* would allow for access to a market of 70–75 million potential readers. Abdul Aziz Hussain, 'Penerbitan buku2 dan majallah2 Melayu di-Singapura di-antara bulan September 1945 dengan bulan September 1958', Honours Thesis, University Malaya Singapore, 1959; Jan van der Putten, 'Configuring Malay Identity through Script', paper presented at a KITLV Workshop, Jakarta, November 2004.

23 A. Samad Ismail, *Memoir A. Samad Ismail di Singapura*, p. 84.

24 Keris Mas, *The Memoirs of Keris Mas*, p. 94.

25 Ibid., p. 105.

26 Arena Wati, *Memoir Arena Wati*, pp. 285–6; Abdullah Hussain, *Sebuah Perjalanan* (Kuala Lumpur: Dewan Bahasa dan Pustaka, 2005), pp. 521, 548, 594–8; A. Samad Ismail, *Memoir A. Samad Ismail di Singapura*, p. 185.

27 Virginia Matheson Hooker, *Writing a New Society: Social Change through the Novel in Malay* (Honolulu: University of Hawaii Press, 2000), pp. 185–6.

28 Apparently, this department and chair were co-funded by Malay teachers, who allowed their salaries to be cut by 1.5 per cent for this purpose; Abdullah Hussain, *Sebuah Perjalanan*, p. 144.

29 Ibid., p. 178.

30 Abdullah Hussain and Nik Safiah Karim, eds., *Memoranda Angkatan Sastrawan '50*, Second edition (Petaling Jaya: Fajar Bakti, 1987), pp. 156–64.

31 Timothy P. Barnard, 'Vampires, Heroes and Jesters: A History of Cathay Keris', in *The Cathay Story*, ed. Wong Ain-ling (Hong Kong: Hong Kong Film Archive, 2002), pp. 124–41.

32 Yusnor Ef, personal communication, December 2003; James Harding and Ahmad Sarji, *P. Ramlee: The Bright Star* (Subang Jaya: Pelanduk, 2002), pp. 102–3; Abdullah Hussain, *Sebuah Perjalanan*, pp. 527–39, 594.

33 Abdullah Hussain, *Sebuah Perjalanan*, p. 617; Rohayati Paseng Barnard and Timothy P. Barnard, 'The Ambivalence of P. Ramlee: *Penarek Beca* and *Bujang Lapok* in Perspective', *Asian Cinema* 13, 2 (2002): 9–23.

34 Abdullah Hussain, *Sebuah Perjalanan*, pp. 603–17; Jamil Sulong, *Kaca Permata: Memoir Seorang Pengarah* (Kuala Lumpur: Dewan Bahasa dan Pustaka, 1993), p. 130.

35 *The Straits Times*, 28 February 1957, p. 4.

36 *The Straits Times*, 4 March 1957, p. 4; Ahmad Sarji, *P. Ramlee: Erti yang Sakti* (Subang Jaya, Selangor: Pelanduk Publications), pp. 190–1, 216, 326–7; Jamil Sulong, *Kaca Permata*, p. 130; *The Straits Times*, 4 March 1957, p. 4; *The Straits Times*, 6 March 1957, p. 5.

37 Harding and Ahmad, *P. Ramlee: The Bright Star*, p. 137; Jamil Sulong, *Kaca Permata*, pp. 130–2; *The Straits Times*, 4 March 1957, p. 4; *The Straits Times*, 6 April, 1957, p. 7; Mohd. Zamberi A. Malek, *Suria Kencana: Biografi Jins Shamsudin* (Bangi: Universiti Kebangsaan Malaysia, 1998), p. 232; Abdullah Hussain, *Sebuah Perjalanan*, p. 609; Barnard, 'Vampires, Heroes and Jesters', p. 129.

38 For more information on such labour issues, and the context, see T. N. Harper, *The End of Empire and the Making of Malaya* (Cambridge: Cambridge University Press, 1998); Abdullah Hussain, *Sebuah Perjalanan*, p. 609.

39 *The Straits Times*, 8 April 1957, p. 4; Abdullah Hussain, *Sebuah Perjalanan*, pp. 539, 612–7.

40 Abdullah Hussain and Nik Safiah Karim, eds., *Memoranda Angkatan Sastrawan '50*; Arena Wati, *Memoir Arena Wati*, pp. 357–60; Sulaiman Jeem and Abdul Ghani Hamid, *Mengenang Pak Zubir* (Singapore: Pustaka Melayu, 1988).

41 Sulaiman Jeem and Abdul Ghani Hamid, *Mengenang Pak Zubir.*

42 Harding and Ahmad, *P. Ramlee: The Bright Star*, pp. 136–8; Mohd. Zamberi, *Suria Kencana*, p. 232–4; Barnard, 'Vampires, Heroes and Jesters', pp. 132–41.

43 Harding and Ahmad, *P. Ramlee: The Bright Star*, pp. 185–6; Barnard, 'Vampires, Heroes and Jesters', pp. 132–41.

44 Said Zahari, *Dark Clouds at Dawn*, pp. 70–6.

8

Civil Society and
the Malay Education Council

E. Kay Gillis

In 1951, the British colonial administration introduced sweeping changes to Malay education in Singapore. The most significant change was that English was to become the main medium of education in Malay schools. The Malay community had strong objections to the new policy and wished to have the decision reversed. After a mass meeting of Malay community organisations, it was decided to form a Malay Education Council whose objective would be to work towards a change of policy. In doing this, the leaders of the Malay community were taking the path of civil society action, a long-familiar tactic in dealing with unpopular policy initiatives in colonial Singapore, and one that would eventually lead to a successful outcome for the Malay Education Council.

This particular campaign was just one of many taking place in Singapore during the 1950s. However, this campaign was extraordinary in that the Malay Education Council was the only organisation prepared to take advantage of the contemporary political situation in Singapore to achieve its objectives. The leaders of the Council began their campaign using traditional methods of negotiation in the informal political sphere. When this was unsuccessful, they switched tactics to find a political way to achieve policy change. They did this by taking advantage of the newly emerged competitive political arena. This was an exciting new development in the history of civil society in Singapore and signalled that a new era of public policy debate had begun. However, this era would prove to be short-lived.

The Malay Education Council and its drive to restore Malay as the medium of education in Malay schools is now only a footnote in Singapore's history. There is little evidence to show that it ever took place and a search for information in the popular history texts of this period proved fruitless. The only real evidence of this campaign is to be found in the Education Department annual reports, and a thesis that was able to incorporate a range of primary resource material from within the Education Department itself.[1] However, the Malay Education Council campaign is important to the history of political development in Singapore because it provides evidence that during one brief period of time, a community organisation was able to overturn public policy by taking advantage of the existence of a competitive political environment. It is also important to note that it was one of the last successful public policy campaigns in Singapore. This chapter will show just how limited the window of opportunity for this particular policy negotiation would prove to be. Following the elections for internal self-government in 1959, the approach to organisational activity changed radically and it became increasingly difficult for any group to influence or even attempt to influence public policy. After 1963, the competitive political environment that had made the Malay Education Council campaign possible began to dwindle and has not yet returned.

Civil society is a much-contested term, and it is important to find a definition that will provide a basis for discussion on the workings of the Malay Education Council. The term is used here in the post-Marxist sense and is defined as a range of voluntary independent groups that are prepared to use political means to influence public policy. Two key words in the definition need further clarification. The word *voluntary* indicates that the members of the organisation have joined of their own accord and that they can change alignment and opinion without fear of the consequences. This freedom of association breeds tolerance and moderation. The *independent* nature of the organisations is dependent on their ability to pursue their own interests. In many authoritarian regimes, policy debate takes place through groups that have been created and controlled by the state. These are not considered to be part of civil society. The definition excludes purely social organisations formed for recreation, entertainment or religious and spiritual purposes. Organisations participate in policy debate through both the formal and informal political spheres. During the colonial period, the absence of a competitive political system meant that organisations used the informal sphere to contest policy. In the 1950s, the emergence of a competitive political sphere created by the Rendel Commission provided the first opportunity for organisations to make use of the formal political sphere.

Civil Society and Imperialism

How realistic is it to talk about organisational activity in a colonial environment? It would seem that the colonial situation is generally unlikely to provide an encouraging political environment for the emergence of civil society. However, the broad legislative arrangements reveal some opportunities for policy debate in the political arena. The presence in the legislative body of nominated members of the public, usually referred to as 'unofficials', stimulated debate on public policy. The presence of an Official Majority meant that these unofficial members could not overturn proposed government legislation.[2] However, the unofficials had some measure of power in policy debate through a provision in the constitution that obliged the governor to report to London on any issue which sparked strong objections from the unofficial members.[3] This was a deliberate measure to prevent an autocratic governor from overriding what was taken to be public opinion. It allowed organisations a significant level of influence in policy debate and encouraged the emergence of civil society. The presence of an Official Majority until 1942 meant that organisations operated within the informal political sphere.

In 1948, the colonial government introduced an Unofficial Majority into the local legislative body for the first time. This provided a more competitive environment for policy debate and encouraged the emergence of a competitive political party system. Elected representation was also introduced in 1948 as a first step towards self-government. Although the British retained discretionary powers that allowed them to overrule policy decisions, these powers were not used lightly or indiscriminately. In 1955, the introduction of the Rendel Constitution created for the first time a Legislative Assembly that consisted of fully elected unofficial members. This provided a competitive formal political sphere for the operation of civil society. The Malay Education Council was able to take advantage of this to influence public policy on Malay education.

The Rise and Fall of Civil Society in Singapore

The residents of Singapore had been active in the informal political sphere in Singapore since 1820, when the first public meeting was held to protest against the imposition of taxes in the port.[4] During the next 50 years, traders and merchants challenged many of the policies laid down by the Board of Control of the East India Company in London or by the Indian Government. They took imaginative and aggressive steps to overturn policies that they considered to be unacceptable.[5] By 1867, the mercantile community had developed a variety of practices and techniques for influencing public policy in the informal political sphere, and had established the first formal organisation, the Singapore Chamber of Commerce, to support its endeavours. At a local level, the traders held public meetings, signed petitions, and encouraged the newspapers to support their position. They also used London-based organisations to support their stand against policies. When the Colonial Office took over the administration of the Straits Settlements in 1867, the mercantile community had established the right to influence public policy. The British seemed to accept this right, and continued down the path of tolerance towards public action. The level of activity tended to ebb and flow over time, but existed throughout the period of British power. Although the Straits Settlements Legislative Council that was formed in 1867 had an Official Majority, the governor's obligation to report to London on any legislation which sparked strong objections from unofficial members gave this nominated group some measure of influence in policy debate. The British took some measures to restrain organisational activity through the introduction of a Societies Act in 1890, but legitimate groups that were politically active in Singapore during the period of British power had little to fear from the legislation.[6] It should be understood, however, that these organisations and activities were largely the sphere of European residents, although some 'respectable' Asians did take part.

In the nineteenth century, there existed a range of commercially oriented groups such as the Singapore Chamber of Commerce, the Singapore Chinese Chamber of Commerce, and the Straits Settlements Association. Other associations representing other interests began to emerge at the end of the nineteenth century. The formation of a number of anti-opium societies led to a long campaign against the sale and distribution of opium. The anti-opium movement in Singapore utilised the worldwide anti-opium movement to support its activities. Several important ethnic organisations were also formed to promote community interests, such as the Straits Chinese British Association, established in 1900, and the Eurasian Association, formed in 1919.[7] Malay interests were represented by the *Kesatuan Melayu Singapura* (KMS), created in 1926. In 1920, the British initiated important political reforms in the Straits Settlements Legislative Council. These reforms provided for representation in the Legislative Council for all racial communities, giving the minority communities, in particular, a voice in policy debate. The Malay and Eurasian communities were allocated one seat each. This allocation reflected the social and economic 'balance of forces' in the community, rather than the racial arithmetic.[8] The British had always encouraged separate ethnic representation in an informal way in order to try to get the views of each community, and the constitutional changes of 1922 formally institutionalised it. The high standard of representation by the unofficial members from the ethnic communities stimulated debate. In particular, minority leaders Mohammed Eunos bin Abdullah and Dr Noel Clarke gave the Malay and Eurasian communities a forceful voice in the Legislative Council. Eunos introduced policy debate on educational issues, and lobbied vigorously for the restoration of Malay rights. The issue most associated with Eunos and the KMS during this period was the provision of land for a Malay settlement at Geylang.[9] Dr Clarke lobbied hard for 'qualified Asiatics' to enter the Malayan Civil Service.[10] The aspirations of the many qualified Eurasians were eventually denied, but a separate Straits Settlements Civil Service (SSCS) was created that would offer cadetships to local candidates with tertiary qualifications.[11]

After the end of the Japanese Occupation, civil society re-emerged in a different form. The rapid growth of nationalism and the British decision to set Singapore on the path of self-determination led to the emergence of a more aggressive style of public action. Trade unions lobbied hard for improved wages and conditions and regularly organised strike action. A unified campaign to protest against the separation of Singapore from Malaya in the Malay Union proposal led to the emergence of multicultural organisations. The British recognised the legitimacy of left-wing organisations, and left-wing representatives were nominated to the Governor's Advisory Council in the immediate post-war period.[12] The introduction of a limited number of elected Legislative Council seats in 1948 encouraged the emergence of political parties. The Malayan Emergency Regulations slowed down left-wing activities from 1948 to 1953 but moderate organisations flourished. After the Emergency Regulations were eased in 1953, the left-leaning organisations re-emerged. Trade union activity led to the introduction of several important pieces of labour legislation, including the Labour Ordinance of 1955, which made provision for an eight-hour working day, and the payment of overtime and sick leave entitlements. Trade unions and student unions often rejected official channels and attempted to win policy decisions through strikes and sit-ins, as in the case of the Hock Lee Bus strike, which began in April 1955 and continued until May 12. As a result of the strike, the bus company was forced to dissolve its in-house 'yellow' union and reinstate sacked strikers. Student unions in the Chinese middle schools managed to prevent the introduction of national service through a series of strikes. Student union activity also helped to raise the profile of Chinese schools and led to important reforms in Chinese education. The competitive political environment and the rapid approach of independence encouraged popular political participation from 1953 until 1959. This high level of group activity provided the backdrop to the Malay Education Council campaign, which began in 1951.

After 1959, this climate of political effervescence began to change. It is important to provide evidence here of the fall of civil society as it will emphasise the small window of opportunity that existed for groups to participate in the formal political sphere. The People's Action Party (PAP) easily won the 1959 election and took power. This appeared to herald the beginning of a golden age of civil society, and association leaders antici-pated a crucial role in policy debate in the final years of British power. The reality, however, was somewhat different. Within four years, associa-tional activity changed radically in both form and content. It was steadily dismantled through regulation, absorption and co-option. By 1975, it had disappeared altogether.

The split in the party in 1961 precipitated the dismantling process. Since its formation in 1954, the PAP had consisted of two wings. Lee Kuan Yew led the moderate faction, and Lim Chin Siong the left-wing faction. The two wings of the party had managed to reach a working compromise which enabled them to remain partners and win the 1959 election. In 1961, however, pressures between the factions began to show and the party split over the issue of merger between an independent Malaya and Singapore. Lim Chin Siong's left-wing faction was against merger and split away from the PAP to form a new party, the Barisan Sosialis (BS). With the departure of the left-wing faction, the PAP lost most of its branch and grassroots support, leaving only the leadership in the hands of the PAP.[13] For the PAP leaders to achieve a merger with Malaya, they needed to win acceptance for it through a referendum, which was held in September 1962. In order to undermine support for their political rivals in the referendum, the PAP used a variety of tactics to discredit and dismantle any groups that supported the BS.

The crisis provided the backdrop to the growing intolerance towards community groups. The leaders needed to control and regulate grassroots consultation. They rapidly established community centres to build up grass-roots support for the PAP, and to provide an alternative channel for dissent. In the name of national integration, the PAP leaders took this opportunity to reduce the power of the ethnic organisations.[14] Rather than abolish these associations, the PAP leaders co-opted ethnic leaders to serve as office bearers in the new government grassroots organisations that provided a conduit for policy transference and the spread of government ideology.[15] These groups and their leaders were influential, and in harnessing their support to the PAP's political objectives, the new channel simultaneously broadened its support and incorporated the existing community elites into the new structure.[16] Through the process of co-option, absorption and de-politicisation, the network of ethnic organisations that had provided support during the Malay Education Council campaign had all but disappeared within ten years. The dismantling of trade unions and student unions took a little longer. Student unions were coerced through arrest and banishment, and students were forced to comply with state-designed codes of behaviour through the introduction of suitability certificates for entry into the local university. Corporate strategies in labour relations led to the replacement of collective bargaining through trade unions with government-sponsored settlement procedures. By 1975, the dismantling of civil society was complete.

Post-War Malay Nationalism

In the post-war period, Singapore had become an important centre for Malay intellectual and nationalist activity. In the previous chapter Timothy Barnard and Jan van der Putten provide us with evidence of the Malay intellectual debates taking place during this period. These debates were stimulated by the work of journalists working on Malay newspapers such as *Utusan Melayu*. It was predominantly through the Malay press that the Malay community at large was exposed to nationalist sentiments. Barnard and van der Putten shows that leaders of the Singapore Malay Teachers' Union were eager participants in the intellectual and nationalist discussions occurring in coffee shops and restaurants in Bussorah Street and North Bridge Road in the late 1940s. Many of the Malay teachers in Singapore were graduates of the Sultan Idris Training College for Malay Teachers at Tanjong Malim in Perak. The college had been an important focus for Malay literature and scholarship since it opened in 1922, and in the post-war period, it was an important centre for the emergence of Malay nationalism. The outpouring of Malay nationalist sentiments and the activism of Malay educational leaders provided a stimulus to the Malay Education Council campaign, which began in 1951.

British Policies on Malay Education

British educational policy until 1942 displayed a 'fundamental inequality' of treatment towards the Malays.[17] Policies dealing with Malay education were adopted to suit rural Malays and were designed to fit students for a career in peasant agriculture. The attempt to impose a rural education on schools in an urban setting denied a generation of young Singapore Malays the opportunity to learn the mix of skills needed for life in an urban community.[18] Malay vernacular schools did not teach English and did not extend beyond primary school. This prevented Malay students from entering commercial or government employment, and condemned students to be 'peons, punkah pullers, motor car drivers and attap cutters'.[19] In the Annual Report for Perak in 1906, E. W. Birch, Resident of Perak, claimed that the objective of Malay education should be 'that Malay children should be taught to be clean, punctual and amenable to discipline' and to make the children 'useful in their homes and callings'. The appointment of Richard Winstedt as Chief Inspector of Schools in 1916 promised to bring important changes to Malay education. Winstedt was acknowledged to be a fine Malay scholar and there is evidence that he understood the problems faced by a Malay student wanting to attend secondary school.[20] Yet despite his knowledge of these problems, Winstedt permitted this system to persist.

An attempt in the 1920s and 1930s to unify politically the ill-assorted settlements of Malaya and Singapore hampered the development of an education system that would serve the needs of the urban cosmopolitan population of Singapore.[21] It was not until the final years before the Japanese Occupation that the government admitted that uniformity of educational policy between the Malay States and Singapore was neither 'necessary nor desirable'.[22] By 1942, however, the British had failed to introduce an educational system in Singapore relevant to the needs of urban Malays.

Significant Shifts in Malay Education Policy

Between 1945 and 1951, the number of Malay schools doubled, from 21 to 42, and attendance at Malay schools also doubled, from 4,102 to 8,505.[23] Despite these encouraging figures, the proportion of Malay students attending Malay schools in fact dropped during this period.[24] The Department of Education interpreted these figures as meaning that a 'large majority of Singapore parents' had shown an 'unmistakable desire' to receive an English education, and announced that government-run Malay schools would make a 'gradual change into English schools'.[25] This heralded a significant departure from traditional policy on Malay schools. The first step was taken in May 1951, when the Department announced that English would become part of the regular curriculum in Malay schools, instead of being offered as an option on Saturday mornings. Within a year, three trained teachers and 86 trainee teachers were teaching English in Malay schools and had introduced a considerable level of English into the system.[26]

This change of attitude was further encouraged by the publication of the Barnes Report on Malay Education in Malaya in 1951. The report was the outcome of a committee composed of Malays and Europeans under the chairmanship of L. J. Barnes.[27] It recommended that the system of separate vernacular schools should be abolished in favour of National Schools open to all races and with English and Malay as the languages of instruction.[28] The Singapore government had not commissioned the Barnes Report and the Department of Education in Singapore was under no obligation to accept its advice. However, its publication stimulated the British to revise Malay education in vernacular schools in Singapore to make it more relevant to the realities of employment in the post-war period.

In 1951, the Education Department announced a new Malay education policy called the Re-Orientation Plan, to be introduced from 1 January 1952.[29] Under the plan, Malay pupils would use Malay as the sole medium of instruction in the first three years, and then would receive all tuition, except Malay language and literature, in English for the remainder of their primary school education.[30] Pupils who completed primary school could qualify for special Malay classes in an English secondary school. The government hoped that this plan would provide Malays with increased employment opportunities and would also allow Malay pupils to pursue post-secondary education.[31] The government believed that the 'salvation of the Malay community from poverty and ignorance lay in the magic formula of English education'.[32] It proposed to implement the plan on 1 January 1952 in Geylang Boys School, Tanglin Tinggi Boys' School, Geylang Craft Centre, Kampong Melayu School and Scotts Road Malay School.[33]

The Malay Education Council

The implementation of the Re-Orientation Plan began as planned in January 1952. Only a few students (550 boys and girls) were affected and there was no serious impact on the Malay community. Two years later, however, the education of more than 1,600 Malay children was affected by the plan. Resentment began to grow and the Malay community began to have serious misgivings about the scheme. Malay leaders feared that the Malay students would adopt new values and lose their Malay habits and customs.[34] They believed that Malay culture and education would face extinction. The plan was perceived as a 'sinister attempt by Government to stifle the Malay way of life'.[35] After two years of operation, the Singapore Malay Teachers' Union (SMTU) asked the Education Department to rescind the plan but did not offer any alternatives.[36] The Singapore branch of the United Malays National Organisation (UMNO) remained silent on the issue and there was no Malay community organisation that could take it up.[37]

In April 1954, five Malay organisations met and formed the Malay Education Council Joint Committee to meet with the Education Department to discuss the Re-Orientation Plan.[38] The organisations were the UMNO, the Peninsula Malay Union of Singapore (PMU), the SMTU, the Federation of Malay Students and the Muslim Society of University of Malaya.[39] These groups represented a broad cross-section of the Malay community and their opinions could be considered to reflect community concerns. The plan was by then in its last two stages and the Department was reluctant to halt its progress.

In August 1954, the Joint Committee decided to organise a meeting of all Malay/Muslim organisations in Singapore to formulate an education plan of its own to be offered as an alternative to the government.[40] It took nearly a year to organise the meeting but in July 1955, 32 Malay/Muslim organisations met to form a new body, the *Majlis Pelajaran Melayu* or Malay Education Council (MEC).[41] The presence of so many important community organisations demonstrated a unity of purpose on the issue within the Malay/Muslim community. The new Council was directed to submit alternative educational proposals to the authorities for their consideration. The committee of the MEC drew up an alternative education plan that demanded the return of Malay as the medium of instruction in Malay schools, and proposed the establishment of Malay secondary schools, a Malay college to train Malay teachers, and a Malay university.[42] In August 1955, the MEC sent a copy of the MEC plan with a covering letter to the Minister of Education, Mr Chew Swee Kee. In the letter, the Council demanded the 'immediate cessation of the Re-Orientation Plan for Singapore Malay Schools'.[43] The Minister of Education met with the leaders of the MEC on two occasions in September and October 1955, and offered to look into Malay grievances. The Department of Education Report of 1956 subsequently stated that as there were 'scarcely any teachers educated above secondary school', many of these demands were impractical.[44]

However, the Education Department did respond to the demand for more Malay teachers, and offered special classes for Malay teachers at the Teachers Training College in 1957. Meanwhile, the Department went ahead with plans to introduce three Malay secondary classes in January 1956 at Siglap Secondary School.[45] The government argued that the school was conveniently located in a Malay area and the principal of the school was a Malay. However, the secondary classes were termed 'Malay' because there were Malay students attending the classes, not because they were taught in the Malay language. The secondary classes proved to be unpopular with parents, and were re-absorbed into the English stream.[46]

In February 1956, the Department of Education responded to the MEC demands by setting up a Malay Education Working Committee (MEWC) to explore ways of improving Malay education and to examine the use of Malay as a medium of instruction in secondary education.[47] The committee as proposed by the Department was representative and was to include the presidents of the MEC and the Singapore Malay Teachers' Union.[48] The MEC leadership and the Singapore Malay Teachers' Union were very suspicious of the composition of the working committee and rejected the invitation to participate in it. There was an attempt at a compromise to appease the two Malay groups but eventually the whole idea was shelved. A half-hearted attempt to form another independent committee also met the same fate.[49] The MEC had been struggling in vain to have its views heard since August 1955. The Council leaders now decided to change tactics and made a decision to politicise the matter. The ruling Labour Front coalition headed by David Marshall was rather vulnerable at this time and this allowed the MEC to take advantage of inter-party competition to pursue its interests.

In 1955, elections under the Rendel Constitution were introduced in Singapore. Through this constitution, the British transferred considerable power to a new, mainly elected legislative body. Following the elections, the Labour Front formed a coalition government with the Malayan Chinese Association (MCA), UMNO and PMU. The UMNO and PMU each had one member in the coalition, and Che Sidek bin Abdul Hamid from the PMU was Assistant Minister of Education. This provided an ideal opportunity for the MEC to pursue its interests through the competitive party system. As the support of the Malay members was vital to the survival of the coalition, the leaders of the MEC were optimistic that the Malay community would be able to extract concessions from it.[50] Singapore UMNO held a key seat in this rather fragile Labour Front coalition, and the party leaders threatened to leave the coalition if the wishes of the MEC were not seriously considered by the Education Department.

In 1956, a White Paper on Education was released and the government encouraged education officials to make concessions to the Malay community.[51] In August 1956, Chief Minister Lim Yew Hock wrote to the MEC and explained that it was prepared to meet any reasonable demands of the MEC, provided that its alternative plan conformed to the bilingual policy outlined in the White Paper.[52] In the letter, he re-iterated the limited employment opportunities available for students educated solely in Malay medium schools. However, the MEC continued to demand a monolingual Malay policy. There was a fundamental disagreement between the two parties involved in the debate that could not be resolved. The government remained convinced that English was the key to the economic advancement of the Malay community and the fostering of integration with the other races.[53] On the other hand, the Malay community believed that the rise of Malay nationalist sentiments and the march towards independence would create a greater need for Malay language education. The time for discussion and negotiation seemed to have come to an end, and the matter of Malay education policy now became a serious political issue.

On 13 October 1956, the Singapore UMNO wrote a letter to the Chief Minister threatening to leave the coalition if the MEC's demands were not met.[54] The resignation of the Singapore UNMO member would cause the coalition to collapse. One month later, MEC leaders met the Chief Minister and there was broad agreement to revert to Malay medium instruction in Malay schools.[55] Through UMNO, the MEC leaders placed political pressure on the Labour Front coalition government in order to achieve their objectives. In November 1956, the Minister of Education presented a new Malay education policy to the Council of Ministers. In his introduction, the minister requested that the Council of Ministers 'approve the restoration of Malay as the medium of instruction throughout the Malay Primary Schools' and the use of Malay as the 'medium of instruction in the proposed Malay Secondary Schools'.[56] With this speech, the government acknowledged that the MEC had achieved its objective.

The MEC demonstrated that it was possible for a community organisation to make use of inter-party political competition to gain influence over policy issues. Although this was a period of intense associational activity, the MEC was the only organisation to do this. Active groups such as trade unions and student unions continued to favour extra-parliamentary tactics for policy change despite the presence of competition in the political arena. Thus the MEC demonstrated a high degree of political awareness on its part. It is interesting to note that this campaign was not only the first to use political competition to achieve its objectives, but very nearly the last.

Within a few years, political competition had all but disappeared, and campaigns of this sort would no longer be part of the political landscape.

The Demise of Political Competition

On 31 August 1963, four days after the announcement of independence through merger with Malaysia, the PAP government called a snap election. It was fiercely contested, and the PAP leaders utilised every advantage at their disposal to achieve victory. They dominated the campaign through their widespread use of government-controlled television and radio, coordinated by the Ministry of Culture. The Barisan Sosialis leaders had the support of the unions, student groups and rural organisations. To defeat the Barisan, the PAP needed to attack the organisations that were the base of Barisan support. Seven left-wing unions had been threatened with deregistration in August 1963, and three days before Nomination Day, the accounts of the three largest pro-Barisan unions were frozen to prevent funds being used to support the BS electoral campaign.[57]

The right-wing Alliance Party failed to win any seats.[58] It was the end of an era for right-wing politics in Singapore. The PAP polled 47 per cent of the vote and won 37 seats out of 51. The Barisan received 34.7 per cent of the vote to win 13 seats to form a sizeable opposition force. The result seemed to signal that Singapore would develop into a two-party state. However, the 1963 elections proved to be the last time that an opposition party had any real opportunity to take power from the PAP. For 13 years from 1968, the PAP held every seat in Parliament.[59] Turnbull suggests that this was a 'voluntary abdication of power by the electorate into the hands of one political group'.[60] Without political competition and with strong constraints on any form of public action, community groups were powerless to influence public policy. The leaders of the Malay Education Council were able to achieve their objectives in 1957 by using the contemporary competitive political system to their advantage. After 1968, this competitive political arena for public policy debate disappeared. Without political competition and with strong constraints on civil society activity, such groups were no longer able to influence public policy.

Closing the Path to Influence

Civil society in Singapore had been strong and effective throughout the period of British power. The beginnings of associational activity were visible in the early period from 1819 to 1867, when the powerful mercantile community forced a series of policy changes on the British regime. After 1867, a range of associations representing a variety of interests contributed to the emergence of civil society as a powerful social and political force. However, the lack of political competition meant that these organisations achieved their objectives by using the informal political sphere. The case study of the campaign fought by the Malay Education Council to influence Malay education policies demonstrates that the leaders of this particular organisation were aware of the opportunities offered by the newly emerged competitive political arena in 1955, and were able to influence public policy by taking full advantage of it. The significance of the Malay Education Council campaign was that it marked a radical change in the style of policy debate.

However, public action such as this was not encouraged after 1959, and by 1975, civil society had been completely dismantled. That only left the competitive political system to provide a pathway for dissent. The success of the Malay Education Council in using inter-party political rivalry in 1955–59 to achieve policy change demonstrated that this was a fruitful avenue to follow. However, this path, too, began to close. Although the 1963 elections resulted in a vigorous two-party Parliament, this was the final opportunity to use inter-party rivalry. For 13 years after 1968, the People's Action Party held all the seats in Parliament. Essentially the path of policy debate was closed to groups except through government-controlled channels. The Malay Education Council campaign for educational policy change demonstrates what might have been possible if competitive politics had been encouraged to flourish.

NOTES

1   Zahoor Ahmad bin Haji Faizal Hussain, 'Policies and Politics in Malay Education in Singapore 1951–1965, with Special Reference to the Development of the Secondary School System', Master of Education Thesis, University of Singapore, 1969.

2   The Legislative Council consisted of the Governor, the Officer commanding the troops in the Straits Settlements, six senior officials, the Chief Justice and four members of the public (referred to as "unofficials"). The composition of the council meant that the official members formed a majority usually referred to as the Official Majority.

3   E. Kay Gillis, *Singapore Civil Society and British Power* (Singapore: Talisman, 2005), p. 6.

4   C. M. Turnbull, *A History of Singapore*, second edition (Singapore: Oxford University Press, 1989), p. 16.

5   Gillis, *Singapore Civil Society*, p.14.

6   Ibid., p. 73.
7   Ibid., p. 61.
8   Ibid., p. 81.
9   *Proceedings of the Straits Settlements Legislative Council* (hereafter, SSLC), 28 January 1929, B 6.
10 Ibid., 6 July 1931, B 153.
11 Ibid., 6 March 1933, B 29.
12 Gillis, *Singapore Civil Society*, p. 118.
13 Ibid., p. 179.
14 Thomas Tan Tsu Wee, 'Political Modernization and Traditional Chinese Voluntary Association: A Singapore Case Study', *Southeast Asian Journal of Social Science* 13, 2 (1985): 72.
15 Ibid., p. 70.
16 Chan Heng Chee, *The Dynamics of One Party Dominance: The PAP at the Grassroots* (Singapore: Singapore University Press, 1976), p. 227.
17 H. E. Wilson, *Social Engineering in Singapore: Educational Policies and Social Change 1819–1972* (Singapore: Singapore University Press, 1978), p. 29.
18 Ibid., p. 30.
19 Sharom Ahmat, 'Singapore Malays, Education and National Development', in *Malay Participation in the National Development of Singapore*, ed. Sharom Ahmat and James Wong (Singapore: Singapore Community Study Centre and Central Council of Malay Cultural Organisations, 1971) p. 7.
20 *Proceedings of the SSLC*, 1917, C 96.
21 Wilson, *Social Engineering in Singapore*, p. 29.
22 *Proceedings of the SSLC*, 1933, B 123.
23 Wilson, *Social Engineering in Singapore*, p. 142.
24 Ibid., p. 142.
25 Colony of Singapore, *Department of Education Annual Report 1951*, p. 15.
26 Wilson, *Social Engineering in Singapore*, p. 144.
27 Federation of Malaya, *Report of the Committee on Malay Education* (Kuala Lumpur: Government Printing office, 1951).
28 Ibid., p. 20.
29 Sharom Ahmat, 'Singapore Malays', p. 7.
30 Colony of Singapore, *Department of Education Annual Report 1951*, p. 27.
31 Ibid.
32 Zahoor Ahmad, 'Policies and Politics in Malay Education', p. 19.
33 Colony of Singapore, *Department of Education Report 1951*, p. 79.
34 Ibid., p.27.
35 Sharom Ahmat, 'Singapore Malays', p. 7.
36 Zahoor Ahmad, 'Policies and Politics in Malay Education', p. 20.
37 Ibid., p. 20.
38 Ibid., p. 21.
39 Ibid., p. 22.
40 Ibid., p. 24.
41 Colony of Singapore, *Department of Education Annual Report 1956*, p. 3.

42 Ibid.
43 Zahoor Ahmad, 'Policies and Politics in Malay Education', p. 27.
44 Colony of Singapore, *Department of Education Annual Report 1956*, p. 3.
45 Ibid.
46 Ibid.
47 *Singapore Free Press*, 16 February 1956.
48 Ibid.
49 *The Straits Times*, 30 July 1956.
50 Zahoor Ahmad, 'Policies and Politics in Malay Education', p. 32.
51 Colony of Singapore, *Department of Education Annual Report 1956*, p. 3.
52 Zahoor Ahmad, 'Policies and Politics in Malay Education', p. 91.
53 Colony of Singapore, *Department of Education Annual Report 1954*, p. 16.
54 Zahoor Ahmad, 'Policies and Politics in Malay Education', p. 101.
55 Ibid., p. 102.
56 Ibid., p. 103.
57 James Minchin, *No Man is an Island: A Portrait of Singapore's Lee Kuan Yew*, second edition (North Sydney: Allen & Unwin, 1990), p. 130.
58 F. L. Starner, 'Singapore Elections of 1963', in *The Malayan Parliamentary Election of 1964*, ed. K. J. Ratnam and R. S. Milne (Singapore: University of Malaya Press, 1967), p. 349.
59 Turnbull, *A History of Singapore*, p. 306.
60 Ibid., p. 310.

9

All Quiet on Jurong Road: Nanyang University and Radical Vision in Singapore

Yao Souchou

On 28 March 1958, the biggest traffic jam in Singapore's history took place along the eleven-and-a-half-mile stretch of Bukit Timah Road and Jurong Road, west of the city. The occasion was the opening of the new Nanyang University (Nantah) founded by the Chinese community; the tens of thousands of guests and well-wishers, some invited but most turning up on their own, started the journey early in the afternoon, intending to reach the campus and catch the official ceremony scheduled to take place at four that afternoon. It was a scene of utter chaos. As the tropical sun began to set, Bukit Timah Road and Dunearn Road were blocked by heavy north-bound traffic, with the confusion worsened by the south-bound traffic from Johor and Bukit Timah Road. The police could not untangle the jam, and 400 extra troops from the paramilitary police reserve unit were called in to help. Despite these reinforcements, the traffic along Jurong Road still came to a standstill. Thousands of people left their cars by the roadside and walked the six miles to the university grounds. The Governor, Sir William Goode, was to open the celebrations at four o'clock; he reached the university two hours later and unveiled the commemorative plaque at seven in the evening.

Thousands eventually arrived in this manner. From the reception marquee they spilled onto the lawn and garden below, and the festivities took much of the sting out of the long, sweaty journey. As they looked up into the night sky, three huge gas-filled balloons lifted off, carrying goodwill messages on long, red, flowing paper strips, and then the fireworks started, filling the sky with myriad flashes of gold and red before trailing off into the far horizon. For the first time in Southeast Asia, a self-funded university had been founded to cater for the thousands of graduates of Chinese secondary schools. As an educational institution, it also carried the long historical ambition of preserving Chinese culture and tradition in the South Seas (*Nanyang*), and producing university graduates who were culturally astute, modern in outlook and employable.

If Nanyang University's inauguration was marked by the problem of traffic control, its ending, too, was foreshadowed on a similar note. But there was no question this time of massive chaos along the ten-mile route from the city to the campus. Early one June morning in 1964, a half-mile-long convoy of 60 police vehicles and Black Maria vans set off for the university at two hours past midnight. The convoy was escorted by Mobile Traffic Police to make sure the road was clear of any other traffic except police vehicles. By three o'clock the convoy had reached the university grounds; a roadblock was set up half a mile away, at the Jurong Police Station. With the exit secured, the pre-dawn crackdown on 'communist subversives' at Nanyang University began.

The 1,300 students were asleep when the police arrived at Nanyang Avenue. For the operation, the Federal authorities[1] called in more than 1,000 police personnel from the Special Branch, the Federal Reserve Unit, the Criminal Investigation Department, the Divisional Police and the Mobile Traffic Squad in order to cordon off the campus. Two hours after the police had entered the campus, the first student detainees were brought out in a van. At the Jurong Police Station roadblock, a Special Branch officer checked all vehicles against a wanted list of names and photographs; students were identified and detained, and 11 others were arrested outside the campus. A total of 51 students were arrested, including four girls. The eight-hour police operation was the biggest since the arrest of more than 100 left-wing unionists and politicians in Operation Cold Store a year earlier. By the time the public woke up, the police convoy had begun to leave the campus, and by ten in the morning, the operation had been completed.

To cast the hectic, unruly movement along the road to the campus, and the final exercise of control, as a metaphor for the rise and fall of Nantah is in no way an overstatement. Nantah's story is one of raw social energies and movements — of new ideas; of social visions always at risk of going awry in the volatile social and political conditions of the time; and of the needs and agendas of the political forces on both sides of the Causeway. It was a time of national struggle and the end of colonialism. Everyone who wanted a stake in the new nation-state was caught up in the changes and what these could bring. Indeed, history made *radicals* of everyone who aspired to power in the post-colonial political order; the 'communist-inspired' Nantah students were not the only ones deserving of the label.

But the story of Nantah also tells of movement of another kind: that of the immigrant imaginary. The Chinese community's ambition to build a university in Southeast Asia was fused with ideas of progressive, culturally-relevant education that are traceable to the modernist reforms in China that began in the late Qing dynasty. Yet the university was also founded to meet the local social, cultural and economic needs of the Chinese. To Nantah's critics, these agendas and needs looked distinctly quixotic; but there is no doubt that for its founders and supporters, the main objectives of 'cultural preservation' and providing tertiary education for graduates of the much-marginalised Chinese schools were realistic and urgent. For all the political controversy surrounding it, Nantah's plan was primarily cultural and pedagogic. Of course, it had always been the fantasy of the Chinese community elite that it could get on with its business of making money without being tainted by wider national politics and the struggle for power, and that setting up a university would be no different. It saw this as the right of good citizens. But in the independent nation, all communities had to come forward to eagerly embrace the agenda of national development. In such a context, the Chinese community's need for cultural preservation, and its insistence on education as a cultural right, looked increasingly like communal self-promotion and out of sync with the national interest. This, as much as the charge of 'communist subversion', spelt the end for Nantah.

Nantah: A Community Project

Chinese vernacular education has a long history in Malaya. Private academies, or *shu kuan*, for fee-paying students first appeared in Penang and Malacca in the early nineteenth century; the earliest was reportedly the Wu Fong Academy founded in Penang in 1819. By 1884, the Straits Settlements of Penang, Melaka and Singapore had about 150 such *shu kuan*, subsidised by community charity. Thus, the Chinese Education Movement in contemporary Malaysia can speak proudly of 180 years of achievement and struggle.[2]

In the beginning, the British colonial attitude was one of very much letting the Chinese community handle its own affairs. In truth, as the historian Tan Liok Ee puts it, '[the] freedom to develop Chinese education was actually official neglect, since the authorities thought that without government assistance, Chinese schools would eventually die out'.[3] In 1924, the colonial government announced that to be eligible for subsidies, vernacular schools had to accept a set curriculum and the registration of suitable teachers. The period 1929–34 saw a worldwide economic recession, with community funding in short supply. To raise funds, students went door-knocking and theatre troupes toured the country. Most schools resisted government subsidies, yet the two decades before the Japanese invasion of 1941 saw a significant expansion in Chinese schools. By 1948, there were 1,364 Chinese schools in the Malay Peninsula, attended by nearly 200,000 students.[4]

The year 1948 was a watershed for Chinese education for another reason, which brings us to our narrative of Nantah. The colonial government announced the beginning of the Emergency to combat the Malayan communists fighting a guerrilla war in the jungle. Many Chinese school teachers and students were caught up in what they saw as a genuine anti-colonial, national liberation struggle. Some were arrested and deported to China. The change in immigration regulations also meant that the schools could no longer recruit teachers from China. From 1949 onwards, several government-sponsored committees recommended the end of vernacular schools and their replacement with a single type of national primary school for all communities. With the incentive of government funding, the ground was set for a struggle over Chinese education for years to come: how to achieve the delicate balance between educational independence, official recognition and financial viability? It was a difficult task, one that was to give Chinese education an almost romantic aura of self-preservation and cultural resistance.

The Emergency also banned graduates of Chinese schools from going to China to attend universities there. The founding of Nantah was thus intended to meet the immediate needs of thousands of young men and women who could not gain admission to the English-language University of Malaya in Singapore. In January 1953, Chinese community leaders announced a plan to set up a Chinese-language university. In the Chinese tradition of communal effort, money was raised from Chinese millionaire philanthropists led by rubber tycoon Tan Lark Sye, who donated $5 million:

his generosity, personal commitment and mercurial temperament were to shape much of the drama of Nantah in the following years. The project 'bought face' for the wealthy through their philanthropy, but it also received community-wide support. After the merchants of the Hokkien Association announced that they were giving 550 acres of rubber-estate land in Jurong to build the campus, the Chinese in Malaya and Singapore went on a fund-raising drive.

There was a great deal of collective spirit and earnestness in the activity. Accustomed to viewing Chinese community undertakings through the prism of personal power and the status of the merchant elite, one tends to forget the potency of cultural identity that bridged and unified the social divide. Nantah was very much that, a symbol of the collective yearning to put down the roots of Chinese culture in Southeast Asia. People I interviewed spoke fondly of the fund-raising drive; they had a term for it, *yi mai* (selling for a cause). The Nanyang Hakka Association held a concert in Kuala Lumpur and tickets, together with bottles of cognac, wall clocks and an assortment of trinkets were auctioned off at a grand dinner the night before. Bottles of Remy Martin went for $1,000 each as rich businessmen dug into their wallets as 'face' demanded of them. The concert and dinner collected more than $15,000. Other concerts and auction dinners were organised by Chinese *she tuan* (voluntary associations) all over Malaya and Singapore. The slogan was, 'Those who have give money, those who have not give labour.' True to this spirit of grassroots engagement, hawkers, rickshaw drivers and labourers donated their earnings for the day. Hair saloons offered *yi jian* and *yi dian* (cut and perm for a cause). On 4 May, Chinese dance hall hostesses in Singapore gave their day to *yi wu* (dancing for Nantah). It was a hugely successful event, collecting some $20,000. One man went to Nan Tien Dance Hall in Chinatown, combining personal pleasure with doing his bit for a good cause, but it was not enough to pacify his wife's rage when he got home, he told me. In Ipoh market in Malaya, one fishmonger nicknamed 'Da Shu Tau' (Big Tree Trunk) put on a raggedy shirt and turned beggar for a day. Wandering from stall to stall, he collected some $1,200; when his shirt and begging bowl were later auctioned, they were bought for $65 by the Ipoh Vegetable Sellers' Association.

The Nantah Spirit: A Genealogy

With its overwhelming community involvement, the building of Nantah spoke of a solidarity and cultural unity not often seen among the usual contentions and differences in wealth and social position among the

Chinese of Malaya and Singapore. To some interviewees, the funding drive was clearly a revelation, showing almost magically that the Chinese could act as one, and thus perhaps serve as a single political force in the struggle to advance Chinese interests in the period of national independence to come. But the enterprise is worth remembering for another reason: it makes a sham of the easy labelling of the university as a hotbed of communist subversion by the authorities, as if the hawkers and dance hostesses who gave up their daily earnings had aimed to bring this about. If communist subversion were not the reason, what then was the nature of the collective zeal over a Chinese-language university? The answer, in a word, is 'culture'.

The provision of tertiary education for Chinese school students and the training of local graduates were undoubtedly the crucial incentives, but there was also the business of culture, which by its very nature cannot be a totally pragmatic affair. Culture and practical reason are intimately linked, as Marshal Sahlins has put it, in shaping the way we think and act.[5] At best we can think of Nantah as located in the interlocking of pedagogical needs, cultural aspirations, and the social and political surroundings of the time. The more conservative view would see the Chinese love of education as having been nurtured by Confucianism from time immemorial, and instilled as it were in their collective psyche. That may be so, but in Malaya, the history of modern Chinese nationalism and the tumultuous history after the ending of World War II were the crucial genealogy that gave Chinese education its particular passion and rigour. This history is central to the story of Nantah, and is worth recounting at some length.

After the Japanese Occupation, British imperial power had lost much of its lustre and real influence. There were stirrings of anti-colonialism and calls for political reform. The winds of change sweeping colonial Asia, the Middle East and Africa, coupled with the weariness of war at home under a new Labour Government, drove Britain towards 'reformation and rationalization of the colonial presence in Malaya'. With broad initiatives linking 'social economic policy with political intentions', the 'British reoccupation of Malaya was conceived as a vast experiment in democracy'.[6] There was the growth of the public sphere, and the lifting of pre-war restrictions on voluntary associations, trade unions and the press.

The new political climate also held something of the political consciousness nurtured by the war. With the departure of the British, the Indian community had most famously lent support to the Japanese-sponsored Indian National Army to fight for India's independence. Radical Malays, on the other hand, looked to Indonesia for inspiration, where at the end of the war Sukarno's guerrillas were fighting against the Dutch. For the Chinese population, the protests against the Sino-Japanese war, which started with the Japanese landing in Tientsin in 1938, had been the crucial political training ground. As the war spread to Central and Southern China — with the Japanese army taking Canton the same year — the news of devastation and the massacres of civilians prompted the Malayan Chinese to organise boycotts of Japanese goods and relief projects that collected funds and materials to be sent back to the mainland. In these activities, local organisers 'jostled with Guomindang and Communist elements'.[7] The war efforts energised a new Chinese patriotism, and more importantly, a political sensibility built on the experience of mass mobilisation and modern, nationalist feelings.

The communist-based organisations had a special place in post-war Malaya and Singapore. Enjoying considerable popular appeal, the communists formed the only effective guerrilla force against the Japanese during the dark years of 1942–45. The retreating British had sought collaboration with the Malayan People's Anti-Japanese Army (MPAJA), the military wing of the Malayan Communist Party (MCP), in organising stay-behind parties for gathering intelligence for the Southeast Asia Command in Ceylon. For its part, the MCP had hoped to strike a bargain with the British and perhaps carve out a legitimate political role in post-war Malaya. In any case, in the relatively liberal climate after the war, organisations with varying degrees of communist influence grew; so, too, did labour unions, student societies and trade associations, whose diverse ideological aims could be loosely described as anti-colonial, democratic-socialist and multi-ethnic. It is problematic to label these organisations as 'communist'; so is tracing their direct or tacit links with the MCP and its off-shoot, the Ex-Comrades Association. This is a controversial issue that is not easily resolved, clouded as it is by state propaganda and erroneous thinking. In this regard, Harper is most astute when he describes these associations as underlined by 'a common ground between the "Eight Points" of the Malayan Communist Party, the republicanism of the Malay left, and the global solidarities of revived trade unionism'.[8] In short, the post-war socialist struggle blossomed in the hothouse conditions of the anti-colonial struggle, nationalism and rising political consciousness generally.

To explain the modern consciousness and desire for progressive education among the Malayan Chinese, we need to go back further. After its founding in 1911, the Chinese Republic faced the turbulent difficulties of a new regime; the political conflict and modern cultural aspirations were inevitably exported to the Chinese in Singapore. Before the revolution, the Qing government had at first left the overseas Chinese community very much to themselves, but at the turn of the century, with the late Qing reform and the stirring of national revolution under Sun Yat Sen, the Chinese government and the revolutionaries both began to compete for political support among the overseas Chinese. The picture of modern Chinese nationalism presents a dramatic contrast to the images more famously depicted of traditional China — the culture-bound, compliant masses, the political influence of the literati, the merchant elite who purchased titles from the government as marks of prestige and honour. China's modern nationalism rose from the ashes of the Opium War (1839–42). Another critical event was the disastrous six months' war with Japan in 1894–95, which saw the annexation of Taiwan and Southern Manchuria by Japan. But the most crucial was undoubtedly the May Fourth Movement of 1919. Energised by anti-Japanese patriotism and the League of Nations' failure to quash Japanese imperial ambitions in China, May Fourth harnessed political reform with a deep conviction in the power of 'modern literature' to liberate Chinese sensibility from — in Lu Xun's potent language — the cannibalistic hold of tradition and mass subservience. The New Cultural Movement signalled an urgent political agenda, as well as a new literary aesthetic. Spreading from China to the South Seas, it took on local issues, just as it had been shaped by the local colour and environment: the influence was not by way of parasitic borrowing. In the Popular Bookshop chain in Kuala Lumpur today, one still finds short stories and essays by Malaysian Chinese writers in anthologies with titles like *Ye Lin Wen Zhang* (*Literary Work of the Coconut Grove*). One sees in such works the enduring traces of May Fourth. In their modern thinking and literary experiment, they also turned their contemplation to what was happening in local society.[9]

So it reflected a convoluted desire indeed when May Fourth was transplanted into the tropics. The yearning for a modern China free from Japanese — and Western — imperialism and endowed with progressive cultural expressions was transformed into a vision for a new society in Malaya. To harness the radical changes in China, to be inspired by what was happening in the homeland, was for the overseas Chinese intelligentsia both logical and sensible. It was still too early to speak of socialism and labour unions, but nascent radicalism and an assault on the *status quo* were some of the important components of the socialist vision of Nantah in later decades.

'Hotbed of Radicalism'

This heritage was to assert a major influence on the cultural and pedagogic ambitions of Chinese schools, shaping as it did the sensibilities of many of the teachers and students. The Chinese Republic was the inspiration,

as mentioned earlier, and so, somewhat inevitably, was the new communist China, whose overthrow of the corrupt Nationalist regime of Chiang
Kai Shek signalled the final transformation that earlier revolutions and
reformers had never completed. Half a century on, it is possible for us
to talk about the 'communist influence' on Chinese schools and Nantah
without tying ourselves into an ideological knot. Chin Peng, the General
Secretary of the MCP, now retired in southern Thailand after the 1989
ceasefire agreement, describes the fervent political imagination and social
realities that drew young people like him — he was 23 when he took up
the top post in 1947 — onto a revolutionary path:

> Conversion to communism is as strong as a religious conversion. It
> provided a faith and belief in a system which, at least to the convert,
> appears as the incontrovertible path to what is right and fair among
> human beings.[10]

Guerrilla war in the jungle was only one highly dramatic articulation
of the vision for Malayan socialism, however. In the 1950s and 1960s,
tough political struggles underpinned by exuberant ideological hope were
also taking place among unionists and students in the cities. If these struggles had communist influence, it was not usually in the form of direct and
explicit links with the MCP or — worse — with paymasters in Beijing or
Moscow, but in broad ideological unity and using a common model for
mass action.

To return to Nantah, one commentator describes the students there as
being 'recruited into [communist] cells [so that they] could agitate efficiently for political changes in the curriculum'. No sympathiser himself, he
nonetheless quickly added that the 'students had genuine grievances' under
colonialism, and later, independent Singapore.[11]

The comment came from the pen of Michael Thorpe, a British Council
lecturer who went to Nanyang University in February 1962 to teach at the
department of modern languages and literature. His account, even for its
imperturbable British views, gives a fascinating picture of student politics
at the campus.[12] Brought up on a diet of the modernist literature of May
Fourth, the young men and women who entered Nantah were no effete products of Confucian subservience and rote learning. 'From the onset,' Thorpe
wrote, 'Nanyang was doomed to become an instrument in the power-struggle
between a west leaning meritocracy and those who, educated in the closed
Chinese system, looked only to China as their legitimate parent.' As Thorpe
began his duties at Nantah, he was, in spite of himself, deeply moved by the
discipline and collective labour of the students that he witnessed.

They were helping to construct the students' union building — an answer to the traditional architecture of the library, with 'columned portico and sweeping green-tiled roofs, dragons breathing at their corners'. Thorpe describes the hectic scene:

> [The student union building] was built on a defensible hill, itself largely
> an artificial product, its top flattened, its slopes graded and smoothed
> with baskets of soil and rubble borne by ant-like battalion of students.
> Slim girls toiled on the slopes under their own weight of earth.

'The organisation, purpose and effort were, indeed, such as build mountains,' Thorpe opined.[13]

To observers like Thorpe, the 'formidable Chinese application' was both impressive and alarming because it was accompanied by a great deal of moral gravity, seemingly the stuff of revolutionaries. The mass labour at the construction site was a collective display of discipline and hardy bodies working as one. Since tough healthy bodies were needed for the building of 'Malayan socialism', and since bodily performance would be shaped by personal values, unsurprisingly, struggle was also launched on the cultural front. This is the other story of Nantah: the campaign against largely Western-inspired 'yellow culture'. The editors of *The Sparks*, a student magazine of the English Society, were certain of the social harm of 'bad films and immoral literature', typical products of 'yellow culture' that lead to 'gangsterism and juvenile delinquency'. Young people turning to gangsterism and juvenile delinquency did not contribute to nation building, and the 'colonialists' were to be blamed for that:

> The morally corrupted people are trouble-makers and parasites of society.
> They cause a loss of man-assets to Singapore which is badly in need of
> them for nation building. We learn from history that it is the colonial-
> ists who were the patrons of yellow culture, who caused us to fall into
> the cultural traps set by them. They were self-interested; they tried to
> prolong their control over the people.[14]

Such was the language of the time. Earnest, full of nationalistic fervour and a trifle naïve, it nonetheless gave vent to the longing for political change that would bring about a socialist future, one that promised equality and justice and escape from poverty which many students knew first hand. Between the waning of the old colonial regime and the coming of the new nation, it was the right time to dream of these things and to strive to realise them. As the students toiled under the tropical sun, untouched by the strength-sapping 'yellow culture', their hardy bodies were symbolic of the urgent practicality: culture, too, must serve the struggle for freedom, dignity and above all, economic security.

Economic security then pervaded much of the talk of social change in Asia and the Nantah students were quick to latch on to the discourse. For many, communism — more the idea and inspiration of it than what happened in China or Russia — was the quickest way to achieve economic equality in Asia; there lay its main attraction. This is worth remembering. From the still-limited literature on the Malayan communists, one gets a strong sense of the grave deprivation of their early youth, as their families tried to carve a living out of small farming plots at the jungle fringe. More than British colonialism, and the bourgeois running-dog government, it was this grinding poverty and hardship that 'politicised and radicalised' them.[15] The 'communist utopia' was to be a land of equality as well as abundance. Han Suyin, who gave lectures and talks at various times in Nantah, travelling from Johor Baru where she had her medical practice, was much remembered by many of the Nantah graduates I interviewed. Hardly a communist, but like many progressive liberals of the time, she had a realistic sense of the problems of Asia, and was drawn to the radical transformations taking place in Mao's China. In her 1960 talk, 'Social Change in Asia', she observed that the 'fundamental differences between Asian countries today are not political', but in the ways of bringing a better life for all:

> To divide the world into communist and anti-communist faiths is to obscure realities, not to explain the monstrous necessity which drives men into action. The differences are in speed and method toward a common aim: food, shelter, social security, a living wage, social justice, education ... In Asia today whichever country or nation is going to achieve this basic social security within the next twenty years for the greatest number of its people, is likely to set the pattern for others. *Not a pattern to imitate exactly, but a frame of reference*, powerful because successful.[16] [emphasis added]

Taming the Radical Beast

'Not a pattern to imitate exactly, but a frame of reference' neatly captures the driving force of Nantah activism and its connection with communism and radical politics. Tracing the origins of this activism, as I have done, to modern China and post-war politics, with its imperative of economic security for the poor, is not to explain away its passion and violence and arguably, its links with the Malayan Communist Party. Half a century on, one should perhaps resist nostalgia for the 'failed revolution'. Yet as we speak of the naïveté and youthful enthusiasm of students in Nantah and the Chinese high schools, we ought not to forget that they were not the only ones seduced by the elegiac vision of a democratic-socialist society.

The PAP leaders then taking Singapore to national independence, too, were inspired by the utopian vision. The young extremists in Nantah may have been too easily swayed by communism, but their energy and drive were still something desirable — if only these qualities could be harnessed and guided down a less revolutionary path. The fortunes of Nantah were famously tied in with the rise of the PAP government, but the story is not just about official suppression and how it brought about the university's ultimate demise.

The history of Singapore from 1954 to 1961, a period covering the founding of the PAP to the departure of its left-wing faction, is generally described by the PAP as being 'astride [the back] of the tiger'.[17] A popular cartoon book depicts Lee with his legs straddling the ferocious beast, right fist in the air clasping the PAP party emblem, ready to land a blow to its head. His clothes in tatters, face grim with determination, it is the visage of a man in the midst of battle as he strikes terror in the enemies visibly cowering under the tiger's belly.[18] Melodramatic at best, the cartoon celebrates the heroism and danger of the PAP enterprise; it was no 'paper tiger' on whose back Lee and his colleagues rode to power.

When he returned to Singapore from his studies in England, the young Lee found himself in a heady atmosphere of anti-colonial nationalism and socialist radicalism. But Lee's politics were of a different ideological hue. At London University and later Cambridge, his major influence was moderate Labour Party 'reformism and social reconstruction', which came to provide the founding vision of his struggle for independence.[19] Nonetheless, Lee was deeply impressed with the energy and commitment of the students and labour organisers he came into contact with. Here is his passionate assessment:

> ... one day in 1954 we came into contact with the Chinese educated world. The Chinese middle school students were in revolt against national service and they were beaten down. Riots took place, charges were preferred in court ... [It was] a world teeming with vitality, dynamism and revolution ... [20]

The commitment and dedication of the left was all the more impressive when contrasted with the English-educated who, like Lee himself, benefited the most from colonial patronage. For Lee, the greatest sins of the English-educated elite were their self-interest and their failure to cast their lot behind the anti-colonial movement. Other observers, particularly Huang Jianli, take issue with this facile dismissal of the English-educated elsewhere in this volume. Nonetheless, Lee understood the dynamism of the Chinese-educated students. He was certain that Singapore's political future would be in the hands of the Chinese radical leftists with whom moderates like him and his colleagues would need to form a political alliance.

Following the PAP's inauguration on 21 November 1954, it took a strong anti-colonial stance, demanding national independence through constitutional means. It called for merger with Malaya with a view to creating a national movement by bringing together all the anti-colonial forces on both sides of the Causeway. With these calls, Lee and his colleagues began building a party with a mass base. For this they relied on the trade unions and Chinese school activists, who brought with them their working-class supporters. The period 1954 to 1961 generally saw collaboration between the PAP moderates and the radical unionists: it made Lee a reluctant suitor of communists and he often had to defend them for the sake of party unity. But the relationship was uneasy and often volatile. It reached a climax in June 1961 when the radical elements led by the charismatic unionist Lim Chin Siong broke with the party and called for the PAP government to resign. Lim, together with other radicals, was later arrested in Operation Cold Store in February 1963.[21]

The PAP harboured a great deal of ambivalence towards the radical left. In 1955, Lee introduced Lim Chin Siong to Chief Minister David Marshall in the latter's office. Pointing to Lim, he said to Marshall, 'Meet the future Prime Minister of Singapore!' He added, 'Don't laugh! He is the finest Chinese orator in Singapore and he will be our next prime minister!'[22] Thus, in a moment of unguarded mirth, Lee gave a sharp evaluation of his nemesis. The political resourcefulness and commitment of the Chinese-educated world that Lim inhabited were both dangerous and something that the PAP desperately wanted. Enjoying popular support, unionists like Lim were able to call mass strikes and, as was often charged, provoke violent confrontations with the police. In the PAP narrative, the workers and high school students barricading themselves in the schoolyards and bus depots, and Nantah extremists quick to riot, were the radical beasts out to destroy the world and had to be tamed.

During the early 1960s, however, the new PAP government was prepared to put up with them and ignore their unsavoury association with the communist-leaning left. A marriage of Machiavellian genius, it clearly could not last. Emboldened by its spectacular electoral success, and with independence almost in its grasp, the PAP government began to move against the enemies lurking threateningly within the camp.

Fall of Nantah

The 1964 police raid on the Nantah campus, ordered by the Federal authorities in Kuala Lumpur, was to cull student activism. But the difficulties went further back; a series of issues had long clouded the position of Nantah in Singapore and Malaya. After the initial euphoria over the founding of the university, the government and education circles began to ask questions about its administration and pedagogic aims. In summary, these were related to:

- how the university was organised and administered;
- the teaching standards and recruitment of lecturers;
- curriculum design and the training of students; and
- whether there was a place for a privately funded Chinese-language university in a multicultural, multiracial society.

Importantly, such questions were often mixed up with the state's own political agendas, which used the problems of Nantah as the basis for its suppressive measures. Nonetheless, these questions were not altogether groundless. As an institution founded by a group of millionaire philanthropists of limited education, it was a wonder that they got Nantah started and managed the complex affairs of university administration for as long as they did. Many of the problems became the focus of the 1959 Prescott Commission Report, the first of the government commissions formed to examine the future of Nantah. The Prescott Commission found the administration and staff morale seriously wanting, and recommended employing more full-time professional administrators to assist the Chairman and the University Council in running the university. On the courses taught, the Commission found them to be 'too heavy', with too many offerings without a judicious balance between those of general education and specialised majors. The Commission concluded that it could not 'in good conscience' recommend the recognition of the university's degrees.[23]

When Tan Lark Sye, the millionaire-founder who was then the Chairman of the University Council, read the report, he thought it 'biased, unjust and cruel'. At a press interview, he stopped 'constantly to blink away the tears in his eyes'.[24] Tan may have had his heart in the right place, but he ran the university like an 'emperor', appointing 'useless people' to key positions, and allowing 'pro-communist elements' to take over the campus, according to the Parliamentary Secretary of Law and National Development, a Nantah graduate himself.[25] The chronology of Nantah's rise and fall occurred almost too neatly. Reading through the government pronouncements and the Prime Minister's speeches of the time, it is clear that 1963–64 was a watershed. Before 1964, the questions were mainly directed at the university's place in independent Malaya, and whether its graduates could find jobs. Lee Kuan Yew himself was often enthusiastic about Nantah's role in 'cultural preservation' for the Chinese, and especially the anti-West, anti-yellow cultural spirit among the Nantah students. However, it soon became clear that the 'cultural preservation' that community leaders like Tan had in mind looked increasingly like 'separate development' and 'self-possessively Chinese', while the students were too aggressively revolutionary for the moderate PAP's liking. Both extreme passions had to be brought in line.

In May 1960, following the fallout from the Prescott Commission Report, Tan resigned from the University Council. Three years later, following the 1963 general election, the government revoked his citizenship. Quite apart from his so-called cultural chauvinism, Tan had urged voters to back Nantah graduates who stood against the PAP in the election. The removal of Tan was meant to be symbolic of the wider attempt to reshape Nantah according to the aims of national development. Now attention could be turned to the student extremists. Among other risky moves, Nantah students were apparently throwing their weight behind the Barisan Sosialis, the only party that could effectively challenge the PAP. In the 1963 general election, busloads of students were reportedly seen going to various electoral areas canvassing for Barisan candidates; and the Secretary-General of the Guild of Nanyang University Graduates, Lim Chien Sen, contested the Hong Lim seat on the Barisan ticket. The Barisan influence was also evident on the Nanyang University Council, where Chia Thye Poh, the Barisan Sosialis Assemblyman for Jurong, was one of the legal representatives of the graduate guild.

After the June 1964 crackdown, the government stated that it backed Kuala Lumpur's action, and was satisfied that in removing the 'communist elements', the Central Government did not 'attempt to interfere with Chinese education in Nanyang University'.[26] The 'communist conspiracy' was the theme of a Government White Paper on 'Communism in the Nanyang University' released immediately after the June arrests, which stated unequivocally that:

> [Student] leadership has been dominated by the underground Communist Party of Malaya whose purpose in exploiting the issues of Chinese education has been to discredit the Malaysian Government and to stir agitation in the Chinese schools.
>
> Their purpose has been the political one of maintaining their political influences and of preparing for their eventual capture of power by carrying out the policy of the Communist United Front …[27]

Communism was portrayed as the sword of Damocles. Operation Cold Store in February the previous year had decimated the radical left, and now the June Nantah crackdown was very much a mopping-up exercise. On 16 July, 20 non-academic staff were dismissed, as were 102 students in what the English daily *The Straits Times* called a 'security clean up'.[28] Another 130 students were expelled in November that year.

In December 1965, the government-appointed Wang Gungwu Curriculum Review Committee released its report. The many recommendations for reform were based on the understanding that Nanyang University should produce graduates who are 'able to guide the course of the country's development and trained to administer the public services and manage the growth of commerce and industry'.[29] When students sent a memorandum of protest over the Committee's recommendations, 16 of them were expelled. For those with an ear for these things, 'channelling the youth energy to public administration and managing the growth of commerce and industry' sharply captures the technocratic rhetoric so beloved of the PAP state. So the Wang Gungwu Committee recommendations were hardly new, but when implemented — with a little help from anti-riot police and security personnel — they were to have far-reaching consequences. In one sense, the Committee report reworked and gave new emphasis to the 'education for national development' theme of the 1959 Prescott Commission Report. Yet it takes no great leap of the imagination to see that this approach to Nantah was also a political stratagem of great significance. 'Education for national development' was a rhetorically seductive phrase; it said so much and yet so little. It spelt the power of the PAP and its suppression of the forces that stood in its way, the subsuming of alternative political imaginations under the unifying needs of the nation-state, and the end of radical vision, made redundant as much by the rise of the PAP as by the changing geo-politics of the region. The final fate of Nantah was an outcome of these forces, more so than the excessive passions of radical students inspired by Mao's China and the struggle in the Malayan jungle or the cankerous incompetence of businessmen trying to run a university.

Conclusion

In 1980, Nantah was merged with the University of Singapore to become the National University of Singapore (NUS). Nanyang Technological University (NTU) now sits on the Nantah campus in Jurong. Established by an Act of Parliament on 1 July 1991, NTU has its origins in the former Nanyang Technological Institute (NTI), whose primary aims of providing tertiary education and research in various branches of engineering and technology were carried over to the NTU. The NTU website comments without a touch of irony:

> Planted on 'Nanyang' soil it is conceivable that NTU looks toward strengthening its affiliation with the alumni of Nantah … A fusion of spirits of old Nantah and NTU will evolve to bring us forth to meet the challenges of the future.

The 'New Nantah' is now efficiently run, its lecturers and professors getting paid on par with NUS levels, and devoted to 'human resource development' for the nation and the job market. The recommendations of the Prescott and Wang Gungwu committees have been fully realised. To the Nantah graduates I talked to, NTU is a disgrace to Nantah's former glory, and no amount of parasitic borrowing could ever recreate the true Nantah Spirit. The sense of loss is not only over the demise of the university, but also the end of the cultural ambition of business tycoons and hawkers and dance hostesses alike: the ambition of cultural citizenship, of community identity, of historical depth and transnational inspirations, including a vision for a socialist future.

NOTES

1   Singapore was then part of the newly formed Federation of Malaysia.
2   Tan Liok Ee, *The Politics of Chinese Education in Malaya, 1945–1961* (Kuala Lumpur: New York: Oxford University Press, 1997).
3   Ibid., p. 25.
4   Ibid., p. 67.
5   Marshal Sahlins, *Culture and Practical Reason* (Chicago: University of Chicago Press, 1976).
6   T. N. Harper, *The End of Empire and the Making of Malaya* (New York: Cambridge University Press, 1998), p. 57.
7   Ibid., p. 67.
8   Ibid., p. 57.
9   D. L. Kenley, *New Culture in a New World: The May Fourth Movement and the Chinese Diaspora in Singapore, 1919–1932* (New York: Routledge, 2003), p. 111.
10 Chin Peng and Ian Ward, *My Side of History* (Singapore: Media Masters, 2003), p. 47. See also Karl Hack and J. Chen, *Dialogues with Chin Peng: New Light on the Malayan Communist Party* (Singapore: Singapore University Press, 2004).
11 Michael Thorpe, '"Penetration by Invitation" — A Lecturer at Nanyang — A Memoir', *Economic and Political Weekly* 1–8 (March 1997): 486.
12 I am grateful to Professor William Newell, who alerted me to the article.
13 Thorpe, 'Penetration by Invitation', pp. 486–7.

14 Ibid., p. 435.

15 A. Khoo, *Life as the River Flows: Women in the Malayan Anti-colonial Struggle (An Oral History of Women from Thailand, Malaysia and Singapore)* (Petaling Jaya: SIRD, 2004).

16 Han Suyin, 'Social Change in Asia', *Suloh Nantah: Journal of the English Society Nanyang University Singapore* 15–16 (1960): 2.

17 John Drysdale, *Singapore: Struggle for Success* (North Sydney: Allen & Unwin, 1984), p. 172.

18 J. Yeoh, *To Tame a Tiger: The Singapore Story* (Singapore: Wiz-Biz, 1995).

19 Michael Barr, *Lee Kuan Yew: The Beliefs Behind the Man* (Richmond, UK: Curzon, 2000), p. 58.

20 Han Fook Kwang, Warren Fernandez and Sumiko Tan, *Lee Kuan Yew: The Man and His Ideas* (Singapore: Singapore Press Holdings, Times Editions, 1998), p. 45.

21 For the career and sad decline of Lim Chin Siong, see Harper, 'Lim Chin Siong and the "Singapore Story"' and C. J. W-L Wee, 'The Vanquished: Lim Chin Siong and a Progressivist National Narrative', in *Lee's Lieutenants: Singapore's Old Guard*, ed. Lam Peng Er and Kevin Y. L. Tan (St Leonards: Allen & Unwin, 1999).

22 Melanie Chew, *Leaders of Singapore* (Singapore: Resource Press, 1996), p. 79.

23 *The Straits Times*, 6 July 1959.

24 *The Straits Times*, 27 July 1959.

25 *The Straits Times*, 13 December 1966.

26 *The Straits Times*, 28 June 1964.

27 Ibid.

28 *The Straits Times*, 17 July 1964.

29 *The Straits Times*, 6 December 1965.

10

The Young Pathfinders:
Portrayal of Student Political Activism

Huang Jianli

In the second half of the twentieth century, student political activism occupied a special place in the history of many countries, and Singapore was no exception. Driven as much by their youthful raw energy, idealism and romanticism as by their freedom from career considerations, family burdens and property ownership, students had occasionally surged to the forefront of national politics and exerted an influence out of proportion to their numbers and became a force to be reckoned with.

Despite it constituting a major fragment of Singapore's history, our understanding of this topic has been shackled. The restrictive templates used in the scripting of Singapore's national history have over-simplified these young pathfinders into a polarised binary of Chinese- versus English-educated student activists. With a particular value system ascribed to these binary entities, the official discourse has placed an overwhelming emphasis on the activism associated with the Chinese middle schools and Nanyang University, while sidelining the less vigorous but nonetheless still significant parallel developments in the English-medium educational institutions as well as ignoring the interactions between them. This paper begins with a brief descriptive outline of student political activism in Singapore from the 1940s to the 1980s, and then proceeds to problematise its portrayal in terms of a simplified binary world.

Outline of Pre-Independence Student Movements

The return of British colonial authorities at the end of World War II and the beginning of the decolonisation process provided the impetus and political space for student politics in Singapore.[1] Although there had been early stirrings of post-war anti-colonial sentiment, the usual marker of the first major student movement is taken to be the May Thirteenth Incident of 1954. The demonstration on 13 May was targeted at the colonial government's drafting of young people into military service against the Malayan Communist Party (MCP), which had mounted an insurrection in the jungles. About 900 students from the Chinese middle schools clashed with riot squads in a march to present a petition for military exemption. More than two dozen people were reportedly injured, and nearly 50 students arrested. Of those arrested, seven were convicted for obstructing the police. In the following days, some students barricaded themselves inside Chung Cheng High School and Chinese High School and threatened to carry out hunger strikes, while others fanned out across Singapore to enlist public support. This event helped to initiate an alliance between the radical Chinese students and their English-educated counterparts.

Activists in the English-medium education stream had been operating at various tertiary institutions. While one centre of activism comprised students studying overseas, who set up the London-based Malayan Forum, the local student hotbed was in the King Edward VII College of Medicine, where some of them initially became involved with the Malayan Democratic Union but were later absorbed into the Anti-British League. The other local centre was the Raffles College at Bukit Timah campus. After the University of Malaya was founded in October 1949 by combining the College of Medicine and Raffles College, the student activists merged and operated through the University of Malaya Students' Union, gaining a controlling influence over student publications such as *Malayan Undergrad*, *The Cauldron*, and *Malayan Orchids*. Apart from demanding a faster pace of decolonisation, the University of Malaya radicals also pushed for the establishment of a political club within the campus. The British authorities granted permission for the formation of the University Socialist Club in February 1953,[2] but their security concerns hovered constantly on the horizon. In 1954, amidst the Chinese schools' May Thirteenth Incident, police raided the University of Malaya hostels at dawn on 28 May and arrested eight members of the University Socialist Club, charging them with sedition for articles published in the undergraduate magazine *Fajar*.

These eight accused students then approached the young lawyer Lee Kuan Yew, who had previously been involved in the Malayan Forum and had just returned home from legal studies abroad. Lee in turn secured the services of and assisted a British Queen's Counsel for a successful defence. This won the admiration of the Chinese middle school activists, who then decided to engage the pair for their own appeal hearing for those convicted of obstructing police during the May Thirteenth Incident. Even though the appeal ended unfavourably, a link between the Chinese- and English-educated activists had been forged and this paved the way for their collaboration in the founding of the People's Action Party (PAP) in 1954.

While the partnership between the Chinese- and English-educated activists was significant, it was the alliance between students and workers that pushed student political activism to its next peak. On 12 May 1955, a couple of thousand students joined nearly 300 labour union strikers at the Hock Lee Bus Company depot, leading to clashes with the police. A policeman, an American correspondent and a student were killed. Threatened with the closure of schools, the students barricaded themselves inside Chung Cheng High School, while the workers threatened a general strike. The David Marshall government, which publicly sympathised with the student and worker protesters, reopened the schools, appointed an all-party committee to examine the problems of Chinese education, and consented to register the Singapore Chinese Middle School Students' Union (SCMSSU).

Having a pan-island middle school union to coordinate their activities had been the students' demand. A pro-tem central committee had drafted the constitution for such a union by January 1955, but the British had rejected its registration. Now with the permission of David Marshall's Labour Front-Alliance government, the inaugural meeting of the SCMSSU was held in October 1955. Despite its initial undertaking to refrain from politics, the SCMSSU quickly positioned itself for greater activism by building up a membership of about 10,000 members and erecting multi-level committees in almost all of the Chinese middle schools.

This was only a temporary victory, however. Barely a year later, after David Marshall had resigned as a result of the failed London constitutional talks, Lim Yew Hock took over and worked with the British to launch a series of counter-subversion measures. He dissolved several alleged communist front organisations in September 1956 (including the SCMSSU), closed two Chinese schools and expelled more than 100 middle school students.

About 5,000 students responded with sit-in protests in six Chinese schools. The police had to be summoned to drive them out with a heavy barrage of tear gas and baton charges. Some students escaped to organise processions in various parts of the city. A two-day curfew was imposed. Labour unions were implicated in these student demonstrations and the Singapore Factory and Shop Workers' Union was subsequently dissolved, and its leaders, including Lim Chin Siong and James Puthucheary, were arrested. By then, Nanyang University (Nantah) had started classes, and the focus of student activism soon shifted to this new institution of higher learning.

Nantah had been established as a community initiative of the Singapore Hokkiens to cater for the growing legions of middle school graduates who had aspirations to further their studies but found their traditional access to Chinese universities being denied after the 1949 communist victory in China. It was a difficult birth, with the university suffering from government non-recognition of its degrees for admission into the civil service and from inadequate standards of university management. When both the S. L. Prescott and Gwee Ah Leng reports turned out to be unfavourable, the students, together with the university founders and sponsors, reacted negatively, but their reactions were initially confined mainly to the pages of student publications.

While tension was building up at Nantah, the Enright Affair erupted at the University of Malaya, sowing the seeds of student protests over the issue of university autonomy and academic freedom for several years to come. In his 1960 inaugural lecture, D. J. Enright, a recently arrived English professor, criticised an ongoing PAP anti-yellow culture campaign for its censorship and its ban on jukeboxes, warning against sterility of the cultural landscape. He was promptly chastised for meddling in local affairs and threatened with revocation of his employment pass. Students protested by staging a mock-funeral procession downtown with a coffin representing the death of 'University Autonomy and Academic Freedom'.

Student political activism rose to a new height following the PAP-Barisan split in 1961. The first sign of the split occurred when the leftists withheld support and caused the defeat of the PAP government candidate during the July 1961 Anson by-election. The formal split came with the formation of the Barisan Sosialis (Socialist Front), which claimed students and workers as major bases of support. Full mobilisation of this opposition front was activated when the PAP government forced the '3–3 Chinese-medium education system' (three years of junior middle and three years of senior middle schooling) to dovetail with the '4–2 English-medium system' (four years of secondary school and two years of junior college education). This realignment was regarded as putting the Chinese-educated at a disadvantage for admission into junior colleges, thus risking higher unemployment and obstructing the potential flow of Chinese middle school students into Nantah. Students of the Chinese middle schools and the Nantah Students' Union petitioned the Minister of Education, voiced forceful opposition in their publications and launched a boycott of the year-end examinations. Lee Khoon Choy, one of the PAP leaders, was transferred quickly to the Ministry of Education as Parliamentary Secretary to handle the demonstrations. He created an opposing Teachers' Union, weeded out principals and teachers sympathetic to the student protests through demotions and transfers, and expelled a large number of boycotting students.[3]

While the educational reform of the middle schools and Nantah constituted the first line of battle, the second was fought over the form of merger with Malaya by which Singapore could secure independence from British rule. Both the design of merger proposed by the government and the format of the national referendum on the issue were attacked vehemently. Nantah students and alumni were mobilised against the June 1962 referendum. Soon after the passage of the merger bill, security forces executed Operation Cold Store on 2 February 1963, leading to more than 100 detentions without trial, including a dozen Nantah students, and the suspension of the Nantah student publication permit. This sparked a major student protest against the indiscriminate use of the Internal Security Act, with the Nantah Students' Union joining hands with the student unions of the Polytechnic and the University of Singapore (formerly the University of Malaya) to issue a manifesto against the arrests and publication ban.

When general elections were called on 21 September 1963, the Barisan Sosialis fielded ten Nantah alumni to stand as candidates and mobilised the general student body to campaign for votes in order to make up for the depletion of the leftists' strength as a result of Operation Cold Store. Soon after the PAP's electoral victory, a big police raid on Nantah campus was launched on the dawn of 26 September, resulting in the arrest of a dozen students and alumni members.[4] The next morning, about 2,000 students held an emergency meeting to launch a classroom boycott from 3 October. Another 800 gathered at City Hall to petition the Prime Minister on 7 October. The government and university authorities ignored these protests and continued their plans to reform Nantah. There was a hiatus after their fourth meeting and the lull was used strategically to mobilise pro-government activists to rival and weaken the Nantah Students' Union. When they next met eight months later, on 5 June 1964, a six-point accord was swiftly announced, vowing to transform the university into a 'purely scholarly institution without any obstruction or influence by any political parties and subversive activities'.

About two weeks later, another large-scale police operation was executed on 27 June 1964, involving more than 1,000 security personnel from various agencies sweeping through the campus and arresting about 50 students. To justify this operation, the Malaysian central government issued a White Paper on 'Communism in the Nanyang University', accusing the Nanyang University Students' Union and the Guild of Nanyang University Graduates of having come under the control of the underground MCP. The paper also alleged that its Vice-Chancellor, Chuang Chu-lin, had succumbed to communist intimidation and was responsible for allowing Nantah to come under communist influence. When students tried to react with a hunger strike on 29 June, a media blackout was imposed. Two weeks later, the university administration, which had been reorganised after the resignation of Chuang, dismissed more than 100 students, administrative staff and canteen workers and served warning letters on another 150-odd students. The Students' Union fought back by leading students and university workers downtown to petition the Chinese Chamber of Commerce and to demonstrate outside the Hokkien Clan Association on 20 July. A parents' forum was also organised to voice grievances against student dismissals in early August, but police interrupted the protest by making more than 40 arrests and subsequently forcibly dissolving the recalcitrant student union. Soon after, stern regulatory measures were put in place to confine the organisation and activities of all student bodies within Nantah, such as restricting membership to a particular faculty or department, imposing faculty advisory roles on meetings and publications, and a whole range of penalties from warning letters to expulsions and detentions. However, as part of a two-pronged approach to limiting student political activism, pro-government student bodies were deliberately set up to recruit their own pool of student supporters to serve primarily as monitors.[5]

Highlights of Post-Independence Activism

Contrary to the government's wishes, student unrest of varying scale continued in the post-independence period, lasting up to the 1980s. Spurred by the PAP's efforts to reform tertiary education in Nanyang University through the Wang Gungwu Report, student protests reached new heights in 1965–66. The Wang Gungwu Committee on curriculum review was convened on 20 January 1965. It met for a total of 12 sessions from 12 February to 25 April, and submitted its final report on 14 May 1965. The recommended changes were extensive, including moving away from a reliance on Chinese as the medium of instruction and embracing Malay and English on a trilingual platform. While the Report was completed when Singapore was still part of the Federation of Malaysia, it was released to the public only on 11 September, after Singapore's shocking and painful exit from Malaysia and its unexpected attainment of nationhood as a tiny island state. With the ground for Malayanisation having shifted abruptly, and with trilingualism being reduced to bilingualism by practical curriculum considerations, massive student demonstrations broke out and vehement charges of Anglicisation were levelled. From October to December 1965 students staged street marches, petitions, and one of the longest boycotts of classes and examinations. The government retaliated with another round of large-scale detentions and expulsion of students.[6]

These Nantah protests over the Wang Gungwu Report and the PAP's university reforms soon overlapped with protests mounted over the Thong Saw Pak Report on Ngee Ann College released in early October 1966. The Chinese-medium college was originally launched by the Teochew-based Ngee Ann Kongsi as a parallel to the Hokkien-initiated Nanyang University. However, the Thong Report blocked this aspiration by recommending (1) the award of diplomas only, (2) barring the use of Chinese as the sole medium of instruction, and (3) the participation of government in its management council. While the Ngee Ann Kongsi accepted the report, the students did not and staged massive protests over the next two months. On 20 October, more than a quarter of the college population gathered at the campus and then took to the streets before storming into the Ministry of Education for a six-hour sit-in. This was followed by fairly large demonstrations at City Hall and during Lee Kuan Yew's opening of the new Nantah library building. On 4 November, 200 demonstrators, together with some representatives from the University of Singapore, the Polytechnic and Nanyang University, clashed with riot police at City Hall, resulting in ten Ngee Ann students being charged with rioting. Threatened with more demonstrations, the police laid siege and charged into the Ngee Ann College Hall on 19 November, ending the student barricade. Eighty-odd students were expelled and a banishment order was served on more than 50 Malaysian students. The Ngee Ann episode ended soon after the government passed legislation in March 1967 to transform this other private, dialect-group educational initiative into an institution of polytechnic learning largely funded and directed by the state.

As the Ngee Ann activism was ending, the Enright Affair re-erupted. Although chastised by the authorities and triggering a storm of protests in

1960, Professor Enright chose to stay on at the University of Singapore, apparently teaching well and inspiring a generation of students in English Literature. However, he clashed again with the authorities over policy matters when Deputy Prime Minister Toh Chin Chye took over the vice-chancellorship in 1968. This time Enright had to leave. Toh's appointment was seen as the PAP government asserting direct control over the university, ensuring that it would not be 'a potential centre of opposition' and 'it was perhaps his job to kill our spirit and make sure we all don't raise independent voices and have an effective union'. A fresh round of student and academic staff protests flared up over the lack of university autonomy and academic freedom. One of the leaders of a rally mounted in the campus quadrangle was Tommy Koh, who was then 'a youthful, left-wing activist, and even when he was a young law lecturer', but who was later persuaded by the establishment to be Singapore's ambassador to the United Nations and then to the United States.[7]

Despite Toh Chin Chye's disciplinary approach, students found the occasional space to organise protests over several external events. In December 1969, about 30 students demonstrated in front of the United States embassy over the My Lai Massacre in Vietnam. They tore up the American flag, petitioned the ambassador, displayed placards and distributed protest letters to the public. On 16 January 1971, a delegation of 15 students from the University of Singapore Student Union (USSU) executive committee and the Democratic Socialist Club protested against the apartheid policy in South Africa and Rhodesia and presented a petition to the Minister for Foreign Affairs and Labour at City Hall. When the *Singapore Herald's* licence was revoked on 28 May 1971, Singapore University students helped to sell the paper in the streets and condemned the government's closure of the newspaper.[8]

Over at Nantah, when Lee Kuan Yew made another attempt to switch its medium of instruction to English in the mid-1970s, the president of the Nantah Student Union, Ho Juan Thai, urged students to protest by writing their examination papers in Chinese instead of English. He was promptly removed from his post as student union leader. Upon graduation, he contested the 1976 general election as a Workers' Party candidate on the grounds of defending Chinese education and cultural identity. He secured 31 per cent of the votes but lost the election and, fearing reprisals, fled to London.[9]

A much better known episode of student activism than the Ho Juan Thai event was the 1974–75 one involving the Juliet Chin-Tan Wah Piow duo, even though this incident has faded into the distant background, given the national amnesia and selective recollections.[10] There was a series of quick escalations of student involvement in the wider society when Juliet Chin and Tan Wah Piow held consecutive leadership of the USSU in 1974–75. They initiated joint action with the student leaders of Nantah, the Singapore Polytechnic and Ngee Ann Technical College to act against the proposed ten-cent rise in bus fare in February 1974. Research committees and protests against fare hikes were organised, including a public petition campaign which garnered 10,000 signatures. In July, they organised protests over a $100 tuition fee hike. The USSU then joined hands with the Singapore Polytechnic Student Union to launch a 'Bangladesh Flood Relief Campaign' in August and to take up the cause of the forced relocation of Tasek Utara squatters in Johore, Malaysia in September. In October, another cause was added to their social agenda: the plight of retrenched American marine workers in Jurong. The USSU set up a retrenchment recruitment centre and challenged the PAP-National Trades Union Congress-affiliated Pioneer Industries Employees Union to secure a better deal for the retrenched workers. Tan Wah Piow was soon arrested on charges of causing a riot on 30 October, in the office premises of the labour union. Five of his student co-leaders were detained and deported, including Juliet Chin. Tan's arrest and trial provoked a wave of protests on and off campus, including a mass rally attended by about 4,000 students, and a two-day boycott of classes in December. Joanna Wong, who worked at the university registrar office for nearly four decades, recalled a worrisome moment when over 2,000 students swarmed the quadrangle in the Bukit Timah campus to demonstrate against the university administration and she was asked to convince Juliet Chin to stop her incitement of freshmen to boycott lectures.[11] On 22 February 1975, Tan was found guilty and sentenced to a year in prison. After his release from prison and just before he was drafted into the armed forces, he escaped to London in 1976, claiming that he had been framed and intimidated by the state. Meanwhile the PAP had moved quickly to amend the university constitution, completely changing the structure, funding and activities of student unions and other student bodies. This was a fatal blow to further student political activism, leading Mary Turnbull to mark 1975 as 'the end of student activism'.[12] In London, in an echo of the Malayan Forum challenge to the British colonial authorities of the early 1950s, Tan Wah Piow led active opposition to the Singapore government from within the Federation of the United Kingdom and Ireland, Malaysia and Singapore Student Organisation (FUEMSSO). In 1986, in a move to pre-empt the possible return of exiled Singapore citizens to challenge its power, the PAP government enacted laws to strip Singapore citizenship from those who had been absent from the country for more than ten years.

While it was true that the campus political activism of the 1950s and 1960s no longer made an overt appearance after the mid-1970s, its impact continued to be felt in an uncanny way through further internal security crackdowns on various segments of society right into the 1980s. Not much is known about the wave of arrests in the second half of the 1970s,[13] but more information is available about the alleged May 1987 Marxist conspiracy, which also carried a resonance of student activism. The latter involved more than two dozen working professionals and church workers, some of whom had student activist pasts while a few were still studying at the Singapore Polytechnic.[14]

On 21 May 1987, 16 people who were mostly from an English-educated, middle-class background and who were engaged in Christian social action programmes were detained without trial for being part of a clandestine communist network. This conspiratorial network was alleged to comprise not only prominent religious organisations but student groupings as well, including the Student Christian Movement of Singapore (SCM), the National University of Singapore Catholic Students' Society and Singapore Polytechnic Catholic Students' Society. Of these initial 16, at least seven had been student union activists in their younger days, five were members of drama group *Third Stage*, one was the sister of expelled USSU president Juliet Chin, and several were helping out with the constitutional political opposition Workers' Party. At one point, the reactions the arrests had provoked among certain sections of the Catholic community threat-ened a collision between the state and church. The urgent attention of Lee Kuan Yew and Archbishop Gregory Yong was required to restore a sense of equilibrium, resulting in the resignation of four leading priests from church bodies and their departure from Singapore in the first half of June.[15]

On 20 June 1987, the government released four of the detainees but arrested six new individuals who were accused of being involved in the same plot. Of these six, five had current or past links to the USSU, SCM or the Polytechnic Students' Union. On 28 and 29 June, a two-part televi-sion broadcast revealed that the leader behind the plot was none other than Tan Wah Piow, the ex-USSU leader who had been jailed for rioting on union premises and who had fled to London just before being enlisted for national service. Some of the detainees were released in mid-July and in the second half of September 1987. However, when nine of those discharged issued a signed statement in April 1988 proclaiming their innocence and ill-treatment during detention, they were promptly re-arrested, except for one who was overseas.[16] All the detainees served varying periods of confine-ment before their eventual release.

Framed in a Simplified Binary World

The above episodic charting of the course of student political activism from the 1940s to the 1980s does not provide full coverage of the young pathfinders who played a critical role in the history of Singapore's formative years. Their detailed stories, with a complete range of nuances about their ideological makeup, cultural values, motivations and activities, have yet to be written. This brief outline, however, is sufficient to allow us to problematise the official scripting of national history that boxed such student activists into a simplified binary frame of 'Chinese- versus English-educated activists'.

The language divide within the Chinese community on the island city-state of Singapore can be traced back to the governing policy of the British colonial authorities. In fulfilling the educational needs of the growing population, they adopted a hands-off approach, devoting resources only to training a small group of English-educated civil servants, doctors and lawyers, and leaving the majority of the Chinese population on their own to organise self-help associations and build Chinese-medium schools for their children. Over the years, even as the differences between the products of the English- and Chinese-medium schools blurred and a small number emerged to straddle the two streams, the educated segment remained conveniently dichotomised as a binary of the Chinese- and English-educated.

The codification of this binary system has been given considerable weighting in the interpretation of student political activism. While the differences in pedagogical approaches and educational values provide an underlying logic in making a distinction between these two groups of student organisations and activities, it is official accounts of the history of Singapore that have greatly accentuated the differences between these activists, ascribed extraneous values to them, and introduced rigidity to the point of making the division almost ahistorical.

Lee Kuan Yew in particular frames his narrative of student activism within the binary framework and readily casts the Chinese-educated activists as the ones succumbing to communist manipulation and subversion. His views apparently took shape rather early, when he first observed the protests and participated in the trials of the Chinese middle school activists during the May Thirteenth Incident of 1954. It was on this occasion that Lee, as an English-educated graduate recently returned from overseas studies in London, was supposedly led into 'a totally different world, one teeming with raw energy and idealism'. 'The world of the Chinese-educated' (which he has tellingly chosen to title chapter 9 of his memoirs) was 'well-organized, disciplined and cohesive' and they were 'resourceful fund raisers'. They had 'remarkable self-control and were capable of mass action, of collective demonstrations of defiance that made it difficult for the government to isolate and pick out the leaders for punishment'. Lee's 'initiation' was into 'a world full of vitality, of so many activists, all like jumping beans, of so many young idealists, unselfish, ready to sacrifice everything for a better society'. He was 'deeply impressed by their seemingly total dedication to the cause of revolution, their single-minded determination to overturn the colonial government in order to establish a new world of equality and fairness'.[17]

These perceived qualities were in total contrast to the group of 'English-educated students who had published *Fajar*' and 'who spoke diffidently, lacked self-confidence, and were psychologically hobbled when they used a language that was not their mother tongue'. Lee regarded many of the English-educated of the 1950s as being 'ill-informed and naïve' and 'simple-minded'. He reckoned then that it would be fatal to cultivate political links only with the English-educated, 'who did not have the convictions or the energies to match, never mind the will to resist' their Chinese-educated counterparts.[18]

While pursuing a vigorous policy of privileging the learning and usage of the English language for all citizens, Lee also subscribed to the belief that the learning of the 'non-mother tongue' had contributed fundamentally to student apathy. In 2000, when writing about 'many tongues, one language', Lee reaffirms:

> When I acted as legal adviser for the Chinese middle school student leaders in the 1950s I was impressed by their vitality, dynamism, discipline and social and political commitment. By contrast, I was dismayed at the apathy, self-centredness and lack of self-confidence of the English-educated students. The nub of the problem was that in our multiracial and multilingual society, English was the only acceptable neutral language, besides being the language that would make us relevant to the world. But it did seem to deculturalise our students and make them apathetic.[19]

Interrogating the Binary Characterisation

The division of student activists into a binary world underpins the storyline of Singapore's national history and distorts our understanding of student political activism in three ways. Firstly, it encourages the tendency to focus our attention almost exclusively on the activism of the Chinese middle schools and Nanyang University, making us forget that the English-educated activists had their own moments of effervescence and also contributed to the political life of Singapore. Secondly, it leads us to ignore the fact that, in the reality of defined space and multilayered interactions, there had been a fair degree of porosity and inter-connectedness in that binary world. Thirdly, it promotes the presupposition that the Chinese-educated students were highly susceptible to communism.

Historian Yeo Kim Wah is probably the first academic to grapple seriously with the simplifications and rigidity of this binary conception. He is a leading authority on the early history of post-war Singapore and wrote the 1973 classic work, *Political Development in Singapore, 1945–1955.* He accepted the fact that there were fundamental differences in the mindset and operational style of the Chinese- and English-educated activists and, for a period of his scholarly life, allowed this binary conception to block out scrutiny of English-educated activism. In his first monograph, he wrote of the language divide as one in which:

> on the one hand, [the Chinese-educated] held the English-educated in contempt for their lack of knowledge of Chinese culture and language, their 'commercial-mindedness', and their receptiveness to 'yellow culture' such as juke-boxes, playboy magazines, sex films and dancing. Above all, the English-educated were considered reactionary because they were believed to have played hardly any part in the anti-colonial struggle. On the other hand, the Chinese-educated intensely resented what they regarded as privileges and preferential treatment enjoyed by the English-educated.[20]

Chapter five of this definitive work deals specifically with 'Student Politics', which in turn is divided into two sub-sections: 'Prewar Student Politics' and 'Postwar Student Politics'. Significantly, both portions centred almost exclusively on student organisations and activities in Chinese schools, leaving the English-educated student activists out in the cold. Yeo himself came to realise this distortion and spent a substantial part of the next stage of his academic life addressing the shortcoming. In the early 1990s, he published two complementary pieces focusing on student politics in the initial years of the English-medium University of Malaya and on how the early English-educated radicals were converted to communism. Through these two updates, we now have a clearer account of the early English-educated activists operating at the tertiary level and a timely reminder that they had appeared even before their Chinese-educated counterparts in articulating anti-colonial nationalist views.[21]

The other major and more recent reinforcement of the binary view of student activism comes from an interview granted by Koh Tai Ann to a group of young local intellectuals seeking out pluralistic voices in Singapore's history, especially in relation to student politics. Koh had opted for an academic career and served in numerous tertiary institutions. When she first entered the University of Singapore as a student in 1964, she plunged into student politics and became a member of the union executive committee and was co-founder of the Democratic Socialist Club, which had been formed to counter the University Socialist Club because the latter, supposedly, had come under the influence of the leftists and Barisan Sosialis. She had helped to run the student union's *USSU Bulletin* and newspaper *The Singapore Undergrad*, as well as the Democratic Socialist Club's newsletter *Socialist Democrat* and official journal *Demos*.[22] There were occasions during the interview when Koh appeared to have remained entrapped in the binary framework put forward by the PAP orthodoxy. She viewed the students of the University of Singapore and Nantah as 'very different, extremely different' and one could tell them apart from the simplicity and uniformity in the way Nantah students dressed and the Spartan conditions of living and eating at Nantah hostels. Ideologically, Nantah students were:

> more socially and community-oriented, more politicised, and certainly more intense and passionate. In fact, Lee Kuan Yew in his way even admired them, and despised the University of Singapore students. He once said ... that SU students were cowards, we don't stand up for our beliefs, whereas the Nantah students would risk jail for their beliefs.[23]

Despite being unable to escape from the restrictive binary framework, her personal experiences and campus knowledge nevertheless allowed her interview to have the effect of subverting the orthodoxy. Almost following up on Yeo Kim Wah's defined period of study which ended in the mid-1950s, Koh's interview provided many useful details and comments which were used earlier in this chapter to highlight the various episodes of student protests among the English-educated from the 1960s to the 1980s, ranging from the Enright affairs to the Juliet Chin-Tan Wah Piow duo and the alleged Marxist conspiracy of 1987. The English-educated was clearly also a force to be reckoned with in the years of anti-colonial struggle and nation building, and student activism was never the exclusive domain of the Chinese-educated.

The second effect of the simplification is the inadequate attention given to the porosity and inter-connectedness between these two worlds. The earlier sections on charting the course of student political activism points out many instances of such interactions. The intertwining of the events of the May Thirteenth Incident of 1954 with the *Fajar* trial, involving the same set of lawyers, was one example. Another instance occurred during the 1963 Operation Cold Store. While Nantah students and alumni were the main targets, the student unions of the Singapore Polytechnic and University of Singapore cooperated to issue a manifesto criticising the government for the detentions and ban on student publications. Similarly, during the protests against the 1965 Wang Gungwu Report on Nanyang University, student representatives from the Ngee Ann College Students' Union, the University Socialist Club of the University of Singapore and the Singapore Polytechnic Political Society jointly petitioned the Singapore Chinese Chamber of Commerce. The uproar over the 1966 Thong Saw Pak Report on Ngee Ann College saw combined student demonstrations at City Hall and even prompted the pro-tem formation of an abortive National Student Action Front for the purpose of uniting students across all tertiary institutions in the country. Juliet Chin and Tan Wah Piow of the University of Singapore were also able to mobilise all four tertiary institutions to coordinate widespread protests against the proposed ten-cent rise in bus fare in February 1974, followed by a joint venture with the Singapore Polytechnic Student Union to organise a Bangladesh Flood Relief Campaign in August.

The third and most problematic aspect of the simplified binary is the presupposition of an equivalent relationship between the Chinese-educated student activists and communism. There is a natural transition in Lee Kuan Yew's *Singapore Story* from praising the sterling qualities of energy, discipline and commitment of the Chinese-educated to viewing them as formidable communist foes. Lee believed that the neglect, self-reliance and marginalisation of Chinese education since the beginning of colonial settlement had provided fertile ground for agents of the Comintern and the communist movement in China to operate in Singapore since the 1930s, and to take advantage of the MCP's reputation in having resisted Japanese forces during the war.[24] Given that Lee's account is essentially post-war, the nexus between the Chinese-educated and communism has been taken as something that was already firmly in place. Not only has that equation been presumed, but other variables such as constitutional radicalism and left-wing nationalist politics were denied space as legitimate tropes to understanding the Chinese-educated activists of the 1950s and 1960s. They were all labelled as 'anti-national' elements, intent on exploiting the anti-colonial movement and Chinese education for the benefit of international communism. The three Cs of communism, chauvinism and communalism were all portrayed as rogues of nation-building, and the Chinese-educated activists as subversive operatives.

It is significant that Lee has found it necessary to confront and delete what was possibly his own early printed denial of a connection between the Chinese-educated and communism by dismissing that past denial as a moment of folly. With reference to the impending appeal trial of students who were involved in the May Thirteenth Incident, Lee was quoted in the *Nanyang Siang Pau*'s 20 September 1954 edition as saying:

> Until now the [colonial] authorities have no evidence of any communist activity in the Chinese schools; but they regard opposition to the government's refusal to allow the students postponement of service as communist activity and under this pretext, they seek to exercise better control over the Chinese schools.

Lee singled this out in his memoir so that he would be able to retract his statement and go on to reinforce the communist puppetry template, claiming that 'I was ignorant, gullible and stupid. I did not know just how efficient the communists were, how their tentacles reached out and controlled every single organization that was bubbling up against the government.'[25]

However, the communist subversion template, initially forged by the British colonial authorities and later reiterated and brandished by the postcolonial Singapore government, had in recent years come under increasing contestation from various quarters that were eager to stake out their own place in history. Those contestations are a separate story, some of which are told in this volume and others elsewhere.[26]

NOTES

1   Most of the information in the first two sections of this paper is taken from extant literature and the following works have been consulted more than others: C. M. Turnbull, *A History of Singapore, 1819–1988* (Singapore: Oxford University Press, 1989); Lee Kuan Yew, *The Singapore Story: Memoirs of Lee Kuan Yew* (Singapore: Times Editions, 1998); Yeo Kim Wah, *Political Development in Singapore, 1945–55* (Singapore: Singapore University Press, 1973); Yeo Kim Wah, 'Student Politics in University of Malaya, 1949–51', in *Journal of Southeast Asian Studies* 23, 2 (1992); Yeo Kim Wah, 'Joining the Communist Underground: The Conversion of English-Educated Radicals to Communism in Singapore, June 1948–January 1951' in *Journal of the Malaysian Branch of the Royal Asiatic Society* 67, Pt. 1 (1994); 'The World of the English-Educated in the 1960s and 1970s: An Interview with Koh Tai Ann', *Tangent* 6 (April 2003); Khe Su Lin, *Lixiang yu xianshi: Nanyang daxue xueshenghui yanjiu, 1956–1964* [*Ideal and Reality: A Study of Nanyang University Students' Union, 1956–1964*] (Singapore: World Scientific Printers, 2006). Where additional details are provided, supplementary citations follow.

2 For early activities of the Socialist Club, see Koh Tat Boon, 'University of Singapore Socialist Club, 1953–1962', Honours Academic Exercise, History Department, University of Singapore, 1972/73.

3 Lee Khoon Choy, *On the Beat to the Hustings: An Autobiography* (Singapore: Times Books International, 1988), pp. 68–70; Sai Siew Min and Huang Jianli, 'The "Chinese-educated" Political Vanguards: Ong Pang Boon, Lee Khoon Choy and Jek Yeun Thong', in *Lee's Lieutenants: Singapore's Old Guard*, ed. Lam Peng Er and Kevin Y. L. Tan (St Leonards: Allen & Unwin, 1999), p. 146.

4 See Yao Suchou's chapter in this volume, 'All Quiet on Jurong Road'.

5 This approach of applying restrictive legislation to student organisations in combination with the formation of pro-party student agencies was very similar to that adopted by the Guomindang in Republican China; see Huang Jianli, *The Politics of Depoliticization: Guomindang Policy Towards Student Political Activism, 1927–1949* (Berne: Peter Lang, 1996).

6 For a detailed discussion on the Wang Gungwu Report, see Huang Jianli, 'Nanyang University and the Language Divide in Singapore: Controversy over the 1965 Wang Gungwu Report', in *Nantah tuxiang: Lishi heliuzhong de shengshi* [Imagery of Nanyang University: Reflections on the River of History], ed. Lee Guan Kin (Singapore: Global Publishing, 2007), pp. 165–220.

7 'The World of the English-Educated in the 1960s and 1970s: An Interview with Koh Tai Ann', *Tangent* 6 (April 2003): 269, 274, 280, 289.

8 Edna Tan Hong Ngoh, '"Official" Perceptions of Student Activism on Nantah and SU Campuses, 1965–1974/75', Honours Thesis, History Department, National University of Singapore, 2001/2, pp. 12, 13. I am also indebted to her for sharing the source materials.

9 In another instance of privileging Chinese student activism over that of the English-educated, this less well-known episode of activism is recorded in Lee Kuan Yew, *From Third World to First: The Singapore Story* (Singapore: Times Editions, 2000), pp. 172, 173.

10 Ibid., p. 137, makes no reference to the Juliet Chin-Tan Wah Piow student activities of the mid-1970s, except to link Tan to Lee's personal authorisation of the Internal Security Department's detentions of the 1987 Marxist conspirators.

11 Interview with Joanna Wong, in *The Straits Times*, 2 February 2001.

12 C. M. Turnbull, *A History of Singapore, 1819–1988*, p. 309.

13 This round of detentions involved as many as 50 people who were said to be associated with a so-called 'Liberation Front'. Detainees included cultural personae, such as Kuo Pao Kun and Yeng Pway Ngon, and those who apparently had been involved in political activism during their student days.

14 For further details beyond the brief exploration here, see Michael Barr's chapter in this volume.

15 Michael Hill and Lian Kwen Fee, *The Politics of Nation Building and Citizenship in Singapore* (London: Routledge, 1995), p. 206; Lee Lai To, 'Singapore in 1987', *Asian Survey* 28, 2 (1988): 202–12; Garry Rodan, 'Singapore's Leadership Transition: Erosion or Refinement of Authoritarian Rule?', *Bulletin*

of Concerned Asian Scholars 24 (1992): 3–17; '"Marxist plot" Revisited: Reactions of the Church in Singapore', in http://www.singapore-window.org/sw01/010521m3.htm, accessed on 8 July 2001.

16 '"Marxist plot" Revisited: Reactions of the Church in Singapore', in http://www.singapore-window.org/sw01/010521m3.htm, accessed on 8 July 2001; 'Was there really a "Marxist Conspiracy"? How can we make sense of this event?' http://www.sintercom.org/sef/ conspiracy.html, updated by Tan Chong Kee on 9 April 1995, accessed on 8 July 2001.

17 Lee Kuan Yew, *The Singapore Story*, pp. 165, 166, 168, 171 and 173.

18 Ibid., pp. 168, 171–3.

19 Lee Kuan Yew, *From Third World to First: The Singapore Story, 1965–2000*, p. 173.

20 Yeo Kim Wah, *Political Development in Singapore, 1945–55*, pp. 177–8.

21 The earlier descriptive outline of Malayan University campus activism drew mainly from Yeo Kim Wah, 'Student Politics in University of Malaya, 1949–51', in *Journal of Southeast Asian Studies* 23, 2 (1992): 346–80 and his 'Joining the Communist Underground: The Conversion of English-Educated Radicals to Communism in Singapore, June 1948–January 1951', in *Journal of the Malaysian Branch of the Royal Asiatic Society* 67, Pt. 1 (1994): 29–59.

22 'The World of the English-Educated in the 1960s and 1970s: An Interview with Koh Tai Ann', *Tangent* 6 (April 2003): 261, 262, 272, 285, 293.

23 Ibid., pp. 263, 264.

24 Lee Kuan Yew, *The Singapore Story*, p. 167. Going much further than Lee were two commissioned works on the history of post-war Singapore — Dennis Bloodworth, *The Tiger and the Trojan Horse* (Singapore: Times Book International, 1986) and John Drysdale, *Singapore: Struggle for Success* (Singapore: Times Book International, 1984). Both embellished their narratives with a blatantly culturalist emphasis and the logic of ethnic primodialism in order to link the Chinese-educated with incipient communist tendencies; see Sai Siew Min and Huang Jianli, 'The "Chinese-Educated" Political Vanguards: Ong Pang Boon, Lee Khoon Choy & Jek Yeun Thong', in *Lee's Lieutenants*, pp. 132–68.

25 Lee Kuan Yew, *The Singapore* Story, p. 173.

26 Contestations through memoirs, archives, novels and theatre are discussed in other versions of this paper. See Huang Jianli, 'Positioning the Student Political Activism of Singapore: Articulation, Contestation and Omission', in *Inter-Asia Cultural Studies* 7, 3 (September 2006): 403–30: Hong Lysa and Huang Jianli, *The Scripting of a National History: Singapore and its Pasts* (Singapore: NUS Press, 2008), chapter 7.

11

The Left-Wing Trade Unions
in Singapore, 1945–1970

Michael Fernandez
and Loh Kah Seng

This chapter seeks to take the history of the left-wing trade union movement in Singapore beyond the question of communist subversion, which
was a product of the Cold War and which has fixated scholars for too
long.[1] The story of the left-wing trade union movement in Singapore is
customarily told from the perspective of the victors, the People's Action
Party (PAP).[2] Their account of the suppression of the unions originates
in the early 1960s, with the PAP government accusing left-wing union
leaders of being front men of the Malayan Communist Party (MCP) or
their pawns. That was a time when virtually every manifestation of union
militancy and left-wing activism was construed as evidence of the power
of the MCP. Our contribution, however, provides a window into the trade
union movement from the inside.[3] It attempts to convey an alternative
reading of the politics of this period, from the perspectives of militants
who were motivated by anti-colonialism and concern for workers, drawn
from oral and biographical accounts and union publications. It is corroborated by other evidence, including newspaper reports and summaries, and
economic statistics and documents from the regimes which mistrusted and
persecuted the movement.

There are encouraging signs in recent years that, thematically, the history of the Singapore left has begun to move beyond communist subversion to anti-colonialism. It has been shown that even the status of Lim Chin Siong — the most prominent pro-communist operative in post-war Singapore — was not clear to either the British or to the Singapore Special Branch, and remains a point of debate among academics.[4] This does not leave Singapore historiography in a postmodern lurch; on the contrary, it offers us the opportunity to tell the story of the left from the point of view of issues which were important to its leaders, and to the workers who supported them, during those years.

'Trade Unionism and Politics are One and the Same'[5]

In the early twentieth century, Chinese workers belonged to associations based on locality, surname and kinship or to guilds comprising workers and employers; not surprisingly these organisations were controlled by the employer. Leading Chinese businessmen collaborated with the British regime, which appointed them to the Legislative Council, the Municipal Commission and the Chinese Advisory Board.[6] Chinese workers could be made to work up to 12–14 hours daily and were given only two holidays a year, during the Lunar New Year, while bus workers were paid low wages and treated as tools.[7] To establish its bargaining power against employers, the labour movement had to be militant and anti-colonial. The British government conceded in 1946 that the unions' militancy was 'a stage in the growth of Unionism in this country which is to be expected'.[8] The movement was essentially engaged in a struggle to restore to the worker his dignity and full rights as a person.[9]

The relationship between politics and trade unionism must be understood in this light. Carl Trocki claims that the left-wing unions placed the political agenda above economic aims.[10] For the unionists, however, 'economic security was given first priority among the aims of our leaders'.[11] James Puthucheary, Lim Chin Siong's deputy in the Singapore Factory and Shop Workers' Union (SFSWU), asserts that 'trade unions should influence political parties and not vice versa'.[12] To the union leaders, the economic and the political were necessarily intertwined: to safeguard workers' interests, labour had to become a primary player in the country's politics. Consequently '[p]olitical agitation is ... inseparable from any labour movement',[13] as 'the fight to improve the working conditions cannot be isolated from the struggle for a pro-workers' Government and a fair and democratic Society'.[14] Yet political action was possible only when union leaders had advanced workers' interests, such as when the Singapore Bus Workers' Union (SBWU) 'took the initiative and lead [*sic*] the workers to raise their living standard'.[15]

In the 1930s, the trade union movement began to establish itself as a permanent voice in Singapore politics. The MCP encouraged the formation of unions along Western lines and, through the Malayan General Labour Union (GLU), organised a number of Malaya-wide strikes for higher wages involving Chinese workers in 1936–37.[16] The movement failed to bridge ethnic divides, however, as the MCP was essentially a Chinese party. In 1940, the British government recognised the legality of trade unions, but this was apparently a propaganda attempt to win over the Malayan working class in the context of the war in Europe.[17] Before the Pacific War, in the absence of official protection, workers' welfare remained largely dependent on the goodwill of employers.

The labour movement's anti-colonialism was heightened by the British capitulation of 15 February 1942. In the post-war years, in Singapore, as in many other developing countries, the movement imagined itself as part of a global labour and anti-colonial movement.[18] Devan Nair recalled that '[t]he names and pronouncements of the Great Titans of this Asian revolution — of men like Soekarno, Mao Tse Tung, Nehru and Gandhi fired our imaginations'.[19] The role of communists at the forefront of international decolonisation inspired anti-colonial politics in Singapore and fused it with the language and spirit of Marxism. For Lim Chin Siong,

> the victory of the Chinese Communist Party [in 1949] ... had far-reaching consequences ... Many Socialists in the world believed that the people in the colonies and the semi-colonies must unite and join forces with the Socialists, headed by Russia.[20]

Most leftists, while sympathetic to communist ideas, were probably not doctrinaire Marxists but socialists. Chen Say Jame, who claimed that he 'found out' who the 'communists' were only after they were detained, insisted that the search for unity made ideological distinctions secondary:

> Many people thought that the MCP was involved, because the MCP could not be seen. But it was not our responsibility to find out who was a communist. At that time, our greatest strength was to unite everyone against the colonial power, that was the most important thing.[21]

Moreover, until the MCP's armed insurrection in mid-1948, the party was legal and popular, too, having endeared itself to the Chinese population through its anti-Japanese activities during the war. To many workers, the MCP appeared to be the most progressive force for resolving their economic problems: low wages, high cost of living, which in December 1946 was 3¼ times that in 1939,[22] and a shortage of rice, their chief staple. The MCP expanded its influence in unions made up of Chinese-speaking industrial workers in small- and medium-sized Chinese firms but was less successful in unions in the Naval Base, the public service such as the Municipality and Public Works Department (PWD), and large commercial firms such as the Singapore Traction Company (STC).[23]

The number of unions climbed from 11 in 1946 to 177 in 1948, with a combined membership of 76,000 (Table 1). Their activism was both anti-colonial and pro-communist. The Singapore GLU, the MCP's labour arm,

Table 1

Number of Trade Unions and Employee Unions in Singapore, 1946–65

Year	Total unions	Total union membership	No. of employee unions	Employee union membership
1946	11	N.A.	8	18,673
1947	163	N.A.	126	96,067
1948	177	76,000	118	74,367
1949	132	51,654	93	47,301
1950	133	53,561	91	48,595
1951	147	63,228	107	58,322
1952	164	69,152	122	63,831
1953	176	78,806	133	73,566
1954	181	81,741	136	76,452
1955	236	145,112	187	139,317
1956	265	163,137	205	157,216
1957	277	147,132	216	140,710
1958	281	135,255	218	129,159
1959	238	152,639	176	146,579
1960	190	150,554	130	144,770
1961	184	170,193	124	164,462
1962	178	194,904	122	189,032
1963	170	148,641	112	142,936
1964	160	163,128	106	157,050
1965	164	119,832	106	113,754

Source: Compiled from *Singapore Annual Reports* 1946–65.

organised 92 strikes in 1946–47. The causes were both economic — for improved wages and working conditions — and political — condemnation of the shipment of British ammunition to Java,[24] support for independence and labour movements abroad and praise of the MCP for its anti-Japanese efforts.[25] The strikes embraced broad sections of the working class, including firemen, hospital attendants, cabaret girls, lightermen and employees of the Singapore Harbour Board (SHB), STC, Naval Base, Municipality, and the PWD. Of the 119 strikes between October 1945 and September 1947, 101 were successful.[26] Politically, the unions were an important part of the broad pan-Malayan alliance of political parties and civil associations pressing for equal rights for the people of Malaya in 1946–48, although the Anglo-Malay collaboration, which endorsed Malay special rights, eventually won out.

The labour movement weakened after 1947, when improvements in the economy reduced labour's willingness to strike.[27] More importantly, to bar the communists, the colonial regime adopted tighter labour laws on the administration and membership of unions. When armed conflict with the MCP broke out in June 1948, the colonial government introduced the Emergency Regulations which, by giving it the power to detain suspected communists without trial, expanded its hardline policy towards the left. The Singapore Federation of Trade Unions, the Singapore GLU's successor, was deregistered in December. Unions were required by law to give two weeks' strike notice, which allowed the management time to employ strikebreakers or resolve disputes in the interim.[28] Many union leaders, fearing to be branded as communists or 'fellow travellers', left the political arena.[29] The unions operating between 1948 and 1953 were non-political and moderate, such as the Singapore Trade Union Congress (STUC) established by V. K. Nair and Lim Yew Hock in May 1951, which predictably failed to appeal to the Chinese unions.

The Mid-1950s: '时势造英雄' (Changing Times Create Heroes)[30]

The movement's revival occurred in 1954. The conventional explanation is that the MCP revived the united front in the more relaxed political situation in Singapore brought about by the Rendel Constitution of 1954, but given the British crackdown on the communists, this theory is unconvincing. Even the insight offered by C. C. Chin in his chapter in this volume, that the MCP's Workers' Committee remained active between 1948 and 1954, offers no support for the contention that the MCP initiated the upsurge in union activity during this period. Rather, his contribution provides a strong argument that the MCP was struggling to maintain its influence over the unions during this period, and that the workers' movement was largely spontaneous and really beyond the control of the MCP. Economic and political circumstances themselves were sufficient to nurture a revival of left-wing politics. Workers continued to receive low pay, and to experience poor working conditions and unsympathetic employers. The rising cost of living was behind most demands for wage increases in the early 1950s. The Weekly Holidays Ordinance obliged shops to close for one whole day per week but violations of the Ordinance were reportedly 'numerous' in 1954, with 250 convictions recorded.[31]

From 1954, the labour movement produced leaders who were charismatic, militant and most importantly, were dedicated to the workers' cause: individuals like Lim Chin Siong, who headed the SFSWU, Fong Swee Suan (SBWU), Sydney Woodhull (Naval Base Labour Union, NBLU), and Jamit Singh (Singapore Harbour Board Staff Association, SHBSA). They came from diverse backgrounds; some were former Chinese middle school students, others members of the University of Malaya Socialist Club and yet others were English teachers.[32] Although portrayed in mainstream history as 'communist front leaders', their leadership was basically a response to the times.

Given the MCP's strong role in the trade union movement of the late 1940s, it is likely that the communists would have retained some influence in this period, but how much is unknown, even today. What is indisputable was the broad coalition of politicians, university and Chinese middle school students, and workers arrayed against the colonial system. In 1954, Chinese school students vigorously opposed British military conscription, with the University of Malaya Socialist Club publishing anti-imperialist editorials, which led to the *Fajar* arrests and trial in July–August. The left supported the party deemed to be the most progressive, and that was the PAP, which comprised the Lee Kuan Yew group and leftists such as Lim Chin Siong, Fong Swee Suan, James Puthucheary, Samad Ismail and Devan Nair.

Understanding the labour movement requires a deconstruction of the terms 'strike' and 'riot'. Strikes were officially defined by their undesired outcomes: the Hock Lee Bus strike of April–May 1955, for instance, is disparaged for the 946,354 man-days lost and naturally degenerated into 'riots', since '[p]ro-communist politicians were most interested in fostering unrest and violence'.[33] This explanation ignores workers' grievances and misrepresents the unions' intent. Lim Chin Siong argued that riots took place not because union leaders incited the workers but because of 'social conditions'; 1955 was a landmark year, with David Marshall's Labour government's pledge to support labour acting as a stimulus to union activism. The mood in many strikes was tense, with employers often refusing to recognise the unions, forming splinter or 'yellow unions' to challenge them, and hiring blacklegs or strikebreakers, often secret society members, to work.[34] As the colonial regime typically supported the employers, union leaders had to call strikes to obtain employers' basic recognition of workers' grievances.[35] Picketers frequently blocked workers who wanted to work or lay on the ground to prevent vehicles from leaving the strike premises. Scuffles were common between the picketers, pro-management workers, blacklegs and police, and reflected the frustrations of workers. It is simplistic to blame the violence solely on communist instigation.

For the left, the Hock Lee Bus dispute was of 'great historical significance', for it 'greatly influenced the trade union movement which due to the Emergency Regulations of 1948 was in a dormant state'.[36] At the heart of the 1955 bus strikes at the Paya Lebar and Hock Lee bus companies was the right of workers to unionise. In February, a strike for pay increases at Paya Lebar Bus Service was countered by the employers who engaged blacklegs to drive the buses. When the strikers picketed in front of the company's gates, they were arrested by the police. The issue of union recognition was fought again in the larger Hock Lee Bus dispute, where 229 employees belonging to the SBWU were dismissed for going on strike. The employers recognised only the Hock Lee Bus Employees' Union, their union. The dismissed workers picketed outside the bus depot and were joined in a show of 'extensive sympathy' by workers from six other bus companies and Chinese middle school students.[37] The tension at the strike was heightened by both sides: while the SBWU attempted to block the buses from leaving, the picketers were manhandled by police trying to clear them on two occasions. Yet when full-scale violence broke out on 12 May, eye-witnesses like Han Tan Juan insisted that the police started it by using water cannons to disperse the picketers.[38] But the concerted efforts of workers and students achieved the dissolution of the 'yellow union' and the reinstatement of the dismissed bus workers.

The militant unions enjoyed a surge in membership in 1955, particularly the SFSWU, whose membership rose from 372 to nearly 30,000, mainly among the poorly unionised or unorganised Chinese workers in small Chinese manufacturing firms. In ten months it became the spine of the left-wing unions. Total union membership swelled from 81,741 to 145,112, representing a third of those gainfully employed. One hundred and eighty-seven of the unions were employee unions with a membership

Table 2
Number and Causes of Strikes in Singapore, 1955–65

Year	No. of strikes	% of strikes for economic reasons*	% of strikes for sympathy	% of strikes for other causes
1955	275	40.0	49.1	10.9
1956	29	58.6	0.0	41.4
1957	27	66.7	3.7	29.6
1958	22	72.7	0.0	27.3
1959	40	70.0	0.0	30.0
1960	45	62.2	0.0	37.8
1961	116	59.5	0.0	40.5
1962	88	73.9	0.0	26.1
1963	47	70.2	0.0	29.8
1964	39	71.8	0.0	28.2
1965	31	90.3	0.0	9.7

Source: Compiled from *Singapore Annual Reports* 1955–65.

* Economic reasons include wage increases, arbitrary dismissal, retrenchment and conditions of service.

of 139,317 (96 per cent of total membership), reflecting the increased assertiveness of labour (Table 1). White-collar workers in European businesses began to organise under the Singapore Business Houses Employees' Union (SBHEU), initially a moderate body.[39] The British saw demands for wage increases as the only legitimate reason for industrial action but to the left, the struggle also encompassed such economic causes as arbitrary dismissal and conditions of service, and political reasons, such as strikes to express sympathy for other unions and to protest against the detention of their leaders.

Of the 1955 strikes, half were sympathy strikes, although in subsequent years, the main causes were economic (Table 2). As seen in the Hock Lee dispute, workers and Chinese school students joined in mutual support. In June 1955, the SFSWU submitted a memorandum calling for Chinese schools to be accorded equal status in the local education system.[40] In the same month, the government arrested Fong Swee Suan and four other unionists who had called for a sympathy strike to support an SHBSA strike (discussed in greater detail below), for threatening internal security and carrying out activities not connected with the labour movement. A Chinese newspaper judged these grounds 'unconvincing' because 'all along the actions of these trade union leaders are in the service of the people'.[41] The SFSWU and SBWU responded with a 15,000-strong protest strike and obtained the detainees' unconditional release.

A major achievement of the unions was their penetration into the government sector. In 1955, the SHBSA still started a peaceful 67-day strike which won public sympathy and, more tangibly, wage increases and shorter working hours. Jamit Singh then worked to unite other unions at the Singapore Harbour Board into the Singapore Harbour Board Workers' Union (SHBWU). In July 1957, the SHBWU started a 'go-slow' to support a labour dispute involving railwaymen in Port Swettenham. When the Harbour Board rejected recommendations made by an official enquiry into the 'go-slow' action, the SHBSA still won the 'moral and political high ground'.[42] Industrial action at the Naval Base showed similar restraint. Sydney Woodhull's achievement for the NBLU was to use strike threats in the volatile labour situation to win from the Admiralty improved salaries and wage increases in 1954–55. In January 1956 the union went on strike for pay increases and protection against redundancy and retrenchment; in April, the Admiralty granted a 15 per cent pay rise, shorter working hours and reduced transport charges.[43]

The efforts of the unions brought tangible benefits to workers and to Singapore's anti-colonial struggle. The 1955 strikes brought about increases in the average weekly and hourly earnings of manual workers by 10 per cent and 14 per cent, respectively (Table 3). Many employers were made to recognise workers' rights to sick benefits, sick pay, free medicine, two weeks' annual leave, and severance pay.[44] The Labour (Amendment) Ordinance (1955), Shop Assistants Employment Ordinance (1957) and Clerks Employment Ordinance (1957) fixed the daily working hours of labourers, shop assistants and clerks at eight hours, made Sunday a non-work day and gave them paid holidays. In 1960, Lee Kuan Yew hailed the successes of the labour movement:

> The days of employers ignoring the laws giving benefits and rights to the workers are on the way out. Gone are the employer's or 'yellow' unions. The intransigence of die-hard employers whose answer to a trade union claim was the use of secret society gangsters is slowly disappearing.[45]

Politically, within the framework of constitutional struggle, the unions' support for a group of English-educated politicians who could deal with the British was vital. Before the 1959 elections, London had chosen Lee Kuan

Yew ahead of Lim Yew Hock as Singapore's future leader.[46] Lee increased in public stature through his association with the left, by maintaining 'I will not fight Communism to support colonialism'.[47]

Contrary to popular misconception, the left was not all-powerful. The unions suffered multiple purges by Chief Minister Lim Yew Hock, who was determined to suppress the left in order to broker an agreement with the British on self-government.[48] In October 1956, the SFSWU and SBWU, '[u]nder the common principle of preserving human rights',[49] supported the Chinese school students in a sympathy strike against the closure of Chinese High School and Chung Cheng High School, which ended in riots. A student participant remembered that riot police surrounded the students gathered in the two schools and used tear-gas to disperse them.[50] Top union leaders, including Lim Chin Siong, Fong Swee Suan, James Puthucheary, Sydney Woodhull and Devan Nair, were detained. Lim Chin

Table 3

Wages in Singapore, 1952–65

Year	Average weekly earnings of manual workers in principal industries ($)	Average hourly earnings of manual workers in principal industries (cts)
1952	31.43	62
1953	31.00	63
1954	33.04	65
1955	36.80	74
1956	37.12	77
1957	37.98	79
1958	36.67	79
1959	36.88	80
1960	38.49	81
1961	38.54	80
1962	42.82	88
1963	43.89	89
1964	43.49	89
1965	44.55	93

Source: Compiled from *Singapore Annual Reports* 1952–65.
Note: A week consists of six working days.

Siong was charged with telling workers at a concurrent mass rally near the Chinese High to *pah mata* ('beat the police up').[51] In 1995 he denied it, saying it would have been 'very foolish and irresponsible on my part'.[52] The SFSWU was deregistered for participating in activities contradictory to the union's rules but its members then joined the Singapore General Employees' Union (SGEU). To obtain full self-government in the London talks, Lim Yew Hock agreed to the establishment of an Internal Security Council (ISC) under what was de facto British control, with the conservative Malaysian government having the decisive vote. When the left, opposing Lee Kuan Yew's agreement on the ISC, attempted to take control of the PAP's executive committee in August 1957, it was struck by a second round of arrests.

The PAP swept the 1959 elections and Lee Kuan Yew became Prime Minister, following which Lim Chin Siong and other top detainees were released. Fang Chuang-Pi, the 'Plen' and leader of a three-man Working Committee of the MCP in Singapore, had supported Lee as the lesser of two evils.[53] The PAP government quickly enacted amendments to the Trade Unions Ordinance, giving the Registrar of Trade Unions vast powers to deregister unions deemed to be acting against workers' interests without giving deregistered unions the right to appeal. The unions were consulted on these amendments and complacently supported them, although the changes 'made arbitrary decisions unassailable by shutting the doors to an appeal to a court'.[54] The government began to deregister splinter unions, amalgamate small unions and affiliate unions to the STUC.

The 1960s Purges: 'Helping People is Not a Matter for Records, but a Matter for Heart'[55]

The rise of the PAP ironically signalled the beginning of the end for the labour movement. Within the PAP, a conflict between the Lee Kuan Yew group and the left over the issue of merger with Malaya led the latter to split from the party to form the Barisan Sosialis in September 1961. This broke up the STUC into the pro-PAP National Trades Union Congress (NTUC) and the left-wing Singapore Association of Trade Unions (SATU). At this point, SATU had the upper hand, with the support of the SGEU, SBWU and SBHEU, led by Lim Chin Siong and others who had joined the Barisan. The government accused SATU of instigating the 77 strikes which occurred in August–December 1961 (compared to 39 in January–July) but revealingly, 61 per cent of the strikes were for economic reasons, predominantly wage increases, dismissals, conditions of service, and retrenchment.[56]

Many of the strikes were called by the formerly moderate SBHEU. With the PAP controlling the unions of the English-educated employees in the public sector through Devan Nair, left-wing unionists such as Dominic Puthucheary (James Puthucheary's younger brother), Woodhull, Kam Siew Yee, Lim Shee Peng, and Tan Jing Quee moved to organise the SBHEU's white-collar workers in the private sector. Under the leadership of Foo Yong Fong and P. Govindasamy, the workers cast away their fear of their European employers to fight for union recognition.[57] A former SBHEU activist emphasised that this was the first time white-collar workers found 'the power of unity and courage to fight' behind 'an organisation that truly led them in their fight for better working conditions, better pay and restoration of their human dignity'.[58] The new activism, manifested in sit-down strikes, go-slows and walk-outs, achieved recognition from such bastions of European business as Guthrie and Company, Robinson and Company and Raffles Hotel. It is best illustrated in the strike against Robinsons in September. When the company dismissed a salesgirl, the employees picketed in front of the company's gates in protest. The government accused the SBHEU of trying to 'trap workers who may have genuine industrial grievances into supporting the political battle that Lim Chin Siong and his friends have to wage' and dispatched the police to forcibly remove the picketers, who locked arms to resist before being ejected.[59] Yet the picket lines re-formed and on several occasions, the picketers persuaded shoppers against entering the store. The management capitulated the following day to cries of *bersatu* (unity) from the employees.[60]

Despite the SBHEU's successes, the left-wing unions were overtaken by political developments for which they were singularly unprepared. The left opposed the British-backed "Grand Design" to establish a Greater Malaysia comprising Malaya, Singapore, the Borneo territories, and Brunei. It sought, rather, merger with Malaya on equal terms, but lacked a strategic plan to achieve this. The left also had to contend with a triple alliance of conservative forces — the Malayan Alliance, the PAP and the British governments — but Fang Chuang-Pi admits that 'no guidelines and methods were available for the effective protection of the left-wing movement'.[61] In contrast, Lee Kuan Yew zealously pursued merger to bring the Alliance government to bear on the left. Concerned by the PAP candidate's heavy defeat in the Hong Lim by-election of April 1961, the Tunku spoke in May of a willingness to bring Malaya, Singapore and the Borneo territories into closer political and economic cooperation within a larger Malaysian federation. This announcement caught the left by surprise, which rejected Malaysia as a neo-colonialist plot but failed to develop a coherent alternative.

At the same time, Lee pressured the British to arrest the leftists under the Preservation of Public Security Ordinance (PPSO). Recent research shows that Lord Selkirk, the British Commissioner in Singapore, and his deputy Philip Moore believed that the Barisan intended to work within constitutional means. For a time, explaining that the left were a political rather than security problem, Selkirk and Moore warded off Lee's calls for mass arrests.[62] However, the left failed to take a persuasive position on the 1962 merger referendum, first supporting an option which might disenfranchise nearly half of the electorate and then telling the people to cast blank votes. The PAP, not surprisingly, won 71 per cent of the vote. In July, London overrode Selkirk and sanctioned the arrests to broker an agreement on merger with the Tunku.[63] The British implicated Lim Chin Siong in an anti-Malaysia revolt in Brunei allegedly organised by the Parti Rakyat Brunei. On 2 February 1963, 'to prevent a Cuba in Singapore', Operation Cold Store detained 113 left-wing political leaders and trade unionists, including Lim.[64] Subsequent British investigations found little evidence of Barisan involvement in the Brunei plot,[65] but the detentions decimated the left. The PAP comfortably won 37 of the 51 seats in the September elections, with the weakened Barisan managing 13.

After Operation Cold Store, the PAP carried out a systematic crackdown on the unions to eradicate alternative sources of power. The government mounted trials of left-wing union leaders for misuse of union funds and deregistered unions whose leaders were found guilty this way. In truth the issue was not, as implied, corruption or the officials' abuse of power but a simple failure to maintain proper documentation from the start, due to a lack of expertise among union officials in these matters and a shortage of funds for engaging accounting clerks.[66] The funds were frequently used to support the families of striking workers and detained union leaders, who were still paid as employed union officials.[67] This suggests that the unions were more concerned with workers' welfare than with legalities or documentation. In addition, as law scholar Shahid Siddiqi noted, deregistration punished the union instead of the officials and disregarded less draconian penalties.[68] The authorities also accused union leaders of involvement in pro-communist activities without putting forward documentary evidence, aiming to recall in public memory the 'revelations' Lee Kuan Yew had made in the 1961 radio talks on merger in 'establishing' the leftists as communists.[69]

In October 1962, Jamit Singh and Yeow Fook Yuen, the treasurer, were charged with misappropriating SHBSA funds. T. T. Rajah, the defense attorney, claimed the money was to help needy union members but there were neither witnesses nor documentary evidence to support this assertion.[70] Jamit Singh protested emotionally, '[h]elping people is not a matter for records but a matter for heart'. In March 1963, Singh and Yeow were convicted of criminal breach of trust and sentenced to 18 and nine months' jail, respectively. After the trial, Jamit Singh was arrested under the PPSO, banished to Malaya and prohibited from returning to Singapore. The SHBSA was deregistered, although Shahid Siddiqi has suggested that it would have been more appropriate to fine the union for failing to supervise Jamit Singh, since the Trade Unions Ordinance did not call for the deregistration of unions which contravened union rules.[71] Jamit Singh's allegation that the trial was a smear campaign and an attempt by the government to capture the union[72] concurs with the subsequent admission by the Deputy Public Prosecutor, Francis Seow, that the trial was intended to reduce Singh's capacity for 'political mischief'. Lee apparently pressured Seow to use a dossier compiled by the Internal Security Department highlighting Jamit Singh's allegedly extravagant lifestyle to incriminate Singh's misuse of union funds.[73] The SHBSA was re-registered in January 1964 under a condition banning 'Communists and political opportunists' from the leadership.[74]

The PAP next moved against the SATU. On 25 August 1963, the Singapore Chinese Chamber of Commerce organised a 'blood debt' rally to press for Japanese compensation for wartime atrocities, an issue which struck an emotional chord with broad sections of the Chinese population. Lee Kuan Yew, attempting to speak at the rally, was booed by large sections of the audience, an act which was plausibly not orchestrated by the unions or SATU's central leadership but spontaneous, reflecting the people's unhappiness with Lee.[75] Three days later, the Registrar of Trade Unions stated his intention to deregister the SGEU, SBWU and SBHEU for displaying anti-Malaysia banners and placards at the rally, deemed as 'communist united front' activities.[76] When the authorities froze the unions' funds, the SATU called a protest strike in October but the police reacted by detaining S. T. Bani, Tan Jing Quee, Wee Toon Lip and 11 other unionists. In November, the SGEU, SBWU and SBHEU were deregistered, breaking the back of the left-wing labour movement, even though district judge J. B. Jeyaretnam ruled the strike as legal, judging that by interfering in the strike, the government had 'entered into the arena of employer-employee relationships', whereupon 'a dispute could well exist between the Government and a trade union'.[77] The deregistration, which left some 60,000 workers without representation, appeared difficult to justify since, after the October arrests, '[t]here was, therefore, no reasons to deprive the workers of the protection of their unions'.[78]

The 1963 NBLU strike revealed the government's machinations against the labour movement.[79] In October, the NBLU launched a strike over annual leave, gratuities and the dismissal of employees. The government and the Admiralty collectively opposed it, with the dockyard accusing the union of using its funds to help the Barisan in the September elections.[80] However, while the NBLU strike was contiguous with the SATU protest strike, the union had given strike notice on 14 September but had held the strike back to seek legal advice on picketing within the Base. The Malayan Trade Union Congress representative, S. J. E. Zaidi, assessed the strike as a genuine industrial dispute.[81]

Lee Kuan Yew intervened personally at the end of October. The Admiralty files record that he was determined not just to end the strike but to break the NBLU leadership.[82] Lee began by accusing the NBLU of calling the strike without a secret ballot by the union members,[83] and Michael Fernandez, the NBLU's new General-Secretary, of pro-communist ties.[84] Lee finally struck a decisive third blow by revealing that the union's Executive Committee had exceeded its term of office by six months. This allowed the Registrar of Trade Unions to declare the strike unlawful and force its termination on 8 November. The NBLU leaders had delayed the election of new office-bearers, a process taking three to four months, after David Marshall had advised that, as in the past several years the elections were seldom held in May, as required by the constitution, it was merely a technical matter.[85] Since the union had given two weeks' notice of the strike, the fact that the government did not prevent it proved an intention to destroy the left-wing leadership.[86] This revelation is made in the Admiralty records:

> Plans were made to use the Government's resources to ensure the isola-
> tion of the NBLU from support by other unions; to build up anti-strike
> leaders in the NBLU; to spread anti-Fernandez propaganda; and to
> provide Police protection for transport conveying the workers to the
> base. (It was noteworthy that the Government propaganda was ruthless,
> and not particularly fussed about accuracy, in denigrating Fernandez and
> de Cruz and building up the opposition party).[87]

The NBLU was deregistered in January 1964, although Shahid Siddiqi proposes that a 'more reasonable remedy would have been to order fresh elections'.[88]

Admittedly the left's downfall was also due to the NTUC's success. Workers ostensibly had become less interested in politics than in making a living. The NTUC led strikes which caused the loss of more man-hours between 1961 and 1963 than the SATU unions, and achieved a rise in 1962 in the average weekly and hourly earnings of manual workers by

11 per cent and 10 per cent, respectively, although the SBHEU must also be given credit for this. These strikes led many workers to believe that the NTUC was independent of the government and served their interests.[89] Nevertheless, the NTUC succeeded because the state had removed the competition. Workers, witnessing the obvious success of the NTUC, did the natural thing. After the October 1963 arrests, 50 branches of the deregistered SATU unions left for the NTUC.[90] By 1966, the 'pro-communist unions' purportedly had only 28,000 members to the NTUC's 150,000.[91] That year, the Barisan resigned from Parliament to take its struggle 'into the streets'.[92] This was a strategic error, for it gave the PAP a complete monopoly of power and condemned many union leaders to long terms of imprisonment without trial. Others, disillusioned by the boycott, accepted the terms put to them by the PAP to obtain their release from prison, upon which they gave up politics for good.

With the NTUC's triumph, the day of autonomous unions was over. Devan Nair declared, 'I do not make any distinction between the PAP and the NTUC ... We were two wings of the same political movement'.[93] Where the left-wing unions had engaged in anti-colonial politics to advance workers' interests, the NTUC supported the PAP's policies of nationbuilding. The NTUC-led honeymoon for workers between 1961 and 1965 did not last. The government began to discipline labour in pursuit of its aim of achieving rapid industrialisation by encouraging foreign multi-nationals to locate in Singapore. Intended to be an obedient workforce engaged in routine factory work, labour could not be allowed to organise independently against employers. In 1966, the government passed the Trade Unions (Amendment) Act which, in requiring unions to take a secret ballot before a strike could be carried out, made swift action against employers impossible.[94] The Industrial Relations (Amendment) Act of 1968 reduced the bargaining power of unions by giving employers greater discretion in the employment of workers. In 1969, a year without new work stoppages, a trade union seminar heralded the 'Modernisation of the Labour Movement'. It marked the end of a decade-long effort by the PAP to discipline the left-wing unions.

Conclusion

The left-wing trade union movement in Singapore lasted only a generation. It faced formidable resistance from employers and governments, which preferred progressive economic growth to strong, autonomous unions. In seeking to establish a political arm, the movement secured allies which did not share its vision of labour as an equal partner with capital. The MCP aimed to establish a different political system. The Lee Kuan Yew group in the PAP used the left as a bridge to the Chinese-speaking masses; upon coming to power they destroyed the unions and moulded labour into a disciplined cog in the industrial economy. But while the unions were inexperienced in politics and over-reliant on moral leadership and worker solidarity, their demise was ultimately due to the state's repressive laws and purges which decimated the leadership, and the manoeuvering of politicians who made them scapegoats for riots and revolts. The labour movement was a victim of the Cold War.

The rise and fall of the left-wing unions is an important part of Singapore's history that has been submerged under the PAP story. The unions' story belongs not to the theme of communist subversion but of the rise of a people uplifted by idealism and anti-colonialism. In the 1950s and early 1960s, unionism was part of a larger movement seeking to create a different society from that which the PAP has since built. The labour movement's emphasis on social justice and worker solidarity and its collaboration with the Chinese school students cut across ethnic, social and occupational divides. It underlined the importance of other ends in life than just material achievement and economic growth. Besides tangible gains, the movement also brought dignity and self-respect to the working class. Together with the Chinese student movement, university students, teachers and others, the unions provided a formidable power base for the PAP and, briefly, the Barisan. The trade union movement bore Singapore out of colonialism into statehood, although it was destined not to survive it.

NOTES

1   The authors are grateful to P. N. Balji, Said Zahari, Wang Gungwu and Sonny Yap for reading drafts of this paper, and to Henry Goh, Lee Tee Tong, Dominic Puthucheary and Tan Jing Quee for their interviews.

2   See John Drysdale, *Singapore: Struggle for Success* (Singapore: Times Books International, 1984); Dennis Bloodworth, *The Tiger and the Trojan Horse* (Singapore: Times Books International, 1986).

3   One of the authors, Michael Fernandez, was variously General-Secretary of the Naval Base Labour Union and the Singapore Commercial House and Factory Employees' Union, as well as an adviser to the Singapore European Employees' Union over 1963 and 1964. He led a 10,000-strong strike at the Naval Base for a month in October–November 1963. He was detained for being a member of the Communist Open Front for nine years from 1964 to 1973, and then again very briefly in 1977. He was, however, never a communist or pro-communist, nor did he ever belong to any Communist Open Front organisation or knowingly work

with any member of the Malayan Communist Party. Prior to his union involvement, Fernandez was a committee member of the University of Singapore Socialist Club and looked after the business matters of its monthly organ, *Fajar*. See Michael Fernandez, oral history interview, 25 May 1981, Oral History Centre, National Archives of Singapore, National Heritage Board. Fernandez also publicly denied being part of the Communist Open Front at the Detention-Writing-Healing Forum organised by *The Necessary Stage* on 26 February 2006. Subsequently, the Ministry of Home Affairs wrote to *The Straits Times* of 8 March 2006 maintaining that Fernandez was not a political dissident or an opposition member engaged in the democratic process but 'belonged to the Communist United Front (CUF) which supported the Communist Party of Malaya (CPM)'.

4   Lim denied being a communist in 1995, in Melanie Chew, 'Lim Chin Siong', in *Leaders of Singapore* (Singapore: Resource Press, 1996). For alternative appraisals of Lim, see T. N. Harper, 'Lim Chin Siong and the "Singapore Story"', in *Comet in Our Sky: Lim Chin Siong in History*, ed. Tan Jing Quee and Jomo K. S. (Kuala Lumpur: INSAN, 2001); and C. J. W.-L. Wee, 'The Vanquished: Lim Chin Siong and a Progressivist National Narrative', in *Lee's Lieutenants: Singapore's Old Guard*, ed. Lam Peng Er and Kevin Y. L. Tan (St Leonards: Allen & Unwin, 1999).

5   Singapore Commercial House and Factory Employees Union (SCHFEU), *Bulletin*, 1 August 1966, p. 1.

6   C. F. Yong, 'Emergence of Chinese Community Leaders in Singapore, 1890–1941', *Journal of South Seas Society* 30, 1 (December 1975): 12–13.

7   Authors' interview with Lee Tee Tong, 28 May 2005.

8   Occupation, Wages, Labour Organisation, *Singapore Annual Report 1946*, p. 45 (henceforth, *SAR*).

9   Authors' interview with Lee Tee Tong.

10 Carl A. Trocki, 'Development of Labour Organisation in Singapore, 1800–1960', *Australian Journal of Politics and History* 47, 1 (2001): 121.

11 Industrial Workers Union, *Anniversary Souvenir Magazine* (Singapore: Industrial Workers Union of Singapore, 1964), p. 64.

12 James Puthucheary, 'Political Role of the Trade Union', *Petir* 3, 6 (4 January 1960): 4.

13 Lim Hong Bee, 'The Labour Movement in Colonial Malaya', *The Straits Times*, 24 July 1946.

14 SCHFEU, *Bulletin*, 1 August 1966, p. 1.

15 *Balian shisi zhounian jiniankan 1948–1962* [*14th Anniversary of the Singapore Bus Workers' Union*], (Singapore: Singapore Bus Workers' Union, 1962), p. 2.

16 Yeo Kim Wah, 'Communist Involvement in the Malayan Labour Strikes: 1936', *Journal of the Malaysian Branch of the Royal Asiatic Society* 49, 2 (1976): 36–79.

17 Charles Gamba, *The Origins of Trade Unionism in Malaya* (Singapore: Eastern Universities Press, 1962), p. 4.

18 Occupation and Wages, *SAR 1946*, p. 43.

19 Devan C. V. Nair, 'An Open Letter to Malayan Socialists', *Not By Wages Alone:*

Selected Speeches and Writings of C. V. Devan Nair, 1959–1981 (Singapore: Singapore National Trades Union Congress, 1982), p. 305.

20 Chew, 'Lim Chin Siong', p. 113.

21 Chen Say Jame, oral history interview, 8 December 1981, Oral History Centre, National Archives of Singapore, National Heritage Board.

22 Occupation and Wages, *SAR 1946*, p. 43.

23 Yeo Kim Wah, *Political Development in Singapore, 1945–55* (Singapore: Singapore University Press, 1973), pp. 216–7.

24 *Malaya Tribune*, 22 October 1945.

25 *Malaya Tribune*, 27 October 1945.

26 Yeo, *Political Development in Singapore*, pp. 215–6.

27 Occupation and Wages, *SAR 1947*, p. 26.

28 Liu Hong and Wong Sin-Kiong, *Singapore Chinese Society in Transition: Business, Politics, and Socio-Economic Change, 1945–1965* (New York: Peter Lang, 2004), p. 175.

29 Occupation and Wages, *SAR 1948*, pp. 32–3.

30 Chen Say Jame, oral history interview.

31 Occupations and Wages, *SAR 1954*, p. 28.

32 Chinese-educated unionists like Lim Chin Siong, Fong Swee Suan and Chen Say Jame were from the Chinese middle schools. Many English-educated unionists, such as P. V. Sharma, Devan Nair, Kam Siew Yee, S. T. Bani and Dominic Puthucheary, came from the Singapore Teachers' Union, where its campaign for equal back-pay for the war period and the Malayanisation of the civil service blooded them in labour activism.

33 Ministry of Education, 'The Hock Lee Bus Riots', National Education website at http://www.moe.gov.sg/ne/sgstory/hockleebusriots.htm.

34 Chew, 'Lim Chin Siong', pp. 114–7.

35 Occupations and Wages, *SAR 1955*, p. 38.

36 *Balian shisi zhounian jiniankan*, p. 9.

37 *Weekly Digest of Chinese, Malay and Tamil Press*, 11 May 1955.

38 'Riding the Tide of Idealism: An Interview with Han Tan Juan', *Tangent* 6 (April 2003): 213.

39 Occupations and Wages, *SAR 1955*, p. 35.

40 *Weekly Digest of Chinese, Malay and Tamil Press*, 2 June 1955.

41 *Sin Chew Jit Poh, Weekly Digest of Chinese, Malay and Tamil Press*, 16 June 1955.

42 Liew Kai Khiun, 'The Anchor and the Voice of 10,000 Waterfront Workers: Jamit Singh in the Singapore Story (1954–63)', *Journal of Southeast Asian Studies* 35, 3 (October 2004): 469.

43 Liew Kai Khiun, 'Raised Voices and Dropped Tools: Labour Unrest at the Harbour and Naval Dockyard in Singapore (1952–72)', Master of Arts Thesis, Department of History, National University of Singapore, 2003, pp. 62–71.

44 James Puthucheary, 'The Struggle for Unity', in *No Cowardly Past: James Puthucheary. Writings, Poems, Commentaries*, ed. Dominic J. Puthucheary and Jomo K. S. (Kuala Lumpur: INSAN, 1998), pp. 136–7; James Puthucheary,

'The Growth and Development of the Trade Union Movement after the Election', in *No Cowardly Past*, p. 128.

45 Speech at the May Day Rally, 1 May 1960, retrieved from STARS, Access to Archives Online (National Archives of Singapore website), www.a2o.com.sg.

46 Albert Lau, '"Nationalism" in the Decolonisation of Singapore', in *The Transformation of Southeast Asia: International Perspectives on Decolonization*, ed. Marc Frey, Ronald Pruessen and Tan Tai Yong (New York: M. E. Sharpe, 2003), p. 196.

47 *Singapore Legislative Assembly Debates*, 16 May 1955, pp. 187–8.

48 Authors' interview with Tan Jing Quee, 27 May 2005. See also Tan Jing Quee, 'Lim Chin Siong — A Political Life', in *Comet in Our Sky*, pp. 72–4.

49 *Weekly Digest of Chinese, Malay and Tamil Press*, 10 October 1956.

50 'Riding the Tide of Idealism', *Tangent*, pp. 214–5.

51 The charge was made by Labour Front Minister for Education Chew Swee Kee in the Legislative Assembly. Lim Chin Siong had been arrested and was absent. *Singapore Legislative Assembly Debates*, 6 November 1956, p. 501.

52 Chew, 'Lim Chin Siong', p. 117.

53 Fang Chuang-Pi, 'The Heavens were Sentient: A Preliminary Response to Said Zahari's Criticism in *Dark Clouds at Dawn*, *Nanyang Siang Pau*, 19 March 2001.

54 Shahid Siddiqi, 'The Registration and Deregistration of Trade Unions in Singapore', Master of Law Thesis, Faculty of Law, University of Singapore, 1968, pp. 29–30.

55 Jamit Singh, *The Straits Times*, 15 February 1963.

56 Labour and Welfare, *SAR 1962*, p. 196. The other 39 per cent were listed under 'Other Causes', but these were left unspecified.

57 Authors' interview with Tan Jing Quee.

58 Authors' email correspondence with Henry Goh, 14 June 2005.

59 *The Straits Times*, 12 September 1961.

60 *The Straits Times*, 13 September 1961.

61 Fang, 'The Heavens were Sentient'.

62 Matthew Jones, 'Creating Malaysia: Singapore's Security, the Borneo Territories, and the Contours of British Policy, 1961–1963', *Journal of Imperial and Commonwealth History* 28, 2 (2000): 96–7.

63 Ibid., pp. 98–9.

64 *The Straits Times*, 3 February 1963.

65 Harper, 'Lim Chin Siong and the "Singapore Story"', pp. 43–4.

66 Occupation and Wages, *SAR 1948*, p. 34.

67 *The Straits Times*, 11 February 1964.

68 Siddiqi, 'The Registration and Deregistration of Trade Unions', pp. 134–5.

69 Lee Kuan Yew, *The Battle for Merger* (Singapore: Government Printers, 1962).

70 Liew, 'The Anchor and the Voice', p. 472.

71 Siddiqi, 'The Registration and Deregistration of Trade Unions', pp. 131–5.

72 *The Straits Times*, 23 January 1963.

73 Francis Seow, *To Catch a Tartar: A Dissident in Lee Kuan Yew's Prison* (New Haven: Yale University Centre for Southeast Asian Studies, 1994), pp. 28–31.

74 *The Straits Times*, 14 January 1964.

75 Authors' interviews with Tan Jing Quee and Lee Tee Tong. The unhappiness with the PAP was due to its policy of economic cooperation with Japan.

76 *The Straits Times*, 30 August 1963.

77 *The Straits Times*, 21 November 1963.

78 Siddiqi, 'The Registration and Deregistration of Trade Unions', pp. 179–80.

79 The account of the strike is based on Michael Fernandez, oral history interview, 25 May 1981, Oral History Centre, National Archives of Singapore, National Heritage Board.

80 ADM 1/28400, Ref. No. CEO/1703B, 30 September 1963.

81 *The Straits Times*, 30 October 1963.

82 ADM 1/28400, Letter from Commodore Superintendent to Admiralty, 21 October 1963.

83 Lee himself knew that the union's constitution only required the elected section representatives to vote, as he had been the NBLU's legal advisor in the 1950s.

84 *The Straits Times*, 29 October 1963. Lee cited Fernandez's close friendship with S. T. Bani and Tan Jing Quee (SATU President and Assistant General-Secretary, respectively). The reality was less sinister: the post of General-Secretary had been vacant following S. Ghouse's arrest during Operation Cold Store, and Bani was contacted in the union's search for a replacement because his father had been NBLU President in the 1950s. Through Bani, Tan Jing Quee got Fernandez, his friend from the University of Malaya Socialist Club, to consider the position.

85 In 1960, the AGM was held in June; in 1961, July; and in 1962, August.

86 Siddiqi, 'The Registration and Deregistration of Trade Unions', p. 155.

87 ADM 1/28400, Appendix K, 'Note of Conversation between Mr Lee Kuan Yew and Mr Moore', 12 November 1963.

88 Siddiqi, 'The Registration and Deregistration of Trade Unions', p. 157.

89 Nair, 'The Growth of the Labour Movement', *Not by Wages Alone*, pp. 8991.

90 *The Straits Times*, 18 October 1963.

91 *The Straits Times*, 4 October 1966.

92 *The Straits Times*, 8 October 1966.

93 Nair, 'Organised Labour in Singapore — Past, Present and Future', *Not by Wages Alone*, p. 206.

94 Siddiqi, 'The Registration and Deregistration of Trade Unions', p. 38.

PART 4

Walking Narrow Paths

12

Singapore's Catholic Social Activists: Alleged Marxist Conspirators[1]

Michael D. Barr

Over the early morning hours of 21 May and 20 June 1987, 22 Singapore citizens were detained by Singapore's Internal Security Department (ISD) as part of Operation Spectrum.[2] They were accused of being part of a Marxist conspiracy 'to overthrow the Government and establish a communist state'.[3] The alleged mastermind was Tan Wah Piow, a former student activist who was then living in *de facto* exile in London. His supposed point man in Singapore was a lay worker in the local Catholic Church, Vincent Cheng. Cheng was supposed to have been manipulating a network of naïve and idealistic agents that extended beyond his Catholic circles to include solicitors, returned students who knew Tan Wah Piow in London, student activists and some people associated with alternative theatre.[4] The detainees were not all Catholics but the core group among those detained included ten people associated with the social work of the Catholic Church. The alleged conspiracy was so extensive that the ISD even interviewed Tharman Shanmugaratnam, now Minister for Finance, for about a week.[5] It was so shadowy that when one of the detainees protested during interrogation that he did not know anything about a conspiracy and did not even know half of his supposed 21 co-conspirators, he was told that he was 'an unconscious conspirator', and might as well admit it.[6]

Yet the words of the then Prime Minister Lee Kuan Yew make clear that he never believed in a Marxist conspiracy. In a private meeting in the midst of the crisis he dismissed the supposed Marxist conspirators as 'do-gooders who wanted to help the poor and the dispossessed'.[7] He even declared that he was not interested in 'Vincent Cheng and his group', but he was more concerned about the 'involvement' of 'several priests'.[8] Yet 20 people, none of them priests, were detained for several months, and two more for several years. Most report being tortured and beaten and all signed confessions dictated by their interrogators, though some recanted their confessions after being released.[9] They were also paraded before the public (via newspapers and three television specials) as subversives and communists.

These extra-judicial arrests proved to be a critical turning point in the Singapore government's management of dissent and public discourse. They marked the beginning of a new era where Singaporeans became conscious of the operation of what later became known as out-of-bounds (OB) markers in politics. On the one hand, people were encouraged to enjoy a new sense of political freedom, but on the other hand, they had the example of Operation Spectrum to remind them of the consequences if they overstepped the mark. Religious institutions, beginning with the Catholic Church, started actively monitoring the activities of their members, priests, ministers and imams to ensure that they stayed within the comfort zone of the government. Secular organisations started following suit.

Each of the disparate individuals who were arrested in Operation Spectrum has his or her own history, but in this paper I restrict myself to an account of the group at the centre of the controversy: the small and — until May 1987 — obscure collection of Singaporeans, some of them Catholics who, according to the government, found Marxism through the channel of Liberation Theology, and were subverting the Catholic Church for revolutionary ends.[10]

The Catholic Activists

In pursuing this project, I have found a line of continuity of Catholic social activism that stretches back to the late 1960s. It would be presumptuous to call this line of continuity an organisation or a group — let alone a conspiracy. Participants have referred to it as 'the movement'. I will adopt this terminology for the sake of convenience, but perhaps it would be more precise to describe it as a subculture that was given a tenuous series of organisational forms within formal Church structures. This subculture was most comfortable with the strands of Catholic thinking that are usually described as progressive, and as the government suggested, it was inspired to some degree by the Marxist-based Liberation Theology that was popular in Latin America and the Philippines at the time. The main inspirational sources for the subculture, however, were explicitly non-ideological. Vincent Cheng was inspired initially by the Community Organisation (CO) methodology developed by Saul Alinsky in Chicago in the late 1930s, though he later became absorbed in *Minjung* theology, which involves a militant and millenarian reading of the Old Testament. Most of the other main figures were inspired by the mainstream Catholic approach of the Young Christian Workers Movement (YCW). As a result, much of the activity was not overtly ideological, being directed predominantly at helping particular groups and individuals to achieve specific goals. Of course, with hindsight, it seems naïve to think that the government would not consider this as constituting threatening political activity, but this was a failing of naïveté that seems to have been almost universal among the laity in the movement.

The priests in the movement were more politically aware, though no more radical, than the laity. Despite the inspirational role played by Liberation Theology,[11] the priests consciously and deliberately eschewed its doctrines — such as class warfare, abolition of private property, revolution, rejection of Church authority[12] — and espoused traditional Catholic social teaching as handed down in Papal and Vatican documents since the end of the nineteenth century. They were confident that as long as they stayed away from overt politics, they were safe from government reprisal.

Background

By the time our story opens in the 1960s, the Catholic Church had been engaged in a sedate but ever-escalating process of review for about 80 years, casting around for new formulae through which to engage society, and particularly the poor and the working classes. In the early 1960s, this process of review culminated in a three-year General Council of the Church known as Vatican II, a massive exercise in reform and reflection that transformed the Church's incremental programme of engagement with the world into a heady potion of change and confusion. This atmosphere had a direct impact on most aspects of the Church, including — and of direct relevance to our story — the training of priests. Among the seminarians affected by these developments were a small group in the Penang seminary who were studying for priesthood in the Archdiocese of Singapore. The most notable members of this group were Vincent Cheng himself and two of the four key priests who were pressured to leave Singapore after the 1987 detentions — Fr Patrick Goh and Fr Edgar D'Souza — but in addition to these key figures, the Penang seminary was also educating at this time two other future priests who were to become active in the movement, though in less central ways — Fr Eugene Vaz and Fr Joseph Tan. These five men, like many others throughout the world, were exposed to a swirl of ideas about the place of the Church in the world. Radical theories such as Liberation Theology did the rounds alongside mainstream Catholic social teaching and ideas of activism associated with the YCW.[13]

At around the same time as the Catholic Church was undergoing this agonising process of metamorphosis, many Protestant churches and the Anglican Church began escalating their social activism, sometimes altering the character of their missionary work from one that was strictly evangelical to one that focused to a greater or lesser degree on temporal issues. An institution affected by this shift in focus was the East Asia Christian Conference (EACC), which shared guilt by association with the alleged Marxist conspirators and was expelled from Singapore at the end of 1987. In the late 1960s, the EACC saw itself as being engaged in a struggle to find a place for Christian mission in industrialising Asia. A practical initiative towards this end — and one with a direct causal connection to our story — was the decision to engage in Industrial Evangelism. The radical departure of Industrial Evangelism from traditional evangelism was that it was not designed to fill pews with converts, but was described in terms of Christian service to society. It was to be facilitated through the establishment of Urban and Industrial Missions (UIM) that would defend and empower urban workers and residents.[14] Industrial Evangelism was a skeleton without flesh, however, and it was up to the personnel on the ground to give it focus and direction. In Singapore, the EACC, through its local affiliate, the National Council of Churches of Singapore (NCCS), turned to one of Saul Alinsky's disciples for assistance.

Saul Alinsky was a self-styled radical organiser in Chicago who had been doing a lot of work with churches since the late 1930s. He had developed an approach to social activism that he called Community Organisation. At the core of this methodology was strategic confrontation: the use of abrasive but legal and non-violent brinkmanship by those without power to build solidarity and win concessions from those with power.[15] Furthermore, it was vital to his methodology that the confrontation be generated by local, natural leaders acting in accord with local values and tradition, and on the priorities identified by the local community.

In the late 1960s, when the EACC decided to build UIMs in Asia, they sent Ron Fujiyoshi, a Hawaiian-born American who had trained with

Alinsky's organisation in Austin, Texas during the 1960s, to Singapore. In 1969, Fujiyoshi set up two UIMs using the CO methodology — the Jurong Industrial Mission (JIM) and a private community centre at Toa Payoh. The two bodies operated under the auspices of the NCCS and flourished for a short time under Fujiyoshi's guidance. The demise of the UIMs came suddenly in 1973, when the government failed to renew Fujiyoshi's visa, effectively expelling him for his activism. This coincided with private expressions of government displeasure to many of the churches about the activities of the UIMs. The churches succumbed to this pressure and withdrew their endorsement and financial support, bringing the experiment to an end.

Convergence in Singapore

The Catholic chapter of our story began in late 1968, when an unassuming nun, whom I shall call 'Sister Samantha',[16] was asked by her religious superior to start a private community centre in Bukit Ho Swee, to be called the Nazareth Centre. Sr Samantha had begun her training as a social worker two years earlier, but running a community centre was unknown territory. She had premises but no appropriate training, no budget, no staff and no idea. Fortunately, help was at hand in the form of a supportive local French Catholic priest, Fr Jean Charbonnier, and a local Australian Anglican priest, Fr James Minchin. These two men had already begun developing socially aware communities of young people within their parishes. Furthermore, Ron Fujiyoshi was already active in Singapore and by this stage the JIM and the private community centre in Toa Payoh were already well-established.

Between them, Fr Charbonnier, Fr Minchin and Ron Fujiyoshi gave Sr Samantha all the help they could, to the point where Fr Minchin remembers them operating in 'loose alliance' through their parishes and the three community organisations. On their advice she appealed to the Catholic Churches in Europe, America and Australia for money. She successfully raised S$60,000 from Australian Catholic Relief, and about another S$40,000 from the Churches in the Netherlands and Germany. Sr Samantha appointed a Chinese-speaking staff member to assist her in her home visits, but because the funds from overseas did not arrive until after she had left the project, she had to beg the Catholic or the Anglican Archbishop every month for money to pay this salary. On some Sundays after Mass, Fr Minchin would send over an enthusiastic group of young volunteers to help with door knocking, a group which was much more helpful than the Catholic seminarians who were sometimes urged to help as part of their pastoral work. Most significant of all, she did an intensive 'in-service' training course in CO under Fujiyoshi.[17] When Vincent Cheng came to work for the JIM in 1971, having taken a year's leave of absence from the local Catholic seminary, Fujiyoshi also trained him in CO,[18] the spirit of which he later passed on to a subsequent generation of young activists.

Pouring Petrol on Fire

Singapore in the late 1960s was still recovering from the shock of separation from Malaysia, and the entire focus of the new nation's energies was devoted to nation building and survival. Workers' rights, press freedoms, free speech, the freedom to have children, and the rights of immigrants were all expendable in the quest for survival.[19] In sharp contradiction of Alinsky's celebration of dissent, Singapore was moving to expel overt politics from the realm of governance as it progressed towards an austere 'administrative state', to use Chan Heng Chee's very appropriate descriptor.[20] The government's priorities were spelt out time and again, including, ironically, in an address by the then Prime Minister Lee Kuan Yew to the EACC when it met in Singapore in 1967. His speech dwelt on the dilemmas of newly de-colonised countries 'catching up' with the West economically; the difficulty of finding leaders able to motivate the populace to join the race for development; and the role of religions in the struggle to move society 'forward to progress and to a higher level of human life'.[21] Armed with a vision of human progress through a collective national struggle led by a natural ruling elite, Lee Kuan Yew envisioned the Christian contribution as helping the government build a sense of solidarity and purpose that would enable the populace to understand — or at least accept — the need for ever greater sacrifices in the struggle for progress. He even hoped that the Christian churches might contribute some real leadership to the role of nation building.[22]

The vision of the EACC was somewhat different. It was all about undermining the meek acceptance of sacrifices by the populace; of building solidarity amongst the poor as they sought better living and working conditions; of defending workers — particularly migrant workers — from exploitation by employers who, from the perspective of the government, were playing a pivotal role in the national development project. Conflict was almost inevitable. It is a testament to Sr Samantha's political innocence that she had only the dimmest idea that her activities would invite scrutiny from the highest levels of government and the security services.

Sr Samantha's application of the CO methodology was innocuous in itself, but it nevertheless made her, in her own words, 'a marked woman'. In 1969, while making arrangements for a delegation to meet a government minister, she was told by an official from the Prime Minister's Office that her 'name is on the Prime Minister's desk'. This followed an occasion when she had arranged with a local Member of Parliament (MP) to meet residents from her community about a municipal problem at his weekly meet-the-people session, only to find the MP phoning her in a panic because over one hundred people had turned up. In an earlier incident, she had received an angry phone call from the local Area Officer of the Housing and Development Board (HDB) because an article had appeared in the Chinese press about another municipal issue. It was assumed (correctly) that she had suggested going to the press. Both these incidents had marked her out as someone to be watched. What were the issues generating this controversy? They were the ordinary fare of municipal administration: blocks of flats without working toilets; rats climbing into ground-floor kitchens; vandalism. And what was the key to Sr Samantha's advocacy? She convinced the local residents to approach the authorities — beginning with the local HDB Area Officer — as a collective with collective complaints, instead of as individuals with a series of individual complaints, and to take ordinary opportunities (such as press articles and delegations) to draw attention to their grievances. This was a very mild, relatively non-confrontational form of Alinsky's methodology, but it was still clearly recognisable as CO because it created a locus of power among the grassroots that was independent of the ruling elite. It began with door knocking to discuss problems and begin identifying local leaders, followed by meetings to discuss action, and finally moved on to (mildly) confrontational actions to seek redress of grievances and generate solidarity. Sr Samantha was clearly heading for a confrontation with the government, but it never reached a head because her health gave out in 1969 and she had to retire from the work. Her superiors in her religious order — almost certainly sensing the dangers ahead — shifted the orientation of her centre from CO to social service.[23]

YCW Networks

A short time later, the subculture of Catholic activism began taking root in Singapore under the guidance of a number of priests whose inspiration came not from Saul Alinsky, but from the example and methodology of Canon Joseph Cardijn, the founder of the YCW.[24] Canon Cardijn was a Belgian priest (later a Cardinal) of working class origins who sought to build lay movements among the working class. Under the direction of the clergy, these groups were to evangelise the working class through the spiritual and intellectual formation of young Christian workers who would then work, and if necessary agitate, for workers' rights. Cardijn was deeply concerned about both the temporal and spiritual welfare of the working class, and regarded the problem of inhumane working conditions (justified by economic liberalism) and the spread of atheism (promoted by communists) as two sides of the same coin.[25] He was determined to build a movement of young Catholics to meet this challenge. He founded his movement in 1924 and received the endorsement of Pope Pius XI a year later. The key structure was and is the small group or cell, and its key methodology is captured in the triple imperative, 'SEE, JUDGE, ACT', which is ubiquitous in writings and conversations about the YCW. Its *modus operandi* was less confrontational than that of CO, but it shared its goal of empowering the powerless.

The role of the chaplain was crucial in the operation of the YCW. It operated under the direct and exclusive authority of the local bishop and the close supervision of a chaplain, who ideally would inspire and spiritually form his charges, but would not be intimately involved in directing activities. Of course the reality on the ground varied according to a range of factors, not least of which was the personalities involved. In Singapore, the mission of the YCW was taken in deadly earnest by its leaders and activists, which, without detracting from the selflessness and zeal of the students and workers who dedicated the early years of their adulthood to its work, was no small tribute to the priests involved. The key YCW priests were:

- Fr Joseph Ho, chaplain of the YCW in the early 1970s and chairman of the Catholic Justice and Peace Commission (JPC) in the mid-1980s;
- Fr Patrick Goh, chaplain of the YCW from 1974 until 1987, chaplain of the Catholic Students' Society (CSS) at the university and Singapore Polytechnic in the mid-1980s, founder of and chaplain to the Jurong Workers' Centre, and member of the JPC at the time of the detentions; and
- Fr Edgar D'Souza, assistant editor of *The Catholic News* from 1979 to 1987.[26]

Looking more broadly than just the YCW priests, we can also identify another priest who was central to the work of the Catholic subculture in Singapore:

- Fr Guillaume Arotcarena, MEP. He was the founder of and chaplain to the Geylang Catholic Centre (GCC) (later called the Catholic Centre for Foreign Workers), and chaplain to the prisons in the mid-1980s.

Of these, the main inspirational figure was Fr Joseph Ho, who was the first local priest to leave the comfort of established presbyteries to live among the poor. The most central figure, however, was Fr Patrick Goh. From the accounts of those who knew him, Fr Goh was an inspirational leader in his own right and a formidable organiser and strategist. He had been raised in poverty and felt the needs of the poor very personally. These four men were all pressured to leave Singapore after the detentions of 1987. Other sympathetic priests in parishes included Fr Joseph Tan, Fr Simon Pereira CSSR and Fr Eugene Vaz. This network of priests, laymen and Church organisations formed the heart of the supposed Marxist conspiracy of 1987.

The organisations under the charge of these priests were institutionally separate from each other, but there was considerable overlap in personnel and activities. Tang Lay Lee, for example, was a law student when she joined the CSS in 1973 and went on to become a member of its executive committee in her final years on campus. Upon graduating in 1977, she was employed as secretary of the Southeast Asian Catholic student groups. From 1979 to 1982, she worked as co-ordinator of the CSS in Singapore. After a break, during which she took up her profession as a lawyer for the first time, she returned to full-time church work as a staff member for the YCW in 1986, where the ISD found her in May 1987. From about 1980 onwards, she also taught English and leadership skills to workers (particularly female immigrant workers) in the evenings as a volunteer for the YCW. She maintained this work even while practising law from 1983 to 1986. Except for her volunteer work and honorary positions, these were official Church positions, answerable to chaplains and ultimately to the Archbishop, for which she was paid a salary of S$500 a month by the Archdiocese.[27]

Vincent Cheng came from a slightly different background. He had been a seminarian for nine years but left without being ordained. He joined Ron Fujiyoshi's work in the JIM in the early 1970s, and then became involved in the Student Christian Movement. In 1976 he joined the JPC as an ordinary member.[28] In 1981 he moved to Thailand where he became co-ordinator of a program that was trying to consolidate the efforts of Catholic social activists in the ASEAN countries. In June 1982 he was invited back to Singapore by Fr Guillaume Arotcarena, who asked him to work full-time in his newly founded GCC, which concentrated on defending Malaysian manual workers and Filipino maids from exploitation and abuse. In 1985 Cheng accepted an invitation to become executive secretary of the JPC. He was occupying this position when he was detained.

The Work

According to the government, the 'Marxist conspirators' intended to overthrow the government, which raises the question: what were they doing in their groups over all those years, and what was it that provoked the official backlash? Fortunately there is sufficient documentary and oral evidence to allow us to paint a fairly complete picture of the group's work in the 1980s. From the descriptions given below, it is easy to see why the government would be upset with the movement's activities and would want to wage a political campaign against it. It is more difficult to see how the work could be regarded as subversive.

Migrant Workers

While the work on behalf of migrant workers was low-profile and not overtly political, it occupied the most energy over the longest time. It had its genesis in the JIM of the late 1960s and was continued by the GCC and the Jurong Workers' Centre, the YCW and the Catholic Welfare Services (CWS). Most of the work consisted of counselling workers on processes by which they could exercise their rights, teaching them English, and assisting them in their dealings with the Ministry of Labour.

The GCC and CWS had a particular focus on the problems faced by foreign maids. As well as providing advice and refuge to abused and frightened maids, the Catholic organisations also acted as a liaison with the Ministry of Labour. Until the detentions, the government had not given any indication that it was concerned with the work of the GCC, and in fact had been co-operating actively with its efforts.[29] It is ironic that one of the core detainees, Ng Bee Leng, was detained for her work with the GCC when her main role was to maintain daily contact with the Ministry of Labour so that the Ministry could assess the individual cases of the maids who had come to the GCC for help.[30]

A lot of the staff and volunteers involved in this work were solicitors who were willing to work for nothing or next to nothing in order to help the less fortunate: people such as Teo Soh Lung in the 1970s, and Tang Lay Lee, Kenneth Tsang and Lim Sok Hoon in the 1980s. Remarkably, there were so many self-sacrificing solicitors willing to donate their evenings that

Teo Soh Lung had no compunction about leaving the work in 1981: 'The Geylang Catholic Centre actually had a whole team of lawyers and I was not indispensable, so I left.'[31]

12-Hour Shift

The campaign against the government's introduction of the 12-hour shift in 1984 was initiated and run by the YCW with input from other sections of the movement. The YCW organised a survey of over 200 workers, 70 of whom were already operating in the 12-hour shift environment. The survey inquired into the workers' patterns of rest days and working weeks, socialising, family time, tiredness, health and opinions about the 12-hour shift.[32] Students assisted in the collection of this data,[33] which was used in conjunction with other research to present a formal submission to Prof. S. Jayakumar, the then Acting Minister for Labour, whose public relations office then entered into a polite correspondence on the matter.[34] The 12-hour-shift issue and the YCW report were given prominent coverage in *The Catholic News* thanks to the presence of Fr Edgar D'Souza as assistant editor, which prompted Lim Boon Heng, a Catholic government MP, to engage the authors in a debate through the letters pages.[35] The report and the subsequent debate in *The Catholic News* also caught the attention of the secular press, both English and Chinese.[36]

Retrenchment

The retrenchment campaign emerged in response to the upsurge in unemployment that accompanied the recession of the mid-1980s. It was basically an effort to highlight the human plight of the unemployed by publicising case studies of real people, and to pressure employers, the trade unions, the government and society as a whole to treat the retrenched and those facing retrenchment with a sense of justice and compassion. The YCW issued a May Day statement on retrenchment in 1985 that was publicised in *The Catholic News*.[37] It also conducted a survey of 31 retrenched workers and used the results as the basis for a 21-page booklet on the subject, marked 'for private circulation'.[38] The campaign was particularly critical of the quiescent role of trade unions and the government.

Industrial Rights

Beyond the particular campaigns outlined above, the YCW was at the forefront of a series of more low-key efforts to raise awareness of industrial relations issues, such as the minimum wage, family wage, workplace health and safety, and workmen's compensation, and to provide leadership training to workers who wanted to agitate for improvements in their conditions of work.

Graduate Mothers Campaign

The movement's response to the then Prime Minister Lee Kuan Yew's eugenics initiatives in 1983 (the most celebrated of which gave mothers who were university graduates priority in enrolling their children in the 'best' schools) was initiated by the Social Awareness Response Committee of the Catholic Students' Society. The CSS printed pamphlets and T-shirts opposing the Graduate Mothers Priority Scheme, which it distributed and sold on campus and in churches.[39] It is notable that the T-shirts and pamphlets were originally produced as part of a joint project between the CSS and the National University of Singapore Students' Union (NUSSU), but the NUSSU was forced to withdraw from the project after the National University of Singapore (NUS) administration forbade their involvement.[40] An earlier joint protest by the students' unions of NUS, Nanyang Technological Institute, Ngee Ann Polytechnic and Singapore Polytechnic withered after a 'three-hour closed door meeting' between the leadership of the four bodies and the Minister of State (Education), Tay Eng Soon.[41]

Education

The movement was also highly critical of streaming in schools, the privileging of Chinese-medium Special Assistance Plan Schools, the Gifted Education Program, and more generally of the educational reforms being introduced in the 1980s.[42] At the heart of its critique lay a rejection of materialism and competitiveness.

Abortion, Family Life, HDB living

The movement also displayed ongoing concern with traditional Catholic social issues, such as abortion and family life, including the effects of HDB living on family and community life.

Conscientising

Overlaying all this work — and the aspect that perhaps did the most to feed conspiracy theories — was the JPC which, with Vincent Cheng as executive secretary, operated in the mid-1980s as a centre of networking and as a source of inspiration and guidance alongside that provided by the chaplains. In the 1980s it took on a quasi-spiritual, quasi-political role of 'conscientising' or consciousness raising about issues of justice and oppression, routinely placing these overtly social and political issues in spiritual and theological contexts. During this time Cheng and the JPC's study-cum-spiritual programme was based heavily on a Korean Protestant approach to social issues called *Minjung* theology [theology of the poor/ oppressed].[43] This theology resonated strongly with the consciousness-raising approaches of the YCW and Saul Alinsky's CO. It was based on a confrontational, millenarian reading of the Old Testament that imbued the socio-political struggle of the marginalised with more than a touch of messianic certainty.[44] *Minjung* theology is not connected with Liberation Theology, though there are similarities in their processes of conscientising the poor and marginalised so that they and their supporters realise the nature and extent of their marginalisation and oppression.[45]

Regardless of the theological sources of the JPC's conscientising, it is clear that there was no subversion in the study groups led by the JPC, not only because neither Cheng nor Fr Joseph Ho believed in subversion, but because a record of one of the networking-cum-soul searching sessions reports at length the contributions of 'Vincent, an active member of the Justice and Peace Commission'.[46] His comments were no more than mildly critical of the priests and hierarchy for being too accepting of the status quo in Singapore and of not giving matters of justice a high priority. His only two statements that related to concrete action were his praise for groups that 'look into the welfare of foreign workers, especially Filipino maids in Singapore', and a recommendation that 'we can have Bible and theological seminars focusing on the Justice Message …'.[47] The level of innocence displayed in this report should not be surprising because the government's published evidence against Cheng (disregarding confessions solicited under painful physical duress) contained nothing more incriminating than an attendance list for a meeting and some notes in Cheng's handwriting planning the agenda of a meeting of the Coalition of Organisations for Religious Development (CORD). The notes reveal nothing more sinister than an intention to discuss 'political participation'.[48] The accusation that these people were engaging in a conspiracy to overthrow the state is therefore difficult to sustain — regardless of which strand of theology is purported to have inspired them.

The Detentions

So why were they arrested? The government's own record of Lee Kuan Yew's face-to-face meeting with Archbishop Gregory Yong and other Church leaders on 2 June 1987 provides some insights into the Prime Minister's thinking:

> PM said that he was not interested in VINCENT CHENG and his group, but he had to deal with them in a way that would make it less likely for others to follow. He was however more concerned about the involvement of several priests [being] Fr EDGAR D'SOUZA, Fr PATRICK GOH, Fr JOSEPH HO and Fr AROTCARENA.
>
> PM said that the problem was not going to be over even if the four priests were disgraced or defrocked ... PM said that he wanted the problem to be resolved in a way that would prevent a kind of 'crack position' when every action of the Church would be suspect.[49]

If we compare the situation in 1987 with that of the early 1970s, the critical difference is that in the 1980s there was a perception that these 'several priests' had emerged as a group of troublemakers and that this threatened to turn a series of uncoordinated 'do-gooder' activities into 'problems' that Lee saw as 'coming from the Church' and which were leading it into 'a collision course with the Government'.[50] The troublemakers had, according to Lee, 'got' the Archbishop and *The Catholic News* through Fr Edgar D'Souza, whom he described as 'a skilful united front operator'.[51] He identified the other trouble makers as Fr Patrick Goh, Fr Joseph Ho and Fr Arotcarena,[52] who between them held responsibility for the YCW, the CSS, the Jurong Workers' Centre and the JPC, and the GCC.

Throughout the private meetings in this period – and especially in the meeting of 2 June – the detainees were routinely dismissed by Lee as being of no interest to him, but he frequently iterated the role of 'these four priests' who, he emphasised, 'the Government had full rights ... to arrest'. He was so much more concerned about the priests because of the potential of 'priests or so-called priests' to bring what he called 'Filipino tactics' into Singapore.[53] By 'Filipino tactics' he was referring to the activities of priests who were motivated by Liberation Theology to engage the Church in revolutionary politics.[54] Yet it is important to note that even this scenario was not, according to Lee, an existential threat. He was not arguing that the Church in Singapore was harbouring revolutionary priests; he merely advised that 'this was something which the Church should monitor'.[55]

If Lee knew that the priests had not been engaged in seditious activities, then why did the government pursue them with such vigour? The answer to this lies not just in imagined threats, but also in political realities. These four priests had displayed a capacity and willingness to voice opposition to government initiatives by organising across social boundaries under the auspices of the Church. Perhaps the best single example of this was the instance when university students distributed leaflets and sold T-shirts through Catholic parishes as part of their campaign against the Graduate Mothers Priority Scheme after the NUS administration had forbidden their sale and distribution on campus.[56] Another example was the involvement of students and *The Catholic News* in the campaign against the 12-hour shift. That it was this political capacity and activity that triggered the government's concern is apparent from the words of Archbishop Yong, as reported in the ISD minutes of the 2 June meeting when he was speaking of his apparent disregard for earlier warnings that had been given by the government:

> ... the Archbishop said that when he was called up in mid-1986 by the MHA [Ministry of Home Affairs], the officials did not tell him that the Catholic activists had links with communists and were using the Church; they merely told him that these activists were involving themselves in socio-political issues.[57]

It was this capacity to engage 'in socio-political issues' that was the government's first-stated and on-going concern. The movement did not threaten the state or the nation, but it did threaten the government's capacity to set the agenda for public discourse. The government had begun encouraging disparate elements of society to contribute to public discourse within the limits it set, but only insofar as it retained control of the agenda. By demonstrating their ability to cross social and institutional boundaries (for instance, from church to campus to shop floor to media) the priests and their lay associates demonstrated a level of independence of thought and action that challenged the government's monopolistic control of the public agenda. Furthermore, a common theme of Catholic activism ever since the 1960s has been its propensity to transform a collection of individual complaints into a collective demand for action. This was the point that drew Lee Kuan Yew's attention to Sr Samantha and the work of the UIMs in the late 1960s and early 1970s. It was this that transformed a merely implicit challenge to the government's agenda into one that was completely explicit.

To make matters even worse, the priests and their lay associates appeared to be acting in wilful defiance of the government.[58] Sr Samantha's failing health, the *de facto* expulsion of Ron Fujiyoshi and a few quiet words with some church leaders had been sufficient to deal with the UIMs in the early 1970s, but in this instance, several warnings had been issued and had not had the desired effect. In fact, they had not been understood or passed on, but the Ministry of Home Affairs thought it was being defied.[59]

Conclusion

It is apparent from this study that it would take a broad canvas to paint the whole picture of the detentions of 1987. From the perspective of the detainees and the priests associated with the movement, they were acting out their social duty as Catholics with the full knowledge and support of the Church. In interview several even volunteered to agree with Lee Kuan Yew's assessment that they were just 'do-gooders who wanted to help the poor and the dispossessed'. As far as we can tell from all available sources, none of them had actually done anything wrong, either in the eyes of the Church or in the eyes of the law. Furthermore all the available evidence suggests that the priests were not teaching and had never taught Liberation Theology or any sort of revolutionary creed. The leap of imagination that pictures them or the lay activists as agents of Liberation Theology baffles them even now, and to this day many of the detainees struggle to understand why they were targeted.

From the government's perspective, its ministers were worried by what they saw as dangerous developments in the Catholic Church at an international level. The Prime Minister was acutely conscious of the popularity of Liberation Theology among radical clergy in the Philippines and Latin America, and claimed to be fearful of a revolutionary situation developing in Singapore. These fears were all about imagined futures, but Lee and his colleagues were above all practical politicians concerned with the day-to-day exercise of power. At this more immediate level the government faced a scenario in which the movement posed a short-term threat to its monopoly on political discourse. This was the government's immediate concern, but its rhetoric and imagination focused on a more fanciful scenario, whereby the Church might become a threat to the state. This was merely an exercise of the official imagination, but that was enough to provide political justification for the detentions.

NOTES

1   This paper was researched and written with financial support from the Australian Research Council and the University of Queensland, and the kind assistance of the National University of Singapore (NUS) Department of History, the Asia Research Institute (NUS), and the Trinity Theological College Library, Singapore. On a more personal note, I wish to thank those people who opened their pasts to me through interviews and by making private archives available. I am particularly grateful to Fr James Minchin for his assistance with this project. He not only made himself available for two interviews but also

welcomed my wife, Shamira, and me into his home and introduced me to his friends. I would also like to thank my wife for her counsel and assistance.

2   *The Straits Times*, 22 May and 21 June 1987.

3   *The Straits Times*, 27 May 1987.

4   *The Straits Times*, 27 May, 21 June and 20 July 1987.

5   Interview with a former detainee, Singapore, 25 March 2003. Some interviews conducted in the course of this research have been de-identified at the request of the interviewee, and in accordance with procedures approved by the Behavioural and Social Science Ethical Review Committee of the University of Queensland.

6   Interview with a former detainee, Singapore, 25 March 2003.

7   Report of Lee Kuan Yew's words in ISD notes of a meeting between the PM and Catholic Church leaders on 2 June 1987 at 3pm at the Istana. This document is marked 'SECRET' but was released to the court as Exhibit 85(d) during the government's legal action against the *Far Eastern Economic Review* in 1989.

8   Ibid.

9   See 'Statement of Ex-Detainees of Operation "Spectrum", Embargoed until 10am 18th April 1988', reproduced in Francis T. Seow, *To Catch a Tartar: A Dissident in Lee Kuan Yew's Prison* (Haven, Conn: Yale Centre for International Area Studies, 1994), pp. 258–61. The statement was signed by nine former detainees.

10 *The Straits Times*, 28 May 1987.

11 Interview with Fr James Minchin, Melbourne, 17 February 2005 and interview with Edgar D'Souza, Melbourne, 16 February 2005.

12 See, for instance, *Church and Society*, published by Frs G. Arotcarena, Edgar D'Souza, Patrick Goh, Joseph Ho, Joseph Tan and Eugene Vaz as the Church and Society Study Group, December 1984. This particular issue contains explicit rejections of: class warfare (p. 15), the inevitability of opposition between capital and labour (p. 14), and violence (p. 19).

13 Interview with Edgar D'Souza, Melbourne, 16 February 2005.

14 East Asia Christian Conference, *God's People in Asian Industrial Society: The Report of the* [1966] *East Asia Christian Conference on Christians in Industry and Lay Training*, ed. Robert M. Fukada (Kyoto: EACC, 1967), p. 119.

15 See Saul D. Alinsky, *Reveille for Radicals* (New York: Random House, 1969), pp. 144–6; and Saul D. Alinsky, *Rules for Radicals: A Practical Primer for Realistic Radicals* (New York: Vintage Books, 1971), pp. 146–8.

16 Interview with Sr Samantha, Singapore, 2 May 2003. Sr Samantha is a member of a religious order and under the order's rules she is not free to allow the use of her name or to allow reference to her order in any publication. The interview was conducted on the understanding that these prohibitions would be respected.

17 Ibid.

18 Vincent Cheng Kim Chuan, 'The Taiping Revolution: A Socio-Ethical Study of Class Struggle', Master of Theology Thesis, Trinity Theological College, Singapore, 1978, p. 256.

19 For the best, dedicated study of this phenomenon, see Chan Heng Chee, *Singapore: The Politics of Survival 1965–1967* (Singapore and Kuala Lumpur: Oxford University Press, 1971).

20 Chan Heng Chee, *Politics in an Administrative State: Where Has the Politics Gone?* (Singapore: Department of Political Science, University of Singapore, 1975).

21 Lee Kuan Yew, *Leadership in Asian Countries* (Singapore: Ministry of Culture, 1967), pp. 1, 3, 7.

22 For a fuller exposition of the author's understanding of Lee's thinking at this time, see Michael D. Barr, *Lee Kuan Yew: The Beliefs Behind the Man* (Richmond, UK: Curzon, 2000), especially chapters 3 and 4, pp. 49–136.

23 Interview with Sr Samantha, Singapore, 2 May 2003.

24 At least three of the four priests at the centre of the alleged conspiracy were inspired directly by Canon Cardijn. These were Fr Joseph Ho, Fr Patrick Goh (each of whom was a chaplain and leader to the YCW) and Fr Edgar D'Souza (who spoke eloquently of Canon Cardijn and his methodology during his interview in Melbourne on 16 February 2005).

25 Joseph Cardijn, *The Hour of the Working Class* (Melbourne: [Young Christian Workers, 1949]), pp. 9–14.

26 Fr D'Souza was not institutionally involved in the YCW but was drenched in Canon Cardijn's teachings and considered himself to be part of the movement. Interview with Edgar D'Souza, Melbourne, 16 February 2005.

27 Interview with Tang Lay Lee, Singapore, 20 April 2004. A salary of S$500 per month in the mid-1980s was meagre for a professional, but more than that paid to most manual workers.

28 Cheng, *The Taiping Revolution*, p. 256.

29 One public indication of the co-operative spirit between the GCC/CWS and the Ministry of Labour was a glowing news feature in *The Sunday Times* [of Singapore] in 1984, which highlighted the work of both the GCC and the efforts of the Ministry to assist maids who had been cheated. In this feature, Fr Arotcarena even expressed his appreciation for the Ministry's diligence in cases where breaches of the law were clear-cut. See 'Centre to fight maid "abuse"', *The Sunday Times*, 5 August 1984.

30 Report in *The Catholic News*, 14 June 1987.

31 Interview with Teo Soh Lung, Singapore, 17 March 2003.

32 The original results from these surveys are held by Sinapan Samydorai, National President of the YCW, 1982–86.

33 Interview with Kevin de Souza, Singapore, 21 March 2003.

34 See *The YCW Report on 12-Hour Shift*, presented to Prof. S. Jayakumar, the then Acting Minister for Labour, by The Young Christian Workers Movement, The Justice and Peace Commission, and The Christian Family Social Movement; and subsequent correspondence. Held by Sinapan Samydorai.

35 See *The Catholic News*, 25 December 1983; and 19 August, 30 September and 28 October 1984.

36 *Singapore Monitor*, 13 December 1983 and 31 October 1984; *The Straits*

Times, 24 December 1983; *Lianhe Zaobao*, 12 November 1983. (Translation of the *Lianhe Zaobao* article was kindly provided by Assoc. Prof. Huang Jianli, Department of History, National University of Singapore.)

37 *The Catholic News*, 27 April 1985.

38 Young Christian Workers Movement (Singapore), *Retrenchment*, October 1985, for private circulation.

39 CSS ExCo, 'Report on the Catholic Students' Society 1983/1984', *Aquinas '84/5*, p. 56.

40 'NUS puts its foot down on sale of T-shirts', *The Straits Times*, 8 November 1984.

41 'Dr Tay calls off discussion on priority scheme', *The Straits Times*, 14 April 1984; 'Students call for delay in priority scheme registration', *The Straits Times*, 1 May 1984; 'We accept need for the scheme, say students', *The Straits Times*, 17 May 1984.

42 *Aquinas '84/5*, pp. 16–39.

43 Interview with a former detainee, Singapore, 27 March 2003; and interview with Fr James Minchin, 17 February 2005.

44 See Crys H. S. Moon, *A Korean Minjung Theology — An Old Testament Perspective* (Maryknoll, NY: Orbis Books, 1985).

45 Donald N. Clark, 'Growth and Limitations of Minjung Christianity in South Korea', in *South Korea's Minjung Movement: The Culture and Politics of Dissidence*, ed. Kenneth M. Wells (Honolulu: University of Hawaii Press, 1995), pp. 87–103.

46 The Aquinas Committee, 'Does Our Church Educate for Justice?', in *Aquinas '84/5*, pp. 46–9.

47 Ibid., pp. 47, 49.

48 *The Straits Times*, 29 May 1987.

49 Capitals present in the original text. In fact Lee stated twice in this meeting that he was 'not interested' in Vincent Cheng and his group. Internal Security Department notes of the meeting between the PM and Catholic Church leaders on 2 June 1987 at 3 pm at the Istana.

50 Ibid.

51 Ibid.

52 Ibid.

53 Ibid.

54 The minutes of the 2 June meeting record Lee's concern thus: 'In the Philippines, the priests had succeeded in using methods perfected in Latin America, and modified to suit Asian conditions.' Ibid.

55 Ibid.

56 'NUS puts its foot down on sale of T-shirts', *The Straits Times*, 8 November 1984.

57 Internal Security Department notes of the meeting between the PM and Catholic Church leaders on 2 June 1987 at 3 pm at the Istana.

58 In the 2 June meeting Lee referred twice to earlier warnings that the government, through ISD and the Ministry of Home Affairs, had passed onto the

Archbishop, but which did not appear to have been heeded. Ibid.

59 *The Straits Times* (27 May 1987) referred to this episode in these terms: 'In July last year [1986], the Home Affairs Minister informed Catholic Archbishop Monsignor Gregory Yong that Catholic organisations were being subverted for subversive political ends. "However, after a brief period of moderation, Vincent Cheng's subversive activities continued unabated," the MHA statement said.' Kevin de Souza also received an unofficial warning from a friend who was studying to be a police officer, but in his naïveté did not realise that it was something more than an expression of concern from a friend. (Interview with Kevin de Souza, Singapore, 21 March 2003.)

13

Internalised Boundaries: AWARE's Place in Singapore's Emerging Civil Society

Lenore Lyons

The period 1987 to 1995 was significant in establishing the organisational and ideological structures that underpin the sphere of civil society in Singapore today. The decade began with an event, commonly referred to as the Marxist conspiracy that was explored in the previous chapter by Michael Barr, which unequivocally demonstrated the authoritarian power of the People's Action Party (PAP). It ended with a much more subtle but no less powerful demonstration of PAP power, namely the Catherine Lim Affair, and the articulation of a new form of political regulation under the rubric of out-of-bounds (OB) markers. These two events illustrate the transition from overt authoritarian control exercised through legal structures such as the Internal Security Act (ISA), to greater reliance on self-regulation by civil society actors themselves. The latter is premised on PAP statements about the need for consultation between the government and non-government sectors based on mutual support for a set of shared national values. According to this view, over time Singapore's active citizenry will rely less on the state to define the boundaries of acceptable activist engagement and will come to depend more on an internalised sense of what is best for the nation.

While several studies have documented the ways in which the political discourses surrounding civil society in Singapore changed during this period,[1] few have explored the impact that these changes had on specific organisations. Using the case study of the Association of Women for Action and Research (AWARE), this chapter examines the ways in which political discourse and action shape the internal workings of a non-government organisation (NGO). The case study of AWARE is particularly telling because it is one of the very few active NGOs to have witnessed both the crackdown on civil society activism sparked by the Marxist conspiracy, as well as the transition to a more moderate form of political regulation under the leadership of Goh Chok Tong. In tracing the history of AWARE's activism during its first decade of operation (1985–95), it is possible to identify the significance that both the Marxist conspiracy and the Catherine Lim Affair had on the everyday workings of Singapore's NGOs. This period is pivotal not only in wider socio-political terms, but also because it laid the foundation for the emergence of a specific organisational culture within AWARE. Many of the lessons learnt and challenges faced during this period proved significant for the way that AWARE faced its second decade.

This analysis is based on narratives about AWARE's early history recounted to me during interviews conducted with AWARE members from 1994 to 1997.[2] While the focus of my interviews was with the meanings and actions associated with being a feminist in Singapore, we also touched on AWARE's early history and the individuals who founded the association. These interviews reveal an unspoken orthodoxy about the history of the women's movement and AWARE's place in it. Two dominant, overlapping narratives emerge: (1) Lee Kuan Yew's role in the founding of AWARE, placing the narrative of the organisation and the women's movement squarely in the role of respondent to the actions of the state; and (2) the fear of being deregistered. Exploring these narratives provides useful insights into AWARE's organisational culture and activism during the late 1990s. It also sheds light on the ways in which state rhetoric is refracted within the inner workings of an NGO. In exploring these narratives I am not suggesting that the stories that members tell about the founding of AWARE are fixed and unchanging; as the broader socio-political context changes, members may become more willing to explore previously taboo topics, or focus on hitherto unexplored issues in the history of AWARE. While I have found that the same foundational narratives continue to circulate, founding members are certainly less reticent in talking about previously sensitive issues. In part this reflects the passage of time, as well as the changing political landscape in Singapore.

In the first part of this chapter, I explore these foundational narratives before turning to a case study of how these narratives shaped AWARE's response to internal conflict in the mid-1990s. This case study reveals the points of contention and convergence between the state's discourses about civil society and AWARE's own model of social activism. It demonstrates that the Marxist conspiracy had a significant impact on Singapore's civil society beyond those individuals who were immediately involved. In the case of AWARE, it became a constant reference point in the group's discussions about civil society and NGO activism throughout the 1990s. Occasional warnings from the ruling elite to AWARE's Executive served to further entrench the meanings and significance that the crackdown had on AWARE's organisational culture. By the end of the decade, and well before Goh Chok Tong publicly used the term, AWARE had internalised the lessons of the Marxist conspiracy and was already modelling the OB markers.

Founding Fathers and Absent Mothers

Formed in 1985, AWARE is an openly multiracial women's rights organisation with research, service and advocacy arms. Full membership to AWARE is open to female Singaporean citizens and permanent residents over 18 years of age. Male Singaporeans, as well as foreign women and men without permanent residency, may join as associate members. The AWARE Constitution states three general objectives of the association:[3] (1) to promote the awareness and participation of women in all areas; (2) to promote the attainment of full equality; and (3) to promote equal opportunities for women. The constraints of the Societies Act mean that in pursuing these goals AWARE adopts an essentially reformist agenda. While the Singapore Constitution guarantees freedom of association (Article 14) in principle, organisations with more than ten members or committees with more than five members are required to register under the Societies Act or the Companies Act. Individuals who participate in groups that are not officially registered face the threat of arrest and imprisonment for participating in 'illegal assemblies'. All registered organisations are expressly prohibited from engaging in 'political activity' and must restrict their activities to issues outlined in their constitutions (see for example Clause 24e in the AWARE Constitution). The government has effectively used the Societies Act to suppress the activities of a number of local groups as well as foreign-based NGOs.[4]

AWARE's greatest role has been in the area of consciousness-raising, counselling and support services, and putting women's issues on the political agenda via public forums, letters to the editors of the major daily newspapers, or private approaches to government ministries. This often requires a back door approach in which AWARE gently and quietly lobbies the state, and sits back as the government takes the praise for its latest idea. Such an approach has seen important reform on matters related to family violence and sex discrimination.[5]

Former Singaporean Prime Minister Lee Kuan Yew's Great Marriage Debate plays a central role in the narratives surrounding AWARE's foundation. At a National Day Rally Speech in August 1983, the then Prime Minister called attention to a trend in which graduate women were delaying or forgoing marriage and childbirth. Lee voiced his fears that in a country whose only resource was its people, a decline in birth rates amongst the well-educated would result in a 'thinning of the gene pool', and thus national economic disaster.[6] Using a eugenicist argument, Lee claimed that while all women can be mothers, better-educated women should be mothers. He cited the 1980 census which showed that while 'uneducated' women were producing an average of three children, those with secondary or tertiary education had 1.65 children. He referred to this as a 'lop-sided procreation pattern' but the issue was dubbed the Great Marriage Debate by the local press.[7]

In November 1984, in reaction to government policies aimed at encouraging graduate women to marry and have children, the National University of Singapore Society (NUSS) held a forum titled 'Women's Choices, Women's Lives'. Several women who later became founding members of AWARE spoke at the forum. Popular memory records that a member of the audience provocatively reminded the speakers that talk was well and good, but 'what are we going to do now?' The challenge to address the issues raised during the forum was taken up by a group that included both the keynote speakers and members of the audience. A pro-tem committee agreed to meet with the objective of determining whether there was a need in Singapore for an association that addressed women's rights and sex discrimination. At this time none of the affiliate members of the government-oriented Singapore Council of Women's Organisations (SCWO), a federation of diverse women's groups, were explicitly oriented towards the goal of improving women's social or legal status. After one year of informal meetings, the Association of Women for Action and Research was formally registered with the Singapore Registrar of Societies.

According to this version of Singapore's feminist history, Lee Kuan Yew, the nation's founding father, was pivotal in putting women's rights issues in the spotlight. In this instance he played the role of protagonist.

This is not a role, however, that he has always occupied. For example, the PAP is lauded for introducing the Women's Charter[8] and giving women access to education and employment opportunities in the immediate post-independence period. This positive portrayal of Lee Kuan Yew and his party is presented in two books that appeared in the early 1990s: one was published under the auspices of the PAP Women's Wing[9] and the other by a government-sponsored umbrella group, the Singapore Council of Women's Organisations.[10] Both texts adopt an upbeat account of women's status; Singaporean women, they claim, 'have come a long way', thanks to the PAP. For example, echoing the view that the state is basically supportive of women's rights, in her book Jenny Lam Lin argues that the labour-intensive industrialisation programme of the 1970s that was promoted by the PAP increased women's participation in the workforce and created a situation in which most women saw themselves as men's equals. The majority of AWARE members I spoke to in the mid-1990s accepted this account — they claimed that the PAP played an active role in eliminating gender inequality and promoting women's participation in education and employment during the 1970s. This belief may in part explain their outrage when during the Great Marriage Debate Lee sought to introduce policies that would overturn these advances. Many of the women expressed their disbelief that a government which had promoted the principles of meri-tocracy and supported women's participation in public life would seek to reinstate women's primary roles as wives and mothers. Middle-class women who had benefited directly from the PAP's push to increase women's labour force participation were dismayed that younger women may not have the same opportunities that they had enjoyed.

One of the consequences of giving Lee Kuan Yew such a prominent place in the telling of women's history in post-independence Singapore is that the state consequently takes on the role of catalyst for the women's movement, making the movement appear more reactive than its history suggests. If we date the beginning of the women's movement from the foundation of AWARE, then it was indeed born as a reaction to state initiatives. This narrative, however, ignores what is arguably the women's movement's greatest single success: the successful struggle against polygamy in the 1950s.[11] During the whole of the 1950s, the Singapore Council of Women (SCW) waged a thankless and apparently fruitless campaign to end polygamy.[12] Then, in the lead up to self-government in 1959, it lobbied all political parties to address the issue of women's rights under marriage. Although none of the political parties at this time gave priority to women's issues, they were increasingly persuaded by the SCW that women's votes would play an important role in the next election. Eventually the PAP included women's rights in their 1959 election manifesto, the only party to do so. When the PAP came to power, the SCW reminded it of its election promises and by 1961 the Women's Charter, which provides provisions against polygamous marriage, was passed into legislation. According to Phyllis Chew, women's votes and the lobbying power of the SCW were crucial to the PAP's success.[13] In popular history, however, the PAP (and rarely the SCW) is positioned as the champion of women's rights, thus relegating civil society to the margins. In the case of the Great Marriage Debate, the PAP and the state once again occupy a central role in popular mythology, to the point where the earlier history is contextualised to a footnote in history.

The narratives that members told me about the founding of AWARE reflected the popular mythology of the central role of the PAP. In these accounts, the history of women's activism outside the formal organisational context of AWARE was largely unacknowledged. The mothers of the nation, including members of the SCW, the National Council of Women (formed in International Women's Year in 1975), and the SCWO were also absent. Similarly, stories about women students and academics at the National University of Singapore who were active in forming discussion groups and producing newsletters on topics related to women's status prior to the NUSS meeting of 1984, were subsumed by the PAP's (and by association, AWARE's) dominant place in the history of feminism. By giving the Great Marriage Debate and Lee's statements about women's roles as mothers such central prominence in the telling of AWARE's history, the organisation over-emphasised the role played by the state and overlooked the existence of a nascent women's movement dating back well before independence. Playing up the power of the state to give (through the Women's Charter) and take away (such as through the Great Marriage Debate), became yet another PAP strategy of control and containment. The PAP's interest in recounting Singaporean women's history represents a case of the government co-opting feminism 'to subserve the party's political purposes'.[14]

In this Big Bang account of Singaporean feminism, the interview respondents felt comfortable in asserting that prior to AWARE, there was 'nothing'. For many founding members, this reflected their own lack of engagement with women's rights or feminist issues prior to AWARE and their lack of involvement with other women's organisations.[15] But it is also based on an assessment of what other women's groups in Singapore were doing at the time of the Great Marriage Debate. AWARE's pro-tem committee spent time considering whether Singapore needed a women's rights organisation. They reviewed the activities of women's groups and decided that not only was there no existing women's rights organisation, but that infiltration or transformation of an existing group would prove troublesome. In their assessment, AWARE would become Singapore's only women's rights organisation.

Being the only women's rights organisation in Singapore carried with it tremendous responsibility. Founding member Vivienne Wee uses the term 'one-organisation movement' to describe this role:

> This is the peculiar thing about AWARE. It is a one-organisation movement that contains within itself [everything] ... In other countries [these women] would ... divide off and be their own thing, but in AWARE the space isn't there ... If you come out and say you are a feminist, of one kind or another, whatever kind, it's like you have to join AWARE. What other organisation is there in Singapore to join?[16]

Very quickly, AWARE found itself to be not simply 'a' Singaporean women's organisation, but 'the' Singaporean women's movement. Not only did this require AWARE to become a place in which all women found their natural (feminist) home, but it also put pressure on the organisation to succeed. To many founding members, collapse would be more than the failure of a women's organisation, it would signal the demise of the entire Singaporean women's movement.[17] Furthermore, for an organisation that owed its existence to a seemingly all-powerful state, the possibility of de-registration was always just around the corner. It is to this second foundational narrative that I turn next.

The Struggle to Overcome

The narratives that are told about AWARE's early years are replete with the imagery of struggle. One founding member reflects:

> We felt that our main struggle was just to keep going, that we had to keep going. If we were not allowed to continue, if we were deregistered as a society, nobody would pick up the pieces and try again. It is like that in Singapore. Once it is gone that is the end of it. So we said, whatever the cost we must keep going, and if it means sometimes we compromise or tone down our demands then we have to do it. We have to be very tactful and we have to think carefully. That we were being reasonable people and that we were making reasonable compromises.[18]

Throughout AWARE's first decade, fear of being 'closed down' (deregistered) was constant within the organisation. Many of these fears had their origins in the Marxist conspiracy, a term used to describe the arrest and detention under the Internal Security Act of 22 people in May 1987 for allegedly threatening the state and national interests.[19] Among those arrested were Catholic social workers and lay workers from the Geylang Catholic Centre for Foreign Workers. This group advocated higher wages, social security benefits, job security and better employment conditions for all foreign workers. At the time of their arrest, the government claimed that Catholic organisations were 'a cover for political agitation' to 'radicalise student and Christian activists'.[20] Those arrested were detained without trial. Some later confessed and were rehabilitated with an agreement not to enter into politics.

Some of those arrested were also members of AWARE. At the time of the arrests, the association's small membership of less than 100 chose to remain silent in order to avoid any suspicion of the organisation's activities. In the weeks that followed the arrests, AWARE's Executive Committee (Exco) was unclear how or if the organisation would be implicated. The government released few details about who had been detained and on what grounds, so fear was rife among the detainees' circle of family, friends and colleagues. The organisation took a low profile, and individuals tried to assess whether they or their fellow members were at risk of being arrested. Some members of the Exco burnt international feminist publications on radical and Marxist feminism for fear that these would taint the organisation with the Marxist brush. Some public forums were cancelled and the release of AWARE's important research report on population matters was postponed.[21] Not all members agreed with the Exco's response, but even though some left AWARE in protest, these internal debates were never made public.

In the mid-1990s, memories of the Marxist conspiracy were still fresh in the minds of founding members, several of whom also served on the Exco at the time of the arrests. During my interviews few were willing to talk about the event and what it meant to AWARE. Their consistent response: 'We can't/don't talk about that.'[22] Despite their refusal to talk about the specifics of the Marxist conspiracy, it was clearly still on their minds and was often alluded to in their discussions about possible threats to the organisation. Many believed that a government crackdown was a real possibility and pointed to the detentions of 1987 as proof of both intent and means. They supplemented their accounts with references to other events. For example, one member related the following story:

> We have these monthly forums and one was on 'Women in Politics',
> and we had one of the pioneer women [a woman involved in the early
> women's movement]. She is in her 70s, and she said, 'I hope one day
> we will see a woman Prime Minister.' So the very next day, the Minister

called me up and said 'Who is this woman?' He didn't even know his history, he didn't even know who she was. So I said she was in her 70s and she had been in the city council. A perfect innocent, she wasn't going to start a new party or an opposition, or whatever. But you could see how suspicious they were.

By 1992 AWARE's membership had trebled, from less than 100 members a few years earlier to almost 300. This jump in membership was due to the organisation's growing public profile, aided by the establishment of a volunteer Helpline service to assist victims of domestic violence, and media attention directed at a number of high-profile AWARE presidents. The organisation's growing size, its recent establishment of a women's centre and administrative office, and its ability to use the print media to promote its cause, increasingly attracted government attention. At the 1993 Woman of the Year award ceremony, Acting Community Development Minister Abdullah Tarmugi, in a veiled reference to AWARE, warned that some younger women preferred a more aggressive approach to social change. His advice was to 'continue to be moderate and avoid being confrontational'.[23] Over the next year, as AWARE campaigned publicly for a change to the medical benefits legislation for civil servants,[24] members of the Exco received phone calls from various unofficial emissaries warning them that the Prime Minister's Office was watching them and that they should tone down their strident criticisms of the government.

In response to these warnings, throughout 1993 and 1994, AWARE's Exco modified its own behaviour and counselled its more vocal members to modify their public statements. Increasing credence was given to self-regulation as a mode of organisational behaviour. As the earlier quotation on survival suggests, the Marxist conspiracy became a trope for an organisational culture in which compromise and moderation became the hallmarks of self-regulation. By the end of 1994, these fears had a more immediate reference point. In November 1994, *The Straits Times* published a commentary by well-known Singaporean novelist Catherine Lim, in which she claimed that Prime Minister Goh Chok Tong's promise of a more consensual leadership style had been abandoned in favour of the authoritarian style of Lee Kuan Yew.[25] Goh's response a fortnight later began what is known as the Catherine Lim Affair, in which Lim was publicly chastised for undermining the authority of the Prime Minister. In his response, Goh outlined the central tenets of a new era of civil society activism — one that was to be based on out-of-bounds markers. These markers identify subjects that the ruling elite considers to be off-limits. They have been described as 'issues that are too sensitive to be discussed in public for fear of destabilising or jeopardising public peace and order'.[26] While the PAP is ultimately responsible for determining the limits of the OB markers, it does so retrospectively, with the result that what actually constitutes unacceptable political engagement is often unclear.

Within AWARE, the OB markers had already become a way of life. Fear of closure, sparked by early warnings, meant that the organisation had already tempered its public statements or limited its activities to avoid criticism. The following quotations highlight the speed with which the language of the OB markers spread from Goh's initial comments in December 1994, through to the Exco and then to other active members. Both quotations come from interviews with non-Exco members in February 1995.

> It's a fine balance. You want to say something but you kind of have to know where the *markers* are. In anything you need to know where the markers are, except in anything you don't really know where they are. So you err on the side of caution. You are always very careful.

To be very 'careful' in this context meant employing a strategy of self-protection:

> Sometimes guerrilla warfare is more successful than outright war. Especially if you are in the minority. When the enemy advances, you retreat. And it's only when you have the chance to come out and do something that is effective. You don't want to be charging into battle and getting killed. How does that help the cause?

In my discussions with members of the Exco, bracketing (putting aside some issues), was extolled as a tactic that ensured AWARE's continued existence. Importantly, while the Catherine Lim Affair and the phrase 'OB markers' were never used in any of our conversations throughout 1995, the Marxist conspiracy was often mentioned in order to demonstrate the PAP's ability to deliver on its threats to deal with unruly NGOs. The significance of the 1987 detentions cannot be underestimated. AWARE was one of the few politicised NGOs in the 1990s that had direct experience of detention and brutal interrogation. When its founding members considered the implications of overstepping the PAP's unspoken markers, they thought about the Marxist conspiracy and not the public knuckle-rapping of Catherine Lim. Throughout the 1990s, AWARE certainly spent considerable time formulating and re-formulating its strategies in anticipation of the state's response. The Exco began to set AWARE's own internal OB markers somewhere within the invisible circle marked out by the state. This proved to be a successful form of state control — AWARE ended up policing its own behaviour without the need for state intervention. This strategy only works where there is a strong organisational ethic that ensures that the majority of members toe the party line. In the case of AWARE, this was made possible by a strong ethics of respect based on the bonds of friendship that tied the Exco and its wider circle of active members together. Used in this context, the concept of respect implied that the views of all AWARE's members were equally validated even though the beliefs of a minority were used as the basis for the organisation's actions.[27] By 1995, however, these bonds were beginning to show signs of strain.

Reinforcing the OB Markers

By April 1995, AWARE's membership stood at 670 and although a large number of these new recruits were 'passive members',[28] it became increasingly evident that fault lines were appearing between some of AWARE's active membership. In mid-1995 a group of members wrote a discussion paper titled 'AWARE Blueprinters Suggestions for Future Directions and Strategies' (hereafter Blueprint). The formation of the Blueprinters working committee occurred after a brainstorming session in 1994 in which members indicated that the organisation was at a crossroads. The Blueprinters presented their ideas to the Executive Committee and a small group of key individuals (mostly founding members or ex-presidents) in April 1995. Despite many reservations from this group, the Blueprint was presented to an Extra-ordinary General Meeting (EOGM) in June 1995.

The Blueprint was presented as a discussion paper which would 'provide a means to chart future directions by providing signposts and reference points to members and the leadership'.[29] The Blueprinters recommended the creation of an AWARE Manifesto and a programme of conscientisation. The manifesto would act as a 'reference point' in AWARE's day-to-day activities, while the conscientisation programme was aimed in the first instance at the Exco in order to educate committee members 'on what feminism is about'.[30]

The Blueprint was rejected by the majority of members who attended the EOGM. Many women objected to what they saw as a homogenising tendency within the document — that is, it prescribed one way of being feminist. Others argued that AWARE was not and had never been a feminist organisation. While the Blueprinters rejected the first claim by arguing that they wanted to explore feminisms, not feminism, they were shocked by the latter suggestion. They claimed that while AWARE had always adopted a 'don't ask, don't tell' strategy with regard to the feminist label, everyone (members, non-members, the state, the media) knew that it was in fact a feminist organisation. When their opponents stated that AWARE was not feminist (although the majority believed that it was), they argued that AWARE had never publicly identified itself with the label. They also believed that in adopting an openly feminist conscientisation programme, AWARE was inevitably embracing such an identity.[31]

The imperative to avoid the negative connotations associated with the term feminism was also linked to wider concerns to ensure that AWARE did not disappear. In the early 1990s the PAP had already warned AWARE in public and in private to tone down its public comments about government policy. Within the Exco, concerns that AWARE might become another victim of government anti-Marxist rhetoric were heightened when the Blueprinters began to use terms such as 'manifesto' and 'consciousness-raising'.[32] The Blueprinters, and some of their younger supporters, were sceptical that the government would want to close AWARE down. They argued that AWARE was too vocal and too visible for de-registration to occur without any fuss. Their more cautious colleagues, however, pointed to the Marxist conspiracy and argued that the government would have no compunction in detaining a small group of radical members and then forcing the deregistration of AWARE on a trumped-up charge.

In the case of the Blueprinters, AWARE's foundational narratives came together to shape the Exco's response to internal conflict. As the one face of feminism in Singapore, AWARE had to necessarily incorporate a range of different views about women's rights activism. In attempting to become all things to all people, it insisted on a policy of ambivalence towards feminism — the organisation provided room for those who openly identify as feminist, as well as those who adopted an anti-feminist (but pro-women's rights) stance. As the Blueprinters pointed out, this strategy also required silence about what feminism means in the Singaporean context. The Exco were concerned that women who were wary of the term could be alienated from the organisation if it were discussed more explicitly.

In addition, the Exco were worried that the language of conscientisation might send potentially risky messages to the government about AWARE's interests and agenda. The additional burden that AWARE carried as a one-organisation movement was that it had a wider social responsibility to all women (as well as its members) to ensure that the organisation was not closed down. Drawing on historical memory of struggle against a paternal (and sometimes malevolent) state, AWARE constantly counselled its members to monitor and modify their behaviour. The Marxist conspiracy and other unspecified warnings became part of the mythology of survival into which all members were inducted. In most instances, these threats did not need to be spelt out — they were part of a wider political culture that younger members were expected to accept. Goh Chok Tong's public treatment of Catherine Lim reinforced the Exco's message that the state had the power to shut AWARE down whenever it liked. His comments regarding OB markers merely provided a common language with which to name an already internalised mode of behaviour.

Conclusion

The narratives that founding members tell about AWARE's first decade reveal an organisational culture built on fear and self-regulation. The first foundational narrative, by drawing on the central role of the Great Marriage Debate in AWARE's formation, served to emphasise the association's status as both a subordinate by-product of the state, and as the exclusive face of the feminist movement in Singapore. In taking on these roles, AWARE became all things to all women, and this required a cautious and ambivalent stance towards feminism. It also placed pressure on AWARE to succeed, because to fail would be to throw away women's chances of achieving gender equality in Singapore. Success, however, was always tenuous. The state's heavy hand in matters of civil society meant that AWARE constantly monitored its own behaviour for fear of attracting the state's wrath. For AWARE, these threats were not unfounded. They had their origin in the second foundational narrative — the fear of de-registration. In recounting the story of AWARE's birth, the central role played by the PAP served to re-inscribe the state's power. When combined with the imagery of struggle, the state became omnipresent. These threats can be overcome, however, when women rally together and put their friendships (and the future of the organisation) before their own needs and interests.

These foundational narratives served as a model of how best to deal with the more politically contentious aspects of the organisation's activities. As the example of the Blueprinters shows, an insistence on compromise built around the bonds of friendship allowed few spaces for alternative voices to be heard or for strategies that question dominant discourses to be developed. Internal tension, because it called into question the ambivalence surrounding feminism and provided the state with an excuse to crack down on the organisation, was to be avoided. Members were reminded that the future of AWARE, and by association the Singaporean women's movement, lay in their hands. More significantly, however, restricting the emergence of alternative voices served to entrench the state's discourse about acceptable civil society activism. By establishing AWARE's own internal OB markers, these foundational narratives demonstrated that having such markers was an acceptable practice. In the case of AWARE, not only did the Marxist conspiracy serve as a trope for the more politically contentious aspects of the organisation's activities (that is, it exemplified self-regulation), but AWARE's response to it further legitimised the organisation's mode of engagement with the state (that is, it entrenched the state's own discourse about acceptable civil society activism). AWARE began to embody the state's rhetoric about a model of civil society in which some topics were always already off-limits.

Internal self-regulation dominated AWARE's activism through the late 1990s, but by the turn of the century, as the founding members adopted a less prominent role in the organisation and as the Marxist conspiracy became a distant memory, AWARE's Executive became more willing to challenge existing orthodoxies. The OB markers have given way to a more inclusivist style of state-civil society engagement built around the rhetoric of active citizenry. This study remains significant, however, in demonstrating how state rhetoric is internalised within the inner workings of one of Singapore's NGOs, and how organisational behaviour in turn legitimises broader patterns of civil society engagement. As AWARE and other NGOs look forward to a new era of state-civil society engagement under the leadership of Prime Minister Lee Hsien Loong, the lessons of the past continue to shape the face of civil society activism.

NOTES

1   See, for example, Terence Lee, 'Gestural Politics: Civil Society in "New" Singapore', *Sojourn: Journal of Social Issues in Southeast Asia* 20, 2 (2005): 132–54; Terence Lee, 'The Politics of Civil Society in Singapore', *Asian Studies Review* 26, 1 (2002): 97–117.

2   Using a purposive sampling strategy, I interviewed 34 AWARE members in 1994. Initial interviews took between one to two hours. I conducted follow-up interviews with most respondents a year later, and again in 1997. For a discussion of the methodological issues associated with this project, see Lenore Lyons, 'Re-Telling "Us": Researching the Lives of Singaporean Women', in *Love, Sex and Power: Women in Southeast Asia*, ed. Susan Blackburn (Clayton: Monash University Press, 2001), pp. 115–28; Lenore Lyons and Janine Chipperfield, '(De)Constructing the Interview: A Critique of the Participatory Method', *Resources for Feminist Research/Documentation sur la Recherche Feministe* 28, 1/2 (2000): 33–48.

3   AWARE, 'Association of Women for Action and Research Declaration and Constitution' (Singapore: AWARE, 1990), p. 1.

4   For further discussion, see Yayoi Tanaka, 'Singapore: Subtle NGO Control by a Developmentalist Welfare State', in *The State and NGOs: Perspectives from*

Asia, ed. Shinichi Shigetomi (Singapore: Institute of Southeast Asian Studies, 2002); Garry Rodan, 'Embracing Electronic Media but Suppressing Civil Society: Authoritarian Consolidation in Singapore', *The Pacific Review* 16, 4 (2003): 503–24.

5   For a discussion of these campaigns, see Lenore Lyons, *A State of Ambivalence: The Feminist Movement in Singapore* (Leiden: Brill Publishers, 2004).

6   *The Straits Times*, 15 August 1983.

7   For further discussion, see Stella R. Quah, *Family in Singapore: Sociological Perspectives* (Singapore: Times Academic Press, 1994), p. 136.

8   The Women's Charter covers laws dealing with marriage, divorce, custody, maintenance, inheritance, property rights and protection against violence (although it is unevenly applied to Muslim women, who are also covered by *Shariah* law).

9   Aline K. Wong and Wai Kum Leong, eds., *Singapore Women: Three Decades of Change* (Singapore: Times Academic Press, 1993).

10 Jenny Lam Lin, ed., *Voices and Choices: The Women's Movement in Singapore* (Singapore: Singapore Council of Women's Organisations, 1993).

11 Ibid., p. 84.

12 Phyllis Ghim Lian Chew, 'The Singapore Council of Women and the Women's Movement', *Journal of Southeast Asian Studies* 25, 1 (1994): 112–40.

13 Ibid.

14 Geraldine Heng, '"A Great Way to Fly": Nationalism, the State, and the Varieties of Third-World Feminism' in *Feminist Genealogies, Colonial Legacies, Democratic Futures*, ed. M. Jacqui Alexander and Chandra Talpade Mohanty (New York: Routledge, 1997), p. 44.

15 It should be noted, however, that through its research programmes AWARE has played an important role in bringing the work of these women's groups to light.

16 Personal communication, February 1995.

17 It could also be argued that AWARE was also the first politicised NGO to emerge post-independence. Constance Singam points out that the implications of AWARE's survival extended beyond its impact on the women's movement to the sphere of civil society as a whole (personal communication, August 2005).

18 The founding members are a small group, and the majority requested anonymity. The use of pseudonyms would potentially identify these women and consequently I have chosen to use the quotations without identifiers.

19 See Michael Barr's chapter in this volume.

20 Michael Haas, 'The Politics of Singapore in the 1980s', *Journal of Contemporary Asia* 19, 1 (1989): 59.

21 AWARE, *Population: An Issue of Current Concern* (Singapore: Association of Women for Action and Research, 1988).

22 None of those detained would agree to speak to me, even though the purpose of my interview was to talk only about their involvement in AWARE, and not about their detention.

23 *The Sunday Times*, 19 February 1993.

24 See, for example, *The Straits Times*, 25 May 2002; *The Straits Times*, 8 September 1997.

25 Lee, 'Gestural Politics: Civil Society in "New" Singapore', p. 143.

26 Ho Kai Leong, *The Politics of Policy-Making in Singapore* (Oxford: Oxford University Press, 2000), p. 186.

27 This interpretation of an organisational ethic is based on a series of interviews with AWARE members conducted between 1994–1998. It is developed more fully in Lenore Lyons, 'Negotiating Difference: Singaporean Women Building an Ethics of Respect', in *Forging Radical Alliances Across Difference: Coalition Politics for the New Millennium*, ed. Steven Schacht and Jill M. Bystydzienski (London: Rowman and Littlefield Publishers, 2001).

28 A term I use to describe members who join but do not take part in any organisational activities.

29 Blueprinters, 'Aware Blueprinters Suggestions for Future Directions and Strategies' (Singapore: AWARE, 1995).

30 Ibid., p. 5.

31 For a discussion of the meanings associated with feminism in Singapore, see Lenore Lyons, 'Believing in Equality: The Meanings Attached to "Feminism" in Singapore', *Asian Journal of Women's Studies* 5, 1 (1999): 115–39.

32 While consciousness raising has a long history in the Western feminist movement, it is also strongly associated with the politics of radical Marxism.

14

History Spiked: Hegemony and the Denial of Media Diversity

Cherian George

The hegemonic project of the People's Action Party's (PAP) has included an illiberal twist on the idea of press freedom. The standard liberal position, famously embodied in the First Amendment to the United States Constitution, prohibits government interference in the free press, which is regarded as a *sine qua non* of democracy. The PAP's position, in contrast, prohibits press interference in the work of an elected government, the embodiment of the people's democratic choice. On the surface, the PAP's press system is unremarkable; it is one of dozens of authoritarian models around the world, all of which involve claims that the suspension of press freedom is in the public interest. What makes the system exceptional is its sheer longevity and stability, maintained with declining levels of overt repression. The picture is all the more striking when set against a vision of what could have been. The current state of affairs was by no means preordained. Until the early 1970s, freedom of the press was fought for within the public sphere, through vigorous debates within newspaper pages and other public fora, and through the actual practices of mainstream media organisations that believed that they had every right to challenge authority. That story has been well and truly spiked. The PAP redirected the press, and discussions about the press, towards an acceptance — sometimes voluntary, sometimes coerced — that freedom of the press had to be subordinated to the agenda of an elected government.

The systematic blockading of the liberal path in the history of Singapore journalism is worth a close look not only because of its extraordinary effectiveness, but also because the country's press has been the subject of much ahistorical and uncritical analysis. The failure to understand just how the prevailing illiberal model came to be has led to a misdiagnosis of its current malaise as well as naïve prescriptions that are no match for the sophistication of the forces arrayed against reform. In particular, both critics as well as defenders of the PAP press system mistakenly assume that it is fundamentally at odds with Western models operating in advanced capitalist societies. Critics argue explicitly, or assume tacitly, that the PAP's grip will weaken the more Singapore media resemble those operating in more developed markets. Lee Kuan Yew and other defenders of the system do not disagree that the Singapore press is un-Western, but differ from the critics in preferring to maintain the distinction. They cite history and culture to justify a less adversarial mode of journalism that is more authentically Asian. This entire discourse overstates the difference between Singapore and the West. It is certainly the case that the legal restrictions on the press in Singapore violate the rights to free expression that were developed in the West. However, what is loosely described as the Western press embodies more than mere political rights. It also represents a form of advanced industrial organisation, driven by commercial and institutional interests. In short, the Western model is as much a capitalist form as a democratic one. To dichotomise the Singaporean and Western models is to obscure the possibility that the former, while clearly un-Western in a democratic sense, is highly Western in terms of political economy. Indeed, this chapter will argue that Lee Kuan Yew has tamed the press in part by riding the Western wave of capitalism, turning the commercial media's profit motive against its democratic mission.

The Pre-PAP Press

Lee Kuan Yew's definitive precept on government-press relations — quoted in his memoirs 30 years later — was stated in 1971, shortly after his government closed down two newspapers and arrested the executives of a third. 'Freedom of the press, freedom of the news media, must be subordinated to the overriding needs of Singapore, and to the primacy of purpose of an elected government,' Lee said.[1] One of the key justifications cited in this speech was Singapore's vulnerability to ethnic conflict, which — as in the Maria Hertogh riots of 1950 and the Prophet Mohammed's birthday riots of 1964 — could be instigated by irresponsible media coverage. Of course, suspending freedom of speech when it poses a direct danger to society or infringes on other rights is not necessarily inconsistent with liberal democracy. Hence, the moves in some free societies to outlaw hate speech, and the judgment that the First Amendment does not afford a man protection in 'falsely shouting fire in a theatre and causing a panic'.[2]

A stronger challenge to the liberal perspective is found in the PAP's discourse on Asian values. The government maintains that Asia applies different — but not unequal — standards, whereby states 'have their own traditions in which rulers have a duty to govern in a way consonant with the human dignity of their subjects, even if there is no clear concept of "rights" as has evolved in the West'.[3] The government highlights cultural differences: the West has an individualistic ethos which views authority as oppressive, while Asia has communitarian traditions that translate into a consensus-seeking approach. From this perspective, freedom from torture and slavery can be described as core human rights, but curbs on press freedom, like detention without trial, are not considered to be definitive breaches of international law or universal principle.[4] The propagators of these ideas said they were responding to post-Cold-War American triumphalism, which produced an assertive and culturally insensitive foreign policy intent on converting the world to American-style liberal democracy. This debate has coloured accounts of Singapore media history and discussions of press freedom. However, the Asian-Western dichotomy breaks down when one looks at the history of the press in Singapore.

If the Asian tradition tends towards consensus seeking and shuns being adversarial, it is difficult to find traces of traditional 'Asian' journalism in pre-PAP Singapore. Independent and adversarial journalism appears to have been the norm through most of the history of the Singapore press. From a legal standpoint, of course, there has never been a time when Singapore newspapers were free from licensing laws. When the British arrived, the templates for censorship had already been developed in India and were applied automatically to Singapore. Thus, as Francis Seow notes poignantly, the history of the loss of press freedom has to recognise that 'one cannot really lose anything which one has never possessed nor appreciate a loss which has never been known, possessed or experienced'.[5] However, a recitation of laws and regulations does not amount to a history, and while the legal framework may appear fundamentally constant, the history of government-press dynamics has been one of change.

Since the 1970s, press freedom has been a virtual non-issue within elite discourse. Before that, the role of the press was a matter of contention. Press laws were actively resisted, debated and fought over. Under the British, English-language newspapers — while protecting the interests of the ruling and commercial classes, and certainly not championing democracy — were eager to brand themselves as fiercely independent. Thus, one of the settlement's earliest newspapers, the *Singapore Free Press*, was so named to celebrate the lifting of certain censorship regulations in the 1830s. Even *The Straits Times* earned a reputation as 'The Thunderer of the East' under the editorship of Alexander William Still from 1908 to 1926.[6] Still had a strong sense of a newspaper's role in serving the public interest — and of its right to define that interest in terms occasionally at odds with the government's agenda. He attacked the performance of the governor, Sir Lawrence Guillemard, in a fashion that Still's successors would find unthinkable. For example, when the press got wind of behind-the-scenes discussions of a proposed constitutional change, and the administration urged editors to defer the debate until its proposals were actually announced (a request that today would probably be acceded to), Still shot back in an editorial: 'That is mere pompous nonsense when addressed to a free people and a free press.'[7]

The Chinese-language press was smaller, due to lower levels of literacy and income within the Chinese-speaking community. Perhaps it is there, rather than in the British-run English-language press, that one would find traces of a style of journalism more in line with the theory of Asian values. However, Chen Mong Hock's 1967 history of early Chinese newspapers suggests no such tradition. Political stands were vigorously asserted, based more on the publisher's own leanings than on the mandate of heaven, either in Singapore or China. The first daily newspaper in Chinese, the *Lat Pau*, founded in 1881, contained a mix of articles not significantly different from that which the English papers carried — editorial comment on political affairs, moralistic social reportage, commercial news, and titillating gossip.[8] As for the Malay-language press, Lily Zubaidah Rahim describes in this volume the radicalism of *Utusan Melayu*, which was founded in 1939 and served as a nerve centre for political activists, student leaders and other figures in the anti-colonial resistance, including one Lee Kuan Yew. Only by excising such significant institutions from the history of the Singapore press does the Asian values theory hold.

Reserve Powers and the 1971 Crackdown

When the PAP came to office, it inherited from the colonial administration reserve powers over the press, principally in the form of licensing. Its desire and ability to retain those powers is perhaps best explained by the position of newspapers during the nationalist movement. Although individual journalists figured prominently among the PAP's early captains, the press as an institution conspicuously missed the boat. The non-English papers spoke to and for their respective linguistic communities, and were therefore not in tune with the PAP's multiracial, secular nation-building agenda. The English papers, which had the potential to unite the communities, probably disappointed Lee Kuan Yew the most, by not seeing beyond the English-educated middle class and by misapprehending his objectives. With hindsight, *The Straits Times* appears to have made an epic miscalculation. Not only was it too slow in localising its management, but worse, it spent the period from March 1959 to January 1973 headquartered in Kuala Lumpur, Malaysia. This was the same period that would later be mythologised as the years that defined and forged a new nation, and when institutions such as National Service, the Economic Development Board, the Housing Development Board and the National Trades Union Congress came into being. *The Straits Times* of today dutifully plays its part in retelling that genuinely dramatic story, but would never be able to claim a heroic role in it. Its move to Malaysia — although quite understandable at the time — seared into Lee's mind the newspaper's image as 'birds of passage'.[9] He and his colleagues could tell themselves that they succeeded in spite of the press, not because of it.

In Lee's memoirs, the chapter on media management is framed in cultural terms, probably because it was written in the wake of the Asian values debate. He contrasts the English-language press, influenced by first British and then American norms — 'always sceptical and cynical of authority' — with the Chinese and Malay press, whose 'cultural practice is for constructive support of policies they agree with, and criticism in measured terms when they do not'. Lee adds that to this day, 'Chinese-educated readers do not have the same political and social values as the English-educated. They place greater emphasis on the interests of the group than those of the individual.'[10] This culturalist thesis is contradicted by Lee's own account of government relations with the Chinese and Malay media. He notes that the two main post-war Chinese papers, *Nanyang Siang Pau* and *Sin Chew Jit Poh*, had 'opportunistic editors working through Chinese journalists of whom most were left-wing and quite a few were Communist Party cadres'.[11] It was their sympathy with the communists that accounted for their strong support of the pre-independence PAP, Lee notes. He also notes that the Maria Hertogh riots were sparked by the Malay-language *Utusan Melayu*, which 'tugged at Muslim emotions in a way the English paper could not'.[12] While the PAP finds it politically convenient to rap English-educated journalists as un-Asian compared with those working in Asian languages, the fact remains that the Chinese and Malay newspapermen account for a larger proportion of the most adversarial confrontations between state and press. While no *Straits Times* editor has ever been locked away, *Utusan*'s editor Said Zahari was detained for 17 years from 1963. And, it was the *Nanyang Siang Pau* that precipitated the most intense attack on press freedom in Singapore history outside of the Japanese Occupation.

That over-eventful month was May 1971. In late April, Lee Kuan Yew accused the Chinese-language press of stoking up chauvinism in its coverage of the decline of Chinese-medium schools. On 2 May, four senior *Nanyang Siang Pau* executives were detained under the Internal Security Act. Shortly after, the English-language *Eastern Sun* was accused of receiving communist funds from Hong Kong. Its senior staff quit, and the paper closed down. Lee Kuan Yew accused the *Nanyang Siang Pau*, *Eastern Sun* and *Singapore Herald* of involvement in 'black operations' against Singapore's security. On 28 May, the *Herald*'s licence was withdrawn; its senior expatriate journalists were expelled from the country. It had been launched only ten months earlier, but in its brief life it 'attracted quite a following, with its lively, entertaining, refreshingly irreverent approach', writes the historian Mary Turnbull.[13] Not surprisingly, this critical month in the history of Singapore's media continues to be subject to differing interpretations. In his memoirs, Lee maintains that he was acting against 'black operations'.[14] Others remember it simply as an act of flagrant censorship against the politically feisty *Herald*.

A slightly different interpretation was provided by a foreign correspondent, Anthony Polsky, who was expelled shortly after the affair. In his analysis, the *Eastern Sun* and the *Herald* would not have been dragged into the web but for *Nanyang Siang Pau*'s intransigence. The government, he said, miscalculated when it assumed that the Chinese paper would be silenced by the arrests. Denying the charges, the paper published a blank editorial column under the headline, 'Our Protest'. The owners, particularly the brother of one of the detained executives, 'began to consider it a question of family honour which required public vindication' and refused to make a deal with the Prime Minister's Office.[15] The paper continued to challenge the arrests in its columns, precipitating something of a crisis of credibility for the government. The *Eastern Sun* was sacrificed as a 'red herring', Polsky says; highlighting its admittedly dubious funding would help persuade Singaporeans of the threat of Chinese communist subversion. Attacking an English-language paper had the additional advantage of appearing even-handed to the Chinese-educated, according to this theory. Whether or not *Nanyang Siang Pau* was the primary target, its conduct confounds the theory that an adversarial stance was limited to the Western-influenced English-language media. As for the two banned English papers, Mary Turnbull notes that the following years did bring forth 'revelations about the role of foreign slush funds in infiltrating the regional press', but concludes that 'there was no evidence that either the *Eastern Sun* or the *Herald* were being influenced by their backers'.[16]

What is also clear is the effect the actions had. 'The events of May 1971 sent shock waves through Singapore and raised concerns about press freedom,' Turnbull says.[17] The *Herald's* managing director, Jimmy Hahn, said that if its permit were withdrawn, Mr Lee would be 'guilty of premeditated murder of a newspaper'.[18] Hyperbole, perhaps, but not ineffective in provoking a sense of moral outrage among readers who had developed emotional ties with the newspaper. The public relations cost of the government's threats included a 'Save the Herald' fund-raising campaign that attracted university students and other educated Singaporeans. It was not just the young republic's democratic credentials that were sullied by the events of May 1971, but also — and perhaps more seriously — its reputation as an investor-friendly economy. The *Herald's* management pointed out that, on top of violating press freedom, the government had decided 'to interfere in a commercial enterprise in an unprecedented manner'.[19] Speaking to the Hong Kong Foreign Correspondents Club, Polsky said that some foreign businessmen were concerned about 'arbitrary Singapore Government interference in the private sector'.[20] The government may have won its battle against the press, but such collateral damage had to hurt at a time when its reputation for economic management was still a work in progress.

A New Path

As a result of the tumult of 1971, Lee Kuan Yew and the PAP appeared to decide that the colonial legacy of reserve powers was inadequate to their nation-building project. That legacy — allowing discretionary licensing and preventive detention — guaranteed that the government would win any fight with any newspaper or individual journalist. For a state content to rule by force, such laws would certainly suffice. For a party with a hegemonic mission, however, recourse to these instruments exacted a heavy cost, demeaning the consensual aspect of its rule and exposing the raw coercive power beneath. Far better to win without a fight than to fight and win. It was no coincidence that the PAP introduced new press laws soon after it wielded the old ones in 1971's unprecedented orgy of aggression against the press, which, while certainly effective, also generated much public debate and disquiet. The PAP applied the lessons learnt from that affair in new press laws enacted in 1974. The Newspaper and Printing Presses Act (NPPA) retained discretionary licensing as its cornerstone but introduced unique legislative innovations, the genius of which remains under-recognised and under-estimated.

In addition to a predictable ban on foreign ownership, which many countries already had, the NPPA made it mandatory for newspaper companies to be publicly listed, and to create management shares to be held by government nominees. Public listing — with ordinary shareholders limited to a 3 per cent stake after a 1977 amendment to the NPPA — meant that Singapore would never again see the likes of the Lee family that published the recalcitrant *Nanyang Siang Pau*. 'I do not subscribe to the Western practice that allows a wealthy press baron to decide what voters should read day after day,' Lee Kuan Yew would later say.[21] (The reader should no longer be surprised that while the offending publishers in 1971 were accused of harbouring Chinese communist and chauvinist agendas, such practices were labelled 'Western' by the time of writing of Lee's memoirs.) As for the management shares, they provided a mechanism for the government to influence a newspaper's workings without interfering with ownership, which could instead be left to the stock market. Management shares were allocated to banks and other members of the business establishment. 'They would remain politically neutral and protect stability and growth because of their business interests,' Lee explained.[22] Management shares have 200 times the voting rights of ordinary shares, giving them effective control of the board and top editorial positions. This is the system under which the Singapore press operates — prosperously — to this day.

To appreciate the genius of the NPPA, one needs to contrast it with what it is not. Other authoritarian governments with an equally strong belief in their need to set the direction for the media have invariably been tempted to take over ownership of newspapers. The Chinese Communist Party is the paramount example. Those that do not nationalise the media operate a violently repressive system of censorship and routinised attacks on the press. Critics of the PAP sometimes liken it to such totalitarian or dictatorial regimes, but the comparison is profoundly misleading, under-estimating the sophistication of the government's press controls. The PAP has achieved what possibly no other authoritarian state has done: effective, near-watertight supervision of the press without either nationalising ownership of the media or brutalising journalists.

The PAP and its supporters may have an alternative interpretation, which is that the cooperative stance of the press is the result of its own enlightened professional judgment, and not of government control. From this perspective, editors have come round to appreciating that the PAP is a good government that, while not infallible, certainly has a track record of incorruptibility and outstanding performance in responding to the public's needs. The absence of visible contention, in other words, is interpreted as genuine consensus. This is undoubtedly an important part of the explanation for the 30-year calm in government-press relations. However, given that other societies with high levels of socio-economic development and political stability have more adversarial media, this cannot be a complete explanation unless one is to believe that Singapore is a heaven on earth, where all antagonisms have vaporised.

The legal framework is only part of the secret. More important is the quality of political judgment that has maintained the press system in a dynamic equilibrium, balancing the political interests of the PAP government, the profit motives of publishers, the professional and pecuniary needs of journalists, and the public's demand for information and analysis. This is not to say that all these stakeholders are happy with the system, all of the time. Rather, it is to point out that none of them has been so unhappy as to throw it out. Discerning consumers of news in Singapore, the main victims of the lack of press freedom, certainly complain about the standard of news media, and are concerned about their credibility. However, they have not been sufficiently outraged to, for example, boycott the mainstream media or to flee in droves to alternative websites that are much more independent of government control — both of which have happened in Malaysia.[23] Indeed, as Garry Rodan observes, media policy in Singapore may have been partly influenced by a conscious desire 'to pre-empt the situation that has occurred in Malaysia where the government-controlled domestic media lost much of their appeal and credibility'.[24]

It is also noteworthy that critics of the press in Singapore attack the press more than the underlying system of laws and regulations. The situation is quite unlike 1971, when, as the 'Save the Herald' campaign demonstrated, critics viewed newspapers as victims of government repression. Today, the public is more inclined to assign blame to the press itself. This is the direct — and, arguably, intended — result of an NPPA regime that has shifted the emphasis from a very public licensing-and-censorship model to one based on behind-the-scenes self-censorship. The traditional political dynamic between press and society has been reframed as a producer-consumer relationship.

More needs to be said about how the state maintains the support of editors and reporters. Most analyses treat this question as unproblematic: media professionals are regarded either as cowards ruled by fear, or as dyed-in-the-wool functionaries eager to do the PAP's bidding. However, both perspectives again underestimate the hegemonic intent of Lee Kuan Yew's brand of authoritarianism. Despite having the power to direct the press on its every move, or to staff it with civil servants, his government went about the more painstaking — but perhaps ultimately more resilient — project of training editors to marry their traditional professional skills with the required political judgment. This project may be underwritten by indubitable coercive power, but the day-to-day coinage comprises persuasion and all the elements of a sophisticated media relations campaign, including the trading of access and prestige for friendly coverage.

Like all authoritarian governments, the PAP coveted the media's power as a propaganda tool. But unlike most authoritarian rulers, Lee Kuan Yew appreciated that this power depended on the media's credibility, which would be crushed by a state that grasps it too lustily. Thus, when retired senior civil servant S. R. Nathan was given the job of executive chairman of the *Straits Times* group in 1982 — the first of a series of former government officials appointed to the most senior levels of management in the Singapore press — Lee reminded him that the flagship newspaper had a 140-year history and should be treated like a china bowl.[25] Calibrated coercion — self-restraint in the use of regulatory muscle — has been a vital part of the PAP's formula for long-term management of the press, post-1971.[26]

The dynamic equilibrium referred to earlier provides journalists with periodic reminders of just who is boss, but also enough leeway to persuade enough of them that there is still a place in Singapore for the professional practice of journalism, and that the space is expanding. Thus, Cheong Yip Seng, the former editor-in-chief of the *Straits Times* group, writes that the newspapers have become 'a little more confident, assertive, and critical'. In an article entitled, 'The Singapore Press: How Free, How Credible?' Cheong acknowledges that the government has 'enormous reserve powers over ownership and control of editorial policy'. But he argues that despite a history of poor press relations, the government 'does not want a docile press' but 'a livelier, more credible press with high professional standards'. Instances of government interference through 'telephone calls to influence treatment of news or to reprimand ... are much fewer nowadays', he adds. He takes comfort from the fact that a new generation of political leaders is emerging, who know they need a more credible mass media to communicate with a more sophisticated electorate. This analysis would be considered standard fare from an SPH editor *circa* 2006. It was in fact written 25 years earlier, in 1981.[27] That the mixture of realism and hope has hardly changed since then underlines the resilience of the PAP system of press management. Realism stands in the way of any foolhardy dream of changing the media system's wider political framework, while hope reassures journalists that there is a professional role for them even within the current boundaries.

Paths Not Taken

The Singapore press since 1971 has lost a number of its older characteristics, for better or for worse. The most consequential change is in its nation-building role. It is not that the earlier press did not believe in nation-building, but that there was never a clear and consistent idea of exactly what kind of nation was being built. The Chinese-language papers were diaspora media focused squarely on nation-building in China. *The Straits Times'* fateful and understandable blunder was to assume — along with most politicians, including in the PAP — that it was building a Malayan nation. In the course of the 1970s, the PAP forcibly focused the newspapers' nation-building energies on the Singapore project. It was an act of political leadership that with hindsight many Singaporeans would agree the PAP was duty bound to undertake.

Second, and more contentious, is the crushing defeat of the idea of the press as an independent guardian of the public interest. Up until 1971, mainstream newspaper editors believed they had a right to contest the government's interpretation of the national interest. They tried to uphold a difference between being pro-Singapore and pro-government, and insisted on the value of strong criticism of government. 'The point is that no feedback is worth a damn unless it is straight from the shoulder. And straight-from-the-shoulder feedback can only be gathered honestly,' said the *Herald's* founding editor, Francis Wong, in a 1971 speech at a university forum two months after the closure of his newspaper.[28] *Nanyang Siang Pau* publisher Lee Eu Seng declared, upon the arrest of his brother and three other executives:

> It is necessary to state very clearly that in Singapore, the newspapers have
> a clear and definite duty to bring to the attention of the government
> (since there is no opposition in Parliament to do so) the wishes, criti-
> cisms and legitimate grievances of the general public.[29]

No newspaper since has made the argument that the press has a national responsibility to play the role of a surrogate opposition. Today, editors continue to profess a pro-Singapore, not pro-PAP, policy. However, they no longer claim the right to define being pro-Singapore in terms that conflict with the PAP's broad agenda. By 1995, Turnbull was able to write that the parameters within which the press operates had been settled. 'The press accepts the premise that it is not the Fourth Estate and has not been elected as politicians have.'[30]

Third, Singapore has witnessed the delegitimisation of non-commercial motives for newspaper publication. This may seem a curious statement when set against PAP politicians' frequent sermonising against the excesses of market-driven media. Rhetoric aside, however, the PAP's policies elevated the profit motive to a status never before seen in Singapore's media history. Prior to the NPPA, it was common for newspapers to be published at a loss by proprietors who craved prestige and influence more than revenue. Thus, the pioneering Chinese-language paper *Lat Pau* was more of a patriotic venture than an entrepreneurial one.[31] Its early 20th century competitors, such as *Thien Nan Shin Pao, Jit Shin Pao* and *Thoe Lam Jit Poh*, were even more ideologically driven in pleading for one side or the other in China's political ferment. Chen notes that 'for the sake of propagating their ideas, the proprietors of these papers were prepared to pour money down the drain'.[32] Looking back in time from the more capitalist 1960s, Chen finds the behaviour of these publishers 'astonishing'. Post-1974 — with privately held newspaper companies outlawed and newspaper directors obliged to serve shareholders, not causes — following the tradition of those early publishers would not just be astonishing, but unthinkable.

Closely related to the delegitimisation of non-commercial motives for newspaper publication is the elevation of objectivity — or at least a highly functional version of it — as the gold standard for journalism. The earlier press, not just in Singapore but worldwide, included a prominent partisan streak.[33] The pedigree of partisan or cause-driven journalism is today denied by the new mainstream, which calls on journalists to set aside their own opinions and values before putting finger to keyboard. While objectivity has its benefits, media scholars have grown increasingly critical of the unthinking and profoundly conservative way it is applied by professional journalists, including in free societies.[34] The injunction against reporting the news from an opinionated standpoint compels reporters to rely on sources. Objectivity urges reporters to pick those sources whom the world outside considers 'authorised knowers'.[35] These tend to be government officials and other institutional newsmakers. This is less of a problem in a plural democracy, but in a highly centralised political system such as Singapore's, objective journalism can turn into an echo chamber for the already-loud government voice. Thus, it is not surprising — and should not be seen as insincere — that the Singapore government has upheld objectivity in its position on the press: 'The local media's role is to report the news accurately, factually and objectively for Singaporeans.' Similarly, it has deemed it 'inappropriate … for the media to editorialise in its reporting of the news' — a distinction that was not observed in the past.[36]

None of the four developments above should be regarded as absolute. If the domestic press corps had been converted totally into willing mouthpieces of the PAP, the ruling party would not need to remind journalists about its philosophy, which it continues to do. Although the dominant ideology, it has not reached the ultimate status of internalised common sense. Instead, PAP speeches continue to assume — probably correctly — that its position runs counter to an intuitive sense in the modern world that the press, whether in Asia or the West, should serve as an independent and fearless check on power. The Singapore press continues to push gently for more debate on national issues, and uses its behind-the-scenes access to persuade officials to be more open with information and tolerant of criticism. Within the newsrooms, editors encourage enterprise and analysis. In their public statements, they sometimes profess support for the consensual, communitarian Asian way. In practice, however, journalism awards that they give out to their staff explicitly credit stories that reveal facts and opinions officials did not want published, and that generate public debate and controversy.[37]

The main acts of resistance to the PAP's hegemonic press system take place outside the mainstream, in alternative media — media that express 'an alternative vision to hegemonic policies, priorities, and perspectives'.[38] One post-independence periodical that fell into this category was *SPUR*, the journal of the Singapore Planning and Urban Research Group, which addressed issues such as housing, identity and nation building. It ceased publication in the mid-1970s. The arts and culture community has spawned the irreverent *Big-O* magazine, and the critical *Focas* journal. Opposition party newsletters, such as the Workers' Party's *Hammer*, continue to circulate. The most resilient platform for alternative media has proven to be the internet, because of its minimal cost of entry and its freedom from discretionary licensing.[39] Before the arrival of the world wide web, Singaporeans, many of them on campuses overseas, used the online forum soc.culture. singapore, and its regional precursor, soc.culture.asean. The birth of the web stimulated more organised efforts, probably starting with the Sintercom site in 1994. A search by a team of sociologists over four months in 2000 found 82 Singapore-based or Singapore-related political websites providing alternatives to dominant discourses. They included the sites of registered opposition parties and civil society groups promoting reform within their areas of concern, such as the Nature Society of Singapore and Action for Aids. There were also religious and linguistic groups claiming fairer treatment, including the banned Unification Church (the 'Moonies'), and a Speak Dialect Campaign resisting the government's promotion of Mandarin among Chinese Singaporeans.[40]

Some of these sites serve purely internal communication needs of their groups, and are more properly described as sites of 'resistance' because they try to insulate their discourse from state domination, rather than of 'contention' in the sense that Sidney Tarrow has used the term, which includes an element of claim-making on external institutions, and thus a desire to enter the public sphere.[41] Among those that fit the latter category is The Online Citizen (theonlinecitizen.com), a website run by a collective of political commentators. Think Centre, a political society that does human rights and pro-democracy work, has its own website (www.think-centre.org) and e-mail list. Another prominent site was the now-defunct Fateha, which challenged the elite's claim to represent Singapore's Muslim community. More irreverent are Sammyboy (www.sammyboy.com), which blends political commentary with reviews of brothels and links to pornography, and the popular satirical site, TalkingCock (www.talkingcock.com). Individual commentators have risen to prominence through political blogs such as Mrbrown.com and Yawningbread.org. These alternative media projects represent a variety of political leanings. However, they are united in rejecting the harmonious consensus and illiberal intent of the PAP's preferred media system. They also share an inability to make huge profits, and an unwillingness to subject themselves to the strictures of objective disinterestedness.

Conclusion

The authoritarian impulse behind Singapore's press system is as old as the hills. What is more novel is the PAP's astute use of global forces pushed by capitalist liberal democracies to reinforce a profoundly illiberal system. While less clever regimes assumed that they had to subvert the press completely in order to assure their preferred results, Lee Kuan Yew recognised that he merely needed to tweak its incentive structure and install the right barriers. If journalism were a river, he didn't need to build a dam; he instead canalised its main channel and closed off its more unruly tributaries. This strategy worked because journalism's main impetus by the late twentieth century was commerce, not ideology. Arguably, the net effect of Westernisation on the Singapore press has been a conservative one, thanks to the twin imports of professional objectivity and commercial organisation, and the marginalisation of more cause-driven and polemical journalism. Worldwide, the press, even when free and left to its own devices, has applied itself more strenuously to the seeking of profits than to campaigning for political change. Lee had seen this in the conduct of the island's most successful newspaper company. *The Straits Times*' mission before independence was to protect its commercial interests — which it thought it would achieve by being anti-PAP — and 'not to uphold press freedom or the right to information'. 'After we became independent in 1965, the *Straits Times* ... did a complete turnaround and supported the PAP,' Lee writes, adding for good measure, 'This did not increase my respect for it.'[42]

This present reading of Singapore's press history corroborates Garry Rodan's thesis, that information control by authoritarian regimes is not necessarily inconsistent with market development. Singapore, in his view, may represent a viable alternative political model for capitalist development, rather than an exception to the rule. Rodan observes that markets are highly seductive for profit-seeking companies, leading to 'widespread self-censorship to avoid confrontation with authoritarian regimes and protect access to those markets'.[43] Furthermore, business attitudes towards press freedom are ambivalent at best. While businesses demand 'transparency', the kind of transparency they require does not amount to general democratic values and practices as much as bureaucratic-rationalist systems that facilitate their operations. Political stability and predictable, reliable legal and supervisory regimes are more relevant to them than press freedom in a political sense. Rodan concludes that 'the best prospects of comprehensive transparency reform rest with the actions of social and political forces not driven principally by instrumental market considerations, but trying to expand the political space of civil society'.[44]

If correct, this analysis suggests that any attempt to reform the media via the mainstream press would be incomplete. The political economy of news production, together with the profession's interpretation of objectivity, has resulted in dominant media that are themselves unconvinced of the need for greater diversity of the sort Singapore once had. They have been at the receiving end of the PAP's assaults on press freedom, but they are not crying out to be saved. The economic monopoly that licensing grants them, and the relative restraint with which the PAP has exercised its more unpleasant powers, mean that they have not done too badly from the closing off of alternative paths in Singapore's press history. The forgotten victims in this story are the alternative media, past and present, who have tried to preserve the tradition of a diverse, unruly and counter-hegemonic public discourse.

NOTES

1 Lee Kuan Yew, *From Third World to First: The Singapore Story: 1965–2000: Memoirs of Lee Kuan Yew* (Singapore: Times Editions and Singapore Press Holdings, 2000), p. 218.
2 *Schenck v United States* (1919).
3 Bilahari Kausikan, 'Asia's Different Standard', *Foreign Policy* 92 (1993): 24–41.
4 Ibid.
5 Francis Seow, *The Media Enthralled: Singapore Revisited* (Boulder, Colorado: Lynne Rienner Publishers, 1998), p. 2.
6 Mary Turnbull, *Dateline Singapore: 150 Years of The Straits Times* (Singapore: Singapore Press Holdings, 1995).
7 Quoted in ibid., p. 78.
8 Chen Mong Hock, *The Early Chinese Newspapers of Singapore 1881–1912* (Singapore: University of Malaya Press, 1967).
9 Lee, *From Third World to First*, p. 214.
10 Ibid., p. 212.
11 Ibid., p. 213.
12 *The Straits Times*, 20 November 1972.
13 Turnbull, *Dateline Singapore*, p. 291.
14 Lee, *From Third World to First*, pp. 215–8.
15 Anthony Polsky, 'Premier Lee Kuan Yew and the Singapore Press Controversy', talk delivered to the Hong Kong Foreign Correspondents Club, 20 July 1971.
16 Turnbull, *Dateline Singapore*, p. 293.
17 Ibid., p. 291.
18 Quoted in Seow, *The Media Enthralled*, p. 85.
19 Ibid., p. 83.
20 Polsky, 'The Singapore Press Controversy'.
21 Lee, *From Third World to First*, p. 218.
22 Ibid., p. 218.
23 Cherian George, *Contentious Journalism and the Internet: Towards Democratic Discourse in Malaysia and Singapore* (Singapore: Singapore University Press, 2006).
24 Garry Rodan, *Transparency and Authoritarian Rule in Southeast Asia: Singapore and Malaysia* (London: Routledge Curzon, 2004), p. 15.
25 Turnbull, *Dateline Singapore*.
26 Cherian George, 'Consolidating authoritarian rule: Calibrated coercion in Singapore', *Pacific Review* 20, 2 (2007): 127–45.
27 Cheong Yip Seng, 'The Singapore Press: How Free, How Credible?' *The Asean Journalist* 1, 1 (1981): 28–9.
28 Francis Wong, 'Nation Building and the Press', talk at Seminar on Mass Media, University of Singapore Student Union, 18 July 1971.
29 Quoted in Seow, *The Media Enthralled*, p. 44.

30 Turnbull, *Dateline Singapore*, p. 387.

31 Chen, *The Early Chinese Newspapers of Singapore*.

32 Ibid., p. 130.

33 See, for example, Mitchell Stephens, *A History of News* (Fort Worth, Texas: Harcourt Brace, 1997).

34 See, for example, Jeremy Iggers, *Good News, Bad News: Journalism Ethics and the Public Interest* (Boulder, Colorado: Westview Press, 1998); Brent Cunningham, 'Re-thinking Objectivity', *Columbia Journalism Review* July–August 2003. Available at http://www.cjr.org/issues/2003/4/objective-cunningham.asp/. Accessed 15 April 2005.

35 Mark Fishman, *Manufacturing the News* (Austin, Texas: University of Texas Press, 1980).

36 Lee Boon Yang, 'Lunch Talk by Minister for Information, Communications and the Arts, Dr Lee Boon Yang, at the Singapore Press Club Lunch', 12 November 2003. Available at http://www.mita.gov.sg/pressroom/press_031112.html/. Accessed 15 April 2005.

37 Cherian George, 'Asian Journalism: More Prized than Preached?' Paper delivered at Association for Education in Journalism and Mass Communication Western conference, December 2002.

38 John Downing, *Radical Media: Rebellious Communication and Social Movements* (Thousand Oaks, California: Sage, 2001), p. v.

39 George, *Contentious Journalism and the Internet*.

40 K. C. Ho, Zaheer Baber and Habibul Khondker, '"Sites" of Resistance: Alternative Websites and State-Society Relations', *British Journal of Sociology* 53, 1 (2002): 127–48.

41 Sidney Tarrow, *Power in Movement: Social Movements and Contentious Politics*, second edition (Cambridge, UK: Cambridge University Press, 1998).

42 Lee, *From Third World to First*, p. 215.

43 Rodan, *Transparency and Authoritarian Rule*, p. 16.

44 Ibid., p. 17.

Bibliography

This consolidated bibliography contains books, chapters and journal articles only. For archival sources, interviews, government publications, websites, newspaper reports, and other sources, see the notes in individual chapters.

Abdullah, Firdaus Haji. *Radical Malay Politics: Its Origin and Early Development.* Petaling Jaya: Pelanduk Publications, 1985.

Abraham, Itty. 'State, Place, Identity: Two Stories in the Making of Region', in K. Sivaramakrishnan and A. Agrawal, *Regional Modernities: The Cultural Politics of Development in India.* Delhi: Oxford University Press, 2003, pp. 404–25.

Acharya, Amitav. *The Quest for Identity: International Relations of Southeast Asia.* Oxford: Oxford University Press, 2000.

Ahmad, Kassim. *Kemarau di Lembah.* Kuala Lumpur: Teks Publishing, 1985.

Ahmat, Sharom and James Wong, eds. *Malay Participation in the National Development of Singapore.* Singapore: Eurasia Press, 1971.

Ahmat, Sharom. 'Singapore Malays, Education and National Development', in *Malay Participation in the National Development of Singapore*, ed. Sharom Ahmat and James Wong. Singapore: Singapore Community Study Centre and Central Council of Malay Cultural Organisations, 1971, pp. 6–13.

Ali, Syed Hussin. 'Pertubuan-pertubuan Bahasa dan Sastera Melayu di Singapura selepas Perang Dunia II (Khasnya Asas 50)'. Honours Thesis, University of Malaya, Kuala Lumpur, 1959.

Alinsky, Saul D. *Reveille for Radicals.* New York: Random House, 1969.

Alinsky, Saul D. *Rules for Radicals: A Practical Primer for Realistic Radicals.* New York: Vintage Books, 1971.

Archives and Oral History Department. *Road to Nationhood: Singapore 1819–1980.* Singapore: Singapore News and Publications, 1984.

Awang, Usman. *Gelombang: Sakaj2 Pilihan, 1949–1960.* Kuala Lumpur: Oxford University Press, 1961.

AWARE. *Population: An Issue of Current Concern.* Singapore: AWARE, 1988.

AWARE. 'Association of Women for Action and Research Declaration and Constitution'. Singapore: AWARE, 1990.

Baker, C. J. 'Economic Reorganization and the Slump in South and Southeast Asia', *Comparative Studies in Society and History* 23, 3 (1981): 325–39.

Ball, S. J. 'Selkirk in Singapore', *Twentieth Century British History* 10, 2 (1999): 162–91.

Barnard, Rohayati Paseng and Timothy P. Barnard. 'The Ambivalence of P. Ramlee: *Penarek Beca* and *Bujang Lapok* in Perspective', *Asian Cinema* 13, 2 (2002): 9–23.

Barnard, Timothy P. 'Vampires, Heroes and Jesters: A History of Cathay Keris', in *The Cathay Story*, ed. Wong Ain-ling. Hong Kong: Hong Kong Film Archive, 2002, pp. 124–41.

Barr, Michael D. *Lee Kuan Yew: The Beliefs Behind the Man*. Richmond, UK: Curzon, 2000.

Barr, Michael D. 'J. B. Jeyaretnam: Three Decades as Lee Kuan Yew's *bête noir*', *Journal of Contemporary Asia* 33, 3 (2003): 299–317.

Bayly, Christopher and Tim Harper. *Forgotten Armies: The Fall of British Asia, 1941–45*. London: Penguin, 2004.

Bedlington, Stanley. 'The Singapore Malay Community: The Politics of State Integration'. Ph.D. Thesis, Cornell University, 1974.

Bellows, Thomas J. 'The Singapore Party System: The First Two Decades'. Ph.D. Thesis, Yale University, 1968.

Bellows, Thomas J. *The People's Action Party of Singapore: Emergence of a Dominant Party System*. Monograph Series Number 14, Yale University Southeast Asian Studies, 1970.

Berman, B. and J. Lonsdale. *Unhappy Valley: Conflict in Kenya and Africa*, vol. 2. Oxford: James Currey, 1992.

Bloodworth, Dennis. *The Tiger and the Trojan Horse*. Singapore: Times Books International, 1986.

Blueprinters. 'AWARE Blueprinters Suggestions for Future Directions and Strategies'. Singapore: AWARE, 1995.

Bose, Sugata. 'Instruments and Idioms of Colonial and National Development: The Indian Experience in Comparative Perspective', in *International Development and the Social Sciences: Essays in the History and Politics of Knowledge*, ed. F. Cooper and R. Packard. Berkeley and Los Angeles: University of California Press, 1997, pp. 45–63.

Boyce, D. George. *Decolonisation and the British Empire, 1775–1997*. New York: St. Martin's Press, 1999.

Braddell, Roland St John. *The Legal Status of the Malay States*. Singapore: Malaya Publishing House, 1931.

Braga-Blake, Myrna, ed. *Singapore Eurasians: Memories and Hopes*. Singapore: The Eurasian Association, 1992.

Burns, Peter Laurie. 'The English Language Newspapers of Singapore, 1915–1951'. Academic Exercise, University of Malaya, 1957.

Butcher, John G. *The British in Malaya, 1880–1941: The Social History of a European Community in Colonial South-east Asia*. Kuala Lumpur; Oxford: Oxford University Press, 1979.

Cardijn, Joseph. *The Hour of the Working Class.* Melbourne: [YCW, 1949].

Chan Heng Chee. *Politics in an Administrative State: Where Has the Politics Gone?* Singapore: Department of Political Science, University of Singapore, 1975.

Chan Heng Chee. *Singapore: The Politics of Survival 1965–67.* Singapore: Oxford University Press, 1971.

Chan Heng Chee. *The Dynamics of One Party Dominance: The PAP at the Grassroots.* Singapore: Institute of Southeast Asian Studies, 1976.

Chan Heng Chee. *The Role of Intellectuals in Singapore Politics.* Occasional Paper Series No. 26. Singapore: Department of Political Science, University of Singapore, 1976.

Chan Heng Chee. 'Political Developments 1965–1979', in *A History of Singapore,* ed. Ernest C. T. Chew and Edwin Lee. Singapore: Oxford University Press, 1991, pp. 157–81.

Chan Heng Chee, *A Sensation of Independence: David Marshall: A Political Biography,* re-issue of 1984 edition with a new acknowledgement. Singapore: Times Books International, 2001.

Chatterjee, P. *Nationalist Thought and the Colonial World: A Derivative Discourse?* London: Zed Books, 1986.

Chatterjee, P. *The Politics of the Governed: Reflections on Popular Politics in Most of the World.* New York: Columbia University Press, 2004.

Cheah Boon Kheng, ed. *A. Samad Ismail: Journalism and Politics.* Kuala Lumpur: Singamal, 1987.

Cheah Boon Kheng. *Red Star Over Malaya.* Singapore: Singapore University Press, 2003.

Chen Mong Hock. *The Early Chinese Newspapers of Singapore 1881–1912.* Singapore: University of Malaya Press, 1967.

Cheong Yip Seng. 'The Singapore Press: How Free, How Credible?' *The Asean Journalist* 1, 1 (1981): 28–9.

Chew, Ernest C. T. and Edwin Lee, eds. *A History of Singapore.* Singapore; New York: Oxford University Press, 1991.

Chew, Melanie. *Leaders of Singapore.* Singapore: Resource Press, 1996.

Chew, Melanie. *Biography of President Yusuf bin Ishak.* Singapore: SNP Publishing, 1999.

Chew, Phyllis Ghim Lian. 'The Singapore Council of Women and the Women's Movement', *Journal of Southeast Asian Studies* 25, 1 (1994): 112–40.

Chik, Ibrahim. *Memoir Ibrahim Chik: Dari Api ke Regimen ke-10.* Bangi: Penerbit Universiti Kebangsaan Malaysia, 2004.

Chin, C. C. 'The Plight of the Chinese during Japanese Occupation', *Journal of the South Seas Society* 52 (1998): 161–88.

Chin, C. C. 'The Revolutionary Programmes and their Effect on the Struggle of the Malayan Communist Party', in *Dialogues with Chin Peng: New Light on the Malayan Communist Party,* ed. C. C. Chin and Karl Hack. Singapore: Singapore University Press, 2004, pp. 260–78.

Chin, C. C. and Karl Hack, eds. *Dialogues with Chin Peng: New Light on the Malayan Communist Party.* Singapore: Singapore University Press, 2004.

Chin Peng and Ian Ward. *My Side of History.* Singapore: Media Masters, 2003.

Chua Beng Huat. 'Multiculturalism in Singapore: An Instrument of Social Control', *Race and Class* 44, 3 (2003): 58–77.

Clark, Donald N. 'Growth and Limitations of Minjung Christianity in South Korea', in *South Korea's Minjung Movement: The Culture and Politics of Dissidence,* ed. Kenneth M. Wells. Honolulu: University of Hawaii Press, 1995, pp. 87–103.

Clutterbuck, Richard. *Conflict and Violence in Singapore and Malaysia 1945–1983.* Revised edition. Singapore: Graham Brash Ltd, 1984.

Connelly, Matthew. *A Diplomatic Revolution: Algeria's Fight for Independence and the Origins of the Post-Cold War Era.* New York: Oxford University Press, 2002.

Cooper, Frederick. *Colonialism in Question: Theory, Knowledge, History.* Berkeley and Los Angeles: University of California Press, 2005.

Cunningham, Brent. 'Re-thinking Objectivity', *Columbia Journalism Review* (July–August 2003). Available at http://www.cjr.org/issues/2003/4/objective-cunningham.asp/. Accessed 15 April 2005.

Darusman, Suryono. *Singapore and the Indonesian Revolution 1945–1950.* Singapore: Institute of Southeast Asian Studies, 1992.

Downing, John. *Radical Media: Rebellious Communication and Social Movements.* Thousand Oaks, California: Sage, 2001.

Drysdale, John. *Singapore: Struggle for Success.* Singapore: Times Book International, 1984; North Sydney: Allen & Unwin, 1984.

Duara, Prasenjit. *Rescuing History from the Nation: Questioning Narratives of Modern China.* Chicago: University of Chicago Press, 1995.

East Asia Christian Conference (ed. Robert M. Fukada). *God's People in Asian Industrial Society: The Report of the* [1966] *East Asia Christian Conference on Christians in Industry and Lay Training.* Kyoto: EACC, 1967.

Emerson, Donald K. '"Southeast Asia": What's in a Name?' *Journal of Southeast Asian Studies* 14 (1984): 1–21.

Emerson, Rupert. *Malaysia: A Study in Direct and Indirect Rule.* New York: Macmillan, 1937. Reprint, Kuala Lumpur: University of Malaya Press, 1964.

Ferguson, James. *Expectations of Modernity: Myths and Meanings of Urban Life on the Zambian Copperbelt.* Los Angeles: University of California Press, 1999.

Fishman, Mark. *Manufacturing the News.* Austin, Texas: University of Texas Press, 1980.

Fong Sip Chee. *The PAP Story: The Pioneering Years (November 1954–April 1968) A Diary of Events of the People's Action Party: Reminiscences of an Old Comrade.* Singapore: Times Periodicals, 1979.

Foulcher, Keith. *'Pujangga Baru': Literature and Nationalism in Indonesia, 1933–1942.* Bedford Park: Flinders University, 1980.

Foulcher, Keith. 'Literature, Cultural Politics, and the Indonesian Revolution', in *Text/Politics in Island Southeast Asia,* ed. D. M. Roskies. Athens, OH: Ohio University Center for International Studies, 1993, pp. 221–56.

Gamba, Charles. *The Origins of Trade Unionism in Malaya.* Singapore: Eastern Universities Press, 1962.

Gamer, Robert E. 'Parties and Pressure Groups', in *Modern Singapore*, ed. Ooi Jin-Bee and Chiang Hai Ding. Singapore: University of Singapore Press, 1969, pp. 197–215.

Gamer, Robert E. *The Politics of Urban Development in Singapore*. London: Cornell University Press, 1972.

George, Cherian. 'Asian Journalism: More Prized than Preached?' Paper delivered at Association for Education in Journalism and Mass Communication Western Conference, December 2002.

George, Cherian. 'Consolidating authoritarian rule: Calibrated coercion in Singapore', *Pacific Review* 20, 2 (2007): 127–45.

George, Cherian. *Contentious Journalism and the Internet: Towards Democratic Discourse in Malaysia and Singapore*. Singapore: Singapore University Press, 2006.

George, T. J. S. *Lee Kuan Yew's Singapore*. London: Andre Deutch, 1974.

Ghosh, Amitav. 'The March of the Novel through History: The Testimony of My Grandfather's Bookcase', in Amitav Ghosh, *The Imam and the Indian*. Delhi: Permanent Black, 2002, pp. 287–304.

Gillis, E. Kay. *Singapore Civil Society and British Power*. Singapore: Talisman, 2005.

Goscha, C. E. *Thailand and the Southeast Asian Networks of the Vietnamese Revolution 1885–1954*. Richmond: Curzon, 1999.

Haas, Michael. 'The Politics of Singapore in the 1980s', *Journal of Contemporary Asia* 19, 1 (1989): 48–77.

Hack, Karl and J. Chen. *Dialogues with Chin Peng: New Light on the Malayan Communist Party*. Singapore: Singapore University Press, 2004.

Han Fook Kwang, Warren Fernandez and Sumiko Tan. *Lee Kuan Yew: The Man and his Ideas*. Singapore: Singapore Press Holdings, Times Editions, 1998.

Han Suyin. 'Social Change in Asia', *Suloh Nantah: Journal of the English Society Nanyang University Singapore* 15–16 (1960): 2–8.

Han Suyin. *My House Has Two Doors*. London: Jonathan Cape, 1981.

Han Tan Juan. 'Riding the Tide of Idealism: An Interview with Han Tan Juan', *Tangent* 6 (April 2003): 210–30.

Harper, T. N. 'Globalism and the Pursuit of Authenticity: The Making of a Diasporic Public Sphere in Singapore', *Sojourn* 12 (1997): 261–92.

Harper, T. N. *The End of Empire and the Making of Malaya*. Cambridge and New York: Cambridge University Press, 1998.

Harper, T. N. 'Empires, Diaspora and the Languages of Globalism, 1850–1914', in *Globalization in World History*, ed. A. G. Hopkins. London: Pimlico, 2001, pp. 141–66.

Harper, T. N. 'Lim Chin Siong and the "Singapore Story"', in *Comet in Our Sky: Lim Chin Siong in History*, ed. Tan Jing Quee and K. S. Jomo. Kuala Lumpur: INSAN, 2001, pp. 1–56.

Heng, Geraldine. '"A Great Way to Fly": Nationalism, the State, and the Varieties of Third-World Feminism', in *Feminist Genealogies, Colonial Legacies, Democratic Futures*, ed. M. Jacqui Alexander and Chandra Talpade Mohanty. New York: Routledge, 1997, pp. 30–45.

Hill, Michael and Lian Kwen Fee. *The Politics of Nation Building and Citizenship in Singapore.* London: Routledge, 1995.

Ho K. C., Zaheer Baber and Habibul Khondker. '"Sites" of Resistance: Alternative Websites and State-Society Relations', *British Journal of Sociology* 53, 1 (2002): 127–48.

Ho Kai Leong. *The Politics of Policy-Making in Singapore.* Oxford: Oxford University Press, 2000.

Holden, Philip. 'Imagined Individuals: National Autobiography and Post-Colonial Self-Fashioning', *Asia Research Institute, Working Paper Series*, 13, Singapore, 2003.

Hong Lysa and Huang Jianli. *The Scripting of a National History: Singapore and its Pasts.* Singapore: NUS Press, 2008.

Hua Wu Yin. *Class and Communalism in Malaysia: Politics in a Dependent Capitalistic State.* London: Zed Press, 1983.

Huangfuguang. 'Twice Imprisonment in Singapore during the British Colonial Rule' in *The Passionate Years*, ed. Luo Wu and Chen Jian. Hong Kong: Witness Publishing House, 2005, pp. 103–32.

Huang Jianli. *The Politics of Depoliticization: Guomindang Policy towards Student Political Activism, 1927–1949*, Berne: Peter Lang, 1996.

Huang Jianli. 'Positioning the Student Political Activism of Singapore: Articulation, Contestation and Omission', in *Inter-Asia Cultural Studies* 7, 3 (2006): 403–30.

Huang Jianli. 'Nanyang University and the Language Divide in Singapore: Controversy over the 1965 Wang Gungwu Report', in *Nantah tuxiang: Lishi heliuzhong de shengshi* [Imagery of Nanyang University: Reflections on the River of History], ed. Lee Guan Kin. Singapore: Global Publishing, 2007, pp. 165–220.

Hussain, Abdul Aziz. 'Penerbitan buku2 dan majallah2 Melayu di-Singapura di-antara bulan September 1945 dengan bulan September 1958'. Honours Thesis, University Malaya Singapore, 1959.

Hussain, Abdullah. *Harun Aminurrashid Pembangkit Semangat Kebangsaan.* Kuala Lumpur: Dewan Bahasa dan Pustaka, 1982.

Hussain, Abdullah. *Sebuah Perjalanan.* Kuala Lumpur: Dewan Bahasa dan Pustaka, 2005.

Hussain, Abdullah and Nik Safiah Karim, eds. *Memoranda Angkatan Sastrawan '50.* Second edition. Petaling Jaya: Fajar Bakti, 1987.

Hussain, Ashfaq. 'The Post-Separation Effect on the Malays and their Response', *Journal of the Historical Society* (July 1970): 67–72.

Hussain, Zahoor Ahmad bin Haji Faizal. 'Policies and Politics in Malay Education in Singapore 1951–1965, with Special Reference to the Development of the Secondary School System'. Master of Education Thesis, University of Singapore, 1969.

Hyam, Ronald. 'Bureaucracy and "Trusteeship" in the Colonial Empire'. In *The Oxford History of the British Empire, vol. IV: The Twentieth Century*, ed. Judith M. Brown. Oxford: Oxford University Press, 1999, pp. 255–79.

Ibrahim, Zuraidah. 'Malay Mobilisers', in *Lee's Lieutenants: Singapore's Old Guard*, ed. Lam Peng Er and Kevin Y. L. Tan. Sydney: Allen & Unwin, 1999, pp. 116–31.

Iggers, Jeremy. *Good News, Bad News: Journalism Ethics and the Public Interest.* Boulder, Colorado: Westview Press, 1998.

Ismail, A. Samad. *Memoir A. Samad Ismail di Singapura.* Bangi: Penerbit Universiti Kebangsaan Malaysia, 1993.

Ismail, A. Samad. 'Our James', in *No Cowardly Past: Writings, Poems, Commentaries*, ed. Dominic Puthucheary and K. S. Jomo. Petaling Jaya: INSAN, 1998, pp. 55–62.

Ismail, A. Samad. 'Lim Chin Siong: Some Memories', in *Comet in Our Sky: Lim Chin Siong in History*, ed. Tan Jing Quee and K. S. Jomo. Kuala Lumpur: INSAN, 2001, pp. 165–7.

Jansen, G. H. *Afro-Asia and Non-Alignment.* London: Faber & Faber, 1966.

Jeem, Sulaiman and Abdul Ghani Hamid. *Mengenang Pak Zubir.* Singapore: Pustaka Melayu, 1988.

Jones, Matthew. 'Creating Malaysia: Singapore's Security, the Borneo Territories, and the Contours of British Policy, 1961–1963', *Journal of Imperial and Commonwealth History* 28, 2 (2000): 85–109.

Jones, Matthew. *Conflict and Confrontation in South East Asia, 1961–65: Britain, the United States, and the Creation of Malaysia.* Cambridge: Cambridge University Press, 2002.

Josey, Alex. *Lee Kuan Yew: The Crucial Years.* Singapore: Times Books, 1980.

Josey, Alex. *David Marshall's Political Interlude.* Singapore: Eastern Universities Press, 1982.

Kadir, Suzaina. 'Islam, State and Society in Singapore', *Inter-Asia Cultural Studies* 5, 3 (2004): 357–71.

Kausikan, Bilahari. 'Asia's Different Standard', *Foreign Policy* 92 (1993): 24–41.

Kenley, D. L. *New Culture in a New World: The May Fourth Movement and the Chinese Diaspora in Singapore, 1919–1932.* New York: Routledge, 2003.

Keris Mas. Tr. Shah Rezad Ibrahim and Nor Azizah Abu Bakar. *The Memoirs of Keris Mas: Spanning 30 Years of Literary Development.* Kuala Lumpur: Dewan Bahasa dan Pustaka, 2004.

Khe Su Lin. *Lixiang yu xianshi: Nanyang daxue xueshenghui yanjiu, 1956–1964* [*Ideal and Reality: A Study of Nanyang University Students' Union, 1956–1964*]. Singapore: World Scientific Printers, 2006.

Khoo, A. *Life as the River Flows: Women in the Malayan Anti-Colonial Struggle (An Oral History of Women from Thailand, Malaysia and Singapore).* Petaling Jaya, Malaysia: SIRD, 2004.

Khoo Boo Teik. *Beyond Mahathir: Malaysian Politics and Its Discontents.* London: Zed Books, 2003.

Khoo, Francis Kah Seng. 'The Presidential Council', *Singapore Law Review* 1 (1969): 14–19.

Koh Tai Ann. 'The World of the English-Educated in the 1960s and 1970s: An Interview with Koh Tai Ann', *Tangent* 6 (2003): 261–94.

Koh Tat Boon. 'University of Singapore Socialist Club, 1953–1962'. Honours Academic Exercise, History Department, University of Singapore, 1972/73.

Kok Pin Loong. 'Aliens Ordinance 1933'. Academic Exercise, University of Singapore, 1972.

Kua Bak Lim, ed. *Who is Who in the Chinese Community of Singapore*. EPB Publishers, Singapore, 1995.

Kumar, Suresh. 'Singapore Indian Association, 1923–1941'. Academic Exercise, National University of Singapore, 1995.

Lam, Jenny Lin, ed. *Voices and Choices: The Women's Movement in Singapore*. Singapore: Singapore Council of Women's Organisations, 1993.

Lam Peng Er and Kevin Y. L. Tan, eds. *Lee's Lieutenants: Singapore's Old Guard*. Sydney: Allen & Unwin, 1999.

Lau, Albert. *A Moment of Anguish: Singapore in Malaysia and the Politics of Disengagement*. Singapore: Times Academic Press, 1998.

Lau, Albert. '"Nationalism" in the Decolonisation of Singapore', in *The Transformation of Southeast Asia: International Perspectives on Decolonization*, ed. Marc Frey, Ronald Pruessen and Tan Tai Yong. New York: M.E. Sharpe, 2003, pp. 180–96.

Lee Khoon Choy. *On the Beat to the Hustings: An Autobiography*. Singapore: Times Books International, 1988.

Lee Kuan Yew. *The Battle for Merger*. Singapore: Government Printing Press, 1961.

Lee Kuan Yew. *Leadership in Asian Countries*. Singapore: Ministry of Culture, 1967.

Lee Kuan Yew. *The Singapore Story: Memoirs of Lee Kuan Yew*. Singapore: Times Editions and Prentice Hall, 1998.

Lee Kuan Yew. *From Third World to First: The Singapore Story: 1965–2000: Memoirs of Lee Kuan Yew*. Singapore: Times Editions and Singapore Press Holdings, 2000.

Lee Lai To. 'Singapore in 1987', *Asian Survey* 28, 2 (1988): 202–12.

Lee, Terence. 'The Politics of Civil Society in Singapore', *Asian Studies Review* 26, 1 (2002): 97–117.

Lee, Terence. 'Gestural Politics: Civil Society in "New" Singapore', *Sojourn: Journal of Social Issues in Southeast Asia* 20, 2 (2005): 132–54.

Lee Ting Hui. *The Open United Front: The Communist Struggle in Singapore, 1954–1966*. Singapore: South Seas Society, 1996.

Lee Yong Hock. 'A History of the Straits Chinese British Association, 1900–1959'. Academic Exercise, University of Malaya, 1960.

Leifer, Michael. 'Communal Violence in Singapore', *Asian Survey* 10, 4 (1964): 1115–21.

Leong Yee Fong. 'Labour and Trade Unionism in Colonial Malaya: A Study of the Socio-Economic and Political Bases of the Malayan Labour Movement, 1930–1957'. Ph.D. Thesis, Universiti Malaya, 1990.

Leong Yee Fong. 'The Emergence and Demise of the Chinese Labour Movement in Colonial Malaya, 1920–1960', in *The Chinese in Malaysia*, ed. Lee Kam Hing and Tan Chee Beng. New York: Oxford University Press, 1999, pp. 169–93.

Li, Tania. *Malays in Singapore: Culture, Economy and Ideology.* Singapore: Oxford University Press, 1989.

Liaw Yock Fang, ed., tr. *The Complete Poems of Chairil Anwar.* Singapore: University Education Press, 1974.

Liew Kai Khiun. 'Raised Voices and Dropped Tools: Labour Unrest at the Harbour and Naval Dockyard in Singapore (1952–72)'. Master of Arts Thesis, Department of History, National University of Singapore, 2003.

Liew Kai Khiun. 'The Anchor and the Voice of 10,000 Waterfront Workers: Jamit Singh in the Singapore Story (1954–63)', *Journal of Southeast Asian Studies* 35, 3 (2004): 459–78.

Lim Choo Hoon. 'The Transformation of the Political Orientation of the Singapore Chinese Chamber of Commerce, 1945–1955', *Review of Southeast Asian Studies* 9 (1979): 3–63.

Liu Hong and Wong Sin-Kiong. *Singapore Chinese Society in Transition: Business, Politics, and Socio-Economic Change, 1945–1965.* New York: Peter Lang, 2004.

Loh Kah Seng. 'Beyond "Rubber Prices" History: Life in Singapore during the Great Depression Years'. Master of Arts Thesis, National University of Singapore, 2004.

Low Choon Sai James, 'Kept in Position: The Labour Front-Alliance Government of Chief Minister David Marshall in Singapore, April 1955–June 1956'. MA Thesis, National University of Singapore, 2000.

Low Choon Sai James, 'Kept in Position: The Labour Front-Alliance Government of Chief Minister David Marshall in Singapore, April 1955–June 1956', *Journal of Southeast Asian Studies* 35, 1 (2004): 41–64.

Lyons, Lenore. 'Believing in Equality: The Meanings Attached to "Feminism" in Singapore', *Asian Journal of Women's Studies* 5, 1 (1999): 115–39.

Lyons, Lenore. 'Negotiating Difference: Singaporean Women Building an Ethics of Respect', in *Forging Radical Alliances across Difference: Coalition Politics for the New Millennium,* ed. Steven Schacht and Jill M. Bystydzienski. London: Rowman and Littlefield Publishers, 2001, pp. 177–90.

Lyons, Lenore. 'Re-Telling "Us": Researching the Lives of Singaporean Women', in *Love, Sex and Power: Women in Southeast Asia,* ed. Susan Blackburn. Clayton: Monash University Press, 2001, pp. 115–28.

Lyons, Lenore. *A State of Ambivalence: The Feminist Movement in Singapore.* Leiden: Brill Publishers, 2004.

Lyons, Lenore and Janine Chipperfield. '(De)Constructing the Interview: A Critique of the Participatory Method', *Resources for Feminist Research/ Documentation sur la Recherche Feministe* 28, 1/2 (2000): 33–48.

MacDougall, John Arthur. 'Shared Burdens: A Study of Communal Discrimination by the Political Parties of Malaysia and Singapore'. Ph.D. Thesis, Harvard University, 1968.

McIntyre, W. D. *Colonies into Commonwealth.* London: Blandford Press, 1966.

Mahadeva, A. 'Remembering Lim Chin Siong', in *Comet in Our Sky: Lim Chin Siong in History,* ed. Tan Jing Quee and K. S. Jomo. Kuala Lumpur: INSAN, 2001, pp. 150–7.

Maier, Henk. *We Are Playing Relatives: A Survey of Malay Writing.* Leiden: KITLV, 2004.

Malek, Mohd. Zamberi A. *Suria Kencana: Biografi Jins Shamsudin.* Bangi: Universiti Kebangsaan Malaysia, 1998.

Minchin, James. *No Man is an Island: A Study of Lee Kuan Yew's Singapore.* Sydney: Allen & Unwin, 1986.

Moon, Crys H. S. *A Korean Minjung Theology: An Old Testament Perspective.* Maryknoll, NY: Orbis Books, 1985.

Mrazek, Rudolf. 'Bridges of Hope: Senior Citizens' Memories', *Indonesia* 70 (October 2000): 40–1.

Nair, C. V. Devan. *Not By Wages Alone: Selected Speeches and Writings of C. V. Devan Nair, 1959–1981.* Singapore: Singapore National Trades Union Congress, 1982.

National Heritage Board. *Singapore: Journey into Nationhood.* Singapore: National Heritage Board and Landmark Books, 1998.

Nehru, Jawaharlal. *India's Foreign Policy: Selected Speeches.* New Delhi: Government of India, 1961.

Oliver, Dawn and Derek Benjamin Heater. *The Foundations of Citizenship.* New York; London: Harvester Wheatsheaf, 1994.

Omar, Ariffin. *Bangsa Melayu: Malay Concepts of Democracy and Community, 1945–1950.* Kuala Lumpur: Oxford University Press, 1993.

Ong Yed Deed. 'The Development of the History Curriculum in the English-Medium Schools in Singapore from 1899 to 1991'. Master of Arts Thesis, Columbia Pacific University, 1992.

People's Action Party. *6th Anniversary Celebration Souvenir 1960.* Singapore: People's Action Party, 1960.

People's Action Party. *Our First Ten Years, 1964.* Singapore: People's Action Party, 1964.

People's Action Party. *15th Anniversary Celebration Souvenir, 1969.* Singapore: People's Action Party, 1969.

People's Association. *The First Twenty Years of the People's Association.* Singapore: [People's Association], 1980.

Peritz, Rene. 'The Evolving Politics of Singapore: A Study of Trends and Issues'. Ph.D. Thesis, University of Pennsylvania, 1964.

Peterson, Herbert Henry. 'The Development of English Education in British Malaya'. Master of Arts Thesis, University of Denver, 1942.

Phang, Andrew Boon Leong. 'Jury Trial in Singapore and Malaysia: The Unmaking of a Legal Institution', *Singapore Journal of Legal Studies* 25 (1983): 50–86.

Poulgrain, Greg. *The Genesis of Konfrontasi.* London: Hurst, 1998.

Pugalenthi, S. R. *Elections in Singapore.* Singapore: VJ Times International, 1996.

Puthucheary, Dominic J. 'James Puthucheary, His Friends, and His Times', in *No Cowardly Past: James Puthucheary. Writings, Poems, Commentaries,* ed. Dominic J. Puthucheary and K. S. Jomo. Kuala Lumpur: INSAN, 1998, pp. 3–27.

Puthucheary, Dominic and K. S. Jomo, eds. *No Cowardly Past: Writings, Poems, Commentaries.* Petaling Jaya: INSAN, 1998.

Puthucheary, James. 'Political Role of the Trade Union', *Petir* 3, 6 (4 January 1960).

Puthucheary, James. 'The Growth and Development of the Trade Union Movement after the Election', in *No Cowardly Past: James Puthucheary. Writings, Poems, Commentaries*, ed. Dominic J. Puthucheary and K. S. Jomo. Kuala Lumpur: INSAN, 1998, pp. 127–9.

Puthucheary, James. 'The Struggle for Unity', in *No Cowardly Past: James Puthucheary. Writings, Poems, Commentaries*, ed. Dominic J. Puthucheary and K. S. Jomo. Kuala Lumpur: INSAN, 1998, pp. 135–8.

Quah, Stella R. *Family in Singapore: Sociological Perspectives*. Singapore: Times Academic Press, 1994.

Rahim, Lily Zubaidah. *The Singapore Dilemma: The Political and Educational Marginality of the Malay Community*. Kuala Lumpur: Oxford University Press, 1998.

Rajakumar, R. 'Malaysia's Jean-Paul Sartre', in *A Samad Ismail: Journalism and Politics*, ed. Cheah Boon Kheng. Kuala Lumpur: Singamal, 1987, pp. 39–42.

Ratnam, K. J. and R. S. Milne, ed. *The Malayan Parliamentary Election of 1964*. Singapore: University of Malaya Press, 1967.

Report of the Constitutional Commission, 1954. Singapore: Singapore Government Printer, 1954.

Rich, Paul B. *Race and Empire in British Politics*. Second edition. Cambridge [England]; New York: Cambridge University Press, 1990.

Rodan, Garry. 'Singapore's Leadership Transition: Erosion or Refinement of Authoritarian Rule?' *Bulletin of Concerned Asian Scholars* 24 (1992): 3–17.

Rodan, Garry. 'Embracing Electronic Media but Suppressing Civil Society: Authoritarian Consolidation in Singapore', *The Pacific Review* 16, 4 (2003): 503–24.

Rodan, Garry. *Transparency and Authoritarian Rule in Southeast Asia: Singapore and Malaysia*. London: Routledge Curzon, 2004.

Roff, William R. *The Origins of Malay Nationalism*. Kuala Lumpur: Oxford University Press, 1967.

Roff, William R. *The Origins of Malay Nationalism*. Second edition. New Haven: Yale University Press, 1994.

Rogers, Marvin L. 'Malaysia and Singapore: 1971 Developments', *Asian Survey* 12, 2 (1972): 168–76.

Roskies, D. M., ed. *Text/Politics in Island Southeast Asia*. Athens, OH: Ohio University Center for International Studies, 1993.

Sahlins, M. D. *Culture and Practical Reason*. Chicago: University of Chicago Press, 1976.

Sai Siew Min and Huang Jianli. 'The "Chinese-Educated" Political Vanguards: Ong Pang Boon, Lee Khoon Choy and Jek Yeun Thong', in *Lee's Lieutenants: Singapore's Old Guard*, ed. Lam Peng Er and Kevin Y. L. Tan. St Leonards: Allen & Unwin, 1999, pp. 132–68.

Said, A. Samad. *Between Art and Reality: Selected Essays*. Kuala Lumpur: Dewan Bahasa dan Pustaka, 1994.

Said, Muhammad Ikaml. 'Ethnic Perspectives on the Left in Malaysia', in *Fragmented Vision: Culture and Politics in Contemporary Malaysia*, ed. F. Loh and J. S. Kahn. Sydney: ASAA, 1992, pp. 254–81.

Samat, Talib. *Ahmad Lutfi: Penulis, Penerbit dan Pendakwah*. Kuala Lumpur: Dewan Bahasa dan Pustaka, 2002.

Sarji, Ahmad. *P. Ramlee: Erti yang Sakti*. Subang Jaya, Selangor: Pelanduk Publications, 1999.

Seah Chee Meow. *Community Centres in Singapore: Their Political Involvement*. Singapore: Singapore University Press, 1973.

Seow, Francis T. *To Catch a Tartar: A Dissident in Lee Kuan Yew's Prison*. Haven, Conn: Yale Centre for International Area Studies, 1994.

Seow, Francis. *The Media Enthralled: Singapore Revisited*. Boulder, Colorado: Lynne Rienner Publishers, 1998.

Siddiqi, Shahid. 'The Registration and Deregistration of Trade Unions in Singapore'. Master of Law Thesis, Faculty of Law, University of Singapore, 1968.

Singapore Chinese Chamber of Commerce. *Fifty-Eight Years of Enterprise: Souvenir Volume of the New Building of the Singapore Chinese Chamber of Commerce – 1964*. Singapore: L. M. Creative Publicity, 1964.

Singapore Chinese Chamber of Commerce. *Singapore Chinese Chamber of Commerce Minutes of the Monthly Meetings, 1906 to 1971*. Singapore: National Archive of Singapore, [1906–71].

Song Ong Siang. *One Hundred Years' History of the Chinese in Singapore*. Reprint edition. Singapore: Oxford University Press, 1984.

Soysal, Y. N. *Limits of Citizenship: Migrants and Postnational Membership in Europe*. Chicago: University of Chicago, 1994.

Starner, F. L. 'Singapore Elections of 1963', in *The Malayan Parliamentary Election of 1964*, ed. K. J. Ratnam and R. S. Milne. Singapore: University of Malaya Press, 1967, pp. 312–58.

Stephens, Mitchell. *A History of News*. Fort Worth, Texas: Harcourt Brace, 1997.

Sulong, Jamil. *Kaca Permata: Memoir Seorang Pengarah*. Kuala Lumpur: Dewan Bahasa dan Pustaka, 1993.

Suryanarayan, V. 'Singapore in Malaysia', *International Studies* 11 (July 1969): 111–25.

Sweeney, George. *Political Parties in Singapore, 1945–1955*. Master of Arts Thesis, University of Hull, 1973.

Tan Hong Ngoh, Edna. '"Official" Perceptions of Student Activism on Nantah and SU Campuses, 1965–1974/75'. Honours Thesis, History Department, National University of Singapore, 2001/2002.

Tan Jing Quee. 'Lim Chin Siong — A Political Life', in *Comet in Our Sky: Lim Chin Siong in History*, ed. Tan Jing Quee and K. S. Jomo. Kuala Lumpur: INSAN, 2001, pp. 56–97.

Tan Jing Quee and K. S. Jomo, eds. *Comet in Our Sky: Lim Chin Siong in History*. Kuala Lumpur: INSAN, 2001.

Tan, Kevin Y. L., ed. *The Singapore Legal System*. Second edition. Singapore: Singapore University Press, 1999.

Tan, Kevin Y. L. 'The Legal and Institutional Framework and Issues of Multiracialism in Singapore', in *Beyond Rituals and Riots: Ethnic Pluralism and Social Cohesion in Singapore*, ed. Lai Ah Eng. Singapore: Eastern University Press, 2004, pp. 98–113.

Tan, Kevin Y. L. and Lam Peng Er, eds. *Lee's Lieutenants: Singapore's Old Guard*. St Leonards, NSW: Allen & Unwin, 1999.

Tan Liok Ee. *The Politics of Chinese Education in Malaya, 1945–1961*. Kuala Lumpur; New York: Oxford University Press, 1997.

Tan Melaka (H. Jarvis, ed., trans.). *From Jail to Jail*. Three volumes. Athens, OH: Ohio University Press, 1991.

Tan, Thomas Tsu Wee. 'Political Modernization and Traditional Chinese Voluntary Associations: A Singapore Case Study', *Southeast Asian Journal of Social Science* 13, 2 (1985): 67–79.

Tanaka, Yayoi. 'Singapore: Subtle NGO Control by a Developmentalist Welfare State', in *The State and NGOs: Perspectives from Asia*, ed. Shinichi Shigetomi. Singapore: Institute of Southeast Asian Studies, 2002, pp. 200–21.

Tarrow, Sidney. *Power in Movement: Social Movements and Contentious Politics*. Second edition. Cambridge, UK: Cambridge University Press, 1998.

Teeuw, A. *Modern Indonesian Literature*. The Hague: Martinus Nijhoff, 1979.

Thio Li-Ann. 'The Constitutional Framework of Powers', in *The Singapore Legal System*, ed. Kevin Y. L. Tan. Second edition. Singapore: Singapore University Press, 1999, pp. 67–122.

Thorpe, M. '"Penetration by Invitation" — A Lecturer at Nanyang — A Memoir', *Economic and Political Weekly* 1–8 (March 1997): 485–91.

Toer, Pramoedya Ananta (W. Samuels, ed., tr.). *The Mute's Soliloquy*. London: Penguin, 1999.

Trocki, Carl A. 'Development of Labour Organisation in Singapore, 1800–1960', *Australian Journal of Politics and History* 47, 1 (2001): 113–26.

Trocki, Carl A. *Singapore: Wealth, Power and the Culture of Control*. London and New York: Routledge, 2006.

Turnbull, C. M. *A History of Singapore, 1819–1975*. Kuala Lumpur: Oxford University Press, 1977.

Turnbull, C. M. *A History of Singapore, 1819–1988*. Singapore: Oxford University Press, 1989.

Turnbull, C. M. *Dateline Singapore: 150 Years of The Straits Times*. Singapore: Singapore Press Holdings, 1995.

Van de Ven, Hans. 'Recent Studies of Modern Chinese History', *Modern Asian Studies* 30, 2 (1996): 225–69.

Visscher, Sikko. 'Business, Ethnicity and State: The Representational Relationship of the Singapore Chinese Chamber of Commerce and the State, 1945–1997'. Ph.D. Thesis, Free University, 2002.

Visscher, Sikko. *The Business of Politics and Ethnicity: A History of the Singapore Chinese Chamber of Commerce and Industry*. Singapore: NUS Press, 2007.

Vlieland, C. A. *British Malaya (The Colony of the Straits Settlements and the Malay States under British Protection, namely the Federated States of Perak, Selangor,*

Negri Sembilan and Pahang and the States of Johore, Kedah, Kelantan, Trengganu, Perlis and Brunei): A Report on the 1931 Census and on Certain Problems of Vital Statistics. London: Crown Agents for the Colonies, 1932.

Wati, Arena. *Memoir Arena Wati: Enda Gulingku.* Bangi: Penerbit Universiti Kebangsaan Malaysia, 1991.

Wee, C. J. W.-L. 'The Vanquished: Lim Chin Siong and a Progressivist National Narrative', in *Lee's Lieutenants: Singapore's Old Guard*, ed. Lam Peng Er and Kevin Y. L. Tan. Sydney: Allen & Unwin, 1999, pp. 169–90.

Wee, C. J. W.-L. 'Our Island Story: Economic Development and the National Narrative in Singapore', in *New Terrains in Southeast Asian History*, ed. Abu Talib Ahmad and Tan Liok Ee. Research in International Studies Southeast Asia Series No. 107. Singapore: Singapore University Press, 2003, pp. 141–67.

Wells, Kenneth M., ed. *South Korea's Minjung Movement: The Culture and Politics of Dissidence.* Honolulu: University of Hawaii Press, 1995.

Wilson, H. E. *Social Engineering in Singapore.* Singapore: Singapore University Press, 1978.

Wok, Othman. *Never in My Wildest Dreams.* Singapore: SNP Editions, 2000.

Wong, Aline K. and Wai Kum Leong, eds. *Singapore Women: Three Decades of Change.* Singapore: Times Academic Press, 1993.

Wright, Richard. *The Colour Curtain: A Report on the Bandung Conference.* Cleveland: World Publishing, 1955.

Yaacob, Ibrahim. *Nusa dan Bangsa Melayu.* Jakarta: N. V. Alma'ariff, 1951.

Yao Souchou. 'Books from Heaven: Literary Pleasure, Chinese Cultural Text and the "Struggle Against Forgetting"', *Australian Journal of Anthropology* 8, 2 (1997): 190–209.

Yeo Kim Wah. 'British Policy Towards the Malays in the Federated Malay States, 1920–40'. Ph.D. Thesis, Australian National University, 1971.

Yeo Kim Wah. *Political Development in Singapore, 1945–55.* Singapore: Singapore University Press, 1973.

Yeo Kim Wah. 'Communist Involvement in the Malayan Labour Strikes: 1936', *Journal of the Malaysian Branch of the Royal Asiatic Society* 49, 2 (1976): 36–79.

Yeo Kim Wah. *The Politics of Decentralization: Colonial Controversy in Malaya 1920–1929.* Kuala Lumpur: Oxford University Press, 1982.

Yeo Kim Wah. 'Student Politics in University of Malaya, 1949–51', *Journal of Southeast Asian Studies* 23, 2 (1992): 346–80.

Yeo Kim Wah. 'Joining the Communist Underground: The Conversion of English-Educated Radicals to Communism in Singapore, June 1948–January 1951', *Journal of the Malaysian Branch of Royal Asiatic Society* 67, 1 (June 1994): 29–59.

Yeo Kim Wah and Albert Lau. 'From Colonialism to Independence, 1945–1965', in *A History of Singapore*, ed. Ernest C. T. Chew and Edwin Lee. Singapore: Oxford University Press, 1996, pp. 117–53.

Yeoh, Brenda. *Contesting Space in Colonial Singapore: Power Relations and the Urban Built Environment.* Singapore: University of Singapore Press, 1996.

Yeoh, J. *To Tame a Tiger: The Singapore Story.* Singapore: Wiz-Biz, 1995.

Yong, C. F. 'Emergence of Chinese Community Leaders in Singapore, 1890–1941', *Journal of South Seas Society* 30, 1 (December 1975): 1–18.

Yong, C. F. *The Origins of Malayan Communism.* Singapore: South Seas Society, 1997.

Yong, M.C. *The Indonesian Revolution and the Singapore Connection.* Leiden: KITLV Press, 2003.

Young, Robert J. C. *Postcolonialism: An Historical Introduction.* Oxford: Blackwell, 2001.

Zahari, Said. *Dark Clouds at Dawn: A Political Memoir.* Kuala Lumpur: Insan, 2001.

Index